W9-ABE-044

Regis College Library
15 ST. MARY STREET
TORONTO, ONTARIO, CANADA
M4Y 2R5

WITHDRAWN

Paul
and the
Parousia

Paul
and the
Parousia

BS
2655
E7
P57
1997

AN EXEGETICAL
AND THEOLOGICAL
INVESTIGATION

JOSEPH PLEVNIK

Regis College Library
15 ST. MARY STREET
TORONTO, ONTARIO, CANADA
M4Y 2R5

HENDRICKSON
PUBLISHERS

© 1997 by Hendrickson Publishers, Inc.
P. O. Box 3473
Peabody, Massachusetts 01961–3473
All rights reserved
Printed in the United States of America

ISBN 1–56563–180–3

First Printing — January 1997

The Scripture quotations contained herein are from the New Revised Standard Version Bible, copyright © 1989 by the Division of Christian Education of the National Council of Churches of Christ in the U.S.A. Used by permission. All rights reserved.

Library of Congress Cataloging-in-Publication Data

Plevnik, Joseph.
    Paul and the Parousia: an exegetical and theological
investigation / Joseph Plevnik.
    Includes bibliographical references and index.
    ISBN 1–56563–180–3
    1. Second Advent—Biblical teaching. 2. Bible. N.T. Epistles
of Paul—Theology. I. Title.
BS2655.E7P57   1996
236′.9—dc20   96–10729
                                                  CIP

CONTENTS

PART TWO: THEOLOGICAL INVESTIGATION

PREFACE

The present book, long in the making, takes up the topic of my doctoral dissertation, directed by Professor Rudolf Schnackenburg almost twenty-five years ago. The dissertation, "The Parousia of the Lord according to the Letters of Paul: An Exegetical and Theological Investigation" (Würzburg, 1971) was never fully published. Over the years I continued to work on the topic, as a number of my published articles attest. My sabbatical leave in 1991–92 enabled me to complete the research and to incorporate scholarly material published on this topic since 1971.

But my old dissertation is barely recognizable in the present book. Not only were new sections added to the original outline but the content also was thoroughly reworked, in line with contemporary scholarship. And my own thinking on a number of topics, above all on 1 Thess 4:13–18 and 5:1–11, has developed. I was driven to complete this work in order to fill the gap in the present New Testament scholarship. While several doctoral dissertations were published in German during this time, nothing comparable to this has appeared in English. The present book thus fills the lacuna in this field of New Testament research.

The book has two parts. The first part (chs. 1–7) deals with the fundamental concepts (ch. 1) and imagery (ch. 2) in Paul's presentations of the parousia and with the exegesis (chs. 3–7) of the key texts dealing with the Lord's coming—1 Thess 4:13–18; 5:1–11; 1 Cor 15:23–28, 50–55; and Phil 3:20–21. The first part is foundational for the second part (chs. 8–13), which deals with theological issues connected with the parousia. The notions discovered in the exegetical part are here assembled and located in a wider stream of Paul's thought, and theological issues are raised under such topics as hope, judgment, the antagonistic aspect of the parousia, living with Christ, the church and the parousia, and Paul's apocalyptic theology.

I would like to express my deepest gratitude to Sr. Eleanor Breen, who before her sudden death faithfully read and corrected my manuscript; to our librarian, Mr. Richard Tetreau, who was helpful with his suggestions; to Sr. Mary Bernita, who read the revised version; and to Sr. St. Claude for her continuing help. I would like to thank all my friends who have read the manuscript, suggested improvements, encouraged me, and put up with me as I was struggling to formulate my thought in readable English. I am very grateful to Mr. Jim Clair, who made it possible for me to have a copy editor look over the book, to Mrs. Ruth Peckover for her help in editing the book, and to Regis College administration for its assistance.

It is my hope that the book will be not only a scholarly contribution on the topic but also of some personal value to the reader and to the preacher. It may provide a timely reading at the close of the second millennium. The times and the seasons, however, are not for us to determine, but a proper preparedness for the Lord's coming is the message of the New Testament, and of Paul in particular. If the Lord's coming may no longer be said to be near, it can still be desired. *Marana tha.*

ABBREVIATIONS AND SHORT TITLES

ANCIENT SOURCES

Old Testament

Gen	Genesis
Exod	Exodus
Lev	Leviticus
Num	Numbers
Deut	Deuteronomy
Judg	Judges
1–2 Sam	1–2 Samuel
1–2 Kgs	1–2 Kings
1–2 Chron	1–2 Chronicles
Neh	Nehemiah
Ps	Psalms
Prov	Proverbs
Isa	Isaiah
Jer	Jeremiah
Lam	Lamentations
Ezek	Ezekiel
Dan	Daniel
Hos	Hosea
Obad	Obadiah
Mic	Micah
Nah	Nahum
Hab	Habakkuk
Zeph	Zephaniah
Hag	Haggai
Zech	Zechariah
Mal	Malachi

New Testament

Matt	Matthew
Rom	Romans
1–2 Cor	1–2 Corinthians
Gal	Galatians
Eph	Ephesians
Phil	Philippians
Col	Colossians
1–2 Thess	1–2 Thessalonians
1–2 Tim	1–2 Timothy
Heb	Hebrews
Jas	James
1–2 Pet	1–2 Peter
Rev	Revelation

Apocrypha

Sir	Sirach
Wis	Wisdom of Solomon
Jdth	Judith
1–4 Macc	1–4 Maccabees

Hellenistic Jewish Authors

Josephus

Ant.	*Antiquities*
J.W.	*Jewish War*

Philo

Cher.	*De Cherubim [On the Cherubim]*
Legat.	*De Legatione [On the Embassy to Gaius]*

Pseudepigrapha

Odes Sol	Odes of Solomon
Ps Sol	Psalms of Solomon
2 Bar.	*2 Baruch (Syriac Apocalypse of Baruch)*
T. Abr.	*Testament of Abraham*
T. Moses	*Testament of Moses*
T. 12 Patr.	*Testament of the Twelve Patriarchs*
T. Jos.	*Testament of Joseph*
T. Reub.	*Testament of Reuben*
T. Sim.	*Testament of Simeon*

T. Levi	*Testament of Levi*
T. Judah	*Testament of Judah*
T. Zeb.	*Testament of Zebulun*
T. Benj.	*Testament of Benjamin*
T. Dan	*Testament of Dan*
T. Napht.	*Testament of Nephtali*
T. Gad	*Testament of Gad*
T. Asher	*Testament of Asher*
As. Moses	*Ascension of Moses*
As. Isa.	*Ascension of Isaiah*
Apoc. Elijah	*Apocalypse of Elijah*
Jub.	*Jubilees*

Qumran

CD	*Damascus Document*
1QM	*War Scroll(Milhamah)*
1QH	*Thanksgiving Hymns (Hodayot)*
1QS	*Manual of Discipline (Rule of the Community, Serek hayyahad)*
1QapGen	*Genesis Apocryphon*
4QEn^{a-c}	*1 Enoch* fragments, Qumran Cave 4
4QShirShabb	*Song of Sabbath Sacrifice, Angelic Liturgy*

Gnostic Writings

Gos. Thom.	*Gospel of Thomas*

SCHOLARLY PUBLICATIONS

AB	Anchor Bible
AGJU	Arbeiten zur Geschichte des antiken Judentums und des Urchristentums
AnBib	Analecta biblica
ATANT	Abhandlungen zur Theologie des Alten und Neuen Testament
ATD	Acta Theologica Danica
BETL	Bibliotheca ephemeridum theologicarum lovaniensium
BEvT	Beiträge zur evangelischen Theologie
BFCT	Beiträge zur Förderung christlicher Theologie
Bib	*Biblica*
BibLeb	*Bibel und Leben*
BibS(F)	Biblische Studien (Freiburg, 1895–)
BNTC	Black's New Testament Commentaries
BU	Biblische Untersuchungen
BZ	*Biblische Zeitschrift*
BZAW	Beihefte zur ZAW
BZNW	Beihefte zur ZNW

CBQ	*Catholic Biblical Quarterly*
CNT	Commentaire du Nouveau Testament
ConB	Coniectanea biblica
DBSup	*Dictionnaire de la Bible Supplément*, ed. L. Pirot and A. Robert.
EBib	Etudes bibliques
EKKNT	Evangelisch-katholischer Kommentar zum Neuen Testament
ETL	*Ephemerides theologicae lovanienses*
FB	Forschung zur Bibel
FRLANT	Forschungen zur Religion und Literatur des Alten und Neuen Testaments
GTA	Göttingen theologische Arbeiten
HNT	Handbuch zum Neuen Testament
HTKNT	Herders theologischer Kommentar zum Neuen Testament
HTR	*Harvard Theological Review*
HTS	Harvard Theological Studies
ICC	International Critical Commentary
JBL	*Journal of Biblical Literature*
JSJ	*Journal for the Study of Judaism in the Persian, Hellenistic and Roman Period*
JSNTSup	Journal for the Study of the New Testament Supplement Series
JSOTSup	Journal for the Study of the Old Testament Supplement Series
JSS	*Journal of Semitic Studies*
JTC	*Journal for Theology and the Church*
JTS	*Journal of Theological Studies*
KBANT	Kommentare und Beiträge zum Alten und Neuen Testament
LTK	*Lexikon für Theologie und Kirche*
MeyerK	H. A. W. Meyer, Kritisch-exegetischer Kommentar über das Neue Testament
MNTC	Moffatt New Testament Commentary
NA	Neutestamentliche Abhandlungen
NCBC	New Century Bible Commentary
NICNT	New International Commentary on the New Testament
NIDNTT	*New International Dictionary of New Testament Theology*, ed. C. Brown
NIGTC	New International Greek Testament Commentary
NJBC	*The New Jerome Biblical Commentary* , ed. R. E. Brown, J. A. Fitzmyer, and R. E. Murphy
NovT	*Novum Testamentum*
NovTSup	Novum Testamentum, Supplements
NTA	*New Testament Abstracts*
NTD	Das Neue Testament Deutsch
NTS	*New Testament Studies*
OTP	*The Old Testament Pseudepigrapha*, ed. J. H. Charlesworth
QD	Quaestiones Disputatae
RB	*Revue biblique*
RechBib	Recherches bibliques
RHPR	*Revue d'histoire et de philosophie religieuses*
RNT	Regensburger Neues Testament

SANT	Studien zum Alten und Neuen Testament
SB	Sources bibliques
SBL	Society of Biblical Literature
SBLDS	SBL Dissertation Series
SBLMS	SBL Monograph Series
SBM	Stuttgarter biblische Monographien
SBS	Stuttgarter Bibelstudien
SBT	Studies in Biblical Theology
SC	Sources chrétiennes
ScEs	*Science et esprit*
SNT	Studien zum Neuen Testament
SNTMS	Society for New Testament Studies Monograph Series
ST	*Studia theologica*
SUNT	Studien zur Umwelt des Neuen Testaments
TDNT	*Theological Dictionary of the New Testament*, ed. G. Kittel and G. Friedrich
TDOT	*Theological Dictionary of the Old Testament*, ed. J. Botterweck and H. Ringgren
THKNT	Theologischer Handkommentar zum Neuen Testament
TI	Rahner, K., *Theological Investigations*
TZ	*Theologische Zeitschrift*
USQR	*Union Seminary Quarterly Review*
WMANT	Wissenschaftliche Monographien zum Alten und Neuen Testament
WBC	Word Biblical Commentary
ZAW	*Zeitschrift für die alttestamentliche Wissenschaft*
ZNW	*Zeitschrift für die neutestamentliche Wissenschaft*
ZST	*Zeitschrift für systematische Theologie*
ZTK	*Zeitschrift für Theologie und Kirche*

LIST OF SHORT TITLES

Aalen, *Begriffe*

>Aalen, S. *Die Begriffe "Licht" und "Finsternis" im Alten Testament und Spätjudentum und in Rabbinismus.* SNVAO II Hist. Filos. Kl. 1951 No. 1. Oslo: Dubwad, 1951.

Aejmelaeus, *Wachen*

>Aejmelaeus, L. *Wachen vor dem Ende.* Helsinki: Finische exegetische Gesellschaft, 1985.

Aland et al. *Greek New Testament*

>Aland, K., M. Black, C. M. Martini, B. M. Metzger, and A. Wikgren. *The Greek New Testament.* 3d ed. Stuttgart: United Bible Societies, 1983.

Alexander, "3 Enoch"

>Alexander, P. "3 (Hebrew Apocalypse of) Enoch." *OTP* 1.223–315.

Allo, *1 Corinthiens*

>Allo, E.-B. *Saint Paul: Première Epître aux Corinthiens.* Paris: Gabalda, 1934.

Allo, *2 Corinthiens*

Allo, E.-B. *Saint Paul: Seconde Epître aux Corinthiens*. Paris: Gabalda, 1956.

Andersen, "2 Enoch"

Andersen, F. I. "2 (Slavonic Apocalypse of) Enoch." *OTP* 1.91–221.

Aono, *Entwicklung*

Aono, T. *Die Entwicklung des paulinischen Gerichtsgedankens bei den Apostolischen Vätern*. Europäische Hochschulschriften XXIII, 137. Bern/Frankfurt/Las Vegas: Lange, 1979.

Bammel, "Judenverfolgung"

Bammel, E. "Judenverfolgung und Naherwartung: Zur Eschatologie des Ersten Thessalonicherbriefes." *ZTK* 56 (1959) 294–315.

Barrett, *1 Corinthians*

Barrett, C. K. *A Commentary on the First Epistle to the Corinthians*. London: A. & C. Black, 1971.

Barth, "Rudolf Bultmann"

Barth, K. "Rudolf Bultmann—an Attempt to Understand Him." *Kerygma and Myth*. 2 vols. Edited by H. W. Bartsch. Volume 2. Pages 83–132. London: S.P.C.K. 1957–62.

Bartsch, *Kerygma und Mythos*

Bartsch, H. W. ed. *Kerygma und Mythos*. 6 vols. Hamburg: Reich, 1948–64.

BAG

Bauer, W., W. F. Arndt, F. W. Gingrich, *A Greek-English Lexicon of the New Testament and Other Early Christian Literature*. Chicago: Chicago University Press, 1957.

Baumbach, "Zukunftserwartung"

Baumbach, G. "Die Zukunftserwartung nach dem Philipperbrief." *Die Kirche des Anfangs: Für Heinz Schürmann*. Edited by R. Schnackenburg, J. Ernst, and J. Wanke. Pages 435–57. Freiburg/Basel/Vienna: Herder, 1978.

Baumgarten, *Apokalyptik*

Baumgarten, J. *Paulus und die Apokalyptik: Die Auslegung apokalyptischer Überlieferungen in den echten Paulusbriefen*. WMANT 44. Neukirchen: Neukirchener, 1975.

Beare, *Commentary*

Beare, F. W. *A Commentary on the Epistle to the Philippians*. London: A. & C. Black, 1959.

Becker, *Auferstehung*

Becker, J. *Auferstehung der Toten im Urchristentum*. SBS 82. Stuttgart: Katholisches Bibelwerk, 1976.

Becker, *Untersuchungen*

Becker, J. *Untersuchungen zur Entstehungsgeschichte der Testamente der Zwölf Patriarchen*. AGJU 8. Leiden: Brill, 1970.

Behm, "κοιλία"

Behm, J. "κοιλία." *TDNT*. 3.786–89.

Beker, *Paul's Apocalyptic Gospel*
> Beker, J. C. *Paul's Apocalyptic Gospel*. Philadelphia: Fortress, 1982.

Beker, *Paul the Apostle*
> Beker, J. C. *Paul the Apostle: The Triumph of God in Life and Thought*. Philadelphia: Fortress, 1980.

Beker, *Sieg Gottes*
> Beker, J. C. *Der Sieg Gottes: Eine Untersuchung zur Struktur des paulinischen Denkens*. SBS 132. Stuttgart: Katholisches Bibelwerk, 1988.

Benoit, *Les Epîtres*
> Benoit, P. *Les Epîtres de s. Paul aux Philippiens, à Philémon, aux Colossiens, aux Ephésiens*. Paris: Cerf, 1959.

Benoit, "Resurrection"
> Benoit, P. "Resurrection: At the End Time or Immediately after Death?" *Concilium* (1970) 103–14.

Berger, "Volksversammlung"
> Berger, K. "Volksversammlung und Gemeinde Gottes." *ZTK* 73 (1976) 167–207.

Best, *Thessalonians*
> Best, E. *A Commentary on the First and the Second Epistles to the Thessalonians*. BNTC. Peabody: Hendrickson, 1972.

Betz, *Nachfolge und Nachahmung*
> Betz, H.-D. *Nachfolge und Nachahmung Jesu Christi im NT*. Tübingen: Mohr, 1967.

Beyschlag, *New Testament Theology*
> Beyschlag, W. *New Testament Theology*. 2 vols. Pages 260–62. Edinburgh: T. & T. Clark, 1895.

Billerbeck, *Kommentar*
> Billerbeck, P. *Kommentar zum Neuen Testament aus Talmud und Midrasch*. 4 vols. Munich: Beck, 1922–28.

Bindemann, *Hoffnung*
> Bindemann, W. *Die Hoffnung der Schöpfung: Römer 8,18–27 und die Frage einer Theologie der Befreiung von Mensch und Natur*. Neukirchener Studienbücher 14. Neukirchen: Neukirchener, 1983.

Black, "ἐξουσίαι"
> Black, M. "Πᾶσαι ἐξουσίαι αὐτῷ ὑποταγήσονται." *Paul and Paulinism: Essays in Honor of C. K. Barrett*. Edited by M. D. Hooker and S. Wilson. Pages 74–82. London: S.P.C.K., 1982.

Blank, *Paulus und Jesus*
> Blank, J. *Paulus und Jesus. Eine Theologische Grundlegung*. SANT 18. Munich: Kösel, 1968.

Bloomquist, *Suffering*
> Bloomquist, L. G. *The Function of Suffering in Philippians*. JSNTSup 78. Sheffield: JSOT, 1993.

Bogaert, *Apocalypse de Baruch*
> Bogaert, P. *Apocalypse de Baruch*. 2 vols. SC 144–45. Paris: Cerf, 1969.

Bonnard, *Philippiens*
> Bonnard, P. *L'Epître de saint Paul aux Philippiens*. CNT 10. Paris: Niestlé, 1950.

Bori, KOINΩNIA

>Bori, P. C. KOINΩNIA: L'idea della comunione nell'ecclesiologia recente e nel Nuovo Testamento. Brescia: Paideia, 1972.

Bornkamm, Paul

>Bornkamm, G. Paul. New York/Evanston: Harper & Row, 1971.

Bornkamm, "Philipperbrief"

>Bornkamm, G. "Der Philipperbrief als paulinische Briefsammlung." Neotestamentica et Patristica: Festschrift für O. Cullmann. Edited by W. C. van Unnik. Pages 192–202. Leiden: Brill, 1962.

Brown, " 'Mystery' "

>Brown, R. E. "The Pre-Christian Semitic Concept of 'Mystery.' " CBQ 20 (1958) 417–43.

Bruce, 1 & 2 Thessalonians

>Bruce, F. F. 1 & 2 Thessalonians. WBC 45. Waco: Word, 1982.

Bultmann, "ἐλπίς"

>Bultmann, R. "ἐλπίς." TDNT. 2.517–23.

Bultmann, Glauben und Verstehen

>Bultmann, R. Glauben und Verstehen: Gesammelte Aufsätze. 4 vols. Tübingen: Mohr, 1964.

Bultmann, "History and Eschatology"

>Bultmann, R. "History and Eschatology." NTS 1 (1954) 5–16.

Bultmann, Synoptic Tradition

>Bultmann, R. The History of the Synoptic Tradition. 1963. Reprint. Peabody, Mass.: Hendrickson, 1994.

Bultmann, "Mythology"

>Bultmann, R., "New Testament and Mythology." Kerygma and Myth. Edited by H. W. Bartsch. 6 vols. London: S.P.C.K., 1953. 1.1–44. Rev. transl. by Fuller in Kerygma and Myth. 2 vols. Edited by H. W. Bartsch. London: S.P.C.K., 1957–62. 1.1–44.

Bultmann, "Neues Testament"

>Bultmann, R. "Neues Testament und Mythologie: Das Problem der Entmythologisierung der neutestamentlichen Verkündigung." Kerygma und Dogma I. Edited by H. W. Bartsch. Hamburg: Reich, 1957.

Bultmann, Offenbarung

>Bultmann, R. Offenbarung und Heilsgeschehen. Munich: Lempp, 1941.

Bultmann, Primitive Christianity

>Bultmann, R. Primitive Christianity in Its Contemporary Setting. New York: World, 1956.

Bultmann, Theology

>Bultmann, R. Theology of the New Testament. 2 vols. London: SCM, 1952.

Burrows, More Light

>Burrows, M. More Light on the Dead Sea Scrolls: New Scrolls and New Interpretations with Translations of Important Recent Discoveries. New York: Viking, 1958.

Byrne, "Philippians"

>Byrne, B. "The Letter to the Philippians." NJBC. 791–97.

Caird, *Paul's Letters*
> Caird, G. B. *Paul's Letters from Prison*. NCBC. Oxford: Oxford University Press, 1976.

Caird, *Revelation*
> Caird, G. B. *The Revelation of St. John the Divine*. BNTC. Peabody: Hendrickson, 1966.

Callan, "Psalm 110:1"
> Callan, T. "Psalm 110:1 and the Origin of the Expectation That Jesus Will Come Again." *CBQ* 44 (1982) 622–36.

Campbell, "KOINΩNIA and Its Cognates"
> Campbell, J. Y. "KOINΩNIA and Its Cognates in the New Testament." *JBL* 51 (1932) 352–82.

Caquot, "גָּעַר"
> Caquot, A. "גָּעַר." *TDOT*. 3.49–52.

Carr, *Angels and Principalities*
> Carr, A. W. *Angels and Principalities: The Background, Meaning, and Development of the Pauline Phrase hai archai kai hai exousiai*. SNTMS 42. New York: Cambridge University Press, 1981.

Carrez, "Résurrection"
> Carrez, M. "Résurrection et seigneurie du Christ 1 Co 15,23–28." *Résurrection du Christ et des Chrétiens. 1 Co 15*. Edited by L. de Lorenzi. Serie Monographique de Benedictina 8. Pages 127–40. Rome: Abbaye de S. Paul, 1985.

Cerfaux, *Christ*
> Cerfaux, L. *Christ in the Theology of St. Paul*. New York: Herder & Herder, 1959.

Cerfaux, *Church*
> Cerfaux, L. *The Church in the Theology of St. Paul*. New York: Herder & Herder, 1959.

Charles, *APOT*
> Charles, R. H. *The Apocrypha and Pseudepigrapha of the Old Testament*. 2 vols. Oxford: Clarendon, 1913.

Charlesworth, "Odes of Solomon"
> Charlesworth, J. H. "Odes of Solomon." *OTP* 2.725–79.

Charlesworth, *OTP*
> Charlesworth, J. H. ed. *The Old Testament Pseudepigrapha*. 2 vols. Garden City, N.Y.: Doubleday, 1983–85.

J. J. Collins, "Apocalyptic Eschatology"
> Collins, J. J. "Apocalyptic Eschatology as the Transcendence of Death." *CBQ* 36 (1974) 21–43.

J. J. Collins, *Apocalyptic Imagination*
> Collins, J. J. *The Apocalyptic Imagination: An Introduction to the Jewish Matrix of Christianity*. New York: Crossroads, 1984.

J. J. Collins, "Apocalyptic Literature"
> Collins, J. J. "Apocalyptic Literature." *Early Judaism and Its Modern Interpreters*. Edited by R. A. Kraft and G. W. E. Nickelsburg. Pages 345–70. Philadelphia: Fortress. Atlanta: Scholars Press, 1986.

J. J. Collins, "Morphology"
> Collins, J. J. "Introduction: Toward the Morphology of a Genre." *Semeia* 14 (1979) 1–19.

J. J. Collins, "Jewish Apocalypses"
> Collins, J. J. "The Jewish Apocalypses." *Semeia* 14 (1979) 21–59.

R. F. Collins, "Integrity"
> Collins, R. F. "A propos the Integrity of 1 Thess." *ETL* 65 (1979) 67–106.

R. F. Collins, "1 Thessalonians"
> Collins, R. F. "The First Letter to the Thessalonians." *NJBC*, 772–79.

R. F. Collins, "Tradition"
> Collins, R. F. "Tradition, Redaction, and Exhortation in 1 Th 4,13–5,11." *L'Apocalypse johannique et l'Apocalyptique dans le Nouveau Testament*. Edited by J. Lambrecht. BETL 53. Pages 225–343. Leuven: Leuven University Press, 1980.

Conzelmann, *1 Corinthians*
> Conzelmann, H. *1 Corinthians: A Commentary on the First Epistle to the Corinthians*. Philadelphia: Fortress, 1975.

Conzelmann, "Gegenwart und Zukunft"
> Conzelmann, H. "Gegenwart und Zukunft in der synoptischen Tradition." *ZTK* 54 (1957) 277–96.

Cosby, "Formal Receptions"
> Cosby, M. R. "Hellenistic Formal Receptions and Paul's Use of *apantēsis* in 1 Thessalonians 4:17." *Bulletin of Biblical Research* 4 (1994) 15–34.

Craig, "1 Corinthians"
> Craig, C. T. "The First Epistle to the Corinthians." *Interpreter's Bible*, vol. 10. Nashville: Abingdon, 1953.

Cranfield, *Commentary*
> Cranfield, C. E. B. *A Critical and Exegetical Commentary on the Epistle to the Romans*. 2 vols. Edinburgh: T. & T. Clark, 1975–79.

Cross, "Divine Warrior"
> Cross, F. M. "The Divine Warrior in Israel's Early Cult." *Biblical Motifs—Origins and Transformations*. Edited by A. Altmann. Pages 11–30. Cambridge, Mass.: Harvard University Press, 1966.

Cross and Freedman, "Blessing of Moses"
> Cross, F. M., and D. N. Freedman. "The Blessing of Moses." *JBL* 69 (1948) 191–210.

Cullmann, *Christ and Time*
> Cullmann, O. *Christ and Time*. Philadelphia: Westminster, 1960.

Cullmann, "Out of Season Remarks"
> Cullmann, O. "Out of Season Remarks on the 'Historical Jesus' of the Bultmann School." *USQR* 16 (1961) 131–48.

Dahl, "Parables of Growth"
> Dahl, N. A. "The Parables of Growth." *ST* 5 (1951) 132–66.

Dahl, *Resurrection*
> Dahl, N. A. *The Resurrection of the Body*. SBT 36. London: SCM, 1962.

Dalton, *Christ's Proclamation*
> Dalton, W. J. *Christ's Proclamation to the Spirits: A Study of 1 Peter 3:18–4:6.* AnBib 23. Rome: Biblical Institute, 1965.

Dalton, "Integrity of Philippians"
> Dalton, W. J. "The Integrity of Philippians." *Bib* 60 (1979) 97–102.

Daube, *Sudden*
> Daube, D. *The Sudden in the Scriptures.* Leiden: Brill, 1964.

de Boer, *Defeat*
> Boer, M. C. de, *The Defeat of Death: Apocalyptic Eschatology in 1 Corinthians 15 and Romans 5.* JSNTSup 22. Sheffield: JSOT, 1988.

de Faye, *Les apocalypses juives*
> de Faye, E., *Les apocalypses juives: Essai de critique litteraire et théologique.* Paris: Fischbacher, 1892.

Deissmann, *Licht*/Deissmann, *Light*
> Deissmann, A. *Licht vom Osten: Das Neue Testament und die neuentdeckten Texte der hellenistisch-römischen Welt.* Tübingen: Mohr, 1923. ET: *Light from the Ancient East. The New Testament Illustrated by Recently Discovered Texts of the Graeco-Roman World.* 1927. Reprint. Peabody: Hendrickson, 1996.

de Jonge, "Christian Influence"
> de Jonge, M. "Christian Influence in the Testaments of the Twelve Patriarchs." *NovT* 4 (1960) 182–235.

de Jonge, "Once More"
> de Jonge, M. "Once More: Christian Influence in the Testaments of the Twelve Patriarchs." *NovT* 5 (1962) 311–19.

de Jonge, *Testaments*
> de Jonge, M. *The Testaments of the Twelve Patriarchs: A Study of Their Text, Composition, and Origin.* Leiden: Brill, 1953.

Delcor, *Livre de Daniel*
> Delcor, M. *Le Livre de Daniel.* SB. Paris: Gabalda, 1971.

Delling, "ἡμέρα"
> Delling, G. "ἡμέρα." *TDNT.* 2.947–53.

de Vaux, *Ancient Israel*
> de Vaux, R., *Ancient Israel: Its Life and Institutions.* New York/Toronto/London: McGraw-Hill, 1961.

Dibelius, *Thessalonicher I/II, Philipper*
> Dibelius, M. *An die Thessalonicher I. und II., An die Philipper.* HNT 11. Tübingen: Mohr, 1937.

Dodd, *Apostolic Preaching*
> Dodd, C. H. *The Apostolic Preaching and its Development.* New York: Harper & Row, 1964.

Dodd, *New Testament Studies*
> Dodd, C. H. *New Testament Studies.* Manchester: Manchester University Press, 1954.

Doughty, "Salvation in Corinth"
> Doughty, D. J. "The Presence and Future of Salvation in Corinth." *ZNW* 66 (1975) 61–90.

Dunn, *Romans 9–16*
> Dunn, J. D. G. *Romans 9–16.* WBC 38A. Dallas: Word Books, 1988.

Dupont, *L'Union*
> Dupont, J. ΣΥΝ ΧΡΙΣΤΩΙ: *L'union avec le Christ suivant saint Paul.* Louvain: Nauwelaerts. Paris: Desclée de Brouwer, 1952.

Dupont-Sommer, *Essene Writings*
> Dupont-Sommer, A. *The Essene Writings from Qumran.* Cleveland: World, 1962. Reprint. Gloucester, Mass.: Peter Smith, 1973.

Dupont-Sommer, *Qumran and the Essenes*
> Dupont-Sommer, A. *The Jewish Sect of Qumran and the Essenes.* London: Valentine, 1954.

Eckart, "Der zweite Brief"
> Eckart, K. G. "Der zweite echte Brief des Apostels Paulus an die Thessalonicher." *ZTK* 58 (1961) 30–40.

Eissfeldt, *Einleitung*
> Eissfeldt, O. *Einleitung in das Alte Testament.* Tübingen: Mohr, 1964.

Ellis, *Paul's Use*
> Ellis, E. E. *Paul's Use of the Old Testament.* London: Oliver & Boyd, 1957.

Ernst, *Gegenspieler*
> Ernst, J. *Die eschatologischen Gegenspieler in den Schriften des Neuen Testaments.* Regensburg: Pustet, 1967.

Fee, *1 Corinthians*
> Fee, G. D. *The First Epistle to the Corinthians.* NICNT. Grand Rapids: Eerdmans, 1987.

Feuillet, "Les 'chefs de ce siècle' "
> Feuillet, A. "Les 'chefs de ce siècle' et la sagesse divine d'après 1. Co. II,6–9." *Studiorum Paulinorum Congressus Internationalis Catholicus.* 2 vols. AnBib 17–18. Rome: Biblical Institute, 1963. 1.383–93.

Feuillet, "Fils de l'homme"
> Feuillet, A. "Fils de l'homme de Daniel et de la tradition biblique." *RB* 60 (1953) 170–202.

Feuillet, "Parousie"
> Feuillet, A. "Parousie." *DBSup.* 6, cols. 1331–419.

Findlay, *Thessalonians*
> Findlay, G. G. *The Epistles of St. Paul to the Thessalonians.* Cambridge: Cambridge University Press, 1911.

Fitzmyer, "Romans"
> Fitzmyer, J. A. "The Letter to the Romans." *NJBC.* 876–82.

Fitzmyer, *Romans*
> Fitzmyer, J. A. *Romans.* AB 33. New York: Doubleday, 1993.

Flanagan, "A Note"
> Flanagan, F. "A Note on Phil 3,20–21." *CBQ* 18 (1956) 8–9.

Foerster, "ἐξουσία"
> Foerster, W. "ἐξουσία." *TDNT.* 2.560–75.

Foerster, "σῴζω, σωτηρία"
> Foerster, W. "σῴζω, σωτηρία." *TDNT.* 7.980–1012.

Fohrer, *Geschichte*

Fohrer, G. *Geschichte der israelitischen Religion.* Berlin: de Gruyter, 1969.

Frame, *Thessalonians*

Frame, J. E. *A Critical and Exegetical Commentary on the Epistles of St. Paul to the Thessalonians.* ICC. Edinburgh: T. & T. Clark, 1912.

Friedrich, "Einschub"

Friedrich, G. "1. Thessalonicher 5,1–11, der apologetische Einschub eines Späteren." *ZTK* 70 (1973) 288–315.

Friedrich, *Briefe*

Friedrich, G. *Die Briefe an die Galater, Epheser, Philipper, Kolosser, Thessalonicher, und Philemon.* NTD 8. Göttingen: Vandenhoeck & Ruprecht, 1990.

Friedrich, "σάλπιγξ"

Friedrich, G. "σάλπιγξ." *TDNT.* 7.71–88.

Froitzheim, *Christologie*

Froitzheim, F. *Christologie und Eschatologie bei Paulus.* FB 35. Würzburg: Echter, 1979.

Furnish, *II Corinthians*

Furnish, V. *II Corinthians.* AB 32A. Garden City, N.Y.: Doubleday, 1984.

Furnish, *Moral Teaching*

Furnish, V. *The Moral Teaching of Paul.* Nashville: Abingdon, 1982.

Furnish, *Theology*

Furnish, V. *Theology and Ethics in Paul.* Nashville/New York: Abingdon, 1968.

Garland, "Composition"

Garland, D. E. "The Composition and Unity of Philippians: Some Neglected Literary Factors." *NovT* 27 (1985) 141–73.

Gerhardsson, *Gospel Tradition*

Gerhardsson, B. *The Gospel Tradition.* Lund: Gleerup, 1986.

Gillman, "Transformation"

Gillman, J. "Signals of Transformation in 1 Thessalonians 4:13–18." *CBQ* 47 (1985) 263–81.

Gillman, "Thematic Comparison"

Gillman, J. "A Thematic Comparison: 1 Cor 15:50–57 and 2 Cor 5:1–5." *JBL* 107 (1988) 439–54.

Gillman, "Future Life"

Gillman, J. "Transformation into the Future Life: A Study of 1 Cor 15:50–53, Its Context, and Related Passages." Ph.D. diss., Catholic University Leuven, 1980.

Gnilka, "Antipaulinische Mission"

Gnilka, J. "Die antipaulinische Mission in Philippi." *BZ* (1965) 258–76.

Gnilka, *Schriftzeugnis*

Gnilka, J. *Ist 1 Kor. 3,10–15 ein Schriftzeugnis für das Fegfeuer? Eine exegetisch-historische Untersuchung.* Düsseldorf: Triltsch, 1955.

Gnilka, *Kolosserbrief*

Gnilka, J. *Der Kolosserbrief.* HTKNT 10/1. Freiburg/Basel/Vienna: Herder, 1980.

Gnilka, *Philipperbrief*

>Gnilka, J. *Der Philipperbrief.* HTKNT 10/3. Freiburg/Basel/Vienna: Herder, 1968.

Godet, *1 Corinthians*

>Godet, F. *Commentary on the First Epistle to the Corinthians.* 2 vols. 1886. reprint, Grand Rapids: Eerdmans, 1957.

Greenfield and Stone, "Enochic Pentateuch"

>Greenfield, J. C., and M. E. Stone, "The Enochic Pentateuch and the Date of the Similitudes." *HTR* 70 (1977) 51–65.

Grelot, *De la mort*

>Grelot, P. *De la mort à la vie éternelle.* Lectio divina 67. Paris: Cerf, 1971.

Grelot, "Messie"

>Grelot, P. "Le Messie dans les apocryphes de l'Ancien Testament." *La venue du Messie.* RechBib 6. Pages 19–50. Brussels: Desclée de Brouwer, 1962.

Gundry, *Sōma in Biblical Theology*

>Gundry, R. H. *Sōma in Biblical Theology with Emphasis on Pauline Anthropology.* SNTSMS 29. Cambridge: Cambridge University Press, 1976.

Guntermann, *Eschatologie*

>Guntermann, F. *Die Eschatologie des hl. Paulus.* NA 13/4–5. Münster: Aschendorff, 1932.

Güttgemanns, *Apostel*

>Güttgemanns, E. *Der leidende Apostel und sein Herr: Studien zur paulinischen Christologie.* FRLANT 90. Göttingen: Vandenhoeck & Ruprecht, 1966.

Hahn, Kertelge, and Schnackenburg, *Einheit der Kirche*

>Hahn, F., K. Kertelge, and R. Schnackenburg. *Einheit der Kirche: Grundlegung im Neuen Testament.* QD 84. Freiburg/Basel/Vienna: Herder, 1979.

Hainz, *Ekklesia*

>Hainz, J. *Ekklesia: Strukturen paulinischer Gemeinde-Theologie und Gemeinde Ordnung.* BU 9. Regensburg: Pustet, 1972.

Hainz, *Koinonia*

>Hainz, J. *Koinonia: "Kirche" als Gemeinschaft bei Paulus.* BU 16. Regensburg: Pustet, 1982.

Hanhart, "Paul's Hope"

>Hanhart, K. "Paul's Hope in the Face of Death." *JBL* 88 (1964) 445–57.

Harder, "φθείρω"

>Harder, G. "φθείρω." *TDNT.* 9.93–106.

Harnisch, *Eschatologische Existenz*

>Harnisch, W. *Eschatologische Existenz: Ein exegetischer Beitrag zum Sachanliegen von 1. Thessalonicher 4,13–5,11.* FRLANT 110. Göttingen: Vandenhoeck & Ruprecht, 1973.

Harnisch, *Verhängnis und Verheissung*
> Harnisch, W. *Verhängnis und Verheissung der Geschichte: Untersuchungen zur Zeit und Geschichtsverständnis im 4. Buch Ezra und in der syr. Baruchapokalypse.* FRLANT 97. Göttingen: Vandenhoeck & Ruprecht, 1969.

Hartman, *Asking for a Meaning*
> Hartman, L. *Asking for a Meaning: A Study of 1 Enoch 1–5.* ConB 12. Lund: Gleerup, 1979.

Hartman, *Prophecy Interpreted*
> Hartman, L. *Prophecy Interpreted: The Formation of Some Jewish Apocalyptic Texts and the Eschatological Discourse Mark 13 Par.* ConB 1. Lund: Gleerup, 1966.

Hay, *Glory*
> Hay, D. M. *Glory at the Right Hand: Psalm 110 in Early Christianity.* SBLMS 18. Nashville/New York: Abingdon, 1973.

Heitmüller, *Wiederkunft*
> Heitmüller, F. *Die Wiederkunft Christi und die damit in Verbindung stehenden Ereignisse.* Hamburg: Evangelischer Verlag, 1948.

Henderson, *Myth*
> Henderson, I. *Myth in the New Testament.* London: SCM, 1956.

Henneken, *Verkündigung*
> Henneken, B. *Verkündigung und Prophetie im Ersten Thessalonicherbrief.* SBS 29. Stuttgart: Katholisches Bibelwerk, 1967.

Héring, *1 Corinthiens*
> Héring, J. *La première Epître de saint Paul aux Corinthiens.* Neuchâtel: Delachaux. Paris: Niestlé, 1949.

Hill, "Christ's Kingdom"
> Hill, C. E. "Paul's Understanding of Christ's Kingdom in 1 Corinthians 15:20–28." *NovT* 30 (1988) 297–320.

Hoffmann, *Toten*
> Hoffmann, P. *Die Toten in Christus: Eine religionsgeschichtliche und exegetische Untersuchung zur paulinischen Eschatologie.* NTA 2. Münster: Aschendorff, 1966.

Holtz, *1 Thessalonicher*
> Holtz, T. *Der erste Brief an die Thessalonicher.* EKKNT 13. Zurich: Benziger, 1986.

Hooker, "Interchange in Christ"
> Hooker, M. D. "Interchange in Christ." *JTS* 22 (1971) 346–61.

Isaac, "1 Enoch"
> Isaac, E. "1 (Ethiopic Apocalypse of) Enoch." *OTP* 1.5–100.

J. Jeremias, *Eucharistic Words*
> Jeremias, J. *Eucharistic Words of Jesus.* London: SCM, 1966.

J. Jeremias, "Flesh and Blood"
> Jeremias, J. "Flesh and Blood Cannot Inherit the Kingdom of God. (1 Cor. XV. 50)." *NTS* 2 (1955–56) 151–59.

J. Jeremias, *Unknown Sayings*
> Jeremias, J. *Unknown Sayings of Jesus.* London: S.P.C.K. 1964.

Jörg Jeremias, *Theophanie*
    Jeremias, Jörg. *Theophanie: Die Geschichte einer alttestamentlichen Gattung*. WMANT 10. Neukirchen/Vluyn: Neukirchener, 1965.
Jewett, "Agitators"
    Jewett, R. "The Agitators and the Galatian Congregation." *NTS* 17 (1970–71) 198–212.
Joest, "Parusie Jesu Christi"
    Joest, W. "Die Kirche und die Parusie Jesu Christi." *Gott in Welt: Festgabe für Karl Rahner*. 2 vols. Edited by H. Vorgrimler. Freiburg/Basel/Vienna: Herder, 1964. 1.536–50.
Johnson, *Origins*
    Johnson, R. A. *The Origins of Demythologizing: Philosophy and Historiography in the Theology of Rudolf Bultmann*. Studies in the History of Religions 28. Leiden: Brill, 1974.
Jonas, *Gnosis*
    Jonas, H. *Gnosis und spätantiker Geist*. 2 vols. Göttingen: Vandenhoeck & Ruprecht, 1934.
Jourdan, "κοινωνία"
    Jourdan, G. V. "κοινωνία in 1 Corinthians 10:16." *JBL* 67 (1948) 111–24.
Kabisch, *Eschatologie*
    Kabisch, R. *Die Eschatologie des Paulus in ihren Zusammenhängen mit dem Grundbegriff des Paulinismus*. Göttingen: Vandenhoeck & Ruprecht, 1893.
Kabisch, *Die Quellen*
    Kabisch, R. *Die Quellen der Apokalypse Baruch*. Jahrbücher für protestantische Theologie 18. Leipzig: n.p., 1892.
Käsemann, "Eine Apologie"
    Käsemann, E. "Eine Apologie der urchristlichen Eschatologie." *Exegetische Versuche und Besinnungen*. Pages 135–57. Göttingen: Vandenhoeck & Ruprecht, 1964.
Käsemann, "Beginnings"
    Käsemann, E. "The Beginnings of Christian Theology." *JTC* 6 (1969) 17–46.
Käsemann, "Primitive Christian Apocalyptic"
    Käsemann, E. "On the Topic of Primitive Christian Apocalyptic." *JTC* 6 (1969) 99–133.
Käsemann, *Romans*
    Käsemann, E. *Commentary on Romans*. Grand Rapids: Eerdmans, 1980.
Kaiser, *Isaiah 13–39*
    Kaiser, O. *Isaiah 13–39*. Philadelphia: Westminster, 1974.
Kee, "Testaments"
    Kee, H. C. "Testaments of the Twelve Patriarchs." *OTP* 1.775–828.
Kee, "Terminology"
    Kee, H. C. "The Terminology of Mark's Exorcism Stories." *NTS* 14 (1967–68) 223–46.

Kehl, *Der Christushymnus*
> Kehl, N. *Der Christushymnus im Kolosserbrief.* SBM 1. Stuttgart: Katholisches Bibelwerk, 1967.

Kilpatrick, "ΒΛΕΠΕΤΕ"
> Kilpatrick, G. D. "ΒΛΕΠΕΤΕ, Philippians 3:2." *In Memoriam Paul Kahle.* Edited by M. Black and G. Fohrer. BZAW 103. Pages 146–48. Berlin: Töpelmann, 1968.

Klauck, *Hausgemeinde und Hauskirche*
> Klauck, H.-J. *Hausgemeinde und Hauskirche im frühen Christentum.* SBS 103. Stuttgart: Katholisches Bibelwerk, 1981.

Klein, "Naherwartung"
> Klein, G. "Apokalyptische Naherwartung bei Paulus." *Neues Testament und christliche Existenz: Festschrift für H. Braun.* Edited by H. D. Betz and L. Schottroff. Pages 241–62. Tübingen: Mohr (Siebeck), 1973.

Klijn, "2 Baruch"
> Klijn, A. F. J. "2 (Syriac Apocalypse of) Baruch." *OTP* 1.615–52.

Klijn, "Sources and Redaction"
> Klijn, A. F. J. "The Sources and the Redaction of the Syrian Apocalypse of Baruch." *JSJ* 1 (1971) 65–76.

Knibb, "Date of the Parables"
> Knibb, M. A. "The Date of the Parables of Enoch: A Critical Review." *NTS* 25 (1979) 345–59.

Knibb, *Ethiopic Enoch*
> Knibb, M. A. *The Ethiopic Book of Enoch: A New Edition in the Light of the Aramaic Dead Sea Fragments.* 2 vols. Oxford: Clarendon, 1978.

Koch, *Rediscovery of Apocalyptic*
> Koch, K. *The Rediscovery of Apocalyptic.* SBT 2/22. Naperville, Ill.: Allenson, 1972.

Koester, "Die ausserkanonischen Herrenworte"
> Koester, H. "Die ausserkanonischen Herrenworte als Produkte der christlichen Gemeinde." *ZNW* 48 (1957) 220–37.

Koester, "Purpose"
> Koester, H. "The Purpose of the Polemic of a Pauline Fragment." *NTS* 8 (1961–62) 317–32.

Kreitzer, *Jesus and God*
> Kreitzer, L. J. *Jesus and God in Paul's Eschatology.* JSNTSup 19. Sheffield: JSOT, 1987.

Kuck, *Judgment*
> Kuck, D. W. *Judgment and Community Conflict: Paul's Use of Apocalyptic Judgment Language in 1 Corinthians 3:5–4:5.* NovTSup 66. Leiden: Brill, 1992.

Kümmel, *Korinther I/II*
> Kümmel, W. G. *An die Korinther I/II.* Tübingen: Mohr, 1949.

Kümmel, *Introduction*
> Kümmel, W. G. *Introduction to the New Testament.* Nashville/New York: Abingdon, 1975.

Kümmel, "Problem"
> Kümmel, W. G. "Das literarische und geschichtliche Problem des Ersten Thessalonicherbriefes." *Heilsgeschehen und Geschichte: Gesammelte Aufsätze 1936–1964.* Pages 406–16. Marburg: Elwert, 1965.

Kümmel, *Promise and Fulfilment*
> Kümmel, W. G. *Promise and Fulfilment: The Eschatological Message of Jesus.* SBT 23. London: SCM, 1957.

Lambrecht, "Christological Use"
> Lambrecht, J. "Paul's Christological Use of Scripture in 1 Cor. 15.20–28." *NTS* 28 (1982) 502–27.

Lambrecht, "Structure"
> Lambrecht, J. "Structure and Line of Thought in 1 Cor. 15:23–28." *NovT* 32 (1990) 143–51.

Laub, *Eschatologische Verkündigung*
> Laub, F. *Eschatologische Verkündigung und Lebensgestaltung nach Paulus.* BU 10. Pages 125–27. Regensburg: Pustet, 1973.

Liddell and Scott, *Lexicon*
> Liddell, H. G., and R. Scott. *A Greek-English Lexicon.* Oxford: Clarendon, 1966.

Lietzmann, *Korinther I/II*
> Lietzmann, H. *An die Korinther I/II.* HNT 9. Edited by W. G. Kümmel. Tübingen: Mohr, 1949.

Lindemann, "Die korinthische Eschatologie"
> Lindemann, A. "Paulus und die korinthische Eschatologie: Zur These einer 'Entwicklung' im paulinischen Denken." *NTS* 37 (1991) 373–99.

Lohfink, *Himmelfahrt*
> Lohfink, G. *Die Himmelfahrt Jesu: Untersuchungen zu den Himmelfahrts- und Erhöhungstexten bei Lukas.* SANT 2. Munich: Kösel, 1971.

Lohmeyer, *Philipper, Kolosser, Philemon*
> Lohmeyer, E. *Die Briefe an die Philipper, an die Kolosser, und an Philemon.* MeyerK 9. Göttingen: Vandenhoeck & Ruprecht, 1964.

Löhr, " 'Herrenwort' "
> Löhr, G. "1 Thess 4,15–17: Das 'Herrenwort.' " *ZNW* 71 (1980) 269–73.

Lohse, *Kolosser und Philemon*
> Lohse, E. *Die Briefe an die Kolosser und an Philemon.* MeyerK 9/2. Göttingen: Vandenhoeck & Ruprecht, 1968.

Lövestam, *Wakefulness*
> Lövestam, E. *Spiritual Wakefulness in the New Testament.* Lund: Gleerup, 1963.

Luedemann, "ἀπάντησις"
> Luedemann, G. "ἀπάντησις." *TDNT.* 1.380.

Luedemann, *Paul*
> Luedemann, G. *Paul, Apostle to the Gentiles.* Philadelphia: Fortress, 1984.

Lütgert, *Die Vollkommenen*

Lütgert, W. *Die Vollkommenen im Philipperbrief und die Enthusiasten in Thessalonich.* BFCT 13/6. Gütersloh: Bertelsmann, 1909.

Luz, *Geschichtsverständnis*

Luz, U. *Das Geschichtsverständnis des Paulus.* BEvT 49. Munich: Kaiser, 1968.

Maier, "Ps 110,1"

Maier, F. W. "Ps 110,1. (LXX 109,1) im Zusammenhang von 1 Kor 15,24–27." *BZ* 20 (1932) 139–56.

Malevez, *Christian Message*

Malevez, L. *The Christian Message and Myth.* London: SCM, 1958.

Marshall, *Thessalonians*

Marshall, I. H. *1 and 2 Thessalonians.* NCBC. London: Marshall, Morgan, & Scott, 1983.

Marxsen, *Introduction*

Marxsen, W. *Introduction to the New Testament.* Philadelphia: Fortress, 1976.

Mattern, *Verständnis*

Mattern, L. *Das Verständnis des Gerichtes bei Paulus.* ATANT 47. Zürich/Stuttgart: Zwingli, 1966.

McDermott, "Biblical Doctrine"

McDermott, M. "The Biblical Doctrine of KOINΩNIA." *BZ* 19 (1975) 64–77, 219–23.

Mearns, "Dating the Similitudes"

Mearns, C. L. "Dating the Similitudes of Enoch." *NTS* 25 (1979) 360–69.

Merklein, *Christus und die Kirche*

Merklein, H. *Christus und die Kirche: Die theologische Grundstruktur des Epheserbriefes nach Eph 2,11–18.* SBS 66. Stuttgart: Katholisches Bibelwerk, 1973.

Merklein, "Ekklesia Gottes"

Merklein, H. "Die Ekklesia Gottes: Der Kirchenbegriff bei Paulus und in Jerusalem." *BZ* 29 (1979) 48–70.

Merklein, "Theologe als Prophet"

Merklein, H. "Der Theologe als Prophet: Zur Funktion prophetischen Redens im theologischen Diskurs des Paulus." *NTS* 38 (1992) 402–29.

Metzger "4 Ezra"

Metzger, B. M. "The Fourth Book of Ezra." *OTP* 1.517–56.

Meyer, "σάρξ"

Meyer, R. "σάρξ." *TDNT.* 7.110–19.

Michaelis, *Philipper*

Michaelis, W. *Der Brief des Paulus an die Philipper.* HNT 11. Tübingen: Mohr (Siebeck), 1935.

Michel, *An die Römer*

Michel, O. *Der Brief an die Römer.* MeyerK 4. Göttingen: Vandenhoeck & Ruprecht, 1957.

Milik, *Books of Enoch*
> Milik, J. T. *The Books of Enoch. Aramaic Fragments of Qumrân Cave 4.* Oxford: Clarendon, 1976.

Miller, "ἀρχόντων"
> Miller, G. "ἀρχόντων τοῦ αἰῶνος τουτοῦ—a New Look at 1 Corinthians 2:6–8." *JBL* 91 (1972) 522–28.

Milligan, *Thessalonians*
> Milligan, G. *St. Paul's Epistles to the Thessalonians.* London: Macmillan, 1908.

Moltmann, *Theology of Hope*
> Moltmann, J. *Theology of Hope: On the Ground and the Implications of a Christian Eschatology.* London: SCM, 1965.

A. L. Moore, *Thessalonians*
> Moore, A. L. *1 and 2 Thessalonians.* London: Nelson, 1969.

A. L. Moore, *Parousia*
> Moore, A. L. *Parousia in the New Testament.* Leiden: Brill, 1966.

G. F. Moore, *Judaism*
> Moore, G. F. *Judaism in the First Centuries of the Christian Era: The Age of the Tannaim.* 3 vols. Cambridge: Harvard University Press, 1927–30.

Morissette, "Psaume VIII,7b"
> Morissette, R. "La citation du Psaume VIII,7b dans I Corinthiens XV,27a." *ScEs* 24 (1972) 313–42.

Morris, *Thessalonians*
> Morris, L. *The First and Second Epistles to the Thessalonians.* Grand Rapids: Eerdmans, 1991.

Moule, "St. Paul and Dualism"
> Moule, C. F. D. "St. Paul and Dualism: The Pauline Conception of Resurrection." *NTS* 12 (1966) 106–18.

Mowinckel, *He That Cometh*
> Mowinckel, S. *He That Cometh.* Oxford: Blackwell, 1959.

K. Müller, "Leiblichkeit"
> Müller, K. "Die Leiblichkeit des Heils 1 Kor 15,25–58." *Résurrection du Christ et des Chrétiens. 1 Co 15.* Edited by L. de Lorenzi. Série Monographique de Benedictina 8. Pages 171–281. Rome: Abbaye de S. Paul, 1985.

U. B. Müller, *Messias und Menschensohn*
> Müller, U. B. *Messias und Menschensohn in jüdischen Apokalypsen und in der Offenbarung des Johannes.* SNT 6. Gütersloh: Mohn, 1972.

Müller-Bardorff, "Einheit des Philipperbriefes"
> Müller-Bardorff, J. "Zur Frage der literarischen Einheit des Philipperbriefes." *Wissenschaftliche Zeitschrift der Universität Jena, Gesellschafts-und sprachwissenschaftliche Reihe* 7 (1957–58) 591–604.

Mundle, "καταντάω"
> Mundle, W. "καταντάω." *NIDNTT.* 1.324–25.

Murphy-O'Connor, "Philippiens"
> Murphy-O'Connor, J. "Philippiens." *DBSup.* 7.1211–33.

Murphy-O'Connor, "Second Corinthians"
Murphy-O'Connor, J. "The Second Letter to the Corinthians."
NJBC. 816–29.

Nebe, *"Hoffnung"*
Nebe, G. *"Hoffnung" bei Paulus: Elpis und ihre Synonyme im Zusammenhang der Eschatologie.* SUNT 16. Göttingen: Vandenhoeck & Ruprecht, 1983.

Neil, *Thessalonians*
Neil, W. *The Epistle of Paul to the Thessalonians.* MNTC. London: Hodder & Stoughton, 1965.

Nelis, "Tag Jahwes"
Nelis, J. "Tag Jahwes." *Bibel-Lexicon.* Edited by H. Haag. Columns 1700–1704. Einsiedeln: Benziger, 1956.

Nepper-Christensen, "Herrenwort"
Nepper-Christensen, P. "Das verborgene Herrenwort: Eine Untersuchung über 1. Thess. 4,13–18." *ST* 19 (1965) 136–54.

Nestle-Aland, *Novum Testamentum*
Nestle-Aland, *Novum Testamentum Graece.* 26th ed. Stuttgart: Deutsche Bibelstiftung, 1979.

Neugebauer, *In Christus*
Neugebauer, F. *In Christus: Eine Untersuchung zum paulinischen Glaubensverständnis.* Göttingen: Vandenhoeck & Ruprecht, 1961.

Nickelsburg, *Resurrection*
Nickelsburg, G. W. E. *Resurrection, Immortality, and Eternal Life in Intertestamental Judaism.* HTS 26. Cambridge: Harvard University Press, 1972.

Nickelsburg, *Jewish Literature*
Nickelsburg, G. W. E. *Jewish Literature between the Bible and the Mishnah: A Historical and Literary Introduction.* Philadelphia: Fortress, 1981.

Oepke, "νεφέλη"
Oepke, A. "νεφέλη." *TDNT.* 4.902–10.

Oepke, "παρουσία"
Oepke, A. "παρουσία." *TDNT.* 5.858–71.

Ollenburger, "Introduction"
Ollenburger, B. C. "Introduction." *Holy War in Ancient Israel.* Ed. by M. J. Dawn. Pages 1–33. Grand Rapids: Eerdmans, 1991.

Panikulam, *Koinōnia*
Panikulam, G. *Koinōnia in the New Testament: A Dynamic Expression of Christian Life.* AnBib 85. Rome: Biblical Institute, 1979.

Pearson, "1 Thessalonians 2:13–16"
Pearson, B. A. "1 Thessalonians 2:13–16: A Deutero-Pauline Interpolation." *HTR* 64 (1971) 79–94.

Perriman, "Paul and the Parousia"
Perriman, A. C. "Paul and the Parousia: 1 Corinthians 15.50–57 and 2 Corinthians 5.1–5." *NTS* 35 (1989) 512–21.

Pesch, *Entdeckung*

>Pesch, R. *Die Entdeckung des ältesten Paulusbriefes, Paulus—neu gesehen: Die Briefe an die Gemeinde der Thessalonicher.* Freiburg: Herder, 1984.

Pesch, *Naherwartungen*

>Pesch, R. *Naherwartungen: Tradition und Redaktion in Mk 13.* KBANT. Düsseldorf: Patmos, 1968.

Pesch, *Lieblingsgemeinde*

>Pesch, R. *Paulus und seine Lieblingsgemeinde: Paulus—neu gesehen, Die Briefe an die Heiligen von Philippi.* Freiburg: Herder, 1985.

Peterson, "Einholung"

>Peterson, E. "Die Einholung des Kyrios (1 Thess., IV,17)." *ZST* 7 (1929–30) 682–702.

Philonenko, *Interpolations*

>Philonenko, M. *Les interpolations chrétiennes des Testaments des Douze Patriarches et les manuscrits de Qumrân.* Cahiers de la *RHPR* 35. Paris: Presses universitaires de France, 1960.

Plevnik, "Authenticity"

>Plevnik, J. "1 Thess 5,1–11: Its Authenticity, Intention, and Message." *Bib* 60 (1979) 71–90.

Plevnik, "Parousia"

>Plevnik, J. "The Parousia as Implication of Christ's Resurrection: An Exegesis of 1 Thess 4:13–18." *Word and Spirit: Essays in Honor of David Michael Stanley, S.J., on His 60th Birthday.* Edited by J. Plevnik. Pages 199–277. Willowdale: Regis College, 1975.

Plevnik, "Pauline Presuppositions"

>Plevnik, J. "Pauline Presuppositions." *The Thessalonian Correspondence.* Edited by R. F. Collins. BETL 87. Pages 50–61. Leuven: Leuven University Press, 1990.

Plevnik, "The Taking Up"

>Plevnik, J. "The Taking Up of the Faithful and the Resurrection of the Dead in 1 Thessalonians 4:16–18." *CBQ* 46 (1984) 274–83.

Plevnik, "Ultimate Reality"

>Plevnik, J. "The Ultimate Reality in 1 Thessalonians." *Ultimate Reality and Meaning: Interdisciplinary Studies in the Philosophy of Understanding* 12 (1989) 256–71.

Plevnik, *What Are They Saying?*

>Plevnik, J. *What Are They Saying about Paul?* New York/Mahwah, N.J.: Paulist Press, 1986.

Plummer, *2 Corinthians*

>Plummer, A. *Second Epistle of St. Paul to the Corinthians.* ICC. Edinburgh: T. & T. Clark, 1966.

Priest, "Testament of Moses"

>Priest, J. "Testament of Moses." *OTP* 1.919–34.

Rahner, "The Church and the Parousia"

>Rahner, K. "The Church and the Parousia of Christ." *TI.* 6.295–312.

Rahner, "Eschatologie"
> Rahner, K. "Eschatologie." *LTK.* 3.1094–98.

Rahner, "Hermeneutics"
> Rahner, K. "The Hermeneutics of Eschatological Assertions." *TI.* 4.323–46.

Rahner, *Theological Investigations*
> Rahner, K. *Theological Investigations.* 20 vols. Baltimore: Helicon, 1961–81.

Rahtjen, "The Three Letters"
> Rahtjen, B. D. "The Three Letters of Paul to the Philippians." *NTS* 6 (1959–60) 167–73.

Reed, "Hesitation Formulas"
> Reed, J. T. "Philippians 3:1 and the Epistolary Hesitation Formulas: The Literary Integrity of Philippians, Again," *JBL* 115 (1996) 63–90.

Ricoeur, *Essays*
> Ricoeur, P. *Essays on Biblical Interpretation.* Philadelphia: Fortress, 1980.

Rigaux, *L'Antéchrist*
> Rigaux, B. *L'antéchrist à l'opposition au royaume messianique dans l'Ancien et le Nouveau Testament.* Paris: Gabalda. Gembloux: Duculot, 1932.

Rigaux, *Paul*
> Rigaux, B. *Paul and His Letters.* Chicago: Franciscan Herald, 1968.

Rigaux, *Thessaloniciens*
> Rigaux, B. *Saint-Paul: Les Epîtres aux Thessaloniciens.* EBib. Paris: Gabalda. Gembloux: Duculot, 1956.

Rigaux, "Tradition"
> Rigaux, B. "Tradition et rédaction dans I Th. V.1–10." *NTS* 21 (1975) 318–40.

Robinson and Koester, *Trajectories*
> Robinson, J. M., and H. Koester. *Trajectories through Early Christianity.* Philadelphia: Fortress, 1971.

Roetzel, *Judgement*
> Roetzel, C. L. *Judgement in the Community: A Study of the Relationship between Eschatology and Ecclesiology in Paul.* Leiden: Brill, 1972.

Russell, *Method*
> Russell, D. S. *The Method and Message of Jewish Apocalyptic.* London: SCM, 1964.

Sayler, *Promises Failed?*
> Sayler, G. B. *Have the Promises Failed? A Literary Analysis of 2 Baruch.* SBLDS 72. Chico: Scholars Press, 1984.

Schade, *Apokalyptische Christologie*
> Schade, H.-H. *Apokalyptische Christologie bei Paulus: Studien zum Zusammenhang von Christologie und Eschatologie in den Paulus-Briefen.* GTA 18. Göttingen: Vandenhoeck & Ruprecht, 1981.

Schenk, *Philipperbriefe*
> Schenk, W. *Die Philipperbriefe des Paulus.* Stuttgart/Berlin/
> Cologne/Mainz: Kohlhammer, 1984.

Schlier, *Apostel*
> Schlier, H. *Der Apostel und seine Gemeinde: Auslegung des ersten
> Briefes an die Thessalonicher.* Freiburg/Basel/Vienna: Herder, 1973.

Schlier, *Galater*
> Schlier, H. *Der Brief an die Galater.* MeyerK 7. Göttingen:
> Vandenhoeck & Ruprecht, 1965.

Schlier, *Geist*
> Schlier, H. *Der Geist und die Kirche,* vol. 4 of *Exegetische Aufsätze
> und Vorträge.* Freiburg/Basel/Vienna: Herder, 1980.

Schlier, *Principalities*
> Schlier, H. *Principalities and Powers in the New Testament.* New
> York: Herder & Herder, 1961.

Schlier, *Römerbrief*
> Schlier, H. *Der Römerbrief.* HTKNT 6. Freiburg/Basel/Vienna:
> Herder, 1977.

Schlink, *The Coming Christ*
> Schlink, E. *The Coming Christ and the Coming Church.* Edinburgh:
> Oliver & Boyd, 1967.

Schmid, "κέλευσμα"
> Schmid, L. "κέλευσμα." *TDNT.* 3.656–59.

Schmidt, "ἐκκλησία"
> Schmidt, K. L. "ἐκκλησία." *TDNT.* 3.501–36.

Schmidt, *Christianisme primitive*
> Schmidt, K. L. *Le probleme du christianisme primitive: quatre
> conférences sur la forme et la pensée du Nouveau Testament.* Paris:
> Leroux, 1938.

Schmithals, *Gnosticism in Corinth*
> Schmithals, W. *Gnosticism in Corinth: An Investigation of the
> Letters to the Corinthians.* New York: Abingdon, 1971.

Schmithals, "Historical Situation"
> Schmithals, W. "The Historical Situation of the Thessalonian
> Epistles." *Paul and the Gnostics.* Pages 123–218. Nashville/New
> York: Abingdon, 1972.

Schmithals, "Irrlehrer"
> Schmithals, W. "Die Irrlehrer des Philipperbriefes." *ZTK* 54 (1957)
> 297–341.

Schmithals, *Paul and the Gnostics*
> Schmithals, W. *Paul and the Gnostics.* Nashville/New York:
> Abingdon, 1972.

Schnackenburg, *Baptism*
> Schnackenburg, R. *Baptism in the Thought of St. Paul.* Oxford:
> Blackwell, 1964.

Schnackenburg, *Church*
> Schnackenburg, R. *The Church in the New Testament.* New York:
> Herder & Herder, 1965.

Schnackenburg, "Einheit"
> Schnackenburg, R. "Die Einheit der Kirche unter dem
> Koinonia-Gedanken." *Einheit der Kirche.* QD 84. Edited by
> F. Hahn, K. Kertelge, and R. Schnackenburg. Pages 52–93.
> Freiburg/Basel/ Vienna: Herder, 1979.

Schnackenburg, *God's Rule*
> Schnackenburg, R. *God's Rule and Kingdom.* Freiburg: Herder.
> Montreal: Palm, 1963.

Schnackenburg, "Kirche und Parusie"
> Schnackenburg, R. "Kirche und Parusie." *Gott in Welt: Festgabe
> für K. Rahner.* 2 vols. Edited by H. Vorgrimler.
> Freiburg/Basel/ Vienna: Herder, 1964. 1.551–78.

Schnackenburg, "Ortsgemeinde"
> Schnackenburg, R. "Ortsgemeinde und 'Kirche Gottes' im ersten
> Korintherbrief." *Ortskirche-Weltkirche: Festgabe für Julius Kardinal
> Döpfner.* Edited by H. Fleckenstein, G. Gruber, G. Schwaiger, and
> E. Tewes. Pages 32–47. Würzburg: Echter, 1973.

Schottroff, *Der Glaubende*
> Schottroff, L. *Der Glaubende und die feindliche Welt: Beobachtungen
> zum gnostischen Dualismus und seiner Bedeutung für Paulus und das
> Johannesevangelium.* WMANT 37. Neukirchen: Neukirchener, 1970.

Schrage, "1 Korinther 15:1–11"
> Schrage, W. "1 Korinther 15:1–11." *Résurrection du Christ et des
> Chrétiens. 1 Co 15.* Edited by L. de Lorenzi. Serie Monographique
> de "Benedictina" 8. Pages 21–45. Rome: Abbaye de S. Paul, 1985.

Schrage, " 'Ekklesia' und 'Synagoge,' "
> Schrage, W. " 'Ekklesia' und 'Synagoge.' " ZTK 60 (1963) 178–202.

Schrage, *Ethics*
> Schrage, W. *The Ethics in the New Testament.* Philadelphia:
> Fortress, 1982.

Schreiner, "Ende der Tage"
> Schreiner, J. "Das Ende der Tage: Die Botschaft von der Endzeit in
> den alttestamentlichen Schriften." *BibLeb* 5 (1964) 180–94.

Schürmann, *1 Thessalonicher*
> Schürmann, H. *Der Erste Brief an die Thessalonicher.* Geistliche
> Schriftlesung. Düsseldorf: Patmos, 1964.

Schwally, *Der heilige Krieg*
> Schwally, F. *Der heilige Krieg im alten Israel.* Leipzig: Dieterich,
> 1901.

Schweitzer, *Mysticism of Paul*
> Schweitzer, A. *The Mysticism of Paul the Apostle.* New York: Holt,
> 1931.

Schweizer, "σάρξ"
> Schweizer, E. "σάρξ." *TDNT.* 7.128–29.

Scott, "He Cometh"
> Scott, R. B. Y. "Behold, He Cometh with the Clouds." *NTS* 5
> (1958–59) 127–32.

Seesemann, *Der Begriff* KOINΩNIA

> Seesemann, H. *Der Begriff* KOINΩNIA *im Neuen Testament.* BZNW
> 14. Giessen: Töpelmann, 1933.

Sellin, *Streit*

> Sellin, G. *Der Streit um die Auferstehung der Toten: Eine
> religionsgeschichtliche und exegetische Untersuchung von 1 Korinther
> 15.* FRLANT 138. Göttingen: Vandenhoeck & Ruprecht, 1986.

Sider, "Resurrection Body"

> Sider, R. J. "The Pauline Conception of the Resurrection Body in
> 1 Corinthians XV.35–54." *NTS* 21 (1975) 428–39.

Sieber, *Mit Christus Leben*

> Sieber, P. *Mit Christus Leben: Eine Studie zur paulinischen
> Auferstehungshoffnung.* ATANT 61. Zürich: Theologischer Verlag,
> 1971.

Staab, *Thessalonicherbriefe*

> Staab, K. *Die Thessalonicherbriefe: Die Gefangenschaftsbriefe.* RNT
> 7/1. Regensburg: Pustet, 1969.

Stolz, *Kriege*

> Stolz, F. *Jahwes und Israels Kriege.* ATANT 60. Zürich:
> Theologischer Verlag, 1972.

Strack and Billerbeck, *Kommentar*

> Strack, H. and P. Billerbeck, *Kommentar zum Neuen Testament aus
> Talmud und Midrasch.* 4 vols. Munich: Beck, 1922–28.

Strecker, "Redaktion"

> Strecker, G. "Redaktion und Tradition im Christushymnus Phil
> 2,6–11." *ZNW* 55 (1964) 63–78.

Tannehill, *Dying and Rising*

> Tannehill, R. *Dying and Rising with Christ.* BZNW 32. Berlin:
> Töpelmann, 1967.

Teichmann, *Vorstellungen*

> Teichmann, E. *Die paulinischen Vorstellungen von Auferstehung und
> Gericht und ihre Beziehung zur jüdischen Apokalyptik.* Freiburg
> i.B./Tübingen: Akademische Verlagsbuchhandlung, 1896.

Theissen, *Psychological Aspects*

> Theissen, G. *Psychological Aspects of Pauline Theology.* Philadelphia:
> Fortress, 1987.

Thornton, *The Common Life*

> Thornton, L. S. *The Common Life in the Body of Christ.* London:
> Dacre, 1963.

Thüsing, *Per Christum in Deum*

> Thüsing, W. *Per Christum in Deum: Studien zum Verhältnis von
> Christozentrik und Theozentrik in den paulinischen Hauptbriefen.*
> NA 1. Münster: Aschendorff, 1965.

Tillmann, *Wiederkunft*

> Tillmann, F. *Die Wiederkunft Christi nach den paulinischen Briefen.*
> BibS(F) 14: Freiburg i.B.: Herder, 1909.

Trilling, *Untersuchungen*

Trilling, W. *Untersuchungen zum zweiten Thessalonicherbrief.* Leipzig: St. Benno, 1972.

Tuckett, "Synoptic Tradition"

Tuckett, C. M. "Synoptic Tradition in 1 Thessalonians?" *The Thessalonian Correspondence.* Edited by R. F. Collins. BETL 87. Pages 160–82. Leuven: Leuven University Press, 1990.

Usami, " 'The Dead Raised' "

Usami, K. " 'How Are the Dead Raised?' (1 Cor 15,35–58)." *Bib* 57 (1976) 468–95.

van der Woude, *Die messianischen Vorstellungen*

Woude, A. S. van der, *Die messianischen Vorstellungen der Gemeinde von Qumran.* Assen: Van Gorcum, 1957.

Vermes, *Dead Sea Scrolls*

Vermes, G. *The Dead Sea Scrolls in English.* Harmondsworth/ Baltimore/Victoria: Penguin Books, 1966.

Vögtle, *Zukunft*

Vögtle, A. *Das Neue Testament und die Zukunft des Kosmos.* Düsseldorf: Patmos, 1970.

Volz, *Eschalogie*

Volz, P. *Die Eschatologie der jüdischen Gemeinde im neutestamentlichen Zeitalter: Nach den Quellen der rabbinischen und apokryphen Literatur.* Tübingen: Mohn, 1934. Reprint. Hildesheim: Olms, 1966.

von Dobschütz, *Thessalonicher-Briefe*

Dobschütz, E. von, *Die Thessalonicher-Briefe.* MeyerK 10. Göttingen: Vandenhoeck & Ruprecht, 1909.

von Rad, "βασιλεύς"

von Rad, G. "βασιλεύς." *TDNT.* 1.565–71.

von Rad, "ἡμέρα"

von Rad, G. "ἡμέρα." *TDNT.* 2.943–47.

von Rad, *Holy War*

von Rad, G. *Der heilige Krieg im alten Israel.* ATANT 20. Zürich: Zwingli, 1951. 3d ed., Göttingen: Vandenhoeck & Ruprecht, 1958. ET: *Holy War in Ancient Israel.* Edited by M. J. Dawn. Grand Rapids: Eerdmans, 1991.

von Rad, *Theology*

von Rad, G. *Old Testament Theology.* 2 vols. Edinburgh/London: Oliver & Boyd, 1965.

von Rad, "Day of the Lord"

von Rad, G. "The Origin of the Concept of the Day of YAHWEH." *JSS* 4 (1959) 97–108. Also in *Theology,* 2.119–25.

Wanamaker, *1 & 2 Thessalonians*

Wanamaker, C. A. *Commentary on 1 & 2 Thessalonians.* NIGTC. Grand Rapids: Eerdmans, 1990.

Weipert, "Heiliger Krieg"
> Weipert, M. "Heiliger Krieg in Israel und Assyrien: Kritische Bemerkungen zu Gerhard von Rads Konzept des 'heiligen Krieges im Alten Testament.' " *ZAW* 84 (1972) 460–93.

Weiser, *Jeremia*
> Weiser, A. *Das Buch Jeremia*. ATD 20. Göttingen: Vandenhoeck & Ruprecht, 1965.

Weiss, *Der erste Korintherbrief*
> Weiss, J. *Der erste Korintherbrief*. MeyerK. Göttingen: Vandenhoeck & Ruprecht, 1910.

Wiefel, "Hauptrichtung"
> Wiefel, W. "Die Hauptrichtung des Wandels im eschatologischen Denken des Paulus." *TZ* 30 (1974) 65–81.

Wikenhauser, *Pauline Mysticism*
> Wikenhauser, A. *Pauline Mysticism: Christ in the Mystical Teaching of St. Paul*. New York: Herder & Herder, 1960.

Wilcke, *Zwischenreich*
> Wilcke, H.-A. *Das Problem eines messianischen Zwischenreiches bei Paulus*. ATANT 51. Zürich: Zwingli, 1967.

Wilckens, "Ursprung"
> Wilckens, U. "Der Ursprung der Überlieferung der Erscheinungen des Auferstandenen." *Dogma und Denkstrukturen: Festschrift für E. Schlink*. Edited by W. Joest and W. Pannenberg. Pages 56–95. Göttingen: Vandenhoeck & Ruprecht, 1963.

Wintermute, "Apocalypse of Elijah"
> Wintermute, O. S. "Apocalypse of Elijah." *OTP* 1.721–53.

Wolff, *Korinther II*
> Wolff, Chr. *Der zweite Brief des Paulus an die Korinther*. THKNT 8. Berlin: Evangelische Verlagsanstalt, 1989.

Woschitz, *Elpis, Hoffnung*
> Woschitz, K. M. *Elpis, Hoffnung: Geschichte, Philosophie, Exegese, Theologie eines Schlüsselbegriffs*. Vienna/Freiburg/Basel: Herder, 1979.

Wright, "Psalms of Solomon"
> Wright, R. B. "Psalms of Solomon." *OTP* 2.639–70.

Young, *Isaiah*
> Young, E. *The Book of Isaiah*. 3 vols. Grand Rapids: Eerdmans, 1969.

Zerwick and Grosvenor, *A Grammatical Analysis*
> Zerwick, M. and M. Grosvenor, *A Grammatical Analysis of the Greek New Testament*. 2 vols. Rome: Biblical Institute, 1979.

Ziegler, *Isaias*
> Ziegler, J. *Isaias*. Würzburg: Echter, 1960.

INTRODUCTION

The parousia of the Lord is a constituent part of Paul's gospel: it stands and falls with the faith in the resurrection and lordship of Jesus. While the Lord's coming is more in focus in his earlier epistles than in his later epistles, it retains its essential theological position in all of the commonly recognized Pauline letters.

When I first began to work on this project, around 1970, I was under the constraint of R. Bultmann's interpretation which demanded that the mythological component of the Lord's parousia be stripped or reinterpreted existentially. This necessitated a certain method of investigation. The present book thus reflects this procedure. Concerning the content of this book, however, several things should be mentioned in this connection.

First, my particular interest here in the imagery Paul employed in talking about the parousia. Since most of the imagery occurs in 1 Thess 4:13–18, the first part of this book therefore contains a discussion of the imagery found in that section. I felt that one has first to understand what the imagery means, before one can attempt to remove it or to reinterpret it.

Secondly, since Bultmann removed not only the imagery of the Lord's coming, but the event itself, I tried to understand the theological significance of the parousia. There is always the danger of throwing out the baby with the bath water. This led me to explore the links of the parousia to other salvific events associated with Easter.

Thirdly, because Bultmann chose the existential interpretation as the carrier of his theological reinterpretation, it became imperative to provide a critical analysis of the philosophical principles that guided his theological interpretation. How tenable are they? Are they adequate for the eschatological affirmations made in the NT? Does the shift from the objective to the subjective leave out something from the original message? Hence the book contains a section dealing with the hermeneutical principles governing the eschatological assertions.

Fourthly, the present book, finally written after the heat of controversy and novelty associated with Bultmann has passed, is not a belated answer to Bultmann, although it does address the problems that he raised. It is, beyond that, an attempt to expose the spiritual riches and the theological significance of the parousia for Christian existence. Hence after the study of some key texts, which provide the meaning in the particular context of the Lord's coming, there is a second part of this book that deals with theological themes such as hope, judgment, being with the Lord, the church, etc. This situates the parousia in the wider streams of Paul's thought. My hope is that this will make the book more faithful to Pauline theology and more useful to the reader.

Fifthly, this book affirms that the Lord's coming is a constituent and permanent part of the Christian faith in the development of Paul' thought. It understands the parousia as the completion of Easter, above all as the completion of the Lordship of Jesus that is associated with Easter. It notes that the earlier Pauline epistles reflect a lively hope in the impending coming of the Lord. The undeniable short horizon of expectation, foreshortened because of the joy of being with the Lord, gives a special focus to this event. The apostle situates his own salvation, as well as the salvation of the faithful whom he had brought to the faith, in relation to this future event. In 1 Thess 4:13–18, as well as in the entire letter, we can still see the central place of this salvific event, while in 1 Cor 15 we can observe the emphasis on the resurrection in the context of the Lord's coming. The expectation that he or his faithful will be alive at that event is found in all his major epistles.

Sixthly, it became obvious to me that one should not give an exposition of this theme apart from Paul's expectation of the day of the Lord. It is this notion that supplies the biblical roots for this event, as well as biblical imagery employed by Paul. In addition, there is the coming of the Son of man, or the coming of the

Messiah, documented in Jewish apocalyptic writings that also provides a stream of tradition on which Paul's imagery draws. It was therefore important to trace the development of this imagery. To what extent the apostle depended on Hellenistic imagery, however, is not clear. The enthusiastic turning to this source by E. Peterson has given way to a more critical appraisal of Hellenistic influence on Paul's presentation of the parousia.

PART ONE

EXEGETICAL FOUNDATION

1

❋

CONCEPTS AND TERMS
OF THE LORD'S COMING

The Lord's coming in the end time, the subject of this investigation, is referred to in 1 Thess 4:15 as "the coming (παρουσία, *parousia*) of the Lord." In the same eschatological discourse, 4:13–5:11, Paul mentions also the "day of the Lord" (ἡμέρα κυρίου, *hēmera kyriou*) (5:2), while in 1 Cor 1:7 he speaks of the "revelation" (ἀποκάλυψις, *apokalypsis*) of the Lord. Related to ἀποκάλυψις, *apokalypsis*, are such words as φανερόω, *phaneroō* (1 Cor 4:5; 2 Cor 5:10; Col 3:4), φανερός, *phaneros* (1 Cor 3:13), φωτίζω, *phōtizō* (1 Cor 4:5), and δηλόω, *dēloō* (1 Cor 3:13). In 2 Thess 2:8 occurs also the combination "the appearance" (ἐπιφάνεια, *epiphaneia*) "in his coming" (τῆς παρουσίας, *tēs parousias*; cf. 1 Tim 6:14; 2 Tim 4:8; Titus 2:13).[1]

Paul's most frequently used expressions for the Lord's coming are ρουσία *(parousia)* and "day of the Lord." The former occurs mainly in the Thessalonian correspondence, while the latter is employed throughout the Pauline epistles. The word ἀποκάλυψις ("revelation"), which in 1 Cor 1:7 refers to the Lord's coming, is usually employed for an event associated with the Lord's coming, such as judgment.[2]

---

[1] Since the authorship of 2 Thess is disputed, we shall not base our argumentation on this epistle. The word ἐπιφάνεια occurs also in the Pastoral Epistles.

[2] Elsewhere in the Pauline writings ἀποκάλυψις refers to the present revelations, as in Rom 16:25; 1 Cor 14:6, 26; 2 Cor 12:1, 7; and Gal 1:12; 2:2.

The language dealing with this event expected in the end time is thus not uniform. Each term is associated with its own imagery. But what images are evoked by these expressions? And what is their background?

A. THE PAROUSIA

The dictionary meanings of the word παρουσία include the presence of persons or things, the position of planets, arrival, coming, advent, and visit.[3] The LXX employs this word only seldom (5 times);[4] it occurs only in its Greek MSS, and always in the sense of coming or arrival or presence. The term occurs in the NT 24 times, of this 11 times (plus 3 times in 2 Thess) in the Pauline epistles. In the Gospels it is found only in Matthew (4 times).[5] In the authentic Pauline epistles it is employed for Paul's coming or for the coming of his associates more frequently than for the coming of the Lord.[6] He uses it in the latter sense in 1 Thess 2:19, 3:13, 4:14, 5:23 and 1 Cor 15:23. The word is employed for the Lord's coming in the earliest letters of Paul, above all in 1 Thessalonians (and in 2 Thess 2:1, 8, 9).

Many scholars regard the word παρουσία as a technical term for the end-time coming of the Lord. This, however, may be truer of its usage in the later NT writings (Matt 24:27, 37, 39; Jas 5:7, 9; 2 Pet 1:16; 3:4, 12; 1 John 2:28)[7] than in Paul's. The apostle uses the word more often for his own coming (2 Cor 10:10; Phil 1:26; 2:12) or for the arrival of his associates (1 Cor 16:17; 2 Cor 7:6, 7) than for the Lord's coming. It is part of his active vocabulary. Thus, only

---

[3] Liddell and Scott, *Lexicon*, 1343; Oepke, "παρουσία"; Feuillet, "Parousie," esp. cols. 1331–35; Rigaux, *Thessaloniciens*, 196–201.

[4] The word παρουσία occurs in Neh 2:6 (variant); Jdt 10:18; 1 Macc 8:12, 15:21; and 3 Macc 3:17.

[5] The word παρουσία is not found in Mark 8:38 (Luke 9:26; Matt 16:27) or in Mark 13:24–27 (Matt 24:29–31; Luke 21:25–28), both of which give a description of the Lord's coming. Instead, the verb ἔρχομαι, *erchomai*, is employed.

[6] Paul employs παρουσία 6 times for his own coming or for that of his associates and 5 times for the Lord's coming.

[7] In the Gospels, the expression "the coming (παρουσία) of the Son of man" occurs in Matt 24:27, 37, 39 ("Q"), while their Lucan parallels (17:26, 30) employ the term "the day (ἡμέρα, *hēmera*) of the Son of man." In the rest of the NT, παρουσία is employed for the coming of the Lord in Jas 5:7, 8; 2 Pet 1:16, 3:4, 12; and 1 John 2:28. 2 Thess 2:12 employs παρουσία also for the coming of Satan.

the particular context determines the meaning of this term. When he refers to the Lord's parousia, Paul employs the word παρουσία with a qualifier. He speaks of the παρουσία "of the Lord" (1 Thess 4:15), "of Christ" (1 Cor 15:23), "of our Lord Jesus" (1 Thess 2:19; 3:13), or "of our Lord Jesus Christ" (1 Thess 5:23).

The following texts contain the term παρουσία together with a description of the event:

> For what is our hope or joy or crown (στέφανος, *stephanos*) of boasting before our Lord Jesus at his coming (ἐν τῇ παρουσίᾳ, *en tē parousia*)? Is it not you? Yes, you are our glory and joy! (1 Thess 2:19–20)[8]

> For this we declare to you by the word of the Lord, that we who are alive, who are left until the coming (εἰς τὴν παρουσίαν, *eis tēn parousian*) of the Lord, will by no means precede those who have died. For the Lord himself, with a cry of command, with the archangel's call and with the sound of God's trumpet (ἐν σάλπιγγι, *en salpingi*), will descend from heaven, and the dead in Christ will rise first. Then we who are alive, who are left, will be caught up in the clouds together with them to meet (εἰς ἀπάντησιν, *eis apantēsin*) the Lord in the air; and so we will be with the Lord forever. (1 Thess 4:15–17)

> And may he so strengthen your hearts in holiness that you may be blameless before our God and Father at the coming (ἐν τῇ παρουσίᾳ) of our Lord Jesus with all his saints. (1 Thess 3:13)

The noun παρουσία comes from Hellenistic Greek. The Hebrew Bible does not have a comparable noun, although it expresses the coming of the Lord (God) with a verb form.[9] The word is not found in Philo, but Josephus employs it for the benevolent presence of Yahweh.[10] The noun occurs twice in the *Testaments of the Twelve Patriarchs*—in *T. Judah* 22:2[11] and in

---

[8] Perhaps 2 Thess 1:6–10 should be mentioned here because of its closeness to the above texts and its full description of the parousia without employing that word:

For it is indeed just of God to repay with affliction those who afflict you, and to give relief to the afflicted as well as to us, when the Lord Jesus is revealed (ἐν τῇ ἀποκαλύψει, *en tē apokalypsei*) from heaven with his mighty angels in flaming fire, inflicting vengeance on those who do not know God and on those who do not obey the gospel of our Lord Jesus. These will suffer the punishment of eternal destruction, separated from the presence of the Lord and from the glory of his might, when he comes to be glorified by his saints and to be marvelled at on that day among all who have believed.

[9] Feuillet, "Parousie," 1333.

[10] *Ant.* 3.80; 9.55; 18.284–86. See Oepke, "παρουσία," 864–65.

[11] In *T. Judah* 22:2 Judah says to his sons, "My rule shall be terminated by men of alien race, until the salvation of Israel comes, until the coming (παρουσίας) of the God of righteousness."

T. Levi 8:15[12]—but its use in the original text here is not certain.[13] It also occurs in *2 Enoch* 32:1, but this apocalyptic book as well is an uncertain witness.[14]

A. Deissmann in 1923 asserted that not only the noun παρουσία but also the imagery of Christ's coming is drawn from the Hellenistic παρουσία as it is described in the papyrus texts of that era. From the time of the Ptolemies until the second century CE the expression παρουσία referred to the visits of kings and emperors to a city. These visits were regarded as epoch-making events. On these occasions the citizens made preparations for the glorious event, minted coins to commemorate it, and counted the years of the new era from that time onward. Often such motifs as a crown, joy, or expectation were associated with such visits. This was also the period of the emperor cult; hence, the imperial visitor was greeted as the "savior" and given divine honors. The Latin equivalent of this παρουσία is *adventus*, and there are extant coins commemorating the coming of Augustus in Corinth or the visits of other Roman emperors. According to Deissmann, the imperial παρουσία must have been well known to the apostle and to the people to whom he preached. It provided Paul with ready imagery for the depiction of the Lord's coming; it facilitated the people's understanding of Christ's return; and it explains Paul's unique depiction of the event in 1 Thess 4:13–18.[15]

E. Peterson in 1929 provided further support for this view from newly discovered papyri, inscriptions, and literary sources,

---

[12] In *T. Levi* 8:15 the patriarch discloses what the seven heavenly men in the vision said about the three offices that will be granted to his posterity. The seven men said, "The third shall be granted a new name, because from Judah a king will arise and shall found a new priesthood in accord with the gentile model and for all nations. His presence (παρουσία) is beloved, as a prophet of the Most High."

[13] On the date of *T 12 Patr.*, see Eissfeldt, *Einleitung*, 855–62. According to Eissfeldt, the underlying text, which was later expanded and revised and now contains many Christian interpolations, derives from the time of the Qumran community. But see de Jonge, *Testaments*; also "Christian Influence" and "Once More." Kee, "Testaments," ascribes the underlying composition to a Hellenized Jew and suggests either 250 BCE or 137–107 BCE as the date of composition. He rejects de Jonge's contention that the entire document is a Christian composition.

[14] Eissfeldt (*Einleitung*, 843–44) dates this writing to the seventh century CE. According to him, its present form is a Christian composition, while the original Hebrew text antedates 70 CE. See also Andersen, "2 Enoch," 94–97.

[15] Deissmann, *Licht*, 314–20; ET: Deissmann, *Light*, 368–73.

both Greek and Latin.[16] According to him, the noun ᾿πάντησις, *apantēsis*, found in 1 Thess 4:17 and in the secular sources dealing with the Hellenistic παρουσία,[17] indicates Paul's dependence here on Hellenistic sources. The ἀπάντησις at the imperial παρουσία provides the image for the meeting between the faithful and the Lord. According to Peterson, at the approach of the imperial visitor the citizens would go out of their city to meet (εἰς ἀπάντησιν) the dignitary and conduct him in a parade to their city. Similarly, Peterson states, at the coming of the Lord the faithful would leave their earthly habitation *(civitas)* and go to meet (εἰς ἀπάντησιν) him and to accompany him joyfully to their earthly city. In 1 Thess 4:13–18 Paul depicts this as follows: The Lord comes from his heavenly abode to the heights above the earth. At the news of his coming the believers leave their earthly city and go up to meet him in the air and to accompany him joyfully to their abode on earth. Peterson describes this as the *Einholung* of the Lord—the bringing of the Lord.

Peterson's explanation was taken up by many scholars.[18] But in 1952 J. Dupont, after reexamining Peterson's arguments,[19] cast serious doubts on his interpretation.[20] According to Dupont, Paul himself did not take the Hellenistic imperial παρουσία as a model of the Lord's coming, although the tradition before him, which he utilized, might have done so. The word παρουσία occurs only in the earliest Pauline epistles, and only in apocalyptic sections, where Hellenistic influence is least likely. The word ἀπάντησις and its synonyms,[21] on which Peterson's argument is based, is scarcely a technical term in Hellenistic παρουσία descriptions, as Peterson claims. It occurs frequently and in a variety of contexts in the LXX and in the

---

[16] Peterson, "Einholung."

[17] The equivalents of ἀπάντησις are the nouns ὑπάντησις, *hypantēsis*, and συνάντησις, *synantēsis*, and the equivalents of ἀπαντάω, *apantaō*, are the verbs ὑπαντάω, *hypantaō*, and συναντάω, *synantaō*.

[18] This view was adopted by Rigaux (*L'Antéchrist*, 262–64), Dibelius (*Thessalonicher I/II, Philipper*, 28), Cerfaux (*Christ*, 32–44), and many others. Oepke ("παρουσία"), Feuillet ("Parousie"), and Best (*Thessalonians*, 199), however, are cautious in this regard. See Dupont, *L'Union*, 48.

[19] Dupont, *L'Union*, 49–73.

[20] It is still advocated by Holtz (*1 Thessalonicher*, 203) and seriously considered by Best (*Thessalonians*, 199).

[21] The synonyms are συνάντησις, ὑπάντησις, and ἀπαντή. Cf. Dupont, *L'Union*, 67–68.

NT.[22] Its underlying Hebrew meaning is "meet," "encounter," or "befall." Only seldom do these texts convey the *Einholung*[23] ("go out to bring," "fetch," "go to get"). Other motifs mentioned by Peterson, such as στέφανος and καύχησις, *kauchēsis* (1 Thess 2:19–20), are employed by Paul also outside his parousia depictions (2 Cor 1:14; Phil 4:1) and are found also in the LXX.[24] The festivities that took place at the imperial presence in the city and that ceased once the imperial visitor departed are thus not the image Paul has of the faithful being with the Lord forever.[25] Paul is thinking of an eternal life with the Lord.

Besides the criticism leveled by Dupont, Peterson's explanation is questionable for other reasons, including the following: (1) Linguistic evidence from the Pauline epistles indicates that the word παρουσία is part of Paul's vocabulary. He employs it more often for the coming of persons than for the coming of the Lord. Thus, Paul does not borrow the word from the Hellenistic sources dealing with the imperial παρουσία. (2) Peterson's explanation gratuitously equates the faithful's earthly dwelling with the *civitas terrena*. This is a metaphorical interpretation of the imagery in the Hellenistic παρουσία. (3) His interpretation entails a shift from a horizontal encounter on earth, to which his Hellenistic sources refer, to a vertical encounter involving earth, heaven, and the clouds as means of transportation. (4) It suggests that the faithful are the agents in this encounter: they will go up in order to bring the Lord with them to their *civitas*, just as the citizens went out of their *civitas* to bring the emperor or the king into their city. But 1 Thess 4:16–17 states that the faithful are acted upon—they will be taken up (ἁρπαγησόμεθα, *harpagēsometha*). The agents here are God and his Christ. Moreover, 4:14 states that God through

---

[22] According to Dupont (ibid., 68), this word and its synonyms occur 129 times in the LXX. The expression εἰς ἀπάντησιν (1 Thess 4:17) occurs only once in the Hellenistic sources adduced by Peterson, as Wilcke (*Zwischenreich*, 144) points out. But εἰς ἀπάντησιν occurs over 60 times in the LXX, translating 49 times the Hebrew לִקְרַאת, *liqra'at*, and occasionally אֶל־פְּנֵי, *'el-penê* or לִפְנֵי, *lipnê*. Εἰς ἀπάντωσιν occurs only 3 times in the NT (Matt 25:6; Acts 28:15; 1 Thess 4:17), and the verb ἀπαντάω only twice (Mark 14:13; Luke 17:13). The expression εἰς ἀπαντήν, which occurs 26 times in the LXX, almost always translates the Hebrew לִקְרַאת, *liqra't*.

[23] In the sense "zur Einholung entgegengehen." Wilcke (*Zwischenreich*, 145) suggests that 1 Sam 18:6 and 2 Sam 19:16 may have this meaning.

[24] Dupont, *L'Union*, 71–73.

[25] Ibid., 78–79.

Jesus brings (ἄξει, *axei*) the deceased faithful. (5) Peterson's explanation leaves unexplained a number of motifs found in 4:16–18,
such as the cry of command, the archangel, ἁρπαγησόμεθα, and
the clouds. (6) It does not account for Paul's insistence that the
dead are first raised (4:16), then taken up. Nor does it clarify the
peculiar representation of the resurrection as a return from the
grave (4:16).

The *Einholung* in 4:13–18 is that of the faithful—not of Christ,
as Peterson suggests.[26] It is the faithful who are taken up by the
clouds and brought to the Lord. And it is God who through Jesus
brings about the *Einholung*. Peterson, relying as he does on the
Hellenistic παρουσία, reverses the traditional explanation and thus
puts the cart before the horse. The Hellenistic παρουσία, if it ever
influenced Paul's presentation of the Lord's coming, provided at
best only a partial imagery for it.

A better source of inspiration, Dupont suggests, is the Sinai
theophany, described in LXX Exod 19:10–18 and LXX Deut 32:2. To
illustrate this, Dupont quotes Exod 19:10–18 and highlights significant resemblances.

> The Lord said to Moses: " . . . Have them wash their clothes and prepare for
> the third day, because on the third day the Lord will come down upon Mount
> Sinai in the sight of all the people . . . When the trumpet sounds a long blast
> (αἱ φωναὶ καὶ αἱ σάλπιγγες, *hai phōnai kai hai salpinges*), they may go up on
> the mountain." . . . On the morning of the third day there was thunder and
> lightning, as well as a thick cloud (ἡ νεφέλη, *hē nephelē*) on the mountain,
> and the blast of trumpets (φωνὴ τῆς σάλπιγγος, *phōnē tēs salpingos*) so loud
> that all the people who were in the camp trembled. Moses brought
> (ἐξήγαγεν, *exēgagen*) the people out of the camp to meet (εἰς συνάντησιν, *eis
> synantēsin*) God.[27]

Here the Lord comes down from heaven upon Mount Sinai.
There are trumpet blasts, voices, thunder, and a thick cloud.
Moses brings (ἐξήγαγεν) the people up the mountain to meet (εἰς
συνάντησιν) the Lord. The agreement in motifs between LXX Exod
19:10–18 and 1 Thess 4:16–17 is thus rather extensive. And the
likelihood that the Sinai theophany is the source of Paul's inspiration is further enhanced by the fact that the Sinai event reverberates in Jewish apocalyptic depictions of the end-time coming of God
(cf. *1 Enoch* 1:3–9). According to Dupont, this grandiose theophany

---

[26] Holtz (*1 Thessalonicher*, 203) still follows Peterson in this regard.
[27] Dupont, *L'Union*, 45, 69, 97–98 (author's translation).

is a much closer and more likely source of inspiration for 1 Thess 4:13–18 than is Hellenistic ceremonial for imperial visits.

Dupont does not state where, according to this scenario, the faithful end up after they have been brought to the Lord. In the Sinai scene the Israelites, having heard on the mountain the law of the Lord, return to their tents. Are the faithful, after they are united with the Lord, then let down to the earth?

On closer inspection, Dupont's suggestion that 1 Thess 4:13–18 is modeled on the Sinai event does not account for a number of features found in 4:16–17. It does not explain any better than the Hellenistic παρουσία the raising of the dead, the insistence that the dead are raised first, the taking up by the cloud, and life with the Lord forever. More to the point, it disregards the different functions the motifs have in the two texts, and the different contexts. At Sinai the cloud is a covering, but in 1 Thess 4:17 it functions as a vehicle;[28] at Sinai the Israelites go up the mountain, but in 1 Thess 4:17 the faithful are snatched up (ἁρπαγησόμεθα) by the clouds and lifted to the aerial heights above the earth; at Sinai the Israelites hear voices, lightning, and thunder, but at the parousia the faithful hear the voice of command (κέλευσμα, keleusma) and the voice of the archangel; at Sinai the Israelites hear the promulgation of the law, but in 1 Thess 4:13–18 the faithful are placed near the Lord forever.

Thus, there are many discrepancies between the two accounts. The Sinai event may indeed be a better source of inspiration for Paul than the Hellenistic παρουσία, as Dupont indicates, but it clearly does not explain everything. Paul may not have been directly influenced by LXX Exod 19:10–18 but, rather, by the apocalyptic depictions of God's end-time coming in which the Sinai depiction was utilized and adapted. And he seems to be using other traditions as well. But he is here reformulating these traditional images in a creative fashion in order to incorporate the features specific to Christ's coming and to Christian hope centered on that coming. Hence, while there is some analogy between 1 Thess 4:13–18 and the Sinai event—as there is between 1 Thess 4:13–18 and the Hellenistic παρουσία—in many respects 1 Thess 4:13–18 is unique. Some of the motifs in 1 Thess 4:13–18 occur also elsewhere in Jewish writings and seem to be typical.

---

[28] Best, *Thessalonians*, 199.

B. THE DAY OF THE LORD

Most Pauline texts dealing with the parousia occur in the context of the end-time judgment (1 Thess 1:10; 2:19; 3:13; 5:1–11, 23). But judgment is associated with the tradition of the day of the Lord, and it incorporates the imagery of the Lord's mighty coming. In fact, Paul uses the terms παρουσία and "day of the Lord" in juxtaposition (1 Thess 4:15; 5:2), and he seems to join the two images also in 1 Cor 4:1–5 and Rom 13:12.[29] That παρουσία and "day of the Lord" are inter-changeable is evident also in the Gospels. In recounting the same apocalyptic discourse in the "Q" source, Matthew employs the phrase παρουσία τοῦ υἱοῦ τοῦ ἀνθρώπου, *parousia tou huiou tou anthrōpou*, while Luke uses ἡμέρα τοῦ υἱοῦ τοῦ ἀνθρώπου, *hēmera tou huiou tou anthrōpou* (Matt 24:27, 37, 39; Luke 17:24, 26, 30).

The phrase "day of the Lord" (ἡμέρα κυρίου) and its variants are thus also employed by Paul for the end-time coming of the Lord. In Rom 2:5 he employs the phrase for God's judgment, while elsewhere[30] he seems to refer to Christ's coming and judgment. In fact, the apostle uses "day of the Lord" more frequently than παρουσία. While the latter occurs only in 1 (and 2) Thessalonians and 1 Corinthians, the former is found in all Pauline epistles.[31] "Day of the Lord" is employed more frequently than παρουσία also in the rest of the NT.[32]

---

[29] In 1 Cor 4:5 Paul speaks of the "coming" of the Lord (ἕως ἂν ἔλθῃ ὁ κύριος, *heōs an elthē ho kyrios*), who will judge and reveal the intentions of the heart. In 1 Thess 5:2 he employs ἔρχεται, *erchetai*, with "day of the Lord." In Rom 13:12 he speaks of ἤγγικεν, *ēngiken*. Matthew in 24:27, 37, 39 employs the term παρουσία, while Luke in the parallel texts 17:24, 26, 30 uses "the day of the Son of man."

[30] Rom 2:16; 1 Cor 1:8; 5:5; 2 Cor 1:14; 1 Thess 5:2 (cf. 2 Thess 2:2). Paul employs at times the phrase ἡμέρα Χριστοῦ Ἰησοῦ, *hēmera Christou Iēsou* (Phil 1:6) or ἡμέρα Χριστοῦ, *hēmera Christou* (Phil 1:10; 2:16) or ἡμέρα ὀργῆς, *hēmera orgēs* (Rom 2:5) or ἡμέρα σωτηρίας, *hēmera sōtērias* (2 Cor 6:2 [twice]), or simply ἡμέρα (Rom 2:16; 13:12; 1 Cor 3:13; 1 Thess 5:4). Sometimes the day is only alluded to (1 Cor 4:1–5).

[31] Paul employs this expression at least 12 times, whereas he uses παρουσία for the Lord's coming only 5 times.

[32] In the NT the following expressions also occur: ἡ ἡμέρα ἐκείνη, *hē hēmera ekeinē* (Luke 17:30, 31; 21:34; John 14:20; 16:23; Acts 2:20; 2 Tim 1:12, 18; 4:8); ἡ ἐσχάτη ἡμέρα, *hē eschatē hēmera* (John 6:39, 40, 44, 54; 11:24; 12:48); ἡμέρα κρίσεως, *hēmera kriseōs* (2 Pet 2:9; 3:7, 10; 1 John 4:17); ἡμέρα ὀργῆς, *hēmera orgēs* (Rev 6:17); τῆς μεγάλης ἡμέρας, *tēs megalēs hēmeras* (Rev 16:14).

Depending on the context, "day of the Lord" can be employed by Paul to mean salvation and/or punishment. The meaning is often indicated by the qualifiers "wrath," "judgment," or "salvation." Thus the apostle mentions "the day of wrath" (Rom 2:5, 16) as well as "the day of salvation" (2 Cor 6:2). The connection with the Lord's coming is at times provided by the verbs "to come" (ἔρχεται, 1 Thess 5:2), "to catch" (καταλάβη, katalabē, 1 Thess 5:4), or "to approach" (ἤγγικεν, Rom 13:12). The exhortation to be irreproachable is found in connection with the parousia (1 Thess 3:13) and with the day of the Lord (1 Thess 5:6–8; Rom 13:13; 1 Cor 1:8). And Paul encourages the faithful about the parousia and the day of the Lord (1 Thess 4:18; 5:11).

The christological focus of the day is clear in such expressions as "the day of Christ" (Phil 1:10; 2:16), "the day of Jesus Christ" (Phil 1:6), "the day of our Lord Jesus Christ" (1 Cor 1:8; 2 Cor 1:14), and "the day of the Lord" (1 Thess 5:2; 1 Cor 5:5; cf. 2 Thess 2:2). But the apostle can also simply use "the day" (Rom 13:12; 1 Cor 3:13).[33] It is, then, the context that supplies the necessary information. Paul's usage overlaps, to some extent, that of the rest of the NT.[34]

"Day of the Lord" occurs in various contexts elsewhere in the NT;[35] it is, therefore, not a Pauline expression. In fact, antecedents of "day of the Lord" are found in the LXX, in the Hebrew Bible, and in extrabiblical Jewish literature. These sources also provide the imagery. "Day of the Lord" thus belongs to Jewish tradition and has its own set of associations.

1. The Old Testament

In the Hebrew Bible we find the expression "the Day of Yahweh" (יְהוָה יוֹם, yôm YHWH), which the LXX translates with ἡμέρα (τοῦ) κυρίου, hēmera (tou) kyriou (Amos 5:18, 20). The LXX

---

[33] The term "the day" occurs where the definite article is not called for by the context. The expression "that day" occurs in 2 Thess 1:10; 2 Tim 1:12, 18; 4:8. See on this Nelis, "Tag Jahwes."

[34] Not found in Paul are variants of "the day of the Lord" such as "the days of the Son of man" (Luke 17:22), "the last day(s)" (John 7:37; Acts 2:17), "the great day" (Jude 6; Rev 6:17; Acts 2:20), and "the day of visitation" (1 Pet 2:12). In Eph 4:30 occurs the expression "the day of redemption," and in 6:13 "the evil day."

[35] Matt 11:22, 24; 12:36; Luke 17:30, 31; 21:34; John 6:39, 40, 44, 54; 11:24; Acts 17:31; Eph 4:30; 2 Thess 2:2; 2 Tim 4:8; 1 Pet 2:12; 2 Pet 2:9; 3:7, 10, 12; 1 John 4:17; Jude 6; Rev 6:17; 16:14.

contains the following variants: ἡμέρα (τοῦ) κυρίου ἡ μεγάλη, *hēmera (tou) kyriou hē megalē* (Zeph 1:14); ἡμέρα ὀργῆς (αὐτοῦ, κυρίου), *hēmera orgēs (autou, kyriou)* (Ps 109:5; Ezek 22:24; Zeph 2:3); ἡμέρα κρίσεως, *hēmera kriseōs* (Isa 34:8);ʹμέρα ἀντα-ποδόσεως, *hēmera antapodoseōs* (Isa 61:2); ἡμέρα τῆς δυνάμεώς σου, *hēmera tēs dynameōs sou* (Ps 109:3); ἡμέρα ἐκείνη, *hēmera ekeinē* (Isa 4:2).[36] These expressions in Greek correspond with the Hebrew variants and convey something of the nature of this particular day. They bring out the aspect of power, of judgment, or of salvation. The day in question is not like any other day; it is a definite (ἐκείνη) day of God's choice. It is the day of God's powerful intervention in the order and affairs of the world. This language occurs in prophetic utterances and in the Psalms. The context is a warning to acknowledge God and/or a reassurance of God's intervention. Associated with this day of the Lord are such motifs as wrath, judgment, retribution, reward, power, deliverance, and the lordship of God.

According to G. von Rad,[37] the day-of-the-Lord concept, which is older than the prophetic writings, originally expressed the expectation that God will intervene on Israel's behalf: Yahweh will take Israel's side and will triumph over its enemies. The day of the Lord will be the day of light and brightness for Israel, and the day of darkness and doom for Israel's enemies. This hope of Israel springs from the knowledge of God's all-conquering, terrible, and irresistible power and from Israel's special bond with Yahweh as its covenant partner. But Amos, in pointing out Israel's sinfulness, turned the brightness of this awaited day into darkness and doom for Israel, and the people's joyful expectation into foreboding. On that day the people will come to know not only God's holiness but also God's justice.

According to Amos 5:18–20, the people who disregard the lordship, righteousness, and holiness of Yahweh, Israel's covenant partner, can only expect disaster: "Alas for you, who desire the day of the Lord! Why do you want the day of the Lord? It is darkness, not light" (Amos 5:18). Elsewhere the prophet depicts the day of the Lord as a mighty manifestation of the lordship and power of God (3:3; 4:13; 5:27). The title "Lord, the God of hosts" occurs

---

[36] See Delling, "ἡμέρα," 947–48.
[37] Von Rad, "ἡμέρα," 944.

frequently in this connection (3:13; 4:13; 5:14, 27; 6:14; etc.). Amos warns that the people will experience the Lord's power as a terrible disaster, and he calls them to conversion (5:4–6, 14–15).

The preexilic prophets echoed Amos's warning. But neither they nor Amos understood the day of the Lord to mean the total destruction of Israel. They thought that in his faithfulness, the Lord would preserve in Israel a remnant who would acknowledge and put their trust in him. And neither Amos nor the preexilic prophets thought that this day would bring the world to its close. They understood it to be an intervention within Israel's history, rather than the end of all history.

The exilic and postexilic prophets reverted to the saving aspect of the day of the Lord. The focus was again on deliverance and restoration:[38] on that day the Lord would come and reveal his glorious lordship and power; he would save Israel and annihilate its foes. The day of the Lord became once again the carrier of hope, encouragement, and consolation. But the judgment and punishment motifs did not totally vanish from the depictions of the day of the Lord; they were merely toned down. The prophets still called for the purification of Israel, required by the holiness of God, which had been profaned among the nations by Israel. Yahweh's righteousness and holiness demands the righteousness and the holiness of Israel. According to Mal 3:2–4, the Lord of hosts will come suddenly to his temple and will purify and refine the sons of Levi so that they will present "right offerings to the Lord" (3:3). Mal 3:5–4:4 depicts the Lord removing all the evildoers and the arrogant from the people of Israel. Isaiah 52:11, 25:6–8; Mal 3–4; and Zech 13:2–9 call for the lifting of ignorance and error.[39] According to Isa 25:7, on that day the Lord will remove the "covering" of the nations—an image for their spiritual blindness and errors.[40]

Amos, and the prophets after him, announced a catastrophe that would take place in the near future (Ezek 34:12; Lam 1:21), or they interpreted a past event in this light and imagery. With the passage of time, however, the end time and the universal character of the day of the Lord became dominant, as is clear in Joel 3 and

---

[38] Ibid., 945.

[39] Schreiner, "Ende der Tage."

[40] Cf. Ziegler, *Isaias*, 83. On the date and authorship of Isa 24–27, see Young, *Isaiah*, 2.254–59; Kaiser, *Isaiah 13–39*, 173–79.

Zech 12–14. The latter mentions perpetual day and light, the waters of paradise, the extinction of all enemies of Jerusalem and Judah, peace, worship of the Lord by the surviving nations, and the universal kingship of the Lord. The apocalyptic literature further developed the picture of the day of the Lord with this end-time meaning.

Central to these depictions of the day of the Lord is the assertion that God comes to establish his power and rule. The oracles of the Lord in Amos mention the creator of the world (Amos 4:13; 5:8–9), the Lord (5:16; 9:6), and the God of hosts (3:13; 4:13; 5:16, 27; 9:5). The latter motif is echoed in Zech 14:15, which depicts the Lord's coming with his mighty heavenly army. In Isa 13 Yahweh employs human armies as his swift and terrible instrument. And in Joel 2:1–11 Yahweh musters natural phenomena, such as swarms of locusts that devour everything before them.

The terrible might of the Lord is brought out by the depictions of cosmic repercussions and convulsions: at his coming the sun, the moon, and the stars are darkened; thick darkness covers the earth; the foundations of the earth tremble; the hills melt like wax; and the earth is rent asunder (Amos 5:18, 20; Joel 2:1–2; Isa 13:6–13). Fear and distress strike everywhere. The Lord's coming is a catastrophe for his enemies, usually the hostile nations, but liberation and deliverance for Israel. According to A. Vögtle, these images convey Yahweh's all-conquering power, with which he establishes in the world his righteous rule through judgment and salvation.[41]

The motifs associated with the day of the Lord may reflect various *Sitze in Leben* in which these traditions were transmitted. S. Mowinckel, emphasizing the kingship motif, suggests a cultic celebration of Yahweh's royal day, his coming as a king.[42] Von Rad, emphasizing the conflict motif, suggests the tradition of the "holy wars."[43] F. M. Cross suggests that the two are complementary,

---

[41] Vögtle, *Zukunft*, 51. According to Vögtle, the purpose of the Lord's coming is indicated either in the depiction of the event or in the accompanying oracle of the Lord. In Ezek 30:19 (cf. v. 25; 32:15) the act of judgment upon Egypt is followed by the statement "Then they will know that I am the Lord."

[42] Mowinckel, *He That Cometh*, 145. For a criticism of this, see von Rad, "ἡμέρα," 944 n. 2. Von Rad disputes the cultic setting of the day-of-the-Lord tradition.

[43] Von Rad, "Day of the Lord."

rather than exclusive. For him, the "holy war" was a feature in the early Israelite cult which reenacted the history of redemption. According to him, this explains the juxtaposition of the kingship, divine-warrior, and cultic motifs in Isa 40:2–6, 42:10–16, 51:9–11, 52:7–12 and Ezek 20:33–42.[44]

The judgment, divine-warrior, and kingship motifs are thus central features of the day of the Lord. They occur also in Jewish and in NT apocalyptic. While, in the OT, political expectations overlap with ethical and spiritual concerns, prophetic speech makes it clear that Yahweh's real enemy is sin. Eschatological features occur especially in Second Isaiah and in later prophets, but the ultimate outcome is not life beyond death or beyond this world but life on earth marked with peace, justice, and holiness. In prophetic utterances the day of the Lord is associated with warnings, exhortations, and reassurances.

2. Jewish Apocalyptic Writings

Jewish apocalyptic provides a contemporary background to Paul's eschatological thinking. E. Käsemann has suggested that Jewish apocalyptic is the mother of Christian theology.[45] J. C. Beker regards it as the (only) proper horizon for interpreting Paul's message of the death and resurrection of Christ.[46]

The apocalyptic thinking provides new dimensions for the day of the Lord. While in prophetic statements oracles are uttered directly by God, in apocalyptic literature the revelation is usually mediated by an otherworldly figure, often by an angel. While prophetic utterances deal with life on earth, apocalyptic literature opens up the vision of a transcendent, eschatological, and supernatural reality,[47] of life beyond this life.[48] And while prophetic speech concerns the peace and prosperity of Israel, apocalyptic writings focus on the ultimate outcome for the good and for the evil, within Israel and elsewhere.

---

[44]Cross, "Divine Warrior," 24–30.

[45]Käsemann, "Beginnings"; also "Primitive Christian Apocalyptic."

[46]Beker, Paul the Apostle, 143–81. According to Beker, "The post-Pauline history of the church shows abundantly that the gospel itself was jeopardized when nonapocalyptic thought forms became its hermeneutical carrier" (p. 181).

[47]J. J. Collins, "Morphology," 10.

[48]J. J. Collins, "Apocalyptic Eschatology."

Especially relevant to this discussion are *1 Enoch, 4 Ezra, 2 Baruch (Syriac Apocalypse of Baruch),* and the *Testaments of the Twelve Patriarchs.*[49]

(a) 1 Enoch

First Enoch is a compilation of apocalyptic writings of many authors from the third century BCE to the first century CE.[50] Within this collection the following "books" have been identified: the Book of the Watchers (chs. 1–36), the Similitudes (chs. 37–71), the Astronomical Book (chs. 72–82), the Book of Dreams (chs. 83–90), and the Epistle of Enoch (chs. 91–107).[51] These books reflect different strata of composition in *1 Enoch.*

The Astronomical Book, 1 Enoch 72–82. According to J. T. Milik,[52] G. W. E. Nickelsburg,[53] and J. J. Collins,[54] the Astronomical Book is the oldest section of the Enochian collection, going back to the third century BCE. It depicts the fixed and divinely ordained order of stars and seasons. But according to this book, the presence of sin in the world disturbs this order, and this confusion in turn contributes to sin in the world. Sinners are warned that punishment and destruction await them, for there will be a day of judgment.

---

[49] On the extent of Jewish apocalyptic writings, see J. J. Collins, "Jewish Apocalypses." On the apocalypse genre, see J. J. Collins, "Morphology," which gives the comprehensive definition of Jewish apocalyptic reached by the SBL Genres Project: " 'Apocalypse' is a genre of revelatory literature with a narrative framework, in which a revelation is mediated by an otherworldly being to a human recipient, disclosing a transcendent reality which is both temporal, insofar as it envisages eschatological salvation, and spatial insofar as it involves another, supernatural world" (p. 9). See also J. J. Collins, "Apocalyptic Literature."

[50] See Milik, *Books of Enoch;* J. J. Collins, *Apocalyptic Imagination,* 33–34; Nickelsburg, *Jewish Literature,* 150–51.

[51] The entire *1 Enoch* is extant only in the Ethiopic version, but substantial fragments from all parts, except the Similitudes, have been found in Aramaic fragments of Qumran; see Milik, *Books of Enoch.* This discovery made possible a more precise dating of individual books and opened the way to the redaction and tradition-critical investigation of this compilation.

[52] Milik, *Books of Enoch,* 7. According to Milik, the Qumran fragments witness to four Aramaic manuscripts containing this book. The oldest of these, 4QEnastr[a], dates from the end of the third or the beginning of the second century BCE, while the latest, 4QEnastr[b], dates from the Herodian period, that is, the early years CE.

[53] Nickelsburg, *Jewish Literature,* 47.

[54] J. J. Collins, *Apocalyptic Imagination,* 46.

The day of judgment is mentioned in 81:4.[55] Enoch, after reading the "heavenly tablets" that contain a record of the deeds of mankind (v. 2), blesses "the great Lord, the king of glory," for creating the world and for having patience with the people (v. 3). Enoch blesses those who die in righteousness and goodness, since the heavenly tablets contain no record against them; they will not come under judgment (v. 4).

The day of judgment is the day of condemnation. It is the ultimate day. The context indicates that it occurs after everyone dies. The righteous are encouraged to persevere until death, since only those who die in righteousness will escape the judgment. The necessity of death for all is a fact (v. 9). On the judgment day, the good will announce righteousness to the good, and the righteous will rejoice and congratulate one another, while sinners and apostates shall die and "go down" (vv. 7–8).

The text exhorts the righteous and warns the sinners. It addresses individuals, rather than Israel. Life in the beyond is affirmed, and Enoch blesses those who will possess it. He blesses God when he sees the ultimate completion. The final judgment will manifest the lordship, the eternal kingship, and the goodness of the Creator. The day of judgment is a day in court.

The Book of the Watchers, 1 Enoch 1–36. First *Enoch* 1–36 is an ancient composition, dating from the third century BCE, with a subsection of an even older date.[56] According to G. W. E. Nickelsburg, literary observations and Aramaic remnants indicate that before 175 BCE this book was a literary unit comprising chs. 81–82, 91, and 92–105.[57] But the five Aramaic MSS containing

---

[55] According to Nickelsburg (*Jewish Literature*, 150 n. 154), chs. 81–82 belong to an early literary unit that comprised chs. 1–36, 81–82, and 92–105. The present position of 81:5–10 in the Astronomical Book may be secondary. Milik (*Books of Enoch*, 13–14) suggests that the passage is later than 164 BCE. Nickelsburg (*Jewish Literature*, 159) leaves the question open, but does not join chs. 81–82 to the earlier text of the Astronomical Book. If Milik is right, the connection of the judgment with the disorder of the seasons may be secondary.

[56] Milik, *Books of Enoch*, 25. According to Milik, the Book of the Watchers had from the second century BCE onward essentially the same form as the extant Greek and Ethiopian versions. About 50 percent of the latter version is present in the Aramaic fragments of Qumran.

[57] Nickelsburg, *Jewish Literature*, 48–49. According to Milik (*Books of Enoch*, 22–23), 4QEn^c probably contained the Book of the Watchers, the Book of Giants, the Book of Dreams, and the Epistle of Enoch. He suggests as the date of this compilation the last third of the first century BCE.

fragments of the Book of the Watchers disclose that the book was a compilation.[58] Chapters 1–5 provide the redactional framework. They now introduce the whole of *1 Enoch*, but originally they introduced only chs. 6–36 or chs. 6–19. Chapters 6–11 are a distinct unit that was incorporated almost unchanged into the present composition.[59]

The pivotal section dealing with the day of the Lord is the oracle in 1:1–9, which provides the framework for all of *1 Enoch*. It is linked with the oracle in 5:4–9. *First Enoch* 1:1–9 describes the "day of tribulation" that was shown in heaven to the patriarch Enoch.[60] The following is a reconstruction of the original text of the Ethiopic version:[61]

> The God of the universe, the Holy Great One, will come forth from his dwelling. And from there he will march upon Mount Sinai and appear in his camp emerging from heaven with a mighty power. And everyone shall be afraid, and Watchers shall quiver. And great fear and trembling shall seize them unto the ends of the earth. Mountains and high places will fall down and be frightened. And high hills shall be made low; and they shall melt like a honeycomb before the flame. And earth shall be rent asunder; and all that is upon the earth shall perish. And there shall be judgment upon all, (including) the righteous. And to all the righteous he will grant peace. He will preserve the elect, and kindness shall be upon them. They shall all belong to God and they shall prosper and be blessed; and the light of God shall shine unto them. Behold, he will arrive with ten thousand million of the holy ones in order to execute judgment upon all. He will destroy the wicked ones and censure all flesh on account of everything that they have done, that which the sinners and the wicked ones had committed against him. (*1 Enoch* 1:3–9, Isaac)

This promise applies to "the elect and the righteous" who, on the day of tribulation, will witness the removal of the ungodly. The vision is given by the angels, and it belongs to the elect in the distant future. The text thus deals with the last judgment. The scene

---

[58] According to Milik (*Books of Enoch*, 22), the oldest fragment, 4QEn[a] dates from the first half of the second century BCE and contains fragments from chs. 1–12. 4QEn[b], written in the mid–second century BCE, contains fragments from chs. 5–14. Both copies were brought to Qumran. The other copies were made in Qumran in the first century CE and formed part of the Enochian collection.

[59] J. J. Collins, *Apocalyptic Imagination*, 36.

[60] Verses 1–6 appear in 4QEn[a] 1 i, and v. 9 in 4QEn[c] 1 i; see Milik, *Books of Enoch*, 141–42, 184–85.

[61] The text is the translation by E. Isaac ("1 Enoch"). On Milik's reconstruction of the Aramaic text for vv. 3–5 from the fragment 4QEn[a] 1 i, and for v. 9 from 4QEn[c] 1 i, see Milik, *Books of Enoch*, 142, 184–85.

depicts the mighty coming of the leader of the heavenly armies: The God of the universe comes forth from his dwelling and marches in power on Mount Sinai. He comes with his heavenly (angelic) army, the "ten thousand million of the holy ones." He is the Lord of the heavenly hosts, who appears "in his camp" (v. 4). At his coming fear seizes everyone. The Watchers are terrified. The whole of nature writhes in convulsion: mountains and high places fall down and melt like a honeycomb before the flame; the earth is rent asunder, and all earth dwellers perish.

First Enoch 5:5–10 deals with the sinners: they who have not been long-suffering, have not kept the commandments of the Lord, and have "spoken slanderously grave and harsh words against his greatness" (v. 4). "Therefore, you shall curse your days, and the years of your life shall perish and multiply in eternal execration; and there will not be mercy unto you. In those days you shall make your names an eternal execration unto all the righteous; and sinners shall curse you continually—you together with the sinners" (5:5–6).

In contrast to these, the elect are promised light, joy, peace, and the inheritance of the earth (v. 7). They shall not be judged (v. 9). The years of their happiness shall be "multiplied forever" (v. 10); no sickness shall touch them; they will complete their full number of days on earth; they will be given wisdom; and they will not resort to sin. The promised completion is eschatological yet this-worldly. After the judgment life on earth continues, but it is not clearly an everlasting life.

The two texts emphasize the majesty, the power, and the holiness of God, which will become manifest at his coming. When God assumes his rule, the righteous will be rewarded with a life of bliss on earth. Despite their present tribulations, the righteous are fortunate, for God will richly reward them. But the ungodly, those who prosper now, must know that punishment lies in store for them.

The motifs in chs. 1–5 are taken up and developed in chs. 6–36.[62] Chapters 6–11, an ancient tradition incorporated by the author of the Book of the Watchers,[63] deal with the state of

---

[62] For the motifs common to chs. 1–5 and 6–36, see Hartman, *Asking for a Meaning*, 139–41.

[63] So Milik, *Books of Enoch*, 25. According to him (p. 24), chs. 6–19 date from the end of the third century BCE, the *terminus ante quem* being the year 164 BCE.

mankind and of the earth before the flood. Evil, violence, and bloodshed on earth were caused by the conspiracy of the angelic Watchers, who descended from heaven, divulged the secrets of heaven, and spawned a hybrid race of giants who went about consuming everything. The whole earth cries to heaven, and the souls of the slain appeal to the angels of heaven.

God then gives instruction to bind the evil Watchers and imprison them until "the day of the great judgment," when they shall be cast into fire (10:7). Four angels are sent from heaven to heal the earth and to destroy "all the spirits of the reprobates and the children of the Watchers" (10:16). They uproot all evil and make it possible for "the plant of righteousness and truth" to appear (10:16). The righteous are spared and are given long life. They "live till they beget thousands of children"; they live until old age in peace (10:17). The whole earth is tilled in righteousness, and the plants yield superabundant fruit. Truth and peace prevail (11:1–2). There is no oppression, sin, godlessness, or uncleanness. And all nations "offer adoration" to the Almighty (10:21).

These chapters, which elaborate on Gen 6:1–4, describe the extermination of all evil from the earth: God has checked the spread of evil and cleansed and restored the earth; his judgment ushers in a chiliastic period of bliss on earth. But the ultimate judgment is yet to come.[64] The text emphasizes the sovereignty of God on earth, yet the Holy One does not come personally to establish his rule. *First Enoch* 10:12–13 mentions the future day of judgment for the evil Watchers: after their imprisonment for seventy generations the Watchers will be led off to the abyss of fire to be tormented forever. Their collaborators will then also be cast into that fiery prison (v. 14). According to Nickelsburg, the author implies that the recent events resemble those of the primordial time. What happened at the flood is happening again in the present: the world has gone astray, but the judgment is close and a new age will dawn.[65]

---

[64] See Nickelsburg, *Jewish Literature*, 51.

[65] Nickelsburg, *Jewish Literature*, 51. Nickelsburg suggests that the author is here making an allusion to the current political oppression. The present power holders are like the giants of old, but they will be obliterated: God will assume his power and cleanse the earth, as he has done before.

In a subsequent dream, Enoch is taken to the very abode of the "Great Glory" (ch. 14), where he hears (chs. 15–16) a more detailed account of the condemnation of the Watchers and their offspring, the giants. He is told that the spirits of the slain giants will roam the earth and destroy without incurring judgment "until the day of the consummation, the great judgment day in which the age will be consummated over the Watchers and the godless" (16:1).

On his guided tour of heaven, Enoch sees a fiery prison for the stars and the hosts of heaven who did not keep the appointed time. They will be bound, kept here in chains for ten thousand years until their guilt is paid for (18:16). The seer is also shown the prison for the fallen Watchers. The Watchers will stay in it "until the great day of judgment in which they shall be judged till they are finished" (19:1).[66] Enoch, alone among human beings, sees the end of everything (19:3).

On his second journey through the regions of heaven, Enoch is also shown the abodes where the spirits of the deceased stay until their judgment (22:4). These spirits are separated according to their future lot, in dark or bright chambers. The first three chambers are dark, the fourth is bright. The first chamber contains those who did not receive their punishment during their life on earth; they are set apart in great pain until "the day of judgment and torment" (22:11). The second chamber contains the spirits of those slain by the sinners (v. 12). The third chamber contains the spirits of the outright sinners and transgressors. The seer is told that these "shall not be slain on the day of judgment nor shall they be raised from thence" (v. 13). The fourth chamber, which is bright and has a "spring of water" (21:2, 9), contains the spirits of the righteous deceased before the final judgment (v. 13).

When Enoch comes to paradise (ch. 24), he sees a high mountain that resembles a throne. The angel Michael explains to him that God will come from this throne "to visit the earth with goodness" (25:3). A special tree is reserved for the righteous after the final judgment, for no mortal is permitted to touch it until the "great judgment, when he shall take vengeance on all and con-

---

[66] Here Enoch is told that the spirits of the Watchers are assuming many different forms and are still defiling humankind by leading it to offer sacrifices to demons (1 Enoch 19:1).

clude (everything) forever" (25:4). Then the tree will be transplanted to the temple of the Lord, the Eternal King (25:5), and give fragrance to the righteous and holy (v. 5), and its fruit shall be food for the elect (v. 6).

After this, Enoch comes to Jerusalem and is shown a deep valley, the place of judgment. Here shall be gathered those who speak unbecoming words against the Lord (27:2). They will be judged in the presence of the righteous (v. 3), who praise the Lord of Glory, the Eternal King. At this point, Enoch again blesses and praises "the Lord of Glory" (v. 5; cf. 22:14; 25:7; 36:4).

The Book of the Watchers thus witnesses to a developed eschatology. It envisages the present state and the future lot of the spirits of the deceased. Here the present state and the future lot are related: the spirit of the evildoers are in a place of darkness and pain, awaiting their future judgment; the spirits of the righteous, however, are in light and await their reward in paradise.

The final judgment is still to come, and it will seal the future forever—both for human and for heavenly spirits in the beyond. No mercy will be shown to the originators of evil in the world—to the Watchers or their children. Human spirits will then receive their just recompense: those who did evil in the world will be punished; those who did good in the world will be rewarded. But the lot of the spirits of the wicked differs. Some of these spirits will be raised from their present abode, judged, condemned, and given over to eternal punishment, while the rest of these spirits will neither be slain nor raised from their present abode. But the spirits of the righteous will be raised from their chambers and will be given a paradise on earth.

The raising of the spirits from the chambers implies the resurrection of the body. This is especially clear in the raising of the spirits of the just. The righteous will live for thousands of generations and beget thousands of children. They will enjoy the fruit of the land. They will live in peace, in wisdom, and free of sin.

The final judgment affects above all the Watchers, their children (the giants, the demons as the disembodied spirits of the giants), and the stars. The Watchers and their human cooperators will then be thrown into the fiery inferno, where they will be forever perishing. The future as the object of hope is the restored paradise on earth.

The Book of Dreams, 1 Enoch 83–90. This book, written between 164 and 160 BCE,[67] contains two dream visions. The second vision, chs. 85–90, deals with the history of the world and with the conclusion of this history, the universal judgment (ch. 90). The history of the world, presented in an animal allegory,[68] recapitulates the account of the fallen Watchers and the spread of sin in the world. The judgment scene deals with the future lot of these originators of evil in the world, and of the blinded sheep. The just are not under judgment. After the judgment the final era begins.

The judgment scene is a day in court. The throne is set up, the Lord of the sheep takes his place on it, the books are unsealed, and the seventy angels stand ready to execute the Lord's judgment. The judgment is held against the fallen stars, the shepherds of the nations, and the blinded sheep. The fallen stars are brought before the judge, are found guilty, and are cast into a fiery abyss (90:24). Next, the seventy shepherds (the angelic rulers of the nations) are brought before the judge. These are found guilty of having killed more than the allotted number and are condemned to the same fate as the previous group (v. 25). Then the blinded sheep (the renegade Jews) are brought before the judge and condemned (vv. 26–27). But these are cast into the abyss in the depth of the earth, prepared especially for them.

After the judgment, the old house (Jerusalem)[69] is demolished, and the Lord builds a new, bigger, and loftier house in another location. All his sheep enter it (vv. 28–29). Even "those which have been destroyed and dispersed, and all the beasts of the field, and all the birds of the sky" are brought in (v. 33). The Gentiles come in and pay homage to the sheep that are inside the house, and they submit to them (v. 30).

All the sheep are snow-white and their wool is clean (they are pure, without sin). The Lord rejoices (v. 33) that the sheep laid down their swords. The eternal era of peace now begins. The eyes of the sheep are opened and they see all goodness. Then a "white

---

[67] Nickelsburg, *Jewish Literature*, 93.

[68] On the symbolism of the Animal Apocalypse, see J. J. Collins, *Apocalyptic Imagination*, 54–55.

[69] So Charles, *Apocrypha*, 2.259; Nickelsburg, *Jewish Literature*, 93; J. J. Collins, *Apocalyptic Imagination*, 55.

bull" is born. It has "large horns," is feared, and is constantly petitioned. After that, all generations are transformed into white bulls, while the first white bull becomes a lamb (vv. 37–38).

This interesting allegorical scene depicts life after the final judgment. It affirms the restoration of life for all, even for those who were destroyed. All are assembled in the new Jerusalem[70] of God's making to live together in peace and understanding. Salvation seems to include the Gentiles, but Israel is given pride of place. There is an allusion here to the appearance of the Messiah. And there is a depiction of the final transformation: the sheep are transformed into the image of the Messiah (the white bull), while the latter is apparently transformed into the image of a lamb (v. 38). The suggestion is that the Messiah, a human ruler,[71] will reign with justice (and peace).[72]

In Nickelsburg's opinion, this vision "transcends the eschatology of Third Isaiah in qualitative and significant fashion."[73] The scene affirms the victory of God beyond this life. But as J. J. Collins points out, the completion is still located on earth.[74] The vision of the New Jerusalem here is a powerful incentive to the righteous to persevere to the end.

The Epistle of Enoch, 1 Enoch 91–107. In 92:1–5 the author of this book,[75] who probably wrote in the early second century BCE,[76] introduces Enoch, who speaks with wisdom to everyone but especially to those who "uphold righteousness and peace" until the end of the age. Enoch has seen the mysteries hidden in heaven and reveals what is in store beyond death.

In the Apocalypse of Weeks the sage reviews the history of the world and gives a preview of the things to come. The entire history is organized in "weeks." The first seven weeks (93:1–10), described as the period of the great apostasy, deal with the world from its beginning to the present generation. At the close of the seventh

---

[70] J. J. Collins, *Apocalyptic Imagination,* 55.

[71] The white bull is born (*1 Enoch* 90:37); cf. Grelot, "Messie," 23.

[72] The change of the white bull into the lamb occurs in Charles's correction of the corrupt text (*1 Enoch* 90:38). But cf. Isaac's translation ("1 Enoch," 71).

[73] Nickelsburg, *Jewish Literature,* 95.

[74] J. J. Collins, *Apocalyptic Imagination,* 56.

[75] Chapters 106–7 are an addition; ch. 108 is an appendix; cf. Nickelsburg, *Jewish Literature,* 151.

[76] Ibid., 149–50.

week, the "elect ones of righteousness" are given a "sevenfold instruction" (v. 10). After that follow three more weeks (91:11–17),[77] in which righteousness is restored by the righteous.

In the seventh part of the tenth week occurs the "eternal judgment" of the Watchers. After that, the first heaven passes away and the "great eternal heaven" begins (91:15–16).[78] Countless weeks of a life of goodness, righteousness, and sinlessness follow (91:17). The focus in this instruction is on the final judgment and on the life beyond death. Sinners are shortsighted: they live in wickedness, thinking that beyond this life, in Sheol, equal fate awaits everybody. To their thinking, the righteous are worse off, for their righteousness prevents them from enjoying life here and now and subjects them to suffering (102:6–11; 103:5–6). But Enoch warns that beyond death is judgment. Nothing is hidden from God (98:6–7): evil deeds are recorded, and those who sin will receive their rightful punishment (98:11, 16; 99:4). The righteous can take comfort in the knowledge that God will vindicate them (99:3).

The "day" here is the "day of great judgment" (94:9; 98:10; 102:5; 104:15). On that day the sinners will be judged, while the righteous will be vindicated (97:5) and protected by the angels (100:5). It will be the day of cursing (102:5), of darkness, of anguish, and of shame (96:2; 98:10; 100:7). It will be the day of destruction, slaughter, and bloodshed (98:10; 99:4, 6). There will be no peace (103:8) and no escape (97:3) for the sinners.

According to 102:1–3, the Most High will then hurl against the sinners his "terror of fire." When he hurls his word against them, the sinners will faint for fear and find no escape. Even the luminaries will "faint, tremble and panic." Then all his angels will fulfill their commands. Sinners will be accursed forever, but the souls of those who have "died in righteousness" will receive "all good things . . . joy and honor" (102:4–5). Their spirits will live and rejoice till the end of generations on earth. They will "shine like the lights of heaven" (104:3). The author of this

---

[77] These weeks are misplaced in the Ethiopic version; see ibid., 154 n. 140; Milik, *Books of Enoch*, 260–70.

[78] So Knibb (*Ethiopic Enoch*, 2.220) and Charles (*APOT*, 2.264), following here the majority MSS (Eth II MSS). Isaac ("1 Enoch," 73) here reads "on" instead of "by" the angels (Watchers); cf. also Nickelsburg, *Jewish Literature*, 146. Milik's (*Books of Enoch*, 267) reconstructed Aramaic text here reads, "And thereafter [the tenth Week] in the seventh part [of which] an eternal Judgment and the (fixed) time of the Great Judgment [shall be executed in vengeance, in the midst of the Holy Ones]."

section expects the restoration of life for the souls of the right-eous in the beyond, although the resurrection is not mentioned explicitly. The righteous will then have a blissful life, whereas the evildoers will be exterminated.

The Similitudes, 1 Enoch 37–71. This book, not found among the Aramaic fragments in Qumran, is commonly dated to the first century CE.[79] The book consists of three "parables" or "similitudes" dealing with Enoch's visions of the heavenly realities. The theme of judgment is introduced in the first parable (chs. 38–44) and then developed in the second (chs. 45–57) and third (chs. 58–64 and 69:26–29)[80] parables. The three presentations cover approximately the same ground and are in many respects parallel.

The key element in these accounts is a transcendent figure, referred to as the "Elect One," the "Righteous One," the "Son of man," or the "Messiah."[81] There is a close resemblance between this figure in the Similitudes and the risen Christ, who is the end-time judge. This figure of heavenly provenance performs the same function in the three parables.[82] Named by the "Lord of the Spirits,"[83] the Elect One acts as the judge of the end time. Some of the features traditionally associated with God are now ascribed to this exalted figure. He is an individual, a human being (Son of man), chosen and named from before the creation by the Lord of

---

[79] According to Milik (ibid., 91–98), the absence of this book among the Qumran documents and its closeness to Christian notions indicate that it is a later Christian composition (3d c.). But see Mearns, "Dating the Similitudes"; Greenfield and Stone, "Enochic Pentateuch"; and Knibb, "Date of the Parables." In contrast to Milik's dating, Mearns, Greenfield and Stone, and Knibb posit the following dates for the composition of the Similitudes: Mearns—40 CE; Greenfield and Stone—the first century CE; Knibb—the close of the first century (after the destruction of the Qumran community). J. J. Collins (*Apocalyptic Imagination,* 143) suggests the early or the mid–first century CE. According to Nickelsburg (*Jewish Literature,* 221–32), the tradition present in the Similitudes existed at the turn of the era.

[80] In *1 Enoch* 65:1–69:25, which is a Noachic section, the speaker is Noah, not Enoch.

[81] The title "the Righteous One" occurs in 38:3, while "the Messiah" is found in 48:10; 52:4.

[82] On the transcendence of this figure, see Grelot, "Messie," 48–49. According to Grelot, this figure does not have a historical role to play in the present world. In the appendix, ch. 71, the "Son of man" is identified with Enoch.

[83] "The Lord of the Spirits" is here the title of God. It is parallel to the title "Lord of Hosts" (*1 Enoch* 39:12), which alludes to Isa 6:3. Cf. Nickelsburg, *Jewish Literature,* 215.

the Spirits. He is endowed with righteousness, holiness, wisdom, and power. He judges the mighty and the sinners and weighs the deeds of the righteous.

The first parable is about the appearance of this figure and of the "congregation of the righteous" (38:3). The secrets of the righteous[84] are then revealed, while the sinners are judged. The righteous are given possession of the land. Their faces begin to shine with the light of the Lord of the Spirits (v. 4). The sinners, however, are driven off the land,[85] and kings and the mighty are given into the hands of the righteous to be destroyed (v. 5). Then the chosen and the holy ones[86] come down from heaven and dwell with the righteous on earth (39:1).

In the second parable (chs. 45–57), the role of the Elect One is enhanced and his mysterious identity is disclosed. The judgment, while primarily attributed to the Lord of the Spirits, is in some respects relegated to the Elect One (45:3; 46:4–6). The day of judgment is the "day of burden and tribulation" for the sinners and the godless, who have been kept for this day in a special place that is neither in heaven nor on earth (45:2–6). On that day the Lord of the Spirits will bring them into his presence for condemnation (v. 6). But the Elect One will sit on the throne of glory and test the deeds of those who, in their tribulation, appealed to God's glorious name.[87] The Lord of the Spirits will then send him to dwell among these supplicants on earth. The heavens will then be transformed into an eternal light, and the earth will become a blessing (vv. 4–5). From then on there will be peace and mercy on earth in the presence of the Lord of the Spirits (v. 6).

In ch. 46 Enoch sees "the One to whom belongs the time before time" (v. 1), whose face resembles a human face, although it is full of grace, like the face of an angel. Enoch is told that this is the Son

---

[84] Knibb (*Ethiopic Enoch*, 2.125). Isaac ("1 Enoch," 30), however, has here "secrets of the Righteous One" and regards the above as a variant reading.

[85] It is the Lord of the Spirits who removes the sinners and the mighty from the earth. He weighs the works of the righteous (*1 Enoch* 38:2); he is the judge of all (41:9), and neither angel nor Satan can hinder him. Cf. also 46:3; 48:9; 50:3–5; 60:1–6; 62:2, 10, 12.

[86] Enoch expresses an intense desire to be among them (39:8). These holy ones are endowed with everlasting righteousness, are aglow with an intense light, and are interceding on behalf of those living on the earth (39:5–7).

[87] In *1 Enoch* 47:1 the sage talks about "the prayers of the righteous" and "the blood of the righteous" ascending from the earth to the Lord of the Spirits.

of man,[88] who will "open all the hidden storerooms" and will be victorious "in eternal uprightness" before the Lord of the Spirits (v. 3). He will remove the kings and the mighty (vv. 4–5) and put them to death forever, since they did not extol the name of the "Lord of the Spirits" (v. 6).

In *1 Enoch* 48:3 the mysterious Son of man is given a name; although he had been named before the creation, his identity was kept hidden in the presence of the Lord of the Spirits (v. 6). He is presented as the Elect One, the mainstay of the righteous and the light of the Gentiles. "All those who dwell upon the earth shall fall and worship before him; they shall glorify, bless, and sing the name of the Lord of the Spirits" (v. 5). The Elect One is endowed with power, wisdom, and glory (ch. 49), and he shall judge the secret things. On the day of judgment the kings and the mighty ones of the earth will be brought low. They will be delivered into the hands of the elect ones and will burn in their presence (48: 8–9); they will never rise up again, having "denied the Lord of the Spirits and his Messiah" (v. 10).

After the judgment the righteous and holy ones undergo a change. They are given light, glory, and honor (50:1). The Lord of the Spirits shows them to others so that the latter may repent. Those who repent are not given any honor but are saved "through his name" (vv. 2–5), while the unrepentant perish. Sheol will then give back "all the deposits which she had received" (51:1). The Lord of the Spirits tells Enoch, "The Elect One shall sit on my throne,[89] and from the conscience of his mouth shall come out the secrets of wisdom . . . and the mountains shall dance like rams . . . and the faces of all the angels in heaven shall glow with joy. . . . And the earth shall rejoice; and the righteous shall dwell upon her" (vv. 3–5).

In another vision Enoch sees the punishment of the mighty, the kings, and the fallen angels. On that day the mighty and the kings are punished by the angels of plague (53:1–5), while the fallen angels are punished by the angels Michael, Raphael, Gabriel, and Phanuel: these seize Azaz'el and his cohorts and cast them into the inferno (54:1–6). The powerful on earth will have to watch the Elect One seated "in the throne of glory"[90] judging Azaz'el and his army "in the name of the Lord of the Spirits" (55:4).

---

[88] In *1 Enoch* 48:6 the Son of man is identified as the Chosen One.

[89] So Charles (*APOT*, 2.218) and Isaac ("1 Enoch," 36).

[90] Knibb (*Ethiopic Enoch*, 2.139), following Berl. and Eth II, has here "the throne of my glory." "My," however, is omitted in BM 485, BM 491, Abb 35¹, Abb 55, and Tana 9.

In the third parable, chs. 58–64 and 69:26–29, Enoch speaks about the glory that awaits the believers and the righteous: life eternal, unhindered peace, and everlasting light before the Lord of the Spirits (58:1–6). The place of completion is the liberated earth, where darkness, death, and oppression have no place.

In the theophany in ch. 60, the "Antecedent of Time" (the "Head of Days") is seated on his glorious throne, surrounded by the whole assembly of heaven, his angels and righteous ones. It is the day of judgment, when the sinners are punished and the elect are given a covenant (60:6). On this day the angels bring measuring ropes to the secret places where the righteous have been buried, so that they may return to life and find hope on the "day of the Elect One" (61:3–5). For the Lord of the Spirits is the master of life: no one perishes before him (v. 6). The righteous are raised in order to be first judged and then given salvation and eternal life. The Elect One, seated on the throne of glory, weighs the deeds of the holy ones in heaven (v. 9).

On the day of judgment the Lord of the Spirits annihilates kings and rulers with the "word of his mouth." These feel pain like that of "a woman in travail" (62:4). The rulers are terrified and downcast at the sight of the Son of man sitting on the throne of glory (v. 5). They fall down before him and plead for mercy (v. 9; cf. 63:1–10), but the Lord of the Spirits drives them away in shame (62:10; cf. 63:10–12) and hands them over to the angels of punishment (v. 11). The elect then rejoice at their vindication and "eat and rest and rise with the Son of Man forever and ever." The righteous are given "the garments of glory," which become "the garments of life from the Lord of the Spirits." These garments never wear out, and their glory never ceases (vv. 14–16).

The Similitudes of Enoch thus speak of the day of the Lord in a variety of synonyms. The term "judgment" is almost always employed for the punishment of the evildoers. Those who are judged are the mighty on the earth, the sinners, and the fallen angels. The righteous are really not judged, although their deeds are tested. They are vindicated. Although the Lord of the Spirits is ultimately in charge, judgment is relegated to the Elect One; it manifests his power, honor, holiness, wisdom, righteousness, and long-suffering.

On the judgment day, when the righteous and the oppressed are given eternal life in peace and joy and security on earth, their appearance becomes changed. They form the congregation of the righteous and the elect and live with the Elect One. The deceased righteous are brought to life to dwell with them, and the holy ones who were kept in heaven will then come down to join them.[91]

(b) 4 Ezra

This book, attributed to Ezra the scribe, is dated around the close of the first century CE. It was written after the destruction of the temple.[92] The book has seven sections, each centered around a vision of the events in the end time: (1) 3:1–5:20, (2) 5:21–6:35, (3) 6:36–9:26, (4) 9:27–10:59, (5) 11:1–12:51, (6) 13:1–18, and (7) 14:1–48. In the book Ezra complains about God's justice in abandoning Jerusalem to its enemies, who are godless and worse sinners than Israel. Ezra is obsessed with this world, but his focus is raised by his heavenly partner, the angel Uriel, to the transcendent wisdom of God, to God's plan of salvation, to the new world, and to the vindication of Zion.

The portrayal of the ultimate reality here is a response to a crisis that caused grief, despondency, fear, and bewilderment in Israel. The scribe is told of the end of this world, of the rise of the new world, and of the messianic reign before the consummation of the world. In the second vision it is God who assures Ezra in these words:

> Behold the days are coming . . . when I visit the inhabitants of the earth, and when I require from the doers of iniquity the penalty of their iniquity . . . and when the seal is placed upon the age which is about to pass away, then . . . the books shall be opened. . . . It shall be that whoever remains . . . shall be saved and shall see my salvation and the end of the world. And they shall see the men who were taken up, who from their birth have not tasted death; and the heart of the earth's inhabitants shall be changed and converted to a different spirit. For evil shall be blotted out, and deceit shall be quenched; faithfulness shall flourish, and corruption shall be overcome, and the truth, which has been so long without fruit, shall be revealed. (5:18–28)

---

[91] The righteous did not perish at their death; their spirits were preserved under the wings of the Lord of the Spirits, and they lived with the holy ones (angels) in heaven. Note the resemblance of this to 1 Thess 3:13.

[92] Nickelsburg, *Jewish Literature*, 286; Metzger, "4 Ezra," 520. On the conflicting nomenclature of 4 Ezra, see ibid., 516.

This vision concerns the *visit* of the Most High on earth at the close of the age for judgment and salvation. The opening of the heavenly records indicates judgment. Evil will then be extinguished, but the survivors will be saved. They receive a new spirit; they see those who were taken alive into heaven; and they are transformed in body and soul: they become not only sinless, faithful, and truthful but also incorruptible.

In the third vision, the scribe is shown the messianic reign before the end of the world and the final judgment: "The city which now is not seen will appear . . . and everyone who has been delivered from the evils that I have foretold shall see my wonders. For my son the Messiah shall be revealed with those who are with him, and those who remain shall rejoice four hundred years" (7:27–28).

After this, everyone, including the Messiah, will die. There will be primeval silence for seven days, after which a new world will rise. The souls of the dead shall leave their chambers, and corruptibility will vanish. The Most High will then take his place on the throne of judgment (vv. 29–35) and weigh all the deeds done in this life. On that day of judgment, the nations will have to look at the Most High, whom they have denied, as well as at hell and paradise (vv. [36]–[39]).[93] In the "splendor of the glory of the Most High" all "shall see what has been determined for them" (v. [42]).

Ezra is told that the Most High has created two worlds—the present world subject to mortality, toil, and corruptibility and the new world of righteousness, liberty, and incorruptibility. The new world is meant for the righteous (v. [96]). In it the righteous will shine like the sun, and they will see the face of their Lord. The judgment day will display to all "the seal of the truth" (v. [104]). It will conclude this world and open the immortal age for righteousness and truth, in which there is no corruption or sin or unbelief (vv. 42[112]–45[115]).

The fifth and the sixth visions contain two parallel presentations of the end-time conflict and the ensuing messianic reign before the end of the world. The interpretation of the eagle vision (12:10–39) discloses that the lion, which confronts and rebukes the

---

[93] The square brackets here and in subsequent references correspond to Metzger's notation in Metzger, "4 Ezra."

eagle (cf. 11:36–46), is the Messiah (12:31–39). Though he comes from the tribe of Judah, he is a preexistent being (v. 32). He will bring the oppressive Gentile rulers before judgment, reprove them, and destroy them (v. 32). But he will spare the remnant of his people and "make them joyful till the end comes, the day of judgment" (v. 34).

The sixth vision brings out the restitution of Zion and the role of the law in the messianic judgment. Ezra has a vision of a man rising out of the sea and flying with the clouds of heaven. At his look everything trembles, and at his voice all melt like wax before the fire (13:2–4). As a countless multitude gathers to make war against him, he takes his seat on a great mountain and with his word subdues all his enemies. He sends forth "from his mouth as it were a stream of fire, and from his lips a flaming breath, and from his tongue . . . a storm of sparks" (v. 10). After that he comes down from the mountain and calls to himself a peaceable multitude (v. 12).

In the interpretation of this vision, 13:25–50, the mysterious figure is revealed as the Son of the Most High (13:32). He is the preexistent deliverer of creation. He reproves the nations for their ungodliness and evil thoughts and destroys them. He brings back the captives and those who have fled to the desert in order to keep the commandments of the Lord, and he spares the remnant of the people.

In 4 Ezra we thus find the expectation of the end of this world, of the messianic reign before the end of the world, and of the rise of the new world. The new world is ushered in with the final judgment. Ezra is urged to look at the world to come, rather than at present troubles. The judgment day will set everything aright. It will be also the day of the resurrection.

The day of the Lord here refers to the last judgment, which is carried out by the Most High after the consummation of the world. It initiates the world to come, life eternal, and the reign of God. The day is anticipated by the coming of the Son and the establishment of the messianic reign.

(c) 2 Baruch (Syriac Apocalypse of Baruch)

Like 4 Ezra, 2 Baruch (Syriac Apocalypse of Baruch) is a response to the fall of Jerusalem and dates roughly from the same period.[94] Contemporary scholarship regards it as a unitary composition.[95] The book contains a flurry of questions about God's justice, Israel, the nations, and the promises of God (3:5–9; 5:1). God is almost always the dialogue partner. In Charles's division of the book (chs. 1–77)[96] into eleven sections,[97] there are three messianic apocalypses (21:1–30:5; 35:1–40:4; 53:1–76:5).[98]

The messianic kingdom is a temporary messianic age on earth, preceding the eternal age to come. At the end of this age, the Messiah returns in glory to heaven (30:1), and the dead are raised (vv. 1b–5). The second messianic apocalypse, chs. 35–40, closes with the Messiah's conquest of the last world empire, Rome, and the end of the corruptible world (40:1–4). The Messiah will judge and kill the last ruler and protect his people in the chosen place until the end of the world. "His dominion will last until the world of corruption has ended, and until the times which have been mentioned before have been fulfilled" (v. 3).

But in the third apocalypse (chs. 53–76) it is not clear whether the vision refers to the messianic reign or to the incorruptible age to come. According to Kreitzer,[99] it refers to the transitional messianic reign. This reign, which resembles the paradise on earth, concludes as follows: "For that time is the end of that which is corruptible and the beginning of that which is incorruptible. . . . Therefore, it is far away from the evil things and near to those which do not die" (74:2–3). Either the passage agrees with the previous apocalypses or it presents an ambiguity tolerated by the author.[100]

---

[94] Nickelsburg, *Jewish Literature*, 287; Klijn, "2 Baruch," 616–17. According to some scholars, *2 Bar.* depends on 4 Ezra, while others suggest a common origin for both books (ibid., 620).

[95] Charles (*APOT*, 1.474) isolates six contributors, each with a somewhat different role for the Messiah and the messianic kingdom. Russell (*Method*, 64–65, 293), Bogaert (*Apocalypse de Baruch*, 1.57–95), Sayler (*Promises Failed?* 11–39), and Kreitzer (*Jesus and God*, 76), however, defend the single authorship of the book.

[96] In each section occurs a reference to Baruch's fasting in preparation for a new revelation. This pattern is supposedly the work of the final redactor.

[97] Chapters 78–87 are regarded by Charles as an appendix.

[98] Kreitzer, *Jesus and God*, 69–70. According to Klijn ("2 Baruch," 619; also "Sources and Redaction," 65–76), the final redactor's theology is discernible in his reinterpretation of traditions—in his rejection of the messianic kingdom on earth. But see Kreitzer, *Jesus and God*, 75–76.

[99] Kreitzer, *Jesus and God*, 75.

[100] According to Klijn ("Sources and Redaction," 75), this reign belongs to this world. It is "a step in the direction of the incorruptible world" but is not the messianic kingdom. But see Kreitzer, *Jesus and God*, 75–77.

The day of the Mighty One, the key to the future, is mentioned in 49:2, 51:4, and 55:6 and refers back to the event depicted in 48:38–41. On that day,

> a change of times will reveal itself openly to the eyes of everyone because they polluted themselves in all those times and caused oppression, and each one walked in his own works and did not remember the Law of the Mighty One. Therefore, a fire will consume their thoughts, and with a flame the meditations of their kidneys will be examined. For the judge will come and will not hesitate. . . . Many will surely weep at that time—more, however, because of the living ones than of the dead. (*2 Bar.* 48:38–41, Klijn)

This day of judgment signals the change of eons, closing the age of corruption, sin, and death and opening the age of incorruption. The judge is the Mighty One, and those under judgment are the transgressors of the law. On that day the books containing the lists of sins will be opened and the treasuries of good deeds disclosed.

Baruch, the scribe, yearns for the future age, when he will be rid of the age of corruption. He asks the Lord, "Reprove the angel of death, and let your glory appear . . . and let the realm of death be sealed so that it may not receive the dead from this time, and let the treasuries of the souls restore those who are enclosed in them . . . show your glory soon and do not postpone that which was promised by you" (21:23–25). But the Lord answers him that the end cannot come until the "number that has been appointed is completed" and "salvation which comes has drawn near" (23:4–7).

For the scribe, the day of the Mighty One is the day of salvation. He asks about the shape of the future life: "In which shape will the living live in your day? Or how will remain the splendor which will be after that? Will they . . . take again this present form and . . . put on the chained members which are evil and by which evil is accomplished? Or will you perhaps change these things which have been in the world, as also the world itself?" (49:2–3).[101]

The Mighty One answers Baruch, "The earth will surely give back the dead . . . not changing anything in their form. . . . For then it will be necessary to show those who live that the dead are

---

[101] Compare this with the questions Paul is addressing in 1 Cor 15:35–57.

living again. . . . And it will be that when they recognize each other . . . then my judgment will be strong" (50:2–4).

The resurrection, which is the restoration of the dead to life, is necessary in order that the living may recognize the deceased. It is followed by the judgment and the transformation. The latter applies to the wicked and the righteous, although in a different fashion. Baruch is told, "The shape of those who act wickedly will be made more evil than it is (now) so that they shall suffer torment" (51:2). The wicked will turn into "startling visions and horrible shapes and . . . will waste away." In contrast to this, the shape of the good will become ever more splendid. The righteous will be "glorified by transformation . . . the shape of their face will be changed into the light of their beauty so that they may acquire and receive the undying world which is promised to them" (v. 3). They will be exalted to "the splendor of angels" (vv. 5, 8–10) or to "any shape which they wished" (v. 10). They will see the paradise, the living creatures under the throne of God, and the hosts of heaven (v. 11).

Baruch therefore counsels the people to grieve for those who sin now, for they will be punished, rather than for those who die now. The judgment is not only the vindication of Israel; it will also touch every sinner within Israel: "A retribution will be demanded. . . . For those who are among your own, you rule; and those who sin, you blot out among your own" (54:21–22). The day of the Mighty One is the day of terror for those who have transgressed, but a revelation of marvelous things to the righteous.

After the judgment the Most High will sit down "in eternal peace on the throne of his kingdom" (73:1). Then joy will be revealed, and illness, fear, and tribulation will vanish; no one will die an untimely death; wild beasts will serve the people; and women will no longer have birth pangs (ch. 73). The age is "the end of what is corruptible and the beginning of what is incorruptible" (74:2–4). It is the beginning of the kingdom of God and the restoration of paradise.

Although the end of the world will be preceded by horrors (25:1–4; 27:1–15), the Most High reassures Baruch that those "found in this land" will be spared (29:2). He promises that the righteous, both living and dead, will share in the bliss and plenty of the dominion of the Anointed One. When he returns with glory, "all who sleep in hope of him will rise," the "treasuries . . . in which the number of the souls of the righteous were kept" will be opened, "and they will go out and the multitude of souls will appear together, in one assemblage, of one mind" (30:1–2).[102] But the wicked and apostate will not share in this messianic bliss; their souls will waste away, and they will know that their torment and perdition have come (vv. 4–5).

The Anointed One is here a warlike figure of the end time. When his time comes, "he will call all nations, and some he will spare, and others he will kill. . . . Every nation which has not known Israel and which has not trodden down the seed of Jacob will live. . . . All those who have ruled over you or have known you, will be delivered up to the sword" (72:2–6). As Ezra, so also Baruch exhorts the people to look at what is to come, to the incorruptible and great (44:3–12), for only such will inherit the promised time (v. 13).

The day of the Mighty One here is thus the final reckoning upon which follows salvation or damnation. It will be a day of impartial justice, the end of this corruptible world, and the beginning of the incorruptible world. The righteous will share in the messianic reign, inherit incorruption, and be transformed into ever more glorious shapes. The Most High will vindicate the righteous in this world and the next.

(d) The Testaments of the Twelve Patriarchs

This book,[103] written in the form of a last will and testament, claims to contain the last words of the twelve sons of Jacob. Each of the patriarchs reviews from his deathbed his life story, draws from it particular lessons, and predicts what his posterity will do and what will happen to it in the future and in the last times.

The writing contains some clearly identifiable Christian sections and other closely integrated Christian modifications, emphases, and themes. Is it a Jewish composition adapted by Christians, or is it a Christian composition utilizing Jewish

---

[102] According to U. B. Müller (*Messias und Menschensohn*, 142–44), *2 Bar.* 30:1 is a Christian interpolation. It speaks of the return of the Messiah to heaven; this is without a parallel in Judaism. Cf. also Klijn, "Sources and Redaction," 65–76.

[103] For a new translation and critical notes, see Kee, "Testaments," 1.775–828.

sources?[104] Its time of composition and place of origin are disputed. H. C. Kee dates the work to the Maccabean period, the second century BCE, and the Christian interpolations to the early second century CE.[105] There are good reasons for regarding the composition as Jewish in origin.[106]

The *Testaments of the Twelve Patriarchs* clearly expects the consummation of time (*T. Reub.* 6:8; *T. Levi* 10:2; *T. Zeb.* 8:2; 9:9; *T. Dan* 5:4; *T. Napht.* 8:1; *T. Benj.* 11:3), the day of judgment (*T. Levi* 3:2, 3; 4:1), the coming of God (*T. Judah* 22:2; *T. Asher* 7:3), and the revelation of salvation (*T. Judah* 22:2; *T. Benj.* 10:5) and mercy (*T. Napht.* 4:5; *T. Zeb.* 8:2). On the day of judgment the spirits of error will be annihilated (*T. Sim.* 6:5).

Salvation is effected by God either by himself or through his angels and his messianic figure. According to *T. Napht.* 8:3–4, God will appear in his kingly power, save Israel, assemble the righteous among the Gentiles, and put the devil to flight (cf. *T. Asher* 7:3, 7). Salvation will lift the oppression of Beliar and his spirits. According to *T. Levi* 2:3, the army from the second heaven will work vengeance on the spirits of error (cf. *T. Levi* 10:12; *T. Zeb.* 9:8), but *T. Dan* 5:10–11 expects the one coming from the tribes of Judah and Levi to make war on Beliar, conquer him, and liberate the captives. According to *T. Zeb.* 9:9, it will be the Lord who will liberate the captives from Beliar (cf. *T. Dan* 5:10). *Testament of Levi* 10:2 states that Beliar will then be bound, while *T. Judah* 25:3 asserts that Beliar and his spirits will be thrown into eternal fire. After that the Lord will bring salvation to Israel and visit all nations (*T. Judah* 22:2).

---

[104]De Jonge (*Testaments;* also "Christian Influence," 184, 187 and "Once More," 313) advocates the Christian origin of *T. 12 Patr.* Philonenko (*Interpolations*), however, regards almost the entire work, including the crucifixion of the Messiah, as a Jewish composition. Kee ("Testaments," 776–78) considers it to be a Jewish composition with some Christian interpolations. According to Becker (*Untersuchungen,* 373), there are three stages of composition: the Hellenistic-Jewish original, the Hellenistic-Jewish expansion, and the Christian redaction. For Becker's critical review of various positions up to 1970, see ibid., 129–58.

[105]Kee, "Testaments," 776–78. Kee's solution is close to Becker's (*Untersuchungen,* 374).

[106]Why would a Christian around 200 CE propagate the expectation of a twofold messianic figure or of two messianic figures, or depict three heavens—the first heaven containing water, etc., the second containing light, Beliar, and his spirits, and the third being the abode of God? Why would a Christian use the name Beliar rather than the established NT name Satan?

The book in its present form clearly expects the resurrection of the dead, but it is not certain that the original composition also held this view.[107] According to *T. Levi* 18:9–12, the expected priestly messianic figure will open the gates of paradise, remove the sword from humankind, clothe the "saints" in righteousness, and grant them to "eat of the tree of life." While the term "saints" may be of Christian origin, perhaps replacing "holy ones," the rest of the text agrees with Jewish expectations of the end time. According to *T. Judah* 25:1, the patriarchs Abraham, Isaac, and Jacob will be "resurrected to life." Verses 4–5 then indicate that resurrection is expected for others as well. After the defeat of Beliar and his spirits, "those who died in sorrow shall be raised in joy; and those who died in poverty for the Lord's sake shall be made rich; and those who died on account of the Lord shall be wakened to life, while the impious shall mourn and the sinners shall weep" (*T. Judah* 15:4–5). This, however, may be a Christian adaptation or expansion.[108]

According to *T. Dan* 5:11–12, the Lord will grant eternal peace to those who call upon him; the saints will refresh themselves in Eden and rejoice in the new Jerusalem forever. *Testament of Benjamin* 10:5–9 states that the Lord will reveal his salvation to all nations; the people will see Enoch, Seth, Abraham, Isaac, and Jacob raised up at the right hand in great joy, and "then shall we also be raised each of us over our tribe, and we shall prostrate ourselves before the heavenly king." It mentions the universal transformation: "Then all shall be changed, some destined for glory, others for dishonor, for the Lord first judges Israel for the wrong she has committed, and then he shall do the same for all the nations" (10:8–9).

The *Testaments of the Twelve Patriarchs* thus expects the day of judgment with which is associated the coming of God, the salvation of the just, and the annihilation of the spirits of error. Salvation is basically seen as lifting the oppression of the spirits of error. In its present shape the *Testaments of the Twelve Patriarchs* expects a priestly messianic figure and the resurrection of the dead. Christian modifications make explicit what is expected of the eschatological figure, Jesus Christ, but they do not mention Christ's parousia.

---

[107] According to Becker (*Untersuchungen*, 401), the original shows no traces of this belief. Kee ("Testaments," 780) notes that in "much of the writing there is no clear evidence of a hope in afterlife."

[108] Note the similarity to the Beatitudes.

C. THE APOCALYPSE

In addition to the terms παρουσία and "day of the Lord," the Lord's coming is referred to as a "revelation," ἀποκάλυψις. While the term παρουσία suggests that the Lord is coming from a distant region, from heaven, and "day of the Lord" implies the implementation of the glory and power and rule of the Lord in the world, ἀποκάλυψις indicates the lifting of a mystery. The present reality of the Lord and of the faithful is wrapped in mystery. Then the glory and power of the Lord and the glorious destiny of the faithful will become manifest. Revelation is a typical Jewish notion—another hint that Paul is here relying on Jewish traditions rather than on Hellenistic parallels. Both moments are found in Jewish apocalyptic.

The noun ἀποκάλυψις occurs in the LXX 4 times[109] and in the NT 18 times (in Paul's writings 7 times—3 of which refer to the end-time event [Rom 2:5; 8:19; 1 Cor 1:7]).[110] Only the context discloses how the word is used. In 1 Cor 1:6–7 Paul employs this noun for the Lord's coming: "The testimony of Christ has been strengthened among you—so that you are not lacking in any spiritual gift as you wait for the revealing (τὴν ἀποκάλυψιν, tēn apokalypsin) of our Lord Jesus Christ." The revealing here refers to the parousia of the Lord. In Rom 2:5 and 8:19 the apostle employs ἀποκάλυψις for a moment of the Lord's coming, such as judgment or the status of the faithful as God's sons. In Rom 2:5 he warns, "By your hard and impenitent heart you are storing up wrath for yourself on the day of wrath, when God's righteous judgment will be revealed (ἀποκαλύψεως, apokalypseōs)." And in Rom 8:19 he affirms, "For the creation waits with eager longing for the revealing (ἀποκάλυψιν, apokalypsin) of the children (τῶν υἱῶν, tōn huiōn) of God." At that moment the true glory and identity of the faithful as "sons of God" will become manifest. But Paul employs ἀποκάλυψις also for his own visions of, and encounters with, the Lord. In Gal 1:12 he employs it for his encounter with the Lord at Damascus, and in Gal 2:2 for a special revelation/instruction that he has received from the Lord.

---

[109] 1 Kgs 20:30; Sir 11:27; 22:22; 42:1.

[110] It occurs in Luke 2:32; Rom 2:5; 8:19; 16:25; 1 Cor 1:7; 14:6, 26; 2 Cor 12:1, 7; Gal 1:12; 2:2; Eph 1:17; 3:3; 2 Thess 1:7; 1 Pet 1:7, 13; 4:13; Rev 1:1. In 1 Pet it is employed consistently for the end-time event.

The verb ἀποκαλύπτω, *apokalyptō*, occurs in the LXX 110 times[111] and in the NT 26 times (in Paul 9 times—twice for the end-time coming).[112]

It is no surprise that ἀποκάλυψις or its synonyms occur also in Jewish apocalyptic writings. The Similitudes of Enoch especially are replete with the vocabulary and the notion of secrecy and revelation of secrets. Thus 1 Enoch 48:7 speaks of the wisdom of the Lord having revealed the Chosen and Mysterious One to the holy and righteous. The angel accompanying the patriarch in the heavens reveals to him the names of the four archangels (40:3–10), the mystery of the Son of man (46:2), and other mysteries of heaven (60:11–24; 61:2–13; 64:1–2). The Son of man himself is a revealer:

---

[111] In the LXX the verb ἀποκαλύπτω translates a variety of Hebrew verbs (nine), most often the verb גָּלָה, *gālâ*. In Leviticus it usually refers to a shameful exposure by a human being. In 1 Kgs 3:7, 21 it is employed for the revelation of the word of the Lord. In 1 Kgs 9:15 the Lord is said to uncover the ear of Samuel (cf. 20:2, 13; 22:8, 17; 2 Kgs 7:27). Ps 28[29]:9 speaks of the voice of the Lord stripping bare (ἀποκαλύψει, *apokalypsei*) the forest. Ps 97[98]:2 asserts, "The Lord has made known (ἐγνώρισεν, *egnōrisen*) his victory, he has revealed (ἀπεκάλυψεν, *apekalypsen*) his vindication in the sight of the nations." And in Ps 118[119]:18 the psalmist prays to God, saying, "Open (ἀποκάλυψον, *apokalypson*) my eyes, so that I may behold wondrous things out of your law."
In Sir this vocabulary refers most of the time to human revelations or disclosures. But Sir 1:6 states, "The root of wisdom—to whom has it been revealed?" In 1:30 the author warns, "The Lord will reveal (ἀποκαλύψει) your secrets (τὰ κρυπτά, *ta krypta*) and overthrow you before the whole congregation." According to 4:18, the wisdom "will reveal the secrets" to those who are faithful, while 42:18 states, "He [the Lord] discloses what has been and what is to be, and he reveals the traces of hidden things."

[112] It is employed in Luke 17:30 for the eschatological revelation of the Son of man. In Rom 8:18 it refers to the disclosure of the future glory. In 1 Cor 3:13 it is a synonym for δηλώσει, *dēlōsei*, referring to the fire on the day of the Lord. In 1 Pet 1:5 and 5:1 it refers respectively to the eschatological salvation and glory. The notion of end-time revelation occurs also in 1 Enoch 38:2–3; 48:2, 6–7; 51:3; 53:6; 62:7; 69:27, 29; 4 Ezra 7:27, 33; and 2 Bar. 29:3. In Rom 8:18 Paul declares, "I consider that the sufferings of this present time are not worth comparing with the glory about to be revealed (ἀποκαλυφθῆναι, *apokalyphthēnai*) to us." And in 1 Cor 3:13 he warns, "The work of each builder will become visible (φανερὸν γενήσεται, *phaneron genēsetai*), for the Day will disclose it (δηλώσει), for it will be revealed (ἀποκαλύπτεται, *apokalyptetai*) with fire." The revelation here pertains to the last judgment, when the good and evil that a Christian worker has done in the community will become manifest. First Corinthians 3:13 discloses that φανερός, φανερόω, and δηλόω are also employed in this association. Paul uses φανερόω in this sense in 1 Cor 4:5 and 2 Cor 5:10 and δηλόω in 1 Cor 3:13. In the Psalms and in Sirach ἀποκαλύπτω is employed also for God's revealing the mysteries of wisdom, the secrets of the past and the future, the hidden thoughts of the heart, and the mystery of salvation.

he reveals "all the hidden storerooms" (46:3) and "all the secrets of wisdom" (51:3). But the Son of man is himself mysterious: he was named in the presence of the Lord of Spirits before the suns and the stars were created (48:1–3; cf. 62:6–7). He shall be the "staff of righteousness" and the "light of the Gentiles," and "all who dwell on earth shall fall down and worship him" (48:4). It was for this reason that the Son of man became the Chosen One. "He was concealed . . . prior to the creation of the world and for eternity" (48:5–6). "He has revealed the wisdom of the Lord of the Spirits to the righteous and the holy ones" (48:7). According to 51:3, the Elect One will sit on God's throne, and from his mouth "shall come out all the secrets of wisdom, for the Lord of the Spirits has given them to him and glorified him." The Elect One is said to "appear" before the Lord of Spirits (52:9; 69:29)—possibly a variant of "reveal."

The Lord of the Spirits reveals to Enoch "the names of the holy who dwell upon earth and believe in the name of the Lord of Spirits forever and ever" (43:4). Enoch is then told and shown the mysteries of lightning and thunder (59:1–3). The elect ones in heaven should "scrutinize the mysteries of righteousness, the gift of faith" (58:5). Now it is only light; darkness has disappeared forever (v. 6).

Thus, the word and the notion of ἀποκάλυψις as employed by Paul are firmly rooted in Jewish traditions. Jewish apocalyptic writings especially contain abundant references to the mysteries and to the revelation of mysteries.[113]

D. THE EPIPHANY

Closely related to ἀποκάλυψις is ἐπιφάνεια, *epiphaneia*.[114] This word occurs in 2 Thessalonians concerning the Lord's coming. The authenticity of this work is debated, but it is considered here since it could belong to Paul. At any rate, ἐπιφάνεια does present another way of referring to the Lord's coming in the early church, for it occurs also in the Pastoral Epistles (1 Tim 6:14; 2 Tim 1:10; 4:1, 8; Titus 2:13).[115] Second Thessalonians 2:8 states, "And then the

---

[113] See also *2 Bar.* 20:4–5; 23:6–7; 29:3–4; 39:7; 42:1; 48:3–4; 51:7–8, 11; 54:4–5; 55:7; 73:1; 81:4; 85:8; 4 Ezra 7:33, 36, 48, 104; 8:54, 62; 10:35, 38; 14:5, 35.

[114] The noun ἐπιφάνεια occurs in the LXX 11 times, while the verb ἐπιφαίνω, *epiphainō*, occurs 22 times, and the adjective ἐπιφανής, *epiphanēs*, 15 times.

[115] The verb ἐπεφάνη, *epephanē*, is employed in this sense in Titus 2:11 and 3:4.

lawless one will be revealed (ἀποκαλυφθήσεται, *apokalyphthēsetai*), whom the Lord Jesus will destroy with the breath of his mouth, annihilating him by the manifestation (τῇ ἐπιφανείᾳ, *tē epiphaneia*) of his coming (τῆς παρουσίας)." The words ἀποκαλύπτω, παρουσία, and ἐπιφάνεια are here employed in close association. The noun ἐπιφάνεια seems to entail the glory of the Lord and the destruction of the evil force at the Lord's coming.[116] It is frequently employed in this sense in 2 Maccabees (2:21; 3:24; 5:4; 12:22; 14:15; 15:27) and 3 Maccabees (2:9; 5:8, 51). In addition, the adjective ἐπιφανής occurs in connection with the day of the Lord in Joel 2:11, 31 and Mal 4:5.

As Dupont has already pointed out,[117] ἐπιφάνεια, as employed in 2 Thessalonians, resembles LXX rather than Hellenistic usage. This indicates that all the terms employed for the Lord's coming by Paul or by the tradition close to Paul are best explained from the Jewish background. According to Dupont, the apostle is either taking up the established early Christian vocabulary or the vocabulary of the LXX and Jewish apocalyptic.[118]

CONCLUSION

While Paul employs the terms παρουσία, "day of the Lord," ᾿ποκάλυψις, and ἐπιφάνεια for the Lord's coming, he uses the first two expressions much more frequently than the last two. The term παρουσία is of Greek origin, while "day of the Lord" and ἀποκάλυψις come from the Jewish background. The word παρουσία is not a technical term: it denotes the Lord's coming only when it is properly qualified; otherwise it means the coming or the arrival of certain persons. Paul employs this word for the Lord's coming only in 1 Thessalonians (and in 2 Thessalonians), but even in 1 Thessalonians, this expression is employed in juxtaposition with "day of the Lord." The imagery of the Hellenistic παρουσία is not clearly evident in 1 Thess 4:16–18, despite Peterson's attempt to interpret the imagery here in this light. The

---

[116] According to Dupont (*L'Union*, 75–76), the τῇ ἐπιφανείᾳ τῆς παρουσίας in 2 Thess 2:8 is not a pleonasm. The ἐπιφάνεια here only poorly resembles the Hellenistic epiphanies, which are all benevolent. The author employs it in dependence on the LXX, where it seems to be a translation of two roots, ירא, *yr᾿* (to fear) and ראה, *r᾿h* (to see) (ibid., 77).

[117] Ibid., 73–77.

[118] Ibid., 7.

imagery can be much better explained from the Jewish background, both biblical and intertestamental. And the fact that
Paul employed other terms for the Lord's coming makes it likely
that his imagery of this event also came from established Jewish
tradition. This is also suggested by the usage found in Matt 24
and Luke 17; the former employs the term παρουσία, and the
latter, "day of the Son of man," referring to the same event.

"Day of the Lord" is an ambivalent term: it can mean salvation
or judgment. It has a long history in the OT and in second temple
period writings, which continued and developed this tradition. It
came to be applied also to the coming of a messianic figure with
judgment, resurrection, and eternal life. The word ἀποκάλυψις is
employed relatively infrequently by Paul in connection with the
Lord's coming. The term clearly refers to the Lord's coming only in
1 Cor 1:7, but its use is important in that it gives evidence of
apocalyptic imagery in Paul's thought about the Lord's coming and
counterbalances the imagery of the Hellenistic παρουσία in Paul's
depictions of this event. In fact, the language of disclosure or
revelation occurs rather frequently concerning the day of the Lord.
And even the term ἐπιφάνεια, found in 2 Thess 2:8, resembles LXX
rather than Hellenistic usage.

2

❋

THE IMAGERY

In 1 Thess 4:16–17 Paul uses the expressions "the cry of command," "the archangel's call," and "the sound of the trumpet of God" to depict the circumstances accompanying the Lord's coming down from heaven. And the apostle mentions the clouds as a means by which the faithful are transported from the earth to the lofty region above the earth, where they meet the Lord. What does this imagery mean? What is its background?

A. THE CRY OF COMMAND

In 1 Thess 4:16 Paul states that the Lord will come from heaven "with a cry of command" (ἐν κελεύσματι, *en keleusmati*). P. Nepper-Christensen writes that after the conjunctive ὅτι, *hoti*, which introduces the imagery of the Lord's coming in v. 16, the clarity of the picture disappears: it is not clear who gives the command, to whom the command is given, or how the command relates to the other two motifs. Do the last two motifs, the voice of the archangel and the trumpet of God, explicate the first one? Is the κέλευσμα taken up by the voice of the archangel and by the trumpet of God? It is also not clear for whom all this is meant.[1] According to J. E. Frame, "It is conceivable that God who raises the dead (v. 14), or Christ the agent in resurrection,

---

[1] Nepper-Christensen, "Herrenwort," 145. On the history of exegesis of this imagery, see Frame, *Thessalonians*.

commands the archangel Michael to arouse the dead and that this command is executed at once by the voice of the archangel who speaks to the dead (cf. 1 Cor 15:52) through a divine trumpet."[2] B. Rigaux leaves the obscure image ἐν κελεύσματι vague and tries to make sense of the other two motifs, the archangel's voice and the trumpet of God.[3] L. Cerfaux does not even mention the κέλευσμα among the images of the Lord's descent.[4] But κέλευσμα is mentioned here, and not by chance or by mistake. It has a definite function in this imagery, as I have shown in a previous article.[5] It occurs consistently in theophanies and in the tradition of the day of the Lord.

The dictionary definitions of κέλευσμα are (a) a command as a directive; (b) a command call as a preset signal to troops, dogs, horses, etc.; (c) din, noise, but with an overtone of command.[6] The word κέλευσμα is a hapax legomenon in the NT. In the LXX κέλευσμα occurs only in Prov 30:21, where it means a command call. It is evident that this word does not belong to the stock expressions of the Hellenistic παρουσία, or of NT apocalyptic, or of OT depictions of the day of the Lord. But the underlying motif of command does occur in OT theophanies or depictions of the day of the Lord.

A clear example is in Ps 104:7: "At thy rebuke they fled, at the sound of thy thunder they took to flight." The rebuke here comes from Yahweh and is directed at the primeval waters of chaos (v. 6). The waters flee from Yahweh's mighty command. In this parallel construction, typical of Hebrew poetry, the "sound of thunder" in the second clause takes up the "rebuke" in the first clause. The two images are here employed synonymously.

The Hebrew word for "to rebuke" is גָּעַר, gāʿar.[7] The word occurs 28 times in the OT—16 times in theophanies or similar presentations. In the latter context, which resembles that of 1 Thess 4:16, it is always Yahweh who gives this rebuke (גְּעָרָה, geʿārâ). Yahweh directs it against hostile waters (Ps 18:16; 2 Sam 22:16;

---

[2] Frame, *Thessalonians*, 174.

[3] Rigaux, *Thessaloniciens*, 542.

[4] Cerfaux (*Christ*, 38) states, "The apocalyptic touches are bold and striking: the voice of the archangel, the sounding of the trumpet of God, the resurrection of the dead, clouds, and Christ's coming down from heaven."

[5] Plevnik, "Parousia"; see also "The Taking Up."

[6] Schmid, "κέλευσμα."

[7] Caquot, "גָּעַר."

Ps 68:31; 104:7; 106:9; Isa 17:13; 50:2; 54:9; Nah 1:4; Job 26:22), against the mighty (Ps 76:7), against the insolent (Ps 119:21), and against his enemies (Isa 66:15). Once it is aimed against Jerusalem, when the latter incurs Yahweh's wrath (Isa 51:20). In these contexts the גְּעָרָה is thus always given by Yahweh, and it is always directed toward the enemies of Yahweh.

The word "rebuke," usually employed to translate גָּעַר does suggest that the word is aimed at an enemy, but it does not always bring out the undertone of command. This undertone is clear from the LXX and the translations made by Aquila, Symmachus, and Theodotion. In fact, whenever the LXX uses not ἐπιτιμάω, epitimaō, or ἐπιτίμησις, epitimēsis, but another synonym to translate גְּעָרָה,[8] Theodotion, Aquila, or Symmachus employs ἐπιτιμάω (cf. Isa 17:13; 50:2; 54:9; 66:15).

According to Kee, in all these texts גְּעָרָה means to overpower "the enemies of God and of his purposes."[9] Through his commanding, mighty, and irresistible word, God is enforcing his rule in the cosmos, in the world, and in Israel. His powerful word pushes back the threat and brings deliverance to the psalmist or to the people of God.

This motif underlying the word גְּעָרָה or גָּעַר occurs also in Jewish apocalyptic texts. In 1 Enoch 101:7 Enoch, in his exhortation, points to the power of the Most High, saying, "Has he not ordered the courses of action and her waters—(indeed) her totality—with sand? At his rebuke they become frightened." In the next chapter Enoch warns the sinners to fear the Most High. He asks, "When he flings his word (voice) against you, will you not faint and fear?" (102:1b). Here God hurls forth his word like a spear. In the parallel construction in v. 1a this word is compared to the "terror of fire" that God pours out upon the enemies. The whole world is terrified at this, but the righteous are told not to fear.

In the Similitudes, this motif occurs in connection with the judgment by the Elect One. On the day of the Elect One, "those who are in heaven above and all the powers received a command—one voice and one light like fire" (1 Enoch 61:6). In v. 2 the Lord of the Spirits sets his Elect One on the throne of judgment

---

[8] The LXX may render גְּעָרָה, geʿārâ with ἀποσκορακισμός, aposkorakismos, or ἀπειλέω, apeileō.

[9] Kee, "Terminology," 236.

and endows him with the spirit of righteousness. On the day of judgment he executes righteous judgment: "The word of his mouth will do the sinners in; and all the oppressors shall be eliminated from before his face." This is the day of God's wrath for the sinners and the day of salvation for the righteous (vv. 11–13).

According to 4 Ezra 12:32, the Messiah, whom the Most High has kept until the end of days, "will come and speak to them . . . denounce them for their ungodliness. For first he will set them living before his judgment seat, and when he has reproved them, then he will destroy them." In the animal imagery of the vision, the Messiah, presented as the lion, roars against and reproves the eagle for his unrighteousness (v. 31). Here it is the Messiah who delivers the rebuke.

In the dream vision in 13:1–13, Ezra sees a figure resembling a man come out of the sea, fly with the clouds of heaven, and alight on a mountain, which he uses as his throne. "And whenever his voice issued from his mouth, all who heard his voice melted as wax melts when it feels fire" (v. 4). When enemy hordes gathered to fight him, "he neither lifted his hand nor held a spear or any weapon of war; but I saw only how he set forth from his mouth as it were a stream of fire, and from his lips a flaming breath, and from his tongue he shot forth a storm of sparks . . . and burned them all up" (vv. 9–11). In the interpretation of this vision, vv. 37–38, this imagery is interpreted as rebuke or reproach. The vision is a prediction. The figure, identified here as "my Son," reproves the assembled nations for their ungodliness, reproaches them for their evil thoughts, and destroys them without effort.

In 2 Bar. 21:19–23 the scribe asks God how long he will put up with mortality and transgression and implores, "Command mercifully and confirm all that you have said that you would do so that your power will be recognized . . . reprove the angel of death, and let your glory appear." Here it is God who reproves. With his mighty command God rebukes the angel of death.

In Pss. Sol. 17:23–24[10] the psalmist entreats God to raise up a king in the line of David who will liberate Israel from the nations and purge it of sinners. He begs the Lord, "Undergird him with the

---

[10] Pss. Sol. is dated to the first century BCE. See Wright, "Psalms of Solomon," 640–42.

strength to destroy the unrighteous rulers . . . to smash the arrogance of sinners like a potter's jar . . . to destroy the unlawful nations with the word of his mouth." Here the king, helped by God, is to destroy the enemy nations with a word of command (cf. also 2:22–23).

According to Kee, this motif occurs in exorcisms described in the Qumran writings and in the NT.[11] In the Qumran writings the Hebrew word גָּעַר is employed. In the *Genesis Apocryphon* Harkenosh, the exorcist, describes his exorcism of Pharaoh as follows:[12] "So I prayed [for him] . . . and I laid my hands on his [head]; and the scourge departed from him and the evil [spirit] was expelled [from him] and he lived" (20:28–29). The powerful word here that expels the spirit that caused the scourge is גָּעַר. Here a human agent, in the course of exorcism and through prayer, pushes back the evil spirit from a man. *War Scroll* 14:9–10 praises God, who delivered the souls from the hosts of Belial: "Thou hast driven his spirits [of destruction] far from [Thine elect]." Here it is God who with his powerful word (גָּעַר) drives back the threatening forces of evil.

Kee suggests that this motif is present also in NT accounts of Jesus' exorcisms, in which Jesus with a single command silences and expels the evil spirit. In Mark 1:21–28 Jesus commands (πετίμησεν, *epetimēsen*) the demon, and the demon comes out of the man, to the amazement of everybody. A similar description occurs in Mark 9:21–25. Jesus can also use his powerful command against the storm (4:35–41) or sickness or death (1:41; 3:5; 5:41; 7:34; 10:52; Luke 7:14).

This motif may also be present under a different image in Rev 2:16 and 19:11–16. In 2:12 the seer, introducing the Lord's message to the church at Pergamum, says, "Words of him who has the sharp two-edged sword." Here the word is a two-edged sword. The Lord threatens this community: "I will come to you soon and war against you with the sword of my mouth" (v. 16). According to 19:11–16, Christ, who is to come to impose his rule on his adversaries, is the "word of God": "From his mouth issues a sharp sword with which to smite the nations" (v. 15). He is the "King of kings and Lord of lords" (vv. 15–16).

---

[11] Kee, "Terminology," 234.
[12] The translation is taken from Vermes, *Dead Sea Scrolls*.

These texts indicate that the word of command is frequently associated with God's establishing his end-time rule. At times God's own mighty word destroys the power of evil, the godless, and the wicked; at times God's agent is endowed with this power. But the command ultimately comes from God and is always directed against God's enemies. It annihilates the nations and brings salvation to Israel; it destroys the sinners and vindicates the righteous. When the word is directed toward Israel, as in Isa 51:20, Israel is under God's judgment; and when, as in Rev 2:16, the word is directed toward the church at Pergamum, that community is under God's indictment. The character of command is maintained throughout, even when other images of power, such as fire or sword, are employed.

This suggests that the κέλευσμα in 1 Thess 4:16 denotes as well the commanding word spoken by God or by his agent. It indicates that the command is not given to the Lord or to the angel, for the overtone of rebuke is always present. Further determination of the meaning in 4:16 must, however, await the exegesis of that passage.

B. THE ARCHANGEL'S CALL

In 1 Thess 4:16 Paul states that the Lord will come down from heaven "with the archangel's call" (ἐν φωνῇ ἀρχαγγέλου, *en phōnē archangelou*).[13] This motif indicates another accompanying circumstance of his coming. The term ἀρχάγγελος, *archangelos* (archangel) signifies a mighty heavenly being, an angel of higher rank or one in charge of other angels. As with the word κέλευσμα, so also here questions arise: What does the voice of the archangel mean? How does it relate to the foregoing and to the following motifs?

In light of the preceding investigation it can be ruled out that it is the archangel who here receives the κέλευσμα. As was established above, the command is always given to an enemy of God; and it always implies rebuke.

The archangel in 1 Thess 4:16 is a minister of God and part of the retinue of the Lord. In 1 Thess 3:13 Paul states that the Lord Jesus

---

[13] The omission of the definite article with ἀρχαγγέλου is curious.

will come "with all his saints" (μετὰ πάντων τῶν ἁγίων αὐτοῦ, *meta pantōn tōn hagiōn autou*), alluding perhaps to angels.[14] And according to 2 Thess 1:7, the Lord Jesus will be revealed from heaven "with his mighty angels." This motif occurs also in the synoptic accounts of the Lord's coming. Luke 9:26 states that the Lord will come in the glory "of the holy angels," while Mark 8:38 and Matt 16:27 mention his coming "with the holy angels." According to Matt 13:41, 49, the Lord will send his angels to gather the elect and to separate the evil from the righteous (cf. Rev 10:7; 11:15).

As before, so also for this imagery we extend our search to the contexts that resemble that of the present passage. The most promising contexts, in addition to those already mentioned, are the theophany and the day of the Lord, in which the Lord is often depicted as coming with his army of angels. Often discussions in Jewish apocalyptic writings and in the Book of Revelation utilize the more specific motif of an archangel or a single angel.

The angelic accompaniment of Yahweh is a stereotyped feature in the theophanies of the OT. Yahweh comes as the leader of the heavenly troops. We find this imagery in the oldest poetry of Israel, in Deut 33:2–3:

> Yahweh from Sinai came
> He beamed forth from Seir
> With Him were myriads of holy ones
> At his right hand proceeded the mighty ones
> Yea, the guardians of the people . . .
> All the holy ones are at Thy hand
> They prostrate themselves at Thy feet
> They carry out Thy decisions.[15]

---

[14] Scholarly opinions are divided on this point. Many exegetes, interpreting the word "saints" from the regular Pauline usage, see here a reference to the deceased faithful (Rigaux, *Thessaloniciens*, 492; Findlay, *Thessalonians*, 77). Others interpret this from the OT imagery (von Dobschütz, *Thessalonicher-Briefe*, 153; Frame, *Thessalonians*, 136, 139; Neil, *Thessalonians*, 74; Best, *Thessalonians*, 152; Marshall, *Thessalonians*, 102–3). Still others include both angels and the deceased faithful in this retinue (Milligan, *Thessalonians*, 45; Morris, *Thessalonians*, 115). But if Paul had taught in Thessalonica that the deceased faithful would come with the Lord, then the difficulty about their presence at the parousia, as stated in 4:14–18, would not have arisen: the deceased would share in the parousia of the Lord (Wanamaker, *1 & 2 Thessalonians*, 145).

[15] This is a restored translation made by Cross and Freedman ("Blessing of Moses").

This poem describes the coming of Yahweh in the company of his host from heaven, the myriads of the holy ones. "The holy ones" here are, in parallel construction, associated with "the mighty ones" and "the guardians of the people." They are Yahweh's faithful ministers, carrying out his decisions.

According to Cross, the motif of angelic accompaniment is rooted in the notion of the heavenly council and is part of the war imagery of early Israel.[16] But whatever the origin of this imagery, the presence of the myriads of these "holy ones" depicts Yahweh's power: he comes as the leader of the powerful heavenly army that carries out his command. The motif thus portrays the power of Yahweh as he comes to establish his rule on earth.

This motif occurs in theophanies, in the holy-war tradition, and in the day-of-the-Lord tradition. Psalm 68:18 says, "The chariots of Yahweh are two myriads, two thousand the bowmen of my Lord when he came from Sinai with His Holy Ones."[17] Zechariah 14:5, which is probably echoed in 1 Thess 3:13, states, "Then the Lord your God will come and the holy ones with him." Here the "holy ones" are angels.

The imagery of Deut 33:2–3 occurs also in *1 Enoch* 1:4–9, which depicts the end-time coming of God: "The God of the universe, the Holy Great One, will come forth from his dwelling. And from there he will march upon Mount Sinai and appear in his camp emerging from heaven with a mighty power. And everyone shall be afraid. . . . Behold, he will arrive with ten million of the holy ones in order to execute judgment upon all." Here the power of God, the "Great One," is visible in the powerful army of angels. God comes as a mighty leader of the heavenly army to execute judgment and destroy the evildoers and the sources of evil—the Watchers and their progeny. He comes "with a mighty power." But the destruction of evil means salvation for the righteous.

In *1 Enoch* 60:1–2 the patriarch narrates the following vision: "The heaven of heavens was quaking and trembling with a mighty tremulous agitation, and the forces of the Most High and the angels, ten thousand times a million and ten million times ten million, were agitated with great agitation." When Enoch fainted at the sight of this (vv. 3–4), the angel Michael said to him, "When

---

[16] Cross, "Divine Warrior," 23–24.
[17] Translated by Cross (ibid., 26).

this day arrives—and the power, the punishment, and the judgment, which the Lord of the Spirits has prepared for those who do not worship the righteous judgment, and for those who take his name in vain—it will become a day of the covenant for the elect and inquisition for the sinners" (vv. 5–6).

In the purely forensic setting, when God is not said to "come forth" in his power, angels function as ministers carrying out the sentence of the Lord of the Spirits (*1 Enoch* 53:3–5; 54:1–6; 56:1–5; 60:1–2; 62:11; 63:1; cf. 100:4; 102:3). Usually these angels are sent out as ministers of punishment, but in some depictions they are sent to help the righteous. Thus in 61:1–5 angels clothe the righteous with the robes of righteousness, which will be their stay on the day of the Elect One. In 100:5 they protect the righteous in the days of vengeance.

In the synoptic depiction of the parousia, angels are the Son of man's retinue or his ministers. Thus, Mark 8:38 states that the Son of man will come "in the glory of his Father with the holy angels" (cf. Matt 16:27). According to Luke 9:26, the Son of man will come "in his glory and the glory of the Father and of the holy angels," while Matt 25:31 states that the Son of man will come in all his glory "and all his angels with him." In the explanation of the parable of the tares, Matt 13:36–43, angels are reapers sent forth by the Son of man to remove from his kingdom "all causes of sin and all evildoers." In the depiction of the parousia in Mark 13:26–27, the Son of man comes "in the clouds with great power and glory" and sends out his angels to "gather his elect from the four winds, from the ends of the earth to the ends of heaven." Luke, in the parallel passage, states, "And then they will see the Son of man coming in a cloud with great power and great glory" (21:27). Matthew has the most explicit presentation of the angels at the parousia: "They will see the Son of man coming on the clouds of heaven with power and great glory; and he will send out his angels with a loud trumpet call, and they will gather his elect from the four winds, from one end of heaven to the other" (24:30–31). All this indicates that angels, besides representing the glory of the Lord, have other specific functions connected with the Lord's coming. Since they are said both to remove evil from the face of the earth and to assemble the elect, their presence in this context is ambivalent.

The term ἀρχάγγελος, which Paul uses in 1 Thess 4:16, is not employed in the Hebrew Bible; the LXX, Second Temple literature, and the NT, however, know of mighty angels from the presence of God. Dan 12:1 mentions ὁ ἄγγελος ὁ μέγας, *ho angelos ho megas*, and *1 Enoch* 20 names seven mighty angels: Uriel, Raphael, Raguel, Michael, Saraqael, Gabriel, and Remiel. *First Enoch* 24:6 singles out Michael as the leader.[18] According to 54:6, Michael, Raphael, Gabriel, and Phanuel, on the great day of judgment and at the command of the Lord of the Spirits, seize Azaz'el and his armies and cast them into the furnace of fire. In 10:4–16 Michael and Gabriel bind Azaz'el and his spawn on earth. In v. 11 Michael is mentioned as a mighty angel who gives command to other angels. Verse 71:13 mentions that "the Antecedent of Time came with Michael, Gabriel, Raphael, Phanuel, and a hundred thousand and ten million times a hundred thousand angels that are countless" (see also vv. 8–9). And the Qumran writings know of various orders of angels (נְשִׂיאִים, *nᵉśî'îm*) and of seven sovereign princes of angels (נְשִׂיאֵי רוֹשׁ, *nᵉśî'ê rôš*).[19] In all these texts angels and the angelic princes are associated with God's coming and God's judgment, rather than with the coming of the Son of man or the Elect One.

It is in the NT accounts that angels or archangels accompany the Son of man at his coming or carry out his commands. The Book of Revelation mentions several archangels as heavenly agents of punishment or salvation. When the Lamb breaks the first four seals, one of the four living creatures near the throne of God calls out, "Come!" upon which a rider on a horse emerges and wreaks destruction upon the unrepentant (6:1–7). At the breaking of the seventh seal, which is the signal for the completion, seven angels, one after the other, blow a trumpet. At the sound of the first six trumpets a disaster strikes the unrepentant of the earth, while the seventh trumpet announces that "the mystery of God will be fulfilled" (10:7). Then loud voices in heaven proclaim, "The kingdom of the world has become the kingdom of our Lord and of his Messiah, and he will reign forever and ever" (11:15). God's temple in heaven opens, the ark of the covenant is seen, and there are "flashes of lightning, rumblings, peals of thunder, an earthquake, and heavy hail" (v. 19). The sequence is: the breaking of a seal by

---

[18] See also *Odes Sol.* 4:8. Charlesworth ("Odes of Solomon," 727) dates this composition in the late first or early second century CE.

[19] 4QShirShabb. On angelic orders and princes, see Alexander, "3 Enoch," 249.

the Lamb; an angelic figure giving a command or blowing a trumpet; and an act of judgment or salvation.

A similar pattern occurs in ch. 15, when seven angels carrying plagues come out of the open temple in heaven. One of the living creatures gives to each of them a golden bowl full of the wrath of God. When a voice from the temple—presumably the voice of God—calls, "Go and pour out on the earth the seven bowls of the wrath of God" (16:1), the seven angels one after the other pour out the bowl of wrath upon the earth. Here we find the following sequence: the commanding voice from the temple; one of the living creatures near the throne of God handing to an angel a bowl of the wrath of God; the angel executing God's judgment.

There are, in addition, angels with special messages in the context of judgment in 14:6–11. In the depiction of the coming of the Son of man on a white cloud, an angel comes out of the temple calling "with a loud voice to the one seated on the cloud, 'Use your sickle and reap' " (v. 15). Then another angel comes out of the temple with a sharp sickle. After that a third angel comes out from the altar with a message for the second angel: "Use your sharp sickle and gather the clusters of the vine of the earth, for its grapes are ripe" (vv. 17–18).

The archangels or angelic figures are armed with special authority. Thus, at the breaking of the sixth seal, an angel "having the seal of the living God" commands the four angels in charge of the winds not to damage the earth "until we have marked the servants of our God with a seal on their foreheads" (7:2–3). When the Beast and its armies are defeated, an angel, standing in the sun, cries with a loud voice to the birds, "Come, gather for the great supper of God, to eat the flesh of kings, the flesh of captains, the flesh of horses and their riders" (19:17–18). At the beginning of the thousand-year reign, an angel comes from heaven with the key to the bottomless pit and with a great chain (20:1) to imprison Satan for a thousand years in the pit.

Thus, the Book of Revelation extensively depicts angels and archangels as ministers of God and of the Lamb. They receive a command or give a command or announce an event. The commands come from the temple or from the Lamb. The archangels are frequently mentioned, either by name or by description. The name

Michael is given special prominence.[20] Yet in none of these depictions do we find the *coming* of Christ (i.e., the Lamb) in the company of angels.

The name of the archangel Michael is also known in Qumran. In the depiction of the eschatological war, angelic powers battle side by side with human warriors; it is a war with the "Prince of the kingdom of darkness" (1QM 1:10). According to 17:5–7, on the day of the defeat of the "Prince of wickedness," God will send eternal help to his redeemed "by the might of the princely angel of the kingdom of Michael."

The angelic accompaniment of God is thus a stereotyped motif in the OT, Jewish apocalyptic, and NT apocalyptic. This army of angels portrays the power and also the glory of the coming Lord. In this context, the archangels usually function as God's powerful ministers of judgment, especially against the fallen angels. In the Book of Revelation, the angels are not only the executioners of the judgment entrusted to the Lamb but also God's messengers. Revelation also mentions archangels. But only in the NT is the angelic accompaniment applied to the coming Son of man, and only in Revelation do mighty angels utter a command or blow a trumpet. In 1 Thess 3:13 Paul may allude to the Lord's coming with his angels.[21] This is certainly done in 2 Thess 1:7.

The image φωνὴ ἀρχαγγέλου, *phōnē archangelou*, in 1 Thess 4:16 is thus best interpreted against this background, especially against the NT depictions that associate angels with the coming of the Son of man. It contributes to the power and the glory of the coming Lord and may also suggest a judicial function. The mention of a single archangel here, as well as the call, may imply a special function, not further explained by the

---

[20] Revelation has the following references to the angelic leaders: the "angel standing in the sun" (19:17); the angel coming "from the altar . . . who had authority over fire" (14:18); "Michael and his angels" (12:7); "another mighty angel coming down from heaven, wrapped in a cloud, with a rainbow over his head; his face was like the sun, and his legs like pillars of fire" (10:1–2); an "angel with a golden censor" (8:3); an "angel ascending from the rising of the sun, having the seal of the living God, and he called with a loud voice to the four angels" (7:2).

[21] The LXX (Zech 14:5) has, καὶ ἥξει κύριος ὁ θεός μου καὶ πάντες οἱ ἅγιοι μετ' αὐτοῦ, *kai hēxei kyrios ho theos mou kai pantes hoi hagioi met' autou*. Paul's wording in 1 Thess 3:13, however, is, ἐν τῇ παρουσίᾳ τοῦ κυρίου ἡμῶν Ἰησοῦ μετὰ πάντων τῶν ἁγίων αὐτοῦ, *en tē parousia tou kyriou hēmōn Iēsou meta pantōn tōn hagiōn autou*. The closeness of the two texts is apparent in the words πάντες-πάντων, ἅγιοι-ἁγίων, and μετ' αὐτοῦ.

text.[22] Further determination of the function of this motif in 1 Thess 4:16–18 must await the exegesis of that passage.

C. THE TRUMPET OF GOD

According to 1 Thess 4:16, the Lord will also come from heaven ἐν σάλπιγγι θεοῦ, *en salpingi theou*—at the sound of the trumpet of God. This is the third image portraying the circumstances of the Lord's coming. It is predominantly an image of sound, as are the first two images. While it is terse and condensed, it may invoke an earlier, more extensive presentation that Paul gave to this community. What does this motif signify? And how does it relate to the two preceding motifs?

The trumpet motif occurs also in 1 Cor 15:52, where the apostle states, "In a moment, in the twinkling of an eye, at the last trumpet (ἐν τῇ ἐσχάτῃ σάλπιγγι, *en tē eschatē salpingi*) . . . the dead will be raised imperishable, and we shall be changed." The trumpet here is "the last trumpet" that signals the ultimate completion. In v. 52 Paul asserts that the trumpet will indeed sound (σαλπίσει γάρ, *salpisei gar*). The evocative nature of this image is apparent.

The LXX translates seven Hebrew words by σάλπιγξ, *salpinx*, but most frequently it translates the word for horn (שׁוֹפָר, *šôpār*).[23] This motif occurs in the holy-war tradition, in cultic tradition associated with the ark of the covenant, in theophanies, and in the day-of-the-Lord tradition. It is thus a widely used motif in contexts that resemble the coming of the Lord in 1 Thess 4:16–18.

According to von Rad, one of the most basic uses of this motif occurs in the depictions of the holy war.[24] When the sound of the horn signaled war (Judg 3:27; 6:34; 1 Sam 13:3), all tribes gathered

---

[22] 2 Thess 1:7–10 seems to support this interpretation. Here the author promises a reward to the faithful and punishment to the persecutors and the like "when the Lord Jesus is revealed from heaven with his mighty angels in flaming fire, inflicting vengeance." This text extols the glory of the Lord at his parousia, and the angelic accompaniment brings out his might and his glory.

[23] Friedrich, "σάλπιγξ," 76.

[24] Von Rad, *Holy War.* For a critique of von Rad's view of the holy war, see Ollenburger, "Introduction," 13–31; Fohrer, *Geschichte,* 109; de Vaux, *Ancient Israel,* 258–67; Weipert, "Heiliger Krieg," 488–93; and Stolz, *Kriege,* 10–12, 203. The OT does not employ the expression "holy war." The first to use this term was Schwally, *Der heilige Krieg.* See on this Ollenburger, "Introduction," 5–6.

in one camp. According to Judg 6:34, it was Yahweh who summoned his people. Deuteronomy 24:14 asserts that Yahweh was present in the camp, while Judg 4:14 states that Yahweh marched at the head of his army. The sound of the horn was employed also to indicate a particular move in the course of the battle. The cultic dimension of this motif is evident from the mention of priests blowing the trumpet (2 Chron 13:14).[25]

The day of the Lord is often presented as a day of battle.[26] According to Zech 9:14, on the day of battle "the Lord will appear over them, and his arrow go forth like lightning; the Lord God will sound the trumpet, and march forth in the whirlwind of the south." The assertion "the Lord God will sound the trumpet" resembles "the sound of the trumpet of God" mentioned in 1 Thess 4:16 at the coming of the Lord.

The trumpet sound may signal redemption or disaster for Israel. In Zech 10:8 the Lord says, "I will signal for them and gather them in, for I have redeemed them" (cf. Isa 27:13). When the day of the Lord is a disaster for Israel, the trumpet blast is a signal and a warning of the approaching disaster (Ezek 33:3, 4; Jer 4:5, 19). In the Dead Sea Scrolls the trumpet motif is a feature of the eschatological battle. This is a battle of the Qumran warriors and spiritual forces. God, his angels, and the "sons of light" fight against Beliar, his hordes, and the "sons of darkness."[27] When the priests sound the trumpet, the troops execute a particular maneuver (1QM 3:1, 3, 8). The inscriptions on the trumpets indicate that these signals are in fact God's commands. On the trumpets summoning the congregation is inscribed, "The called of God" (v. 2); on those calling the commanders of the army is written, "The princes of God" (v. 2); and on those signaling attack is engraved, "Formation of the divisions of God for vengeance of His wrath on the sons of Darkness" (v. 8).[28]

The NT employs the trumpet motif to depict the Lord's parousia in Matt 24:31, 1 Thess 4:16, 1 Cor 15:52, and Rev 11:15. According

---

[25] On the resurgence of this notion in prophetic writings and in Qumran, see de Vaux, *Ancient Israel*, 258–67.

[26] Von Rad, *Theology*, 2.119–25.

[27] According to de Vaux (*Ancient Israel*, 267), three out of five explicit citations of the OT here refer to texts dealing with the holy war (Num 10:9; Deut 7:21–22; 20:2–5).

[28] According to de Vaux (ibid., 267), these "visionary dreams are mingled with practical arrangements that could be taken straight from a Roman military text-book."

to Matt 24:31, the Son of man "will send out his angels with a loud trumpet call, and they will gather his elect from the four winds, from one end of heaven to the other." Here the trumpet signal has a positive meaning. In the Book of Revelation this motif acquires a thematic expansion. In Rev 8:2, 6, 7, 8, 10, 12; 9:1, 13, 14; and 10:7 the trumpet sound is a stereotyped motif in the descriptions of punishments that precede the conclusion of this age; in 11:15 it is the signal for the ultimate completion. Here it is the seven angels who, one after the other, blow the trumpet. But each act is initiated by the Lamb, to whom is entrusted the mystery of completion—the scroll sealed with seven seals. The last trumpet signals the inauguration of the kingdom of God and of the Lamb. At the signal of the first five trumpets a particular agent of disaster is unleashed; at the sound of the last two trumpets, the action is initiated by the command of a mighty heavenly being.

At the sixth trumpet the seer "heard a voice from the four horns of the golden altar before God, saying to the sixth angel who had the trumpet, 'Release the four angels who are bound at the great river Euphrates.' So the four angels were released . . . to kill a third of mankind" (9:13–16). At the sound of the seventh trumpet loud voices in heaven exclaim, "The kingdom of the world has become the kingdom of our Lord and his Messiah, and he will rule forever and ever." It is the time for judgment and reward. Further voices and actions are then recorded in heaven: the twenty-four elders fall down before God and worship him for having assumed his power; the temple of God in heaven is opened and the ark of the covenant is seen; there are flashes of lightning, peals of thunder, and an earthquake (11:15–19).

The phrase "the trumpet of God" is not found here. The seventh trumpet, however, signals the ultimate completion. The mighty angel standing on the sea and land declares, "In the days when the seventh angel is to blow the seventh trumpet, the mystery of God will be fulfilled" (10:7). But the trumpet motif is not employed in the depiction of the ultimate event in 19:11–21.

The trumpet motif thus seems to describe the power of God, which summons and releases a force for judgment or salvation. It suggests that God enforces his rule in the world. In 11:15 it ushers in the rule of God and of his Christ. The expression "at the last trumpet" in 1 Cor 15:52 may suggest something similar to this: it is the last trumpet, the one that inaugurates the completion. The context indicates that the ultimate completion here includes the kingdom of God, the resurrection of the dead, and the transformation of all.

In light of this, the phrase ἐν σάλπιγγι θεοῦ (1 Thess 4:16), which occurs in paratactic arrangement with the preceding two circumstantial clauses, probably indicates God's end-time intervention in power. The Lord's coming is a coming in the power of God. Together with the archangel motif, the trumpet of God reinforces the command and power expressed by the κέλευσμα: Jesus comes in the power, authority, and glory of God! Through his coming, God will ultimately bring to himself those who believe in Christ.

D. THE CLOUD

The cloud image occurs in 1 Thess 4:17, not in v. 16. It thus does not indicate the attendant circumstances of the Lord's coming, as in the synoptic parousia depictions, which depend on Dan 7:13. All the Synoptics state that the Lord will come "on the clouds of heaven" (Mark 13:26; Matt 24:30; Luke 21:27). This is also the picture in Rev 1:7: "Look! He is coming with the clouds; every eye will see him, even those who pierced him, and on his account all the tribes of the earth will wail."[29] In 14:14–16 the cloud appears to be the seat of the Son of man, while in 10:1 the cloud seems to enwrap the mighty angel coming down from heaven.[30] But according to 1 Thess 4:17, the believers—those still living and those that have been brought to life again—will at the Lord's coming be taken up "in the clouds (ἐν νεφέλαις, en nephelais) to meet the Lord" in the aerial heights. This image is unique in the NT. In view of its specific function here, it is necessary to investigate the cloud image not in connection with the Lord's coming from heaven but, rather, in connection with assumptions.[31]

According to Lohfink,[32] in Greco-Roman antiquity the taking up is of two types: the heavenly journey and the assumption.[33] The

---

[29] Cf. Matt 24:30.

[30] See Scott, "He Cometh," 131; Pesch, Naherwartungen, 171; Oepke, "νεφέλη," 910; Feuillet, "Fils de l'homme," 187–88; Delcor, Livre de Daniel, 155; Jörg Jeremias, Theophanie, 17, 33, 36; Volz, Eschatologie, 204.

[31] Plevnik, "The Taking Up," 280–81.

[32] Lohfink, Himmelfahrt, 32–78.

[33] Lohfink employs the word Entrückung, which is here translated as "assumption."

heavenly journey is not necessarily associated with death; it can occur either in a trance or at death. But in both cases it involves only the spirit. In a trance the spirit of the living person is transported into heaven, while the body remains on earth. After the trance the spirit returns to the body. At death, however, the soul leaves the body, which is then buried, and journeys alone to heaven, never to return to the body. In the assumption, however, a mortal human being is taken up *body and soul* into paradise or to some other place in the beyond to enjoy a higher life forever. An assumption thus presupposes that the person is *alive* when taken up. It is an exceptional conclusion of life on earth, one that does not involve death. This is to be distinguished from an ascension, in which a *heavenly* being after an appearance on earth *returns* to heaven, its proper abode.

In the heavenly journey the focus is on the *journey*. In the assumption, however, the focus is on the *departure* and the *destination*; the event is told from the point of view of the witnesses on earth, and the emphasis is on the sudden disappearance, which is interpreted as an assumption and exaltation.

The OT and Judaism, according to Lohfink, reveal four ways in which someone can be taken up: (a) the journey to heaven; (b) the assumption of the soul after death; (c) the assumption of the whole person, body and soul, into heaven; and (d) the ascension.[34] In the assumption of the soul after death, the soul leaves the body and the corpse is buried. An assumption here indicates the natural end of life on earth and some type of continuation of life in the beyond.

The assumption of the whole person—type (a)—in the OT and Judaism corresponds to the Greco-Roman assumption. The taking up of the whole person, body and soul, into paradise implies the end of the present life on earth. Translation can be to heaven or to a place other than heaven. This type of taking up occurs in 4 Ezra and 2 Baruch and is associated with Moses, Enoch, Elijah, and the Messiah.[35]

The cluster of motifs associated with these presentations are by and large the same.[36] Lohfink mentions the following motifs: mountain, funeral pyre, lightning, storm, wind, wagon, eagle, cloud,

---

[34] Only (c) has parallels in the ascension and assumption accounts in the NT. See Plevnik, "The Taking Up," 279.

[35] Lohfink, *Himmelfahrt*, 55–70.

[36] Ibid., 42–49, 72–74.

heavenly confirmation through subsequent appearances, adoration by the witnesses, and the institution of a cult. The latter, however, is absent in the OT and Jewish accounts because of their strict monotheism. In biblical accounts and in Judaism it is God who takes up the person, although God makes use of such things as storm, wind, cloud, wagon, or angels.

The technical term for an assumption in these Jewish sources is לָקַח, lāqaḥ. In Hellenistic literature, according to Lohfink, three groups of verbs and nouns express the notion of לָקַח. The first group refers to the act of disappearance and contains such terms as ἀφανίζω, aphanizō, ἀφανὴς γίγνομαι, aphanēs gignomai, ἄφαντος γίγνομαι, aphantos gignomai, and ἀφανισμός, aphanismos. The second group depicts the seizure and employs the words ἁρπάζω, harpazō, ἀναρπάζω, anarpazō, συναρπάζω, synarpazō, and ἁρπαγή, harpagē. Its Latin equivalent is rapio, rapior. The third group deals with the translation and contains such words as μεθίσταμαι, methistamai, and μετάστασις, metastasis.[37]

Type (b) in Jewish accounts, the assumption of the soul alone, presumes that death has occurred. Type (c), the assumption of the whole person, however, presupposes not death but life: life is not terminated but changed; it continues from then on in a more exalted form with God in heaven.[38] This type of assumption entails a direct translation from this life on earth to the eternal life with God. The one who is assumed does not have to taste death, and conversely, the one who has died cannot be assumed.[39] One has to be alive in order to be taken up.

This pattern of assumption occurs also in the NT. Luke employs it in the depiction of the ascension of Jesus in Luke 24 and Acts 1. In both texts, the evangelist states that Jesus was first raised from the dead and appeared to his disciples, then he was taken up into heaven body and soul. This pattern occurs also in Rev 11:3–13. Here the two prophetic witnesses who came from heaven to earth were killed for their testimony. The account states that they were first brought back to life, then they were taken up by a cloud to heaven.[40]

---

[37] Ibid., 41–42.

[38] Ibid., 73 nn. 252 and 253.

[39] Ibid., 74.

[40] In Rev 12:5 the male offspring of the woman is immediately at his birth "caught up to God and to his throne" and thereby spared death.

This understanding is of crucial importance for the situation that Paul faced in Thessalonica. The cloud in 1 Thess 4:17 is associated with the taking up of living persons body and soul into heaven or into the mode of life associated with the risen Lord. This motif is not usually employed for a state of trance, nor for the ascent of the soul after death. It functions, rather, as a vehicle for transporting a living human being, body and soul, from the earth into heaven.[41] In vv. 16–17 the living faithful are taken up by the clouds to be with the Lord forever, and the text does not mention a return to the earth. As in Rev 11:3–13, the deceased faithful are here first brought back to life, then they are taken up by clouds and transported near to the Lord. This pattern suggests an elevation from life on earth to a life like that of the risen Lord, with whom they live forever.

CONCLUSION

The images of the cry of command, the archangel's call, and the trumpet of God in 1 Thess 4:16–18 depict the Lord's coming from heaven, while the image of the cloud depicts the taking up of the faithful. None of these images fits well the Hellenistic παρουσία. In fact, the first three are used in the OT and in Jewish apocalyptic literature in depictions of theophanies or the day of the Lord.

The cry of command (κέλευσμα) corresponds in these depictions to גָּעַר, gāʿar, or גְּעָרָה, geʿārâ, which is usually translated as "rebuke." The LXX, Aquila, and Symmachus translate it as ἐπιτιμάω, ἐπιτίμησις, in which the command overtone is more pronounced. Thus, גְּעָרָה is a cry of command. This command is, in the context of theophanies and the day of the Lord, always given by God. Since the Lord's coming depicted in 1 Thess 4:13–18 mentions only the Lord's descent, the command can scarcely be given to him. It must be a command coming from God or a command given by the Lord himself. And since such a command is always given to a hostile force or to a hostile people, it is not given by God to Jesus, nor is it a command for the dead to rise, as has been suggested in the past. The cry of command thus expresses above all the power of the Lord,

---

[41] Or from heaven to the earth; but this pattern is not present in 1 Thess 4:13–17.

who is coming to push back the power of evil and to establish his rule in the world and in the cosmos.

The archangel's call evokes the angelic accompaniment, which traditionally expressed the power of God in his coming as the leader of heavenly armies to establish his rule over hostile forces and sinners in the world. The mention of a single and powerful archangel suggests that this figure is functioning here in a specific way—probably carrying out the command of the Lord. In the intertestamental literature and in the Book of Revelation such angelic figures usually enforce the judgment of God.

The trumpet of God signals this powerful event, the ultimate completion, when the Lord comes with divine power to assume his rule over the whole of creation (Rev 11:15) and to establish the kingdom of God. Like the other two, this motif expresses the power of the Lord. The three motifs thus state in different ways the power of the Lord at his coming for judgment and salvation and thereby reinforce one another.

The cloud motif, however, belongs to the depiction of the taking up. It therefore does not belong to the imagery of the Lord's descent from heaven, although in the synoptic portrayals of the parousia the Son of man is depicted as coming on the clouds of heaven. The cloud here serves as a vehicle of transportation between earth and heaven, and in this it fulfills its traditional function. In 1 Thess 4:17 it carries the living faithful, who have been joined by the resurrected faithful, to the exalted Lord. The suggestion is that this is the ultimate change of existence—the end of existence here on earth and the beginning of eternal life with the exalted Lord.

3

⚙

THE PAROUSIA DEPICTION IN
1 THESSALONIANS 4:13–18

First Thessalonians 4:13–18, the first part of the extensive eschatological section, 4:13–5:18, contains the most explicit and extensive description in Pauline letters of the parousia of Christ. It is Paul's most important description of the Lord's coming, containing the apostle's response to the grief and anxiety in the Thessalonian community about the future of the deceased faithful. It answers the question, How will the dead participate in the Lord's coming?

The passage has been the subject of scholarly interest for a variety of reasons. The very fact that this problem arose in Thessalonica suggests to some exegetes that Paul, before this, did not preach the resurrection of the dead.[1] Others focus on the expectation of the approaching parousia or on the problems caused by its delay.[2] Others investigate here the interim state of the deceased before the Lord's parousia.[3] Still others probe the text for the messianic millennial reign,[4] Paul's anti-Gnostic polemic,[5] the shift in Pauline eschatology,[6] the presence of a

---

[1] Guntermann, *Eschatologie*, 38–51. This is echoed by Wilckens, "Ursprung," 58–59, and by Luedemann, *Paul*, 219.

[2] See Rigaux, *Thessaloniciens*, 222–27.

[3] Hoffmann, *Toten*.

[4] Wilcke, *Zwischenreich*.

[5] Schmithals, "Historical Situation," 164–67; Harnisch, *Eschatologische Existenz*, 23–29. For the older views on this topic, see Kabisch, *Eschatologie*, 24–31 and Lütgert, *Die Vollkommenen*, 79–81.

[6] Hoffmann, *Toten*, 326–31.

pre-Pauline tradition,[7] or Pauline apocalyptic.[8] The focus of the present investigation is the parousia itself, above all the peculiar depiction of this event in 4:16–17.

A. THE CONTEXT AND THE STRUCTURE OF 1 THESSALONIANS 4:13–18

First Thessalonians 4:13–18 belongs to the section of ch. 4 in which Paul addresses questions raised by the community. K.-G. Eckart[9] suggested that certain passages in this letter should be excised[10] and that the remnant of the letter makes up two letters. According to him, 4:13–18 belongs to the second letter, which contains the following parts: 3:6–10, 4:13–5:11, 4:9–10a, and 5:23–26, 28. Eckart's assertions, however, have been demolished by W. Kümmel,[11] who reaffirmed the unity of 1 Thessalonians. W. Schmithals, although accepting the validity of Kümmel's arguments, suggested a division of 1 and 2 Thessalonians into several letters. According to him, 1 and 2 Thessalonians make up four letters.[12] In Schmithals's arrangement, 1 Thess 4:13–18 belongs to the second letter (which contains 1 Thess 1:1–2:12 and 4:2–5:28) and was preceded by the first letter (which contains 2 Thess 1:1–12 and 3:6–16).[13] His division, however, did not receive scholarly consensus.[14]

---

[7] J. Jeremias, *Unknown Sayings*, 80–83; Nepper-Christensen, "Herrenwort"; Luz, *Geschichtsverständnis*, 326–31.

[8] Hartman, *Prophecy Interpreted*, 181–90.

[9] Eckart, "Der zweite Brief," 33–34. According to Eckart, 1 Thess is composed of two epistles, the first comprising 1:1–2:12, 2:17–3:4, and 3:11–13; and the second, 3:6–10, 4:13–5:11, 4:9–10a, and 5:23–26, 28.

[10] Eckart (ibid.) excises 2:13–16, 3:5, 4:1–8, 10b–12, and 5:12–22, 27 as not concrete enough and having an elevated style. Kümmel ("Problem," 408–12), however, shows that the style in these sections is Paul's. According to him, lack of concreteness is typical for traditional passages dealing with exhortation. See also Schmithals, "Historical Situation," 126–29.

[11] Kümmel, "Problem," 413–14. See also Luz, *Geschichtsverständnis*, 318.

[12] The first letter comprises 2 Thess 1:1–12 and 3:6–16; the third letter, 2 Thess 2:13–14, 2:1–12, and 2:15–3:3(5), 17–18; and the fourth letter, 1 Thess 2:13–4:1. See Schmithals, "Historical Situation," 212–13.

[13] For a similar division of 1 Thess, see Pesch, *Entdeckung*, 23–67.

[14] Schmithals, "Historical Situation," 212–14. For the opposite view, see Kümmel, *Introduction*, 260–62; Luz, *Geschichtsverständnis*, 318–19; and Rigaux, *Paul*, 168–69.

With the exception of Eckart, Schmithals, W. Harnisch, and R. Pesch, the integrity of 1 Thessalonians is presently upheld by most scholars,[15] and here it will be assumed. Thus, all of 1 Thessalonians is regarded here as providing the epistolary context of 4:13–18. That 5:1–11 is a later interpolation was suggested by G. Friedrich,[16] but his argumentation has not obtained scholarly agreement.

The present epistle discloses that the Lord's coming has been in the forefront of Paul's thinking.[17] Whatever the subject he touches on here—be it the greeting of the community (1:2–3), their acceptance of the faith (1:9–10), his hope concerning their ultimate salvation (2:19–20), his own behavior toward them (2:9–12), or his prayers on their behalf (3:11–13; 5:23–24)—his referent is the parousia of Christ. The Lord's coming may not be the main theme of this epistle, but it comes close to being so. The entire letter radiates Paul's ardent hope that he and the Thessalonians will participate in this event.

First Thessalonians is an encouraging letter. Beginning with 4:1 Paul affirms several times the community's Christian existence, even as he spurs the faithful on to new efforts. Thus in v. 1 he urges, "Just as you are doing, you do so more and more," and in v. 10 he confirms, "Indeed you do love all the brothers throughout Macedonia," and then exhorts, "But we urge you, beloved, to do so more and more." This tone is present also in the eschatological section, 4:13–5:11. In 4:18 he concludes with the exhortation "Encourage one another with these words," while in 5:11 he restates this exhortation and confirms what the Thessalonians are doing: "Encourage one another and build up each other, as indeed you are doing" (cf. also 5:4–5, 9–10).

The section 4:13–18 is linked with the immediately preceding and following sections through a similar beginning: "Now concerning (περὶ δέ, peri de) . . . " (4:9; 5:1). But whereas in the flanking passages the apostle sees no need to write to them, in 4:13 he states just the opposite: "We do not want you to be uninformed." Thus, 4:13–18 deals with what Paul regards as an urgent matter: it touches the very hope of Christians and must be clarified.

---

[15] See Wanamaker, 1 & 2 Thessalonians, 34–37.
[16] Friedrich, "Einschub," 314–15; also Briefe, 206–8.
[17] See Plevnik, "Ultimate Reality," 262.

There is perplexity and grief in the Thessalonian community about whether the deceased faithful will share in the Lord's coming.[18] Verse 14 discloses that, for some reason, the Thessalonians thought that death had robbed fellow Christians of their promised future, of their participation in the Lord's parousia. The apostle, in his response, dispels this ignorance, which has caused them such grief and such a profound sense of loss. In v. 13 he states, "That you may not grieve as others do who have no hope." The advice in v. 18—"Therefore encourage one another with these words"—concludes the instruction. Verses 13–18 are thus a unified composition. Verse 5:1 begins a new section, as περὶ δέ, peri de, and the new subject, the times and seasons, indicate.

The instruction in 4:13–18 has two parts. The first part, vv. 13–14, is an argument from the knowledge mediated by faith (v. 14), that the God who has raised Jesus from the dead will also bring the deceased faithful with Jesus. The second part, vv. 15–18, is the assurance guaranteed by the word of the Lord that the living faithful will have no advantage over the dead (v. 15). This reassurance is followed up by the depiction of the Lord's coming from heaven, when the deceased faithful will share with the living in the joyful union with the Lord (vv. 16–17).

B. THE FIRST RESPONSE

In 1 Thess 4:13–14 Paul alludes to the situation in the Thessalonian community: the grief about the faithful who have died before the Lord's coming. This is not so much the common human experience of losing a dear one as it is losing the hope that arises from their faith. The words περὶ τῶν κοιμωμένων, peri tōn koimōmenōn ("concerning those who are asleep")[19] refer to the deceased faithful who had hoped to share in the Lord's coming (v. 13). The apostle here hastens to instruct the surviving believers lest they grieve "as others do who have no hope." He sees that their sorrow springs from a lack of knowledge in this regard. He draws

---

[18] Lindemann ("Die korinthische Eschatologie," 377–78) suggests that "the deceased" (τοὺς κοιμηθέντας, tous koimēthentas) in 1 Thess 4:14, 15 refers only to the deceased Christians. But see Merklein, "Theologe als Prophet," 403.

[19] On this metaphorical expression see Rigaux, Thessalonicien, 529–32; Holtz, 1 Thessalonicher, 188.

the assurance (v. 14) from the death and resurrection of Christ: the participation of the deceased faithful in the Lord's coming is implied by that event, which already has shaped their faith and hope. They need only understand what Christ's resurrection means for them.

1. The Nature of Grief

The deceased here are the believers in Thessalonica who have died since Paul's founding visit to this community. That they are believers is implied by the words τοὺς κοιμηθέντας διὰ τοῦ Ἰησοῦ, *tous koimēthentas dia tou Iēsou* ("those who have died through Jesus"), which we take as belonging together,[20] and clearly stated by the phrase οἱ νεκροὶ ἐν Χριστῷ, *hoi nekroi en Christō* ("the dead in Christ"), in v. 16.[21] The apostle here talks about the believers, as the entire context clearly indicates.

But why do the Thessalonian Christians grieve as they do? Do they perhaps fear that the living will for a time enjoy some sort of advantage over the dead in attaining the ultimate completion? Is this the hopelessness and the grief that Paul addresses so seriously here? It seems that much more is involved here than this. But then, how do they imagine their participation in the Lord's coming?[22] Why do they imagine it as they do? And how did Paul present this event when he preached to them earlier?

It appears that the Thessalonian Christians fear that the deceased faithful will not be united with Christ, as the living would be, at his coming. For some unexplained reason they think that death has robbed the deceased of this. Do they, then, not believe in the resurrection of the dead? Did the apostle not talk to them about the resurrection of the dead?[23] Do some in the community deny the

---

[20]Many exegetes link διὰ τοῦ Ἰησοῦ to the verb, ἄξει, that follows. While this may be preferable on grammatical grounds, it clashes with the concluding words σὺν αὐτῷ, *syn autō*. See Plevnik, "Parousia," 210–12. On recent positions on this issue, see Sieber, *Mit Christus Leben*, 26–29; Froitzheim, *Christologie*, 196; Luedemann, *Paul*, 217–20.

[21]Most exegetes link ἐν Χριστῷ in v. 16 to οἱ νεκροί; cf. Merklein, "Theologe als Prophet," 403 n. 4.

[22]For a survey of various explanations, see Luedemann, *Paul*, 206–12. Cf. also Merklein, "Theologe als Prophet," 404 n. 5.

[23]On these possibilities see Luedemann, *Paul*, 212. Cf. also Merklein, "Theologe als Prophet," 404 n. 6. According to Holtz (*1 Thessalonicher*, 191–92), the Thessalonians had difficulties accepting the resurrection of the body.

resurrection of the dead? Is the resurrection of the dead the real problem Paul is addressing here?

According to Schmithals[24] and Harnisch,[25] Paul did preach the resurrection of the dead to the Thessalonians but his preaching was undermined by Gnostic agitation in the community. This hypothesis, however, has failed to receive scholarly consensus[26] and does not account for the shape of Paul's answer here.

P. Hoffmann[27] and U. Luz[28] insist that the Thessalonians continued to believe in the resurrection of the dead[29] but they became perplexed by the notion of the messianic interregnum. The notion of a millennial reign is documented in *Pseudo-Philo*, 4 Ezra, and *2 Baruch* and implies two resurrections. The dead, accordingly, would be raised only at the second resurrection and would thus be robbed of sharing in the messianic reign.

There are several difficulties with this view as well. One is that these writings, and the notion of the messianic reign in particular, arose after and in response to the destruction of the second temple. Another is that according to *2 Bar.* 30:2, the dead witnesses to the faith are raised in order that they may enjoy the messianic reign. Still another is that Paul, in his letter to the Thessalonians, does not address this problem. Luz, who agrees with U. Wilcke[30] that Paul does not mention this view in his writings, holds it possible that the Thessalonian community might have been influenced in this regard by Jewish notions.[31] But then, why does Paul here or elsewhere not take issue with this view? Besides, the messianic reign, in its Christian interpreta-

---

[24] Schmithals, "Historical Situation," 161–64.

[25] Harnisch, *Eschatologische Existenz*, 23.

[26] According to Luz (*Geschichtsverständnis*, 320–21), Schmithals assumes that Paul has misunderstood the situation; he speaks here to the congregation, which, swayed by the Gnostics, is grieving for its dead. According to Harnisch, however, Paul is not comforting but warning the congregation not to grieve as others do. But if the Gnostics have undermined the resurrection faith, why does Paul here not talk about the resurrection? See Luedemann, *Paul*, 206–9.

[27] Hoffmann, *Toten*, 232.

[28] Luz, *Geschichtsverständnis*, 319. According to Luz, Wilcke proves only that written documentation containing the expectation of the messianic reign comes from the period after the destruction of the temple, not that such ideas arose after 70 CE.

[29] Rigaux (*Thessaloniciens*, 526–27), as well, is firm on this point; against Guntermann (*Eschatologie*, 38–51).

[30] Wilcke, *Zwischenreich*, 48.

[31] Luz, *Geschichtsverständnis*, 319 n. 8.

tion presented in the Book of Revelation, implies the resurrection of the faithful. In Rev 20:4 the seer says, "I also saw the souls of those who had been beheaded for their testimony to Jesus. . . . They came to life and reigned with Christ a thousand years." What is clear, however, is that the Thessalonians regard participation in the Lord's coming as a salvific event, as both Hoffmann and Luz emphasize.[32] It is also clear that here Paul is not merely emphasizing what is already known to the Thessalonians, but is providing new information.[33]

Some scholars have suggested that Paul's phrase "grieve as others do who have no hope" is alluding to the contemporary cosmic pessimism among pagans.[34] In this view, the faithful in Thessalonica have fallen back into pagan pessimism. But the difficulty with this solution is that statements expressing pagan pessimism can easily be balanced by those expressing some hope in the afterlife. There is no evidence here that the Thessalonians share in, or that Paul is here addressing, this pessimism.[35] An argument one way or the other based on the particle $\kappa\alpha\theta\dot{\omega}\varsigma$, kathōs, in v. 13 is not possible, as Hoffmann observes.[36] And as Rigaux,[37] Hoffmann,[38] Luz,[39] T. Holtz,[40] and others rightly note, the apostle here speaks from and about the hope that springs up from the faith that is centered on Christ. In 1:3 he presents Christian existence as marked by a "steadfastness of hope in our Lord Jesus Christ" (cf. also 1:10; 5:9). And throughout the letter this hope is focused on the parousia of Christ (2:19; 3:13). Pagans would scarcely share in this expectation.

2. The Inference from Christ's Resurrection, 1 Thessalonians 4:14

After the remarks in v. 13 Paul gives his first answer, in v. 14: "For since we believe that Jesus died and rose, even so God will

---

[32] Ibid., 320; Hoffmann, Toten, 232.
[33] Merklein, "Theologe als Prophet," 405.
[34] See Henneken, Verkündigung, 75–76.
[35] Ibid.
[36] Hoffmann, Toten, 210.
[37] Rigaux, Thessaloniciens, 532–33.
[38] Hoffmann, Toten, 209–11.
[39] Luz, Geschichtsverständnis, 318.
[40] Holtz, 1 Thessalonicher, 189.

bring those who have died (διὰ τοῦ Ἰησοῦ) with him." The words
διὰ τοῦ Ἰησοῦ ("through Jesus") probably refer to the preceding
participle, κοιμηθέντας ("those who have died") rather than to the
ἄξει that follows.[41] They make explicit the relationship to Christ
among those who have died.[42] But scholarly opinion on this point
is evenly divided. The compound sentence is an anacoluthon with
several shifts between the first (conditional) clause and the second
(result) clause:

(a) The first clause begins with "since we believe," but the second clause does
not follow up with "so, also, we believe."

(b) The first clause states that Jesus himself "rose" (ἀνέστη, anestē) from the
dead, but the second clause implies that it was God who raised Jesus from
the dead.

(c) The first clause argues from Jesus' resurrection, but the second clause
concludes with God's bringing (ἄξει) the deceased with Jesus;[43] the
resurrection of the deceased faithful is passed over.[44]

It seems that the apostle, in his rush to reach the end, skips
over his own thought. But the inference in v. 14 represents a
theological argument typical of Paul: what happened to Christ will
also happen to Christians. As R. Schnackenburg[45] notes, "The
death which they experience through the will of Jesus can no
more remain without the resurrection than it could in his case."
Schnackenburg's paraphrase, however, applies better to 2 Cor 4:14

[41] The latter is already qualified by σὺν αὐτῷ.

[42] See Sieber, *Mit Christus Leben*, 26–29; Hoffmann, *Toten*, 213–15; Luedemann, *Paul*, 218; and Holtz, *1 Thessalonicher*, 193. But Sieber's and Luedemann's argument that Paul placed διὰ τοῦ Ἰησοῦ forward since he already has a modifier (σὺν αὐτῷ) of ἄξει does not resolve the redundancy of διὰ τοῦ Ἰησοῦ and σὺν αὐτῷ if they both refer to ἄξει.

[43] Merklein, "Theologe als Prophet," 405; Laub, *Eschatologische Verkündigung*.

[44] Merklein ("Theologe als Prophet," 407–8) suggests that the grief of the Thessalonians was not caused by their ignorance of the resurrection but by their inability to integrate the parousia and the resurrection. According to Luedemann (*Paul*, 219), however, "Paul did not preach the resurrection of the dead (relating to Christians) during his first proclamation." Merklein's view is to be preferred, although it is not without some difficulties. My view, that the real problem in Thessalonica touched the taking up, does not exclude some prior preaching of the resurrection.

[45] Schnackenburg, *Baptism*, 157–58. Schnackenburg shows that this Pauline principle is applied to sacramental participation, to ethics, and to eschatology. Cf. Tannehill, *Dying and Rising*, 132. For a different interpretation, see Luedemann, *Paul*, 219.

than to 1 Thess 4:14. In 2 Cor 4:14 Paul mentions the resurrection in both clauses: "We know that the one who raised the Lord Jesus will also raise us with Jesus."

The shift from "Jesus rose" to the implied "God raised him" reflects Paul's usual formulation. For the apostle, it is God who raised Jesus from the dead (Rom 4:25; 6:4; 8:11; 10:9; 1 Cor 6:14; 2 Cor 1:9; 4:14; Gal 1:1; 1 Thess 1:10). It may be that the first clause in 1 Thess 4:14 is a fragment of an early credal statement.[46] But, for the apostle, the ground of the hope that is directed toward the ultimate salvation is God, more precisely God's salvific action in Jesus. Paul regards the resurrection of Jesus as an act of God that promises life to all human beings (1 Cor 15:20–22). The condition for obtaining life is faith, belonging to Christ.

"With him" (σὺν αὐτῷ), i. e., with Jesus, implies that the deceased faithful will be brought by God, in the company of Jesus, to wherever God is taking them. The formulation does not explicitly mention the destination. Hoffmann suggests that σὺν αὐτῷ here indicates togetherness with Jesus, or in Jesus' company.[47] According to him, the verb ἄξει in the clause ἄξει σὺν αὐτῷ cannot be further determined, for vv. 16–17 do not give us any hints in this regard. Hence, the ultimate destination cannot be inferred here.

The entire clause, "bring with him" (ἄξει σὺν αὐτῷ), is part of the shift from the resurrection to the parousia. It indicates that the grief of the Thessalonians concerns the participation of the deceased faithful in the Lord's coming. Moreover, the argumentation in v. 14 is elliptic. We observed above that it leaps over the resurrection of the deceased faithful. Could it be that the ultimate destiny is also part of an ellipsis here? The difficulty with this is that in vv. 16–17 the ultimate destiny is not so clearly indicated as the resurrection. In v. 17 the apostle concludes, "And so we will be with the Lord forever." This may still be part of an ellipsis, as Paul tries to respond to the grief in the community. The community is disconsolate at the thought that the deceased faithful will not be with the Lord.

---

[46] The presence of this set phrase here (cf. 1 Cor 15:3–5) may have induced the shifts in the result clause, where the apostle slips into his own way of formulating and makes the inference fit the specific problem in Thessalonica. According to Holtz (1 Thessalonicher, 190), however, 1 Thess 4:14 contains not a credal fragment but Paul's own formulation.

[47] Hoffmann, Toten, 216. According to Hoffmann, σὺν αὐτῷ here does not mean "at the same time as" but, rather, "together with," or "in the company of."

Fortunately, a parallel statement in 2 Cor 4:14 supplies the missing links. It provides the conclusion missing in 1 Thess 4:14. Curiously, the parallelism between 1 Thess 4:14 and 2 Cor 4:14 has not been explored in exegesis. We quote this text to fill out the thought in 1 Thess 4:14. In 2 Cor 4:13–14 Paul states, "But just as we have the spirit of faith that is in accordance with the scriptures . . . we also believe, and so we speak, because we know that the one who raised the Lord Jesus will raise us also with Jesus, and will bring us with you into his presence." Paul here asserts his own resurrection (God will raise him) and the destination (God will bring him with Jesus into his presence [σὺν Ἰησοῦ ἐγερεῖ καὶ παραστήσει σὺν ὑμῖν]). He will not be worse off than the Corinthians for experiencing death. He will be raised and then brought, together with the living Corinthians, into the presence of God! Here the ultimate goal is clearly stated to be the presence of God. Second Corinthians 4:14 thus provides an excellent parallel to 1 Thess 4:14 and supplies the missing links, the resurrection and the destination. This makes it possible to complete Paul's thought in 1 Thess 4:14b: God will *raise the dead* and bring them in Jesus' company *into his presence.* This is also congruent with the apostle's pictorial presentation of the parousia in 1 Thess 4:16–17. It suggests what E. von Dobschütz,[48] Frame,[49] Rigaux,[50] and previous interpreters have maintained: the bringing of the faithful with Jesus into God's glory. This is intimated by the taking up of the faithful in v. 17, which resembles the assumption depictions in the OT and in pagan antiquity. In the assumptions, a living person is taken up into the life beyond. That person leaves behind the present existence on earth to live a new and higher life forever in the beyond.

The parousia, then, involves God's sending the risen Jesus from heaven in order that he may bring into heaven the deceased faithful. The governing image here, as we have argued earlier,[51] is

---

[48] von Dobschütz, *Thessalonicher-Briefe,* 191–92. According to von Dobschütz, the parousia of Jesus is here presented as a bringing *(Abholung)* of the faithful: Jesus comes to bring the faithful with him into God's presence.

[49] Frame, *Thessalonians,* 170–71. According to Frame, " Ἄγειν refers to the final act when Jesus the victor over enemies . . . accompanied by his saints, leads the way heavenward to hand over the kingdom to God the Father."

[50] Rigaux, *Thessaloniciens,* 537. According to Rigaux, in 2 Thess 2:8 and 1 Cor 15:24–28 Paul states not that God will bring back the deceased from heaven but that God will bring them to heaven with him. The focus is on reunion with Christ.

[51] See ch. 2, sec. d.

not the *Einholung*[52] of Christ, the going out by the faithful to bring Christ into their earthly city, but rather the *Einholung* of the faithful by Christ. It is Christ who comes to bring the faithful home. The action is God's action through Jesus. The context in vv. 13–18 and the parallel in 2 Cor 4:14 suggest that the ultimate goal of Christ's parousia is to bring the faithful into God's presence.

This goal implies the resurrection, at least in the sense depicted in v. 16. It was not possible to imagine anything else, for the dead (corpses) are not taken into heaven. Yet Paul does not state, as he should in strict parallelism, that as Jesus had been raised from the dead, so also the deceased faithful will be raised from the dead. The point at issue in v. 14 is not the resurrection of the dead but the participation of the dead in the Lord's parousia.[53] It is the inclusion of the deceased in this end-time act of God through Christ that is affirmed here. But what this implies, and how it will take place, is then brought out in vv. 17–18.

The gathering of the deceased from their graves has always been depicted in Jewish apocalyptic as God's act, although angels could be involved in it. In the texts dealing with the messianic figure (the Elect One or the Son of man) as the judge in the end time, the deceased are brought to life and come from east and west, from north and south, from the depths of the sea, and from the graves in the desert (*1 Enoch* 61:5). This gathering takes place on earth.

Texts dealing with the messianic reign are ambiguous about the resurrection of the dead.[54] According to Rev 20:4–6, the faithful witnesses, those who have been beheaded for their testimony to Jesus, are brought back to life and share in the thousand-year messianic reign before the end time. The deceased faithful are given a privileged but temporary status.

But the picture in *2 Bar.* 29–30 is unclear: those participating in the messianic reign are the surviving righteous, although it is possible that Baruch also envisions the resurrection of the righteous,

---

[52] This is the image used by Peterson ("Einholung," 682–702). Holtz (*1 Thessalonicher*, 199) still employs this image, while Sieber (*Mit Christus Leben*, 31) regards it as "untenable."

[53] Luedemann, *Paul*, 219; Merklein, "Theologe als Prophet," 405–6. But while Luedemann concludes that Paul did not preach before this the resurrection of the dead, Merklein concludes that he did.

[54] They are usually dated to after the destruction of the second temple.

of those who have died hoping in the Messiah.[55] And according to
the depiction in 4 Ezra 7:26–30, the survivors enjoy the messianic
reign for four hundred years. At the end of this reign, everyone,
including the Messiah, dies. A primeval silence descends on the
entire earth and lasts for seven days. After this the dead are raised
(vv. 30–35[44]).

None of these depictions agrees with 1 Cor 15:24–27, where the
apostle asserts that Christ must reign until he has put all his
enemies under his feet. Here the presupposition is that Christ began
to reign at his exaltation (Phil 2:11). The completion of this reign
entails the annihilation of death and, hence, the resurrection of
the dead (cf. 1 Cor 15:54–55).

Paul's understanding of the end-time events thus contains no
hint of a messianic interregnum, and he is here not responding
to such an idea in the Thessalonian community. That this community is affected by such ideas is thus an unverifiable hypothesis. First Thessalonians 4:14, 17 and 2 Cor 4:14 indicate that the
faithful will be united with Christ and that Christ will bring them
into God's presence.[56]

3. The Theological Foundation of Hope

It was noted above that 1 Thess 4:14 contains a typically
Pauline argumentation from Christ's death and resurrection. The
inference εἰ . . . οὕτως καί, ei . . houtōs kai, asserts a fundamental
parallelism between what happened to Christ and what is to
happen to the Christian. The rule "What happens to Christ happens also to the Christian" expresses solidarity with Christ.

When this principle is invoked for the future fulfillment, it
serves as the foundation of hope. In this context, Christ's resurrection serves as the guarantee of the future resurrection.[57] The
inference expresses the apostle's conviction that the believer
presently lives in the wake of the Christ-event and is profoundly
affected by it. Not only is the believer's life patterned after
Christ's; it also shares in Christ's death and resurrection. In this

---

[55] So also Wilcke, Zwischenreich, 42–43.

[56] In 2 Cor 4:14 we are told that Paul himself will be raised from the dead and
brought into God's presence.

[57] Schnackenburg (Baptism, 157) points out this basic feature in Pauline theology. Cf. also Tannehill, Dying and Rising, 7, 75, 130.

understanding, the Christ-event in the past is not an isolated happening or a random event but an event involving and affecting others. It imbues others with life (1 Thess 5:9–10). In particular, Christ's resurrection works the resurrection of others (1 Cor 15:20–22).

This theological inference is evident in 1 Thess 4:14 despite the multiple shifts and leaps of thought. The inference here from Christ's resurrection to Christ's parousia is based on the knowledge of God's saving intent in Christ. It is a knowledge mediated by faith, as is clearly stated also in 2 Cor 4:13–14. This knowledge concerns not only the parallelism between Christ and the faithful but also the work of Christ in the completion of salvation. It concerns God's future action through the risen Lord. And it concerns God's will that those who belong to Christ be with Christ.

That the sharing in the ultimate completion through and with Christ is indeed God's will for the faithful is restated in 1 Thess 5:9–10, where Paul declares, "For God has not destined us for wrath but to obtain salvation through our Lord Jesus Christ, who died for us so that whether we wake or sleep we might live with him." The guarantee here is in God, more precisely in God's deed for them in Jesus and in God's placing them in Christ. The latter is but an additional guarantee of the ultimate fulfillment. As Jesus was by the will of God raised from the dead, so also the faithful who are in Christ will, at the coming of Christ, be raised from the dead and brought with him into God's presence (cf. 2 Cor 4:14).

Paul here takes the present sharing in the Christ-event for granted. The deceased for whom the Thessalonians grieve are believers in good standing: they are "the dead in Christ" (1 Thess 4:16). According to the apostle, those who have been united with Jesus in life and death will be united with Jesus also in the promised fulfillment (cf. 4:1, 10; 5:4–5).

The presence at the parousia of Christ is thus implied by Christ's resurrection. This link is evident also in 1:10, which states that the faithful are awaiting from heaven God's Son, whom God has raised from the dead. The parousia is the completion of the lordship with which the Father endowed Jesus by raising him from the dead (1 Thess 1:10; Rom 1:3–4; Phil 2:11). Those who have shared in the Easter event will also share in its completion.

C. THE SECOND RESPONSE

The basic reassurance has been given: at the ultimate completion, God will bring the deceased faithful with Jesus into his
presence. But how, precisely, will the deceased faithful share in this
redeeming event? So far Paul has argued from an understanding in
faith of the Easter reality. Now he appeals to the authority of the
Lord (v. 15) and unfolds the scenario of the parousia, in which the
deceased are taken up together with the living into the ultimate
reality (vv. 16–17).

1. Declaration on the Word of the Lord, 1 Thessalonians 4:15

First Thessalonians 4:15 contains another general assurance:
"We who are alive, who are left until the coming of the Lord, will
by no means precede those who have died." This is not drawn from
faith but is based on a word of the Lord: "For this we declare to you
on the word of the Lord." This is a rare instance of Paul's
appealing to a saying of the Lord.

The phrase ἐν λόγῳ κυρίου, en logō kyriou ("on the word of the
Lord"), occurs only here in the NT. Does it introduce a logion of
Jesus spoken before Easter? Does it refer to a disclosure of the
exalted Lord? Does it contain a quotation?[58] The preposition ἐν,
translated here as "on," seems to imply a summary paraphrase
rather than a quotation. And λέγομεν, legomen, suggests that Paul
himself is formulating the statement. It is, however, clear that Paul
regards this as reflecting the mind of Jesus. Yet there is no
documented evidence of such a logion from Jesus before Easter.
And it is scarcely likely that the apostle, who in his letters only
seldom quotes a logion of Jesus, would put this logion on the lips of
Jesus. Nor is it likely that he quotes a community saying that was
put on the lips of Jesus by others. At any rate, there is no hint that
Paul recognizes this as a community tradition. And as B. Henneken
remarks, to regard the expression ἐν λόγῳ κυρίου as a stylistic
characteristic of apocalyptic utterings is unwarranted, since there
are no parallels to this in any of the eschatological passages in

---

[58] Merklein ("Theologe als Prophet," 410) regards v. 15b as Paul's quotation of
a logion of Jesus. But this scarcely agrees with the basic statement in v. 16 that at
Christ's coming, first the deceased faithful will be raised up.

Pauline writings.[59] Only an examination of the ways Paul introduces quotations of Jesus and the post-Easter tradition can determine the meaning of ἐν λόγῳ κυρίου here.

One clear instance of Paul's quoting the words of the earthly
Jesus is the eucharistic text 1 Cor 11:23–26, to which there are
parallels elsewhere in the NT (Matt 26:26–29; Mark 14:22–25; Luke
22:14–20). Here the apostle indicates that he is quoting a tradition
(παρέλαβον . . . παρέδωκα, parelabon . . . paredōka), that the tradition goes back to the Lord (ἀπὸ τοῦ κυρίου, apo tou kyriou),[60] and
that it conveys the words of the Lord spoken the night when he
was betrayed (ἐν τῇ νυκτὶ ᾗ παρεδίδετο, en tē nykti hē paredideto).
The actual words are introduced with εἶπεν, eipen (v. 24) or λέγων,
legōn (v. 25), which serve as quotation marks. But the wording in
1 Thess 4:15 has none of these characteristics: it does not refer to a
tradition (παρέλαβον . . . παρέδωκα); it does not indicate that such
a tradition goes back to the Lord (παρέλαβον ἀπὸ τοῦ κυρίου); it
does not give the context in which the logion was spoken by the
Lord; and it does not have εἶπεν or λέγων to mark the actual logion.

In 1 Cor 9:14 Paul alludes to a command of the Lord, saying,
"In the same way, the Lord commanded (διέταξεν, dietaxen) that
those who proclaim the gospel should get their living by the
gospel." The word διέταξεν is not followed by εἶπεν or λέγων, and
the context in which the command was given is not mentioned. It
is followed, rather, with an indirect object (τοῖς τὸ εὐαγγέλιον
καταγγέλλουσιν, tois to euangelion katangellousin) and the content of
the command (ἐκ τοῦ εὐαγγελίου ζῆν, ek tou euangeliou zēn). The
apostle is not quoting a logion of the Lord; rather, he is appealing to
a command of the earthly Jesus, which he is paraphrasing. Such a
command is documented elsewhere (Luke 10:7; Gal 6:6; 1 Tim 5:18).

An appeal to the Lord is made in 1 Cor 14:37, where Paul states,
"Anyone who claims to be a prophet, or to have spiritual powers,
must acknowledge that what I am writing to you is a command of
the Lord." But the text does not contain a quotation and does not
appeal to the earthly Jesus. It refers, rather, to the risen Lord, who
speaks to the community through his prophets. Those who are

---

[59] Henneken, Verkündigung, 82, 92–95.
[60] On the tradition involved in the eucharistic text, see J. Jeremias, Eucharistic
Words, 138–203. That Paul did not directly receive this from the Lord is held by most
scholars; see Fee, 1 Corinthians, 548. The text of 1 Cor 11:23–26 describes the context
of the eucharist and the pronouncements of Jesus over the bread and wine.

prophets and possess spiritual powers from the Lord should be able to confirm that Paul, as well, is here speaking the mind of the Lord. This recognition is mediated by the spirit of prophecy.

Another appeal to the Lord occurs in 1 Cor 7:10, 12, where Paul, giving practical guidelines to the married and to the single, clearly distinguishes between his own counsel and the command of the Lord (v. 25). When he lays down his own rules and gives his advice, he speaks "as one who by the Lord's mercy is trustworthy" (v. 25) and has "the Spirit of God" (v. 40). Thus in vv. 8–9, where he gives his own counsel to the unmarried, he asserts, "I say" (λέγω δέ, *lego de*). But in v. 10, where he lays down the law for the married, he says, "To the married I give this command (παραγγέλλω, *parangellō*)—not I but the Lord (οὐκ ἐγὼ ἀλλὰ ὁ κύριος, *ouk egō alla ho kyrios*)—that the wife should not separate from her husband." This rule is explicitly identified by Paul as a command (ἐπιταγή, *epitagē*) of the Lord (cf. v. 25). It is a command of the historical Jesus,[61] and its content is documented elsewhere in the NT (Matt 5:31–32; 19:9; Mark 10:11–12; Luke 16:18). The command is not a direct quotation—it is not introduced by εἶπεν or λέγων. It is, rather, Paul's summary of the content of the command, as in 9:14. But the distinction in 7:12 between Paul's own counsel and the Lord's command is the reverse of that in v. 10. In v. 12 the apostle says, "To the rest I say—I and not the Lord (λέγω ἐγώ, οὐχ ὁ κύριος, *lego egō, ouch ho kyrios*)."

First Corinthians 7:10 and 9:14 thus disclose that the apostle can regard a statement that he makes as the words of the Lord without reproducing the exact quotation. When he does quote a logion of Jesus, he employs εἶπεν or λέγων, as in 1 Cor 11:23. When he quotes a post-Easter tradition, he indicates such a tradition with παρέλαβον . . . παρέδωκα, as in 1 Cor 15:3. And when such a tradition goes back to Jesus, Paul says, παρέλαβον ἀπὸ τοῦ κυρίου ὃ καὶ παρέδωκα, *parelabon apo tou kyriou ho kai paredōka*, as in 1 Cor 11:23.

This suggests that in 1 Thess 4:15 as well, Paul is not quoting directly the words of Jesus. The words εἶπεν or λέγων do not occur here. Nor is he quoting a post-Easter tradition, since παρέλαβον . . . παρέδωκα does not occur. He is, however, relying on the exalted

---

[61] Conzelmann (*1 Corinthians*, 120) suggests that this command also comes from the exalted Lord.

Lord for the assertion involved. In all other cases Paul deals with the arrangement in the community, but in 1 Thess 4:15 he assures the community about the final completion. The question here deals with post-Easter anxieties, rather than with a problem that Jesus faced before Easter. Thus, the best possibility for the origin of this saying is a special revelation of the Lord to Paul (cf. 1 Cor 2:9–10; 2 Cor 12:1–10).

That 4:15 is not a direct quotation from the Lord is also indicated by the formulation.[62] The word περιλειπόμενοι, *perileipomenoi*, occurs in the NT only here and in v. 16;[63] in v. 15 it probably anticipates v. 16. It does not mean, as in the OT, a remnant left after a process of selection. Nor does it mean, as in apocalyptic, the remnant that escapes the trials of the end time. Here it refers to the present believers who fully expect to live to see the Lord's coming.[64] The phrase "those who are left" is specified by "until the coming of the Lord." The implication is that most will live that long. The rest of the vocabulary in v. 15 is Pauline.[65] Most scholars today have abandoned the notion that v. 15 contains a logion of the historical Jesus.[66]

The words "we, who are alive, who are left until the coming of the Lord" imply that Paul himself expects to be alive at the Lord's coming. He also expects that the faithful in Thessalonica to be alive at that time. His own anticipation of this is amply documented in 1 Cor 7:26, 29.

---

[62] That 1 Thess 4:15 is neither a direct quotation from the Lord nor a received tradition is held by Hartman (*Prophecy Interpreted*, 188), Nepper-Christensen ("Herrenwort," 140–45), J. Jeremias (*Unknown Sayings*, 81), and Luz (*Geschichtsverständnis*, 328–29). Luedemann (*Paul*, 221–38) suggests a Jewish apocalyptic tradition behind 1 Thess 4:16–17.

[63] This may be another indication that 1 Thess 4:16–17 was not part of a prevalent apocalyptic tradition.

[64] Holtz, *1 Thessalonicher*, 195.

[65] The word παρουσία occurs in 1 Thess 2:19, 3:13, 4:15, 5:23 and 1 Cor 15:23; cf. 2 Thess 2:1, 8, 9. In the Gospels, the word is employed only by Matthew (24:3, 27, 37). It seems to be Paul's favorite word in 1 Thess, where it is consistently employed for the Lord's coming. The verb φθάνω, *phthanō*, occurs 5 times in Paul, twice in 1 Thess. In the rest of the NT it occurs only twice. Forms of the participle κοιμηθείς, *koimētheis*, occur in 1 Thess 4:14 and in 1 Cor 15:18, while other forms of the verb κοιμάομαι, *koimaomai*, occur in 1 Thess 4:13 and 1 Cor 7:39, 11:30, 15:20, 51. The rest of the vocabulary in 1 Thess 4:15 (οἱ ζῶντες, *hoi zōntes*, κύριος) is common usage in Paul; cf. Luedemann, *Paul*, 22.

[66] That 1 Thess 4:15 contains a logion of Jesus, or, rather, a community's construction, is maintained by Holtz (*1 Thessalonicher*, 196–99).

2. The Scenery of the Parousia, 1 Thessalonians 4:16–17

The assertion in 1 Thess 4:15 is followed in vv. 16–17 by a pictorial presentation.[67] This structure occurs also in 1 Cor 15:51–52: in v. 51 the apostle first gives his disclosure (μυστήριον, *mystērion*), saying, "We will not all die, but we will all be changed," then in v. 52 he depicts the end-time event at which the dead are raised imperishable and the living are all changed.[68] Both texts contain an authoritative disclosure about an eschatological reality. Both texts deal with the parousia and the resurrection. And both times the apostle speaks as the interpreter of the ultimate reality in a matter of great importance for the faithful.[69] There are also, however, significant differences between the two texts. And structural similarity here does not settle the problem of tradition.

Unlike 1 Cor 15:51–52, 1 Thess 4:16–17 provides a scenic and sequential presentation of the Lord's coming, in which time and place play an important role. It begins with ὅτι ("that"), which resumes the ὅτι in v. 15. The imagery in vv. 16–17 depicts how the deceased faithful will, after all, participate in the taking up at the Lord's coming. This is done by the three pointers, "first" (πρῶτον, *prōton*), "then" (ἔπειτα, *epeita*), and "together with" (ἅμα σύν, *hama syn*). The sequence of these events is crucial. The first act at the Lord's coming from heaven[70] is that the deceased faithful are brought back to life; then only, once they have been reunited with the living, is everyone taken up by the clouds to meet the Lord. These pointers, clearly inserted by Paul himself, insist on this sequence of acts. The surviving faithful have no advantage over the deceased: the latter are brought to life, join the living, and are, together with the living, taken up by the clouds.

---

[67] So also Löhr, "Herrenwort," 269, and Nepper-Christensen, "Herrenwort," 149.

[68] Luedemann, *Paul*, 225. Löhr ("Herrenwort," 270–73) posits a common logion behind 1 Thess 4:15–17 and 1 Cor 15:51–52, but the reconstruction is improbable.

[69] For the latest attempt to argue from the similarity of structure, see Merklein, "Theologe als Prophet," 413–19.

[70] The Lord's coming down from heaven is a stereotyped presentation in the NT. The Synoptic Gospels mention that the Son of man will come on the clouds of heaven (Mark 13:26 par Matt 24:30, Luke 21:27; Mark 14:62 par Matt 26:64); cf. also Rev 1:7; 14:14. But the Pauline presentation in 1 Thess 4:16–17 does not mention the clouds. Is it because it mentions the clouds in connection with the taking up?

This presentation thus discloses how it will be possible for the deceased to share in union with the Lord. Paul here affirms that they can be taken up by the clouds—for they will be brought to life. Once they are alive, they can be taken up. And since they will be brought to life before the taking up, they can join the living for the taking up. As a result, the bringing of the deceased to life is here portrayed as a return to this life. This is another difference between 1 Thess 4:16–17 and 1 Cor 15:50–52.

As noted earlier, Lohfink, after examining the assumption accounts in the OT and in pagan antiquity, observes that to be assumed body and soul into heaven, one has to be alive. The dead are not assumed. Assumption is transportation of a *living* person from the present mode of life on earth to life in the beyond.[71] If the Thessalonians were told by Paul earlier, as they most likely were, that they would be taken up at the Lord's coming, then the death of some of the members of the community would have caused them grief and concern. They would infer from Paul's earlier depiction that the deceased could not be taken up, that they could not participate with the living in the union with the Lord. Death has robbed them of this.

The difference between Paul's answer in this instance and that in 1 Cor 15:50–56 is shaped by the unique nature of the problems facing Paul each time. The resurrection in 1 Thess 4:16 is a return to this life, whereas in 1 Cor 15:50–56 Paul insists that the resurrection does not mean a return to this life. Equally pronounced is the difference between this description and that in the synoptic accounts. In the Gospels it is the Lord who comes on the clouds, but in 1 Thess 4:16–17 it is the faithful who are taken up by the clouds. The Lord's coming on the clouds is not mentioned here! In the Gospels the angels gather the faithful, but in 1 Thess 4:16–18 the faithful are gathered by the clouds. The apostle's depiction of the parousia elucidates what he said to the Thessalonians earlier. It was this portrayal that had caused trouble to start with. By making the scenery more explicit—inserting into it the resurrection of the deceased faithful and a sequential order—he shows how the deceased faithful will, after all, be able to share in the Lord's coming and be with the Lord.

---

[71] Lohfink, *Himmelfahrt*, 37–71. See Plevnik, "The Taking Up," 274–83.

3. The Imagery

The investigation, carried out in ch. 2, of the various motifs Paul employs in his portrayal of the Lord's coming has shed considerable light on the meaning and function of this imagery in 1 Thess 4:16–17. It is now possible to answer at least some of the questions that have been repeatedly asked: Who gives the command? What is the command all about? To whom is it given? How does it relate to the archangel's call and to the trumpet of God?[72]

It was observed that the three prepositional phrases in v. 16, each beginning with the preposition ἐν, relate to the descent of the Lord from heaven. The formulation is terse; each clause contains an image devoid of all detail. The scenery presumes an earlier, more extensive depiction.

(a) We discovered that the cry-of-command (κέλευσμα, *keleusma*) motif corresponds to the גְּעָר, *gāʿar*, the command-rebuke motif that occurs in theophanies and in the tradition of the day of the Lord. This motif emphasizes the compelling power of the command. Earlier we noted that in such contexts it is always God who gives the command. Through this command God is enforcing his authority over the disobedient and opposing elements of nature, people, or spirits. This suggests that in 1 Thess 4:16 as well, the command comes from God or from Jesus invested with such power. That the coming Lord is so invested Paul states in 1 Cor 15:25, 27 and Phil 3:21. It also suggests that the Lord is coming to exercise this power of subjugation to enforce God's reign. Hence, the Lord is not the object of the command. For the same reason, the archangel is not the object of that command. Since the text here is so terse and truncated, no further information is given on the specific object of this command. It is unlikely, lacking further information, that the command deals directly with the resurrection of the dead.[73] The

---

[72] NT apocalyptic likes to speak in images and voices (sounds)—the two are linked. Thus in Rev we hear voices of the elders in heaven (5:8–10; 11:16), voices of angels (5:11–12), the voice of a mighty angel (7:2; 10:3–4; 14:6–7, 8, 9, 15, 18), a voice from heaven (10:4; 14:13), voices of the four living beings (5:8, 14; 6:2, 3, 5, 7), the voice from the temple (16:1, 17), the trumpets sounded by the seven angels (8:7, 8, 10, 12; 9:1, 13; 11:15), the acclamations by the heavenly beings (4:8), etc.

[73] This opinion was already expressed by Teichmann (*Vorstellungen*, 22–23). Tillmann (*Wiederkunft*, 152) suggests that the command is given by God to Christ and is the starting point of the parousia. Similarly, Neil (*Thessalonians*, 101) and Dibelius (*Thessalonicher I/II, Philipper*, 26). But according to Milligan (*Thessalonians*, 60), the command is given by the archangel or by the Lord.

subjugation of the oppressor, however, means liberation of the oppressed. In 1 Cor 15:25, 27 the power of the expected Lord is brought to bear against the power of death and creates the possibility of life that is finally free from corruption and dying. In Phil 3:21 the power of the Lord brings about the transformation of the present existence into the exalted existence of the risen Lord. The basic notion underlying this motif is the power and authority of the coming Lord to remove what does not conform to the kingdom of God.

(b) The archangel's voice, mentioned in 1 Thess 4:16, is related to the cry of command. Our investigation in ch. 2 has shown that angelic accompaniment is another stereotyped motif in theophanies and in the tradition of the day of the Lord. It expresses the overwhelming power and glory of Yahweh and thus is related to the κέλευσμα motif. But only in the NT do we find the angelic retinue as part of the depiction of the exalted Lord's coming in the end time. It is found in the synoptic accounts of the Lord's coming (Matt 24:31; 25:31; Mark 8:38; 13:27; Luke 9:26) and in 2 Thess 1:7–10. This motif also implies that the Lord will remove all opposing forces in the cosmos. It depicts the unheard-of power and authority of the exalted Lord and fits well with the κέλευσμα motif.

In 1 Thess 4:16, however, Paul mentions a single angelic figure, an archangel. This suggests that the apostle may have in mind apocalyptic depictions. Archangels are mentioned in 1 Enoch and in the Book of Revelation, usually in connection with the final judgment, where they carry out specific orders. Revelation also frequently mentions single angelic figures giving commands (Rev 6:1, 3, 5, 7; 8:7, 8, 10, 12; 9:1, 13; 11:15) or executing commands, either of the Almighty or of the Lamb. The command is either a call, like "Come!" (6:1, 3, 5, 7), or a trumpet sound (8:7, 8, 10, 12; 9:1, 13; 11:15).

First Thessalonians 4:16 simply states that the Lord comes at or with the call of an archangel. What the call signals we are not told, for the imagery here offers a bare minimum of information. It is not possible to state that the call is a summons to the angels and the saints to participate in the Lord's coming.[74] In contrast to the κέλευσμα motif, the source of this voice is identified as an

---

[74]Tillmann (Wiederkunft, 154) suggests that the archangel's voice is a call to the angels and the saints summoning them to participate in this event.

archangel, but further identification is not possible, although some suggest the archangel Michael.[75]

The general apocalyptic background suggests that the call of the mighty archangel has a function similar to that of the κέλευσμα. Here it joins the cry of command and enhances its power aspect.[76] Like the cry of command, the angelic power is (usually) directed toward evil forces. It is not possible to be more specific.[77]

Perhaps the closest text to 1 Thess 4:16–17 is 2 Thess 1:7–10. According to this text, "the Lord Jesus is revealed from heaven with his mighty angels (μετ' ἀγγέλων δυνάμεως αὐτοῦ, met' angelōn dynameōs autou) in flaming fire, inflicting vengeance." Here as well, the exalted Lord is accompanied by angels, the power (δυνάμεως) of the angels is noted, and the angels appear to execute the command of the exalted Lord. If this epistle was in fact written by Paul, as many scholars still maintain, then the significance of this passage for interpreting 1 Thess 4:13–18 increases. It would be the only other Pauline passage that describes in some detail the Lord's coming and that also mentions angels as the exalted Lord's retinue. And this passage clearly depicts the parousia as bringing both punishment and salvation. The text is congruent with 1 Thess 4:16–17.

But there are also considerable differences between the two presentations. Second Thessalonians 1:7–10 mentions angels, not an archangel. It emphasizes the punishment of nonbelievers and of those who have rejected the gospel, while this feature is not explicitly stated in 1 Thess 4:16–18. It states that the angels come "in flaming fire," while 1 Thess 4:16 mentions only the arch-

---

[75] Neil (*Thessalonians*, 101) and Staab (*Thessalonicherbriefe*, 37) identify the archangel as Michael. For Rigaux (*Thessaloniciens*, 543), however, the absence of the article makes this identification hazardous. Rigaux has doubts that the Thessalonians were familiar with Jewish angelology.

[76] According to Frame (*Thessalonians*, 174) and Kabisch (*Eschatologie*, 239), the trumpet sound is not God's voice but the voice of an archangel, who is the messenger or the voice or the trumpet of God.

[77] Milligan (*Thessalonians*, 60) suggests that the voice of an archangel is a more specific explanation of the preceding κέλευσμα. Like Rigaux, he doubts that any specific archangel is thought of here. According to Milligan, φωνὴ ἀρχαγγέλλου should be translated as possessive: "a voice such as an archangel uses." Moore (*Thessalonians*, 71) agrees with Rigaux and Milligan but points out that in Rev 1:10 and 4:1 a voice like the sound of a trumpet is mentioned. According to Morris (*Thessalonians*, 142–43), "Some archangel will add his voice to the call that wakes up the dead."

angel's call. And it contains visual imagery, while 1 Thess 4:16 has sound imagery.

(c) The third motif, the trumpet of God,[78] resembles the call of the archangel in that it gives the source of the trumpet sound. It associates the trumpet call with God, as the voice is associated with the archangel. Although OT imagery in the tradition dealing with the day of the Lord supports the image of God blowing the trumpet (Zech 9:14; 10:8), the Dead Sea Scrolls indicate that others blow the trumpets that give a signal from God. In the war in the end time, it is the priests who blow the trumpets that convey a command of God. Thus, those who are called to action by a particular trumpet are said to be "the called of God" (1QM 3:2), or "the princes of God" (v. 2), or "the formation of the divisions of God for vengeance of His wrath on the sons of darkness" (v. 8), etc. In the Book of Revelation it is the chosen angels who blow the trumpets. Here the seventh trumpet sound signals the coming of the rule of God and of the Lamb. With this signal God assumes his supreme power and begins to reign (Rev 11:15). It is the time for God's wrath and for God's reward of the faithful.

In 1 Cor 15:50–52 the trumpet—the last trumpet—signals God's reign and the events associated with its inauguration. But that reign is associated with the subjugation of powers hostile to God (vv. 25–27, 54–55). The trumpet in 1 Thess 4:16 is similarly associated with the exalted Lord's coming to assume his rule.

Like the κέλευσμα and the archangel's call, the trumpet of God is an auditory motif. It likewise may evoke associated imagery, recalling to the Thessalonians the depictions that Paul must have given them earlier. It also expresses the circumstances and the purpose of the Lord's coming, as the preposition ἐν suggests.[79] In 1 Thess 4:16 the trumpet-of-God motif appears to reinforce the two preceding motifs. In literature the piling up of synonymous imagery has the effect of strengthening the statement. The repetition does not so much add extra information as emphasize the existing assertion. Here it portrays in visual and sound imagery the glory and irresistible power of the exalted Lord as he comes for judgment and salvation. There

---

[78] See ch. 2.

[79] It is tempting to relate these eschatological sound images to the awakening of the dead (1 Thess 4:16).

is an overtone of judgment in this imagery, as the apocalyptic background suggests.

(d) The cloud motif in 1 Thess 4:17, as was noted in ch. 2, does not belong to the description of the Lord's coming down from heaven but, rather, to the scene of the taking up of the faithful in response to his coming. In this respect, Paul's description diverges significantly from the synoptic depictions of the parousia (Matt 24:30; 26:64; Mark 13:26; 14:62; Luke 21:27), from Revelation (Rev 1:7; 14:14, 16), and from Dan 7:13–14. This puts in question the apostle's reliance on Dan 7[80] or on the synoptic accounts.[81]

In the context of the taking up, the cloud functions as a vehicle of transportation between earth and heaven, while in the synoptic accounts it functions as a vehicle of transportation between heaven and earth. It is associated with the somatic reality and should be distinguished from the cloud that shrouds the presence of God. Thus the cloud is mentioned in connection with the coming of the Son of man, or, less frequently, with the coming of angels (Rev 10:1), or with the taking up of Jesus or other living human beings. The Son of man as a living human being comes down from heaven on a cloud, and the risen Jesus ascends into heaven on a cloud (Acts 1:9). The two witnesses in Rev 11:12 are first brought to life and then taken up by a cloud into heaven. The living faithful in 1 Thess 4:17 are similarly taken on a cloud into heaven. The cloud is never employed for a journey to a place midway between heaven and earth, and still less for a return journey from such a place.

In this function, the cloud is not an ordinary cloud. It is a cloud of heaven. In the taking up the cloud does not merely transport a person in the present earthly condition into heaven, for this would mean importing mortality and corruptibility into heaven. The cloud functions, rather, as a visible means of exaltation from one mode of existence to another, implying a change of existence. Yet the cloud indicates that the whole human being is taken up into heaven; the souls of the dead are not taken up by a cloud into heaven or any other place.

---

[80] The reliance of Paul in 1 Thess 4:14–17 on Dan 7:13 is maintained by Hartman (*Prophecy Interpreted*, 189–90).

[81] Does Paul here suppress the cloud image so as not to clash with the imagery associated with the taking up?

4. The Provenance of the Parousia Imagery

Deissmann,[82] Peterson,[83] Cerfaux,[84] Holtz,[85] and others hold that Paul's portrayal of the parousia in 1 Thess 4:13–18 draws on the depictions of the Hellenistic imperial παρουσία.[86] The imposing spectacle of an imperial παρουσία, familiar to Paul and his audience, provides Paul with this imagery. According to this model, Paul is here depicting the bringing (die Einholung) of the Lord: as the citizens go out of the city to meet the coming dignitary and accompany him into their city, so also the faithful go out (or up) to meet the coming Lord in order to accompany him to their earthly abode. The apostle thus adapts this scenery in order to portray the coming of Christ in the end time.

But our investigation has confirmed the conclusions of Dupont,[87] according to whom the source of imagery for Paul is OT and Jewish apocalyptic rather than the Hellenistic imperial παρουσία. The key word in Peterson's analysis of the Hellenistic παρουσία and of 1 Thess 4:13–18, ἀπάντησις, is well known in the LXX and has good Hebrew equivalents,[88] and thus cannot sustain Peterson's argument that it is a technical term in the Hellenistic παρουσία. Nor is the phrase εἰς ἀπάντησιν a technical term, since it occurs only once in these texts.[89] Moreover, Peterson's explanation of the parousia depiction in 1 Thess 4:13–18 as the bringing of the Lord (die Einholung des Kyrios) does not agree with the imagery of the text. The entire scene deals with the bringing of the *faithful*, not with the bringing of the Lord. Verse 14 clearly indicates that God will bring the faithful with Jesus (into his presence). In vv. 16–17 the faithful are the object of divine action: the deceased are raised, and the living and those brought to life are taken up.

Dupont's suggestion that the depiction of the theophany on Mount Sinai in LXX Exod 19:10–18 is the source of the imagery in

---

[82] Deissmann, Light, 368–73.

[83] Peterson, "Einholung," 682–702.

[84] Cerfaux, Christ, 32–44

[85] Holtz, 1 Thessalonicher, 203

[86] See ch. 1.

[87] Dupont, L'Union, 77–79.

[88] See Wilcke, Zwischenreich, 144–47.

[89] Ibid. On modern scholars who have adopted Peterson's view, see Cosby, "Formal Receptions." Cosby mentions Mundle, I. H. Marshall, and F. F. Bruce.

1 Thess 4:16–17 is also unsatisfactory.[90] There are too many elements in 1 Thess 4:16–18 that do not fit that pattern and imagery.[91] Moreover, many motifs are not found in both depictions or have a different meaning in each case. Thus the archangel and the κέλευσμα are not found in the Sinai scenery, while the cloud has a different function. The Israelites, after their meeting with the Lord, return to their tents, but in 1 Thess 4:18 the faithful are with the Lord forever. It appears that the apostle draws on the developed imagery available to him in Jewish and Christian apocalyptic and that he uses this imagery in a creative fashion. This is especially evident in the peculiar portrayal of the resurrection as a restoration of life, and of being taking up.

5. Tradition or a Saying of Jesus?

We discovered that the appeal to the word of the Lord in 1 Thess 4:15 does not suggest that Paul is here quoting a dominical saying. Neither the introduction nor the vocabulary in v. 15 allows such a conclusion.[92] Some suggest that vv. 16–17 contain a saying of Jesus or an early church tradition. J. Jeremias[93] makes a strong case for taking vv. 16–17a as an unknown saying of Jesus, and v. 17b as Paul's own inference from the saying.[94] According to him, in vv. 16–17a only the modifications αὐτὸς ὁ κύριος, autos ho kyrios, ἐν Χριστῷ, en Christō, and ἡμεῖς, hēmeis, come from Paul. But Jeremias's solution needs to be modified. The introduction, ἐν λόγῳ κυρίου, en logō kyriou, does not suggest a quotation. And the pointers πρῶτον, prōton, ἔπειτα, epeita, and ἅμα σύν, hama syn are common Pauline words.[95] They point to the

---

[90] Dupont, L'Union, 69.

[91] In the NT, the term εἰς ἀπάντησιν (or εἰς ὑπάντησιν, eis hypantēsin) occurs at Jesus' triumphal entry into Jerusalem (John 12:13), in the parable of the Ten Virgins (Matt 25:1, 6), and in Acts 28:15, where Christians in Rome come out to meet Paul. In all these texts it means "to meet." It is always associated with the coming out (ἐξῆλθον εἰς ὑπάντησιν, exelthon eis hypantēsin, John 12:13; ἦλθαν εἰς ἀπάντησιν, ēlthan eis apantēsin, Acts 28:15; ἐξέρχεσθε εἰς ἀπάντησιν, exerchesthe eis apantēsin, Matt 25:6). The verb ἀπαντάω has the simple meaning "to meet" (Mark 14:13; Luke 17:12).

[92] On the analysis of the vocabulary in v. 15, see Luedemann, Paul, 222.

[93] J. Jeremaias, Unknown Sayings, 80–83.

[94] For vocabulary analyses of vv. 16–17, see Luz, Geschichtsverständnis, 328–29; Luedemann, Paul, 222–25. According to these, the two verses contain largely non-Pauline vocabulary.

[95] See the previous footnote.

current situation in Thessalonica rather than to a situation in the life of Jesus.[96]

According to Luz,[97] the pointers πρῶτον, ἔπειτα, and ἡμεῖς οἱ, *hēmeis hoi*, are Pauline expressions, but ἅμα σὺν αὐτοῖς, *hama syn autois*, comes from the pre-Pauline tradition. Luz offers the following reconstruction of the saying: "The Lord will descend from heaven with a cry of command, with the archangel's call, and with the trumpet of God. The dead in the Lord will rise. Those who are left shall be taken up with them in the clouds to meet the Lord in the air."

In contrast to Jeremias, Luz credits this saying to a recent pre-Pauline tradition that dealt with the delay of the parousia:[98] the community put this saying on the lips of Jesus, and Paul apparently assumed that it came from Jesus. But this does not agree with Paul's way of introducing traditions that go back to Jesus (cf. 1 Cor 7:10; 9:14; 11:23) or community traditions (1 Cor 15:3). Thus, nothing here suggests that Paul regards this as a community tradition.

According to Luz, Paul and others already faced this problem earlier—especially if the expression ἅμα σὺν αὐτοῖς belongs to tradition. But Luedemann shows[99] that ἅμα σὺν αὐτοῖς is a good Pauline expression and agrees with the perspective in v. 15. And if the problem had occurred earlier, why did the apostle then not forestall it in his mission to Thessalonica?

Harnisch suggests several stages in the development of this pre-Pauline tradition. The first stage is a Jewish affirmation of the descent of the Son of man and of the rapture of the remnant. The second is a logion of Jewish-Christian provenance about the resurrection of the dead, the parousia, and the taking up of the faithful. The third contains the Pauline clarifications πρῶτον, ἔπειτα, and ἡμεῖς οἱ ζῶντες, *hēmeis hoi zōntes*.[100] But this reconstruction of tradition likewise does not do justice to Paul's way of ascribing a logion to Jesus.

---

[96] For the setting in the life of Jesus, see Holtz, *1 Thessalonicher*, 196.

[97] Luz, *Geschichtsverständnis*, 328–29.

[98] Ibid., 329. Koester ("Die ausserkanonischen Herrenworte," 233–34) attributes this logion to the creative imagination of the early community. According to him, the community formulated the saying on its own and then attributed it to Jesus.

[99] Luedemann, *Paul*, 223–24.

[100] Harnisch, *Eschatologische Existenz*, 42–45; R. F. Collins, "Tradition," 331–32.

Luedemann's reconstruction of the pre-Pauline tradition is virtually identical with Luz's, except for the phrase "together with," which he ascribes to Paul's redaction. According to him, Paul found the following wording: "The Lord will descend from heaven with a cry of command, with the archangel's call, and with the sound of the trumpet of God. And the dead will rise. Those who are left will be caught up into the clouds to meet the Lord in the air."[101]

Luedemann regards this tradition as a "miniature apocalypse."[102] But according to him, vv. 16–17 are not a unified tradition, for the rising of the dead and the withdrawal contradict each other, since in the tradition "it is assumed that those who have risen will *not* be carried off to the Lord (Paul's understanding is *different*)."[103] Fourth Ezra 13:3, for instance, speaks of the Son of man who comes out of the heart of the sea, flies with the clouds of heaven, and alights on a high mountain. As he comes down the mountain, the remnant of the people come to him. This is the beginning of the messianic reign. But 4 Ezra is not a good model. The text comes from a later period and later experience—the destruction of the temple. It portrays a messianic interregnum at the end of the ages, which is followed by a primeval silence in which everyone dies. Then occurs the resurrection of the dead (7:32–33). It cannot be shown that the pre-Pauline tradition behind 1 Thess 4:16–17 dealt with these issues.

And it is not certain that Jewish apocalyptic at that period dealt with the advantage of the survivors in the end time. An appeal to *2 Bar.* 29–30 is hazardous, for the text comes from the period after the destruction of the temple, probably ca. 100 CE. According to Luedemann, this tradition states, "The righteous, both those still alive and those who have died, will participate in the time of salvation, which is inaugurated by the arrival of the Messiah. The dead are raised after the arrival of the Messiah. Both groups, survivors and resurrected, will be transformed after the judgment" (50:8).[104]

Thus, according to Luedemann, 1 Thess 4:16–17 agrees in structure with Jewish apocalyptic tradition of that time, except for

---

[101] Luedemann, *Paul,* 225.

[102] The descent of the Lord (καταβήσεται, *katabēsetai*) and the mystery of the end time, disclosed in 1 Thess 4:16–17, confirm this formal designation.

[103] Luedemann, *Paul,* 226.

[104] Ibid., 229–30.

the ἀπάντησις, which Paul imports from the Hellenistic depictions of the imperial παρουσία.[105] Accordingly, the faithful are taken up by the clouds to meet the Lord in the air, and then accompany him to the earth. "The notion of withdrawal does not compete or conflict with the notion of the resurrection. Rather, withdrawal involves nothing more than a sudden change of location."[106]

In this reconstruction, the tradition consisted of a saying of the Lord and the apocalyptic core. The former was "understood as a saying of the raised Christ . . . spoken by a prophet." Paul, to be sure, understands the entire λόγος κυρίου, logos kyriou, as the saying of the risen Christ.[107] In order to assure the faithful who have died a share in the fellowship with the κύριος, the apostle "consciously inverts the order of events in the Jewish substratum . . . by having the resurrection occur prōton and by letting the withdrawal occur epeita."[108]

In this explanation, however, the assurance of fellowship with Christ scarcely demands the inversion of the order, for it is not dependent upon the taking up. The withdrawal, as understood by Luedemann, is not an exaltation but a momentary taking up to meet the coming Lord, followed by a return to the earth; it does not involve a change of existence. Besides, why ascribe this text to a prophet rather than to Paul himself? Paul also was a prophet, as H. Merklein[109] demonstrates. Why could Paul not have put the risen Lord's logion into this medium?[110]

There are reasons to believe that the apostle had a hand elsewhere in the formulation of this text. The terse formulation in v. 16 of the attendant circumstances of the Lord's coming bears his imprint. And the taking up of the faithful was part of his previous eschatological instruction to the Thessalonians—the very part that is now causing difficulties in Thessalonica. Finally, the non-Pauline

---

[105]Ibid., 230. Thus Luedemann agrees with Peterson's solution (Luedemann, "ἀπάντησις").

[106]Leudemann, Paul, 230. "Those who survive to the end of time will be withdrawn for the reception of the Son of man. At the gateways of the world they will ceremoniously receive the one who is portrayed as a person of high rank. They will then return with him to the world, where the resurrection of the dead will occur."

[107]Ibid., 231.

[108]Ibid., 233–34.

[109]Merklein, "Theologe als Prophet," 419–24.

[110]The non-Pauline vocabulary here can be explained as deriving from the apocalyptic imagery.

expressions may be accounted for by the uniqueness of this depiction in apocalyptic language.

Hence, the possibility here of a revelation from the exalted Lord to Paul remains real. Paul would, in this case, use the imagery he employed earlier in Thessalonica. This would agree with his prophetic endowment, with which, armed by the authority of the Lord, he unveils the hidden mysteries (cf. 1 Cor 14:26, 30).[111] He not only unfolds the mystery of the ultimate fulfillment but also addresses existential concerns of his communities. The possibility of a revelation is enhanced by the fact that the apostle himself talks of repeated visions and revelations of the ultimate reality (1 Cor 2:7–13; 2 Cor 12:1–7).

6. The Resurrection of the Dead

This investigation has brought out that the taking up of the deceased faithful is the main reassurance in 1 Thess 4:13–18. The Thessalonians think that death has robbed their brothers and sisters in faith of their privilege of sharing in the Lord's parousia. The dead, as everyone knows, cannot be taken up. And Paul has talked about the taking up. The Thessalonians mourn their dead, thinking that these have been deprived of participation in the taking up and, ultimately, in the parousia and the life with the Lord. Hence, the apostle places the resurrection before the taking up and depicts the resurrection as a return to this life.

Hoffmann[112] and Luz[113] show that the anxiety in Thessalonica concerns the salvation of the deceased. Death somehow endangers the ultimate goal, to be with the Lord. But it remains unclear how, precisely, salvation is endangered. Neither scholar links it to the taking up. Both of them introduce here the notion of the messianic interregnum.[114] In that scheme, the living faithful would, at the coming of Christ, be rewarded with the messianic kingdom, while the deceased would be raised at the end of this reign, at the general resurrection. Although Hoffmann finds no evidence that the apostle himself held this idea, Luz suggests that

---

[111] Merklein, "Theologe als Prophet," 423.
[112] Hoffmann, Toten, 232, 234.
[113] Luz, Geschichtsverständnis, 319–20.
[114] Hoffmann, Toten, 232; Luz, Geschichtsverständnis, 319.

1 Cor 15:23–24 contains a hint in this regard.[115] This, however, is far from clear.

The suggestion, made in this investigation, about the taking up offers another plausibility. It explains well the grief of the Thessalonians for their deceased, for they think that these are prevented by death from participating in the parousia and life with Christ. In this explanation the taking up is not merely a momentary lifting to the heights above the earth, followed by a return to the earth, but a translation from the life here on earth to the eternal life with the risen Lord in heaven.[116] It is the *Einholung* of the faithful. It is the end of this life on earth and the beginning of a higher life. Hence, Paul reassures the Thessalonians, saying, "And so we will be with the Lord forever" (1 Thess 4:17).

The apostle here depicts the resurrection as a return to this life, for this enables the deceased to participate in the taking up. The resurrection itself is not the central issue. It has here only one function: to make it possible for the deceased to be taken up. Once we understand the situation from this perspective, we need not read 1 Thess 4:16–17 in the light of 1 Cor 15:50–56, as has often been done in the past.

In 1 Cor 15:50–56 the apostle emphasizes that the resurrection involves a transformation and that the transformation is necessary for entering into the kingdom of God. In 1 Thess 4:16–17, however, the apostle talks about the translation. But the taking up is never a mere change of location; it implies an exaltation. The Jewish background of this scheme, at any rate, indicates that those who are taken up enter thereby a higher form of life near to God. Enoch, Elijah, and Moses did not return to earth after they were taken up into heaven. And according to 1 Thess 4:17, those taken up at the coming of the Lord are with the Lord forever. They have been lifted from the life on earth to share in the life of the risen Lord, by the power of God. The transformation is thus implied in the imagery of translation and exaltation. The sharing of life with the risen Lord forever also suggests such a change.[117]

Paul certainly spoke to the Thessalonians of the resurrection of Jesus, together with its implication for the final destiny of the

---

[115] Luz, *Geschichtsverständnis*, 319, 347.
[116] See Gillman, "Transformation"; see also Plevnik, "The Taking Up," 282.
[117] See Plevnik, "The Taking Up," 280–83.

faithful, when he first came to Thessalonica (1 Thess 1:9–10). But he strongly focused his teaching on the parousia, as the many parousia references in 1 Thessalonians indicate (1:10; 2:19; 3:13; 4:13–5:11; 5:23). He was under the impression that he was living at the end of this age (see 1 Cor 7:29, 31). According to 1 Cor 7:31, "the appointed time has grown short" and "the form of this world is passing away."[118] First Thessalonians 4:13–18 indicates that Paul himself expects to live to see the Lord's coming.

In this fervent expectation of the end, the apostle emphasized that the faithful should be holy and blameless for the Lord's coming (1 Thess 3:13; 5:23). He did not prepare them for death but for the encounter with the coming Lord. He did not bring out what would happen to those who died before the Lord's coming. That question probably did not come up. He did, however, talk about the resurrection of the dead, since he understood Christ's resurrection as bringing life to everyone (1 Cor 15:20–22).[119] Thus, the unexpected deaths in the community triggered a crisis, not because Paul did not mention the resurrection but because of his portrayal of the taking up at the Lord's coming.

CONCLUSION

To the dismayed faithful in Thessalonica, who mourn the death of their fellow believers, thinking that death has robbed them of sharing in the final destiny, Paul first gives his assurance by drawing on the knowledge in faith that God, who raised Jesus to life, will also bring the deceased believers with Jesus to their final destiny. This is his interpretation of the Easter event for the future of Christian existence, and his testimony in faith. Easter determines and opens the future of the faithful. Death is no obstacle to the power of God manifest in the resurrection of Jesus (cf. Rom 8:38) and cannot separate the faithful from Christ. Their belonging to Christ, and hence also their ultimate destiny, are not threatened by

---

[118] In view of this, Paul advises the Corinthians not to get married.

[119] Rigaux, *Thessaloniciens*, 526. According to Rigaux, it is possible that the hope of sharing in the ultimate completion was not clearly enough presented to the Thessalonians. They were ignorant not about the fact of the future resurrection but about its effect. Rigaux disagrees with Guntermann's contention (*Eschatologie*, 39) that Paul could not have preached the resurrection of the dead prior to his writing 1 Thess.

physical death (1 Thess 4:14). The ground of hope here is God—God's deed in Jesus Christ.

For the concrete depiction of the future completion, the apostle draws on the word of the Lord—probably on a revelation of the exalted Christ. He reassures the Thessalonians that at the Lord's coming, the living will be no better off than the deceased. The extent of this word is probably vv. 16–17b, while v. 15 is an antecedent summation. But in his formulation Paul makes free use of existing apocalyptic imagery. That Paul is here quoting a community tradition is less likely. It is, however, almost certain that the apostle earlier taught the Thessalonians in these terms and that his teaching about the taking up caused the present anxiety in the community about the fate of the deceased faithful. To reassure them, Paul here restates the core of this teaching but clarifies it by making certain adjustments. By inserting the restoration of the deceased to life and by pointing out the sequence of acts with πρῶτον, ἔπειτα, and ἅμα σύν, he shows how the deceased believers will also be present for the taking up.

The real problem in the Thessalonian community concerns the taking up. The apostle taught them that at the Lord's coming, they will all be taken up. The unspoken assumption was that they will be alive at the Lord's coming. Thus, when some of the believers died, there was perplexity and grief in the community at their unforeseen loss; for one had to be alive in order to be taken up. The dead are not taken up. How, then, will the deceased faithful participate at the Lord's parousia? Did God revoke his promise in Christ?

In response, Paul asserts that before the living will be taken up at the Lord's coming, the deceased faithful will be brought to life. This will qualify them for the taking up. After that, everyone, those raised to life and the living, will be taken up to meet the coming Lord and to be with him forever.

The taking-up motif here makes it unlikely that the apostle thinks of the parousia as the *Einholung*—the bringing in—of the Lord, modeled on the Hellenistic παρουσία. Verse 14, but also the scene in v. 17, indicate rather the *Einholung* of the faithful. The faithful do not go up; they are lifted up by the power of God. This presentation depicts how a person is elevated from this life on earth to the life like that of the risen Christ.

The resurrection, as depicted here, is thus a return to this life, in seeming contradiction to the presentation in 1 Cor 15. But

1 Thess 4:13–18 and 1 Cor 15:50–56 are each tailored to their own situations. The issue in 1 Thess 4 is the taking up or the sharing of the dead in the parousia of the Lord. The issue in 1 Cor 15 is the reality of the resurrection of the dead and the nature of the resurrected body. In 1 Thess 4 the resurrection restores the deceased to life and thus renders them capable of the taking up. Paul does not reflect on the quality of the risen life, for that is not the issue here; he only shows how the deceased faithful will share in the taking up and in the union with the Lord.

Yet the imagery in 1 Thess 4:16–17 does imply a change in the quality of life. The one who is here taken up is elevated by the power of God to the life like that of the risen Christ. This is eternal life. But the apostle does not reflect on the degrees of glory or bliss; he only asserts that the faithful will be with the risen Lord forever. For Paul, the ultimate completion is something very personal: it is centered on the Lord. The hope of the faithful is to be united with the Lord. And this is also the hope of Paul. But such a hope, borne by love, cannot abide a separation in time and space. It tends to bridge the gap and to foreshorten the distance in time and space. It brings the faithful and the Lord closer together.

Paul here comes closer than usual to depicting the future completion in apocalyptic language. But he is not taken into heaven, like Enoch, and shown in detail the drama of the ultimate completion. He is not feeding their curiosity. His depiction gives to the Thessalonians only what they need in order to live in confident hope of the completion. It is an understanding provided by faith and supplemented by revelation.

4

⚙

THE TIMES AND SEASONS,
1 THESSALONIANS 5:1–11

In 1 Thess 5:1–11, the second half of the eschatological section, 4:13–5:11, Paul addresses the next question presented to him
by the Thessalonians.[1] It concerns "the times and the seasons" of
the completion.[2] But here the apostle does not employ the word
παρουσία; he talks in a threatening tone about "the day of the
Lord." He warns that the day of the Lord "will come like a thief
in the night," with dire consequences for all who are not ready.

This question reflects the community's interest in the date of
the completion and perhaps a concern for their own fate, but
not grief and perplexity, as in 4:13–18. According to Kümmel,
4:13–18 deals with a difficulty caused by the delay of the
parousia, while 5:1–11 encounters the danger of taking the delay
for granted.[3] But it is not clear that the Thessalonians have taken
the delay for granted or have drawn from it consequences for
their spiritual life. What is clear, however, is that Paul here
warns of spiritual dangers.[4]

---

[1] In 1 Thess 3:6 Paul mentions that Timothy has returned with good news from
the Thessalonian community.

[2] The question concerns the living and might have been connected with the
previous question about the fate of the deceased: will the Lord come in their
lifetime, or will they suffer the same fate as the deceased brethren?

[3] Kümmel, "Problem, 414.

[4] Such warnings occur also in the Synoptic Gospels (Luke 12:35–48; 17:24–30;
21:34–36; Matt 24:27, 37–39, 43–51; 25:1–13, 42–51; Mark 13:33–37.

A. THE STRUCTURE AND THE AUTHENTICITY OF
1 THESSALONIANS 5:1–11

As in 4:13, so also here Paul introduces a new subject with περί, *peri*. The adversative δέ, *de* indicates not only a new subject but also a different tone. This is clear from the apostle's words, "You do not need to have anything written to you" (v. 1) and "For you yourselves know well" (αὐτοὶ γὰρ ἀκριβῶς οἴδατε, *autoi gar akribōs oidate*, v. 2). The subject is the times and the seasons (τῶν χρόνων καὶ τῶν καιρῶν, *tōn chronōn kai kairōn*) of the ultimate completion. It sounds as if he were dismissing the question that the Thessalonians put to him.[5] Harnisch speaks here of *praeteritio*.[6] In fact, v. 2 does not deal with the stated subject matter, the date, but with the coming of the day of the Lord like a "thief in the night." Verse 3 then spells out what this metaphor means: a sudden, unexpected, and inescapable disaster for those who talk of, and rely on, "peace and security." Paul warns, "The day of the Lord will come like a thief in the night. When they say, 'There is peace and security,' then sudden destruction will come upon them, as labor pains come upon a pregnant woman, and there will be no escape!" (v. 3).

But with v. 4 Paul backs off from this threat. He makes it clear over and over again that this threat is not meant for the community and that they are in good standing.[7] He concludes with general encouragement in v. 11: "Therefore encourage one another and build up each other, as indeed you are doing."

Wedged between these reassurances is the apostle's exhortation in vv. 6–8. Speaking in the first person plural, he says that since we are children of the light and of the day, we must live a life of faith, love, and hope.[8] It could be that the exhortation to vigilance was Paul's original intention in this section, but having opened with

---

[5] The apostle is responding either to a set of questions that Timothy brought back from Thessalonica and that he communicated to Paul orally (Rigaux, *Thessaloniciens*, 552; Laub, *Eschatologische Verkündigung*, 158) or, less likely, to a situation in the community that somehow came to his attention (Schmithals, *Paul and the Gnostics*, 164–65, and, in dependence on Schmithals, Harnisch, *Eschatologische Existenz*, 52–54). See Plevnik, "Authenticity," 71.

[6] Harnisch, *Eschatologische Existenz*, 52–84.

[7] Depending on how his assurances are divided, there are at least five assurances given in this section. See below.

[8] According to Gerhardsson (*Gospel Tradition*, 133), the exhortation is given in a "particularly gentle pastoral tone due to the hortatory subjunctive."

the prospect of a disaster, he has to clear away the fear that God destines them for destruction (vv. 4–5 and 9–11).

Paul concludes with the assurance that God has destined them to be with the Lord Jesus. They must believe this, and they must encourage one another in this regard (vv. 10–11). The reference "whether we are awake or asleep" in v. 10 concludes not only this section but the entire passage 4:13–5:11.[9]

The sudden shift in tone in 5:1–3 from that in the preceding section has led some interpreters, most recently Friedrich, to conclude that 5:1–11 is a later interpolation.[10] But Friedrich's suggestion has not received scholarly consensus.[11] The vocabulary, the theology, and the rhetorical shifts in this passage speak, rather, in favor of the authenticity of the section. The presence of some non-Pauline vocabulary here no more justifies ascribing this passage to an interpolator than does the non-Pauline vocabulary in 4:13–18. And it is scarcely likely that a later interpolator would first insert a statement such as that in 5:2–3 and then try to tone it down by the many reassurances in vv. 4–10.[12]

B. THE QUEST FOR THE DATE AND THE DAY OF THE LORD, 1 THESSALONIANS 5:1–3

Paul begins by redirecting a quest for the date of the Lord's coming. The pair of words χρόνοι, *chronoi*, and καιροί, *kairoi* (v. 1) is Semitic and apocalyptic in tone.[13] The expression is known to the Thessalonians and is perhaps part of their own question to Paul, but it could also be Paul's own formulation. The Lord had

---

[9] Holtz, *1 Thessalonicher*, 182–83; Wanamaker, *1 & 2 Thessalonians*, 189. According to Wanamaker, Paul, by referring back to 4:13–17, pulls the eschatological exhortation together, ending on a powerful note of hope for both the living and the dead.

[10] Friedrich, "Einschub"; *Briefe* 203–51, esp. 206–8.

[11] See Rigaux, "Tradition"; Plevnik, "Authenticity," 72–74; R. F. Collins, "Tradition," 154–72; Gerhardsson, *Gospel Tradition*, 127.

[12] See Plevnik, "Authenticity," 72–74; Gerhardsson, *Gospel Tradition*, 127; Rigaux, "Tradition," 320; R. F. Collins, "Integrity," 81–84.

[13] Rigaux ("Tradition," 322) regards it as a hendiadys. The pair occurs in LXX (and Theodotion) Dan 2:21 and 7:12. It appears in a parallel construction in Wis 7:18, and in the NT in Acts 1:7 and 3:20–21. Cf. also von Dobschütz, *Thessalonicher-Briefe*, 204; Hoffmann, *Toten*, 229; Schlier, *Apostel*, 85; Wanamaker, *1 & 2 Thessalonians*, 178.

not come yet, and this gave rise to the speculation about the date of his coming. It seems that Paul interpreted this question from the Thessalonians as an idle curiosity, perhaps as an attempt to secure their own future. No doubt he had met such questions earlier and could recognize them for what they were. He therefore refuses to be drawn into such speculation, regarding it as neither necessary nor helpful for Christian existence. Besides, he has had no special revelation on the Lord's coming, although he ardently awaits it. And he imparts this yearning to the faithful.

The phrase ἡμέρα κυρίου, hēmera kyriou must have been known to the Thessalonians. It is the Jewish equivalent of the parousia and refers to God's coming for judgment or salvation.[14] In the "Q" apocalypse, Luke 17:22–37, the day of the Lord, which is the day of the Son of man's coming, is likened to the flood in the time of Noah and to the ruin of Sodom. The flood is mentioned frequently in Jewish apocalyptic literature as a prototype of the end-time condemnation.[15] It is found also in the NT, together with Sodom (and Gomorrah).[16] In 1 Thess 5:2 Paul employs ἡμέρα κυρίου for the first time in this letter but takes it for granted that the Thessalonians understand it. He no doubt used it earlier when he introduced the Thessalonians to the faith. Here he reminds them of his previous instruction on this topic.

We have seen earlier[17] that ἡμέρα κυρίου is an ambivalent expression, meaning salvation or damnation. It is salvation to one (Israel) but destruction to another (the hostile nations), or what is salvation at one time (when Jerusalem is pleasing to the Lord) is destruction at another (when Jerusalem is displeasing to the Lord). The Lord's coming and total destruction of the unprepared, which are depicted here, are also present in the Q synopsis in Matt 24:23–39 par Luke 17:22–37.[18]

---

[14] In the "Q" apocalypse, Matthew uses the word παρουσία, and Luke employs the expression ἡμέρα, hēmera or ἡμέρας, hēmeras for the same event, the terrible end-time coming of the Son to those who seek peace and security (Matt 24:27 par Luke 17:24; Matt 24:37 par Luke 17:26; Matt 24:39 par Luke 17:30).

[15] 1 Enoch 10:2; 54:7–10; 89:1–6; 106:15; 4 Ezra 3:9; 2 Bar. 56:15; Jub. 4:23–24; 5:20–27.

[16] Sodom (and Gomorrah) are mentioned in Matt 10:15, 11:23–24; Luke 10:12, 17:29; Rom 9:29; 2 Pet 2:6; Jude 7; and Rev 11:8.

[17] See ch. 1.

[18] Instead of "peace and security," Luke 17:27, 28 presents life as usual: eating and drinking, marrying, buying and selling, planting and building. Some of this is present also in 1 Thess 5:6–8.

The phrase ἡμέρα κυρίου contains motifs common to the holy-war imagery that depicts a personal coming of the Lord.[19] But for Paul and the NT, the coming of the Lord is the coming of Christ (cf. Matt 24:27, 37, 39; Luke 17:24, 26, 30; 1 Cor 1:8; 5:5; 2 Cor 1:14; Phil 1:6; etc.). It is the day of Jesus Christ's coming, or of his appearance for salvation and judgment.[20] That both judgment and salvation are present in this image is clear from 1 Cor 3:12–15, 4:4–5 and 2 Cor 5:10;[21] and that the Lord's coming also implies judgment is clear from 1 Thess 1:10, 3:13 and 5:23.[22] The idea of coming is suggested in the warning of 1 Thess 5:2, "The day of the Lord will come (ἔρχεται, erchetai) like a thief in the night," and in v. 3, "Then sudden destruction will come[23] upon (ἐφίσταται, ephistatai) them." In judgment or war, the coming is associated with surprise, suddenness, and swiftness. The verb ἐφίστημι, ephistēmi, means "to come upon," "to fall upon," "to strike," or "to smite."

The disaster on the day of the Lord is brought out in vv. 2–3. The coming "like a thief in the night" is made explicit in v. 3: "Then sudden destruction (ὄλεθρος, olethros) will come upon them, as labor pains come upon a pregnant woman, and there will be no escape!" The Lord's day is a sudden and inescapable disaster.

With ὅταν . . . τότε, hotan . . . tote, Paul juxtaposes security ("peace and security") and disaster. But the security is false. Εἰρήνη καὶ ἀσφάλεια, Eirēnē kai asphaleia, occurs in the NT only here. This hendiadys highlights the conviction of security. But "peace" is not the peace that God gives and Paul wishes for the community (1:1; 5:23). It is a false and reckless security of the godless, who disregard the holiness and the sovereignty of God (1 Cor 7:29–31; cf. Luke 17:27, 28–29).

That Paul has the godless and the sinners in mind here is clear from vv. 4–7. In a play on words, he mentions those who belong to darkness and to the night, who sleep and drink. He contrasts to these those who belong to the light and to the day, who are vigilant

---

[19] See von Rad, *Holy War;* also "Day of the Lord." According to von Rad, *Theology,* 2.120: "Yahweh comes in person to the battle." See also ch. 1.

[20] Yet the theocentric aspect of the final judgment is present as well; see 1 Cor 3:16; Rom 2:5–11; 14:10–12.

[21] Cf. also Matt 24:17–31; Luke 17:22–37; 21:25–28

[22] In 1 Thess 3:13 and 5:23 Paul prays that the Thessalonians will be blameless at the coming of the Lord.

[23] In Luke 17:22, 24, 26, 30, for instance, other words are used for the presence or arrival of the Son of man, such as "seeing," "revealing," etc.

and sober. This combination of security and the sudden sweep of the disaster is typical of the NT apocalyptic (Matt 24:23–39; Luke 17:22–37) and of the parables of vigilance (Luke 12:35–48; 21:34–36) and repentance (Luke 13:1–9).

The motif of false security occurs also in OT prophetic literature. Jeremiah thunders against the prophets and priests who deceive and soothe the people with the assurance "peace, peace" (Jer 6:14), just as war, God's punishment, threatens their very existence[24] (cf. also Jer 4:10; Ezek 13:10). Ezekiel 38:14–16 describes God's sudden sweep upon the unsuspecting and secure Israel: "On that day when my people Israel are living securely (ἐπ' εἰρήνης, ep' eirēnēs) you will rouse yourself and come from your place . . . you will come up against my people Israel, like a cloud covering the earth. In the latter days I will bring you against my land, so that the nations may know me . . . when I display my holiness before their eyes."

The adjective αἰφνίδιος, aiphnidios, when employed in connection with the day of the Lord or judgment or war, expresses suddenness.[25] It is associated in 1 Thess 5 with the verb ἔρχεται, erchetai (v. 2) or ἐφίσταται (v. 3).[26] The calamity falls upon or strikes with explosive suddenness and unexpectedness (Mal 3:1–2; Ps 64:5, 8; Prov 3:25; 6:15; etc.).[27] This motif is also present in the synoptic parables about vigilance. Thus in Luke 12:46 Jesus states, "The master of that slave will come on a day when he does not expect him, and at an hour that he does not know" (cf. Matt 24:50). According to D. Daube, not to know is typically associated with what is sudden and disastrous.[28] Night also is a typical image of not knowing: it covers up the stealthy approach of disaster; it lulls the unsuspecting victim.

The image "thief in the night" also implies a sudden and unexpected evil. It occurs in Matt 24:43; Luke 12:39; 2 Pet 3:10; and

---

[24] Weiser, Jeremia, 55.

[25] Synonyms for αἰφνίδιος, aiphnidios are ἄφνω, aphnō, ἐξαίφνης, exaiphnēs, ἐξάπινα, exapina. In the NT, αἰφνίδιος occurs only in Luke 21:34 and in 1 Thess 5:2. The word ἄφνω is found only in Acts (3 times), while ἐξαίφνης occurs once in Mark, twice in Luke, and twice in Acts; ἐξάπινα occurs once in Mark. All these synonyms for αἰφνίδιος in the NT are used in connection with a startling, stunning, and wondrous event. Cf. Daube, Sudden, 28–34.

[26] Both verbs occur in Luke 21:34, 35. Cf. Daube, Sudden, 28.

[27] Ibid., 4–5.

[28] Ibid., 28–29. Daube refers also to Jer 8:15 (14:19): "We look for peace, but find no good, for a time of healing, but there is terror instead."

Rev 3:3, 16:15, and it thus belongs to the Christian vocabulary and imagery. This image is implied in the gospel text: "If the owner of the house had known at what part of the night-watch (ποίᾳ φυλακῇ, poia phylakē) the thief was coming, he would have stayed awake" (Matt 24:43). The interpretation of the parable in Matt 24:44 applies to the coming of the Son of man: "Therefore you also must be ready, for the Son of man is coming at an unexpected hour." The image "thief in the night" thus expresses unexpected danger.

In the exhortation to vigilance in Luke 21:34–36 occurs a cluster of motifs: thief, night, vigilance, readiness, and the coming of the Lord. There is a wide agreement in vocabulary between the passages in 1 Thessalonians and Luke: αἰφνίδιος (Luke 21:34); ἐφίσταται (ἐπιστῇ, epistē, Luke 21:34); ἐκφύγωσιν, ekphygōsin (ἐκφυγεῖν, ekphygein, Luke 21:36); ἡμέρα κυρίου (ἡμέρα ἐκείνη, hēmera ekeinē, Luke 21:34); and μεθυσκόμενοι, methyskomenoi; μεθύουσιν, methyousin (μέθη, methē, Luke 21:34). According to L. Hartman, the two texts depend on the same tradition.[29]

The image of travail in 1 Thess 5:3 is unrelated to the messianic woes. According to Rigaux, this image of a woman who is suddenly convulsed with inescapable birth pangs passed as a technical term into Christian vocabulary. In the OT this motif had been used in a variety of ways in eschatological passages dealing with the day of the Lord.[30] Thus Isa 13:8, which describes the destruction on the day of the Lord: "Pangs and agony will seize them; they will be in anguish like a woman in travail" (cf. Hos 13:13; Isa 26:17; 66:8; Jer 6:24; 13:21; 22:23; 30:6; Ps 48:6). The motif occurs also in Jewish apocalyptic (1 Enoch 62:4; 4 Ezra 4:40, 42) and in the Qumran literature (1QH 3:7–10; 5:30–31). It expresses a dangerous situation, intense pain, inevitability, and suddenness.[31] The best parallel to 1 Thess 5:3 is Isa 13:8 and the related tradition in Jer 6:24 (cf. Jer 50:43; LXX 27:43), where the referent is the crisis of those who must bear condemnation by Yahweh. While Isa 13 is directed against

---

[29] Hartman, Prophecy Interpreted, 192. Hartman suggests that חבל, ḥbl, when vocalized as חֶבֶל, ḥēbel, means "travail" but that when vocalized as חֶבֶל, ḥebel, it means "snare." But see Tuckett, "Synoptic Tradition," 174; cf. also Aejmelaeus, Wachen, 121.

[30] So Rigaux, Thessaloniciens, 559.

[31] Ibid., 325. For a discussion of the history of this motif, see Harnisch, Eschatologische Existenz, 60–77.

Babylon, Jer 6 is spoken against Zion. The metaphor is employed in prophetic and apocalyptic literature to express the inevitable and the unavoidable, as in Isa 26:18 and 66:9. But the texts in 4 Ezra 4:40–42 and 16:36–40, despite what Harnisch says, are scarcely a proof that Paul depends on Jewish apocalyptic tradition for the use of this image.[32] *First Enoch* 62:1–6, however, is very much to the point. The context here is the judgment that the Lord of the Spirits has entrusted to the Son of man: "On the day of judgment all the kings, the governors, the high officials, and the landlords shall see and recognize him—how he sits on the throne of glory. . . . Then pain shall come upon them as on a woman in travail with birth pangs—when she is giving birth (the child) enters the mouth of the womb and she suffers from childbearing . . . they shall be terrified and dejected; and pain shall seize them when they see that Son of Man sitting on the throne of glory" (vv. 3–5). But the situation here, unlike that in 1 Thess 5:2–3, is forensic.

C. THE AFFIRMATION, 1 THESSALONIANS 5:4–6a

With v. 4 Paul backs off from the statement he made in vv. 2–3. He does not deny that the day of the Lord will come suddenly and will bring disaster to those basking in the sun of false security. He is aware of comparable warnings in prophetic literature and in Jesus' sayings. He himself spoke in such terms to the Thessalonians earlier, for only this supposition explains his statement "You know it perfectly well" (ἀκριβῶς οἴδατε).[33] But here the apostle states that this is not how the day of the Lord will come to the Thessalonians: they are not under judgment. The Lord will indeed come like a thief in the night to those who belong to darkness, but not to those who belong to the light. Paul then reassures the Thessalonian community several times in different terms:

(1) "But you, beloved, are not in darkness, for that day to surprise you like a thief" (v. 4)

(2) "You are all children of light" (v. 5a)

---

[32] Harnisch, *Eschatologische Existenz*, 75. In Jewish apocalyptic writings, speculation about the completion differs markedly from that in the NT. Harnisch's conclusion goes beyond the evidence he assembled on this point.

[33] See Plevnik, "Pauline Presuppositions," 53–54.

(3) "and children of the day" (v. 5b)

(4) "We are not of the night" (v. 5c)

(5) "or of darkness" (v. 5c)

(6) "But since we belong to the day" (v. 8)

(7) "For God has destined us not for wrath but for obtaining salvation" (v. 9)

After the first three assurances Paul changes from "you" to the inclusive "we" (v. 5c): we are not displeasing God, we are not under judgment. Statement (1) is in the negative, denying that the faithful in Thessalonica are in darkness. Statements (2) and (3) are positive, affirming that the Thessalonians belong to the light and to the day. Statements (4) and (5) are negations, restating in chiastic order (4) and (3).[34] Statement (6) is part of an exhortation, while (7) gives the ground of hope in God's action on their behalf in Jesus Christ and resembles 4:14. These statements, and the concluding exhortation in v. 11, make up an extensive reassurance of the community.

In the course of this reassurance, the apostle resorts to a play on words. He begins with the word "night" in v. 2. Paul picks it up again with the word "darkness" (1). In (4) and (5) he explicitly links darkness to night to say that the thief comes at night, hence to those who belong to the darkness. All this sounds somewhat contrived, since in v. 2 "night" expresses the *manner* of the day of the Lord's coming (as "a thief in the night") while in vv. 4–6 "night" refers to the *object* of the thief's coming (those who belong to the night and to darkness).

In (2) and (3) Paul restates the content of (1) by employing a Semitic turn of phrase ("sons of . . . "). In (4) and (5) he restates in negative terms and in chiastic order (3) and (2), using a Greek turn of phrase ("not of . . . "). The play on words occurs once more, in the figurative use of the words "awake" and "asleep" in v. 10. In this splurge of metaphors and turns of phrase, it is difficult to determine the exact meaning of "light," "day," or "darkness." The metaphors here are mixed. Three items, however, deserve comment: the phrases "sons of light" and "sons of the day," and the meaning of "darkness" in v. 5.

---

[34] See Wanamaker, *1 & 2 Thessalonians*, 183.

The Hebrew turn of phrase "sons of light" is now well known from the Dead Sea Scrolls[35] (1QS 1:9; 3:13, 24, 25; 1QM 1:13; etc.). Members of the Qumran community regarded themselves as the "sons of light" and outsiders as the "sons of darkness" (1QS 1:10; 1QM 1:1, 7, 16; etc.). The "sons of darkness" were under the dominion of the spirit of darkness (1QS 3:25–27), and their deeds were in darkness (1QM 15:9). Members considered themselves the true inheritors of the promises and as the end-time community of salvation. This terminology is also employed in the NT (Matt 8:12; 13:38; Luke 10:6; 16:8; John 12:36; Eph 5:8; etc.). In the parable of the Dishonest Steward in Luke 16:8, for instance, τοὺς υἱοὺς τοῦ φωτός, tous huious tou phōtos, are contrasted with οἱ υἱοὶ τοῦ αἰῶνος τούτου, hoi huioi tou aiōnos toutou.

The symbolism of light and darkness is archetypal. According to S. Aalen, this antithetical imagery was fundamental to the Jewish understanding of God and the world.[36] Light was associated with salvation and well-being, and darkness with misfortune and ruin. Light comes from God, who is the light of Israel, guiding his people (2 Sam 22:29; Isa 50:10).[37] At the eschatological reversal there will be only light.[38] Light was associated with "the end of mourning," with the end of death and dying, as in the Book of Revelation.

But light and darkness also acquired religious and ethical connotations. Light became associated with the law and Wisdom.[39] In T. Levi 19:1 the children of Levi have to choose between light or darkness, between the law of the Lord and the works of Belial. The alternative of light/darkness is tantamount to that of God's law/works of Belial.

In Qumran literature, Belial and darkness go together. "Sons of darkness" are the outsiders; they belong to the dominion of the spirit of darkness (1QS 3:25–27), and their deeds are in darkness (1QM 15:9). Members of the community, however, are walking in the ways of light (1QS 3:20) and life. They are still exposed to the darkness, to the dominion of Belial, and to temptations (CD 4:15–17; 1QS 3:21–23), but in the end time the powers of darkness will be

---

[35] See Lövestam, Wakefulness, 52.

[36] Aalen, Begriffe.

[37] Lövestam, Wakefulness, 8.

[38] According to Isa 60:19–20, there will no longer be the rising and the setting of the sun and moon, for the Lord himself will be the everlasting light.

[39] Lövestam, Wakefulness, 9–11.

conquered (1QM 1:10, 16),[40] and the times of darkness brought to an end (1QM 1:8–9). Jewish apocalyptic literature associates the present time with darkness (T. Levi 18:4). According to 1 Enoch 58:1–6, the blessed will be "in the light of the sun and the elect ones in the light of eternal life. . . . There shall be light that has no end . . . for already darkness has been destroyed" (cf. 108:11–15).[41]

That the apostle also shares these ideas is clear from 2 Cor 6:14–7:1 and Rom 13:12.[42] Second Corinthians 6:14–15 contains this exhortation: "Do not be mismatched with unbelievers. For what partnership is there between righteousness and lawlessness? Or what fellowship is there between light (φωτί, phōti) and darkness (σκότος, skotos)? What agreement does Christ have with Beliar? Or what does a believer share with an unbeliever?" The authenticity of this text has been disputed. In Rom 13:12, however, Paul clearly indicates that he shares the ethical and religious connotation of light and darkness. There he urges the Romans, "Let us then lay aside the works of darkness (τοῦ σκότους, tou skotous) and put on the armor of light (τοῦ φωτός, tou phōtos) . . . put on the Lord Jesus Christ, and make no provision for the flesh, to gratify its desires." Here ἡμέρα is clearly used in the eschatological sense. Because this day has drawn near, the faithful are to awake from sleep, put away the deeds of darkness, and clothe themselves with the armor of light.[43] The affinity between Rom 13:11–14 and 1 Thess 5:8 has been noted by scholars.[44]

According to E. Lövestam, in Jewish and NT writing, בֵּן/υἱός, bēn/huios, with the genitive is also employed in order to indicate the eschatological heritage. In Matt 23:15, for instance, Jesus states that the Pharisees have made their proselyte υἱὸν γεέννης, huion geennēs. בֶּן-הָעוֹלָם הַבָּא, ben hāʿôlam habbāʾ indicates the one who inherits and who is destined for the future world.[45] It may be that

---

[40]Ibid., 14–15.

[41]On rabbinic literature, see ibid., 20–24.

[42]On the Pauline or non-Pauline origin of this section, see Furnish, II Corinthians, 375–78. Scholarly opinion on this is divided, and the possibility that Paul reworked a tradition cannot be dismissed. The affinity with the Qumran thought here is striking. Cf. Murphy-O'Connor, "Second Corinthians," 823.

[43]Lövestam (Wakefulness, 50–58) brings out strong affinities between 1 Thess 5:4–8 and Rom 13:11–14. Cf. also Frame, Thessalonians, 184; Rigaux, Thessaloniciens, 563.

[44]Lövestam, Wakefulness, 43, 45, 50.

[45]Ibid., 52–53.

the phrase υἱοὶ ἡμέρας, *huioi hēmeras*, in 1 Thess 5:5 also has this meaning—those who belong to, or are destined for, the eschatological day. Verse 5a gives the assurance (γάρ) that the day will not catch them unprepared.[46] The day will not surprise them. The day of the Lord is their day: "It indicates that the readers belong to, are inheritors of, and are destined for the eschatological day to come."[47] According to 1:10, Christian existence implies waiting for God's son from heaven, "Jesus, who rescues us from the wrath that is coming."

This supports the contention of Lövestam that υἱοὶ φωτός, *huioi phōtos* is not identical with υἱοὶ ἡμέρας, *huioi hēmeras*. The word ἡμέρα has the eschatological meaning in 5:2 as well as in v. 4, while the phrase υἱοὶ φωτός in v. 5 refers, rather, to the present Christian existence and takes up οὐκ ἐστὲ ἐν σκότει, *ouk este en skotei*, in v. 4. According to Rom 13:11–14, the faithful, in view of the approaching day, must put on the armor of light. The phrase υἱοὶ ἡμέρας in 1 Thess 5:5 is Paul's ad hoc formulation, interpreting the phrase υἱοὶ φωτός in an eschatological sense.[48]

D. THE EXHORTATION, 1 THESSALONIANS 5:6b–8

Having affirmed the Thessalonian community in vv. 4–5, Paul then advises it concerning a responsible way of awaiting the Lord's coming: "So then (ἄρα οὖν, *ara oun*) let us not fall asleep as others do, but let us keep awake and be sober; for those who sleep (οἱ καθεύδοντες, *hoi katheudontes*) sleep at night (νυκτός, *nyktos*), and those who are drunk (οἱ μεθυσκόμενοι, *hoi methyskomenoi*) get drunk at night (νυκτός, *nyktos*). But since we belong to the day (ἡμέρας ὄντες, *hēmeras ontes*), let us be sober (νήφωμεν, *nēphōmen*), and put on the breastplate of faith and love, and for a helmet the hope of salvation" (vv. 6–8). This section bears strong affinities with Rom 13:11–14. This text indicates that the awaiting of the Lord's coming and the readiness for it go hand in hand (see also 1 Thess 3:13; 5:23; 2 Cor 5:10; Rom 13:11–14). The apostle either urges the faithful to be blameless or prays that they may be found blameless at the Lord's coming.

---

[46] Ibid., 53.
[47] Ibid.
[48] Schlier, *Apostel*, 87.

"So then" as used here draws out the exhortation. It takes up the words "night" and "day" from the affirmation in vv. 4–5 and continues the play on words. It associates "night" with drinking and sleeping, and "day" with vigilance and soberness. The exhortation is first formulated in negative terms as "let us not fall asleep," then in positive terms as "let us keep awake and sober." It is justified (γάρ, gar) in v. 7 with the truism "For those who sleep sleep at night, and those who are drunk get drunk at night."

The exhortation continues the word play in vv. 4–5. The reason is that the exhortation is still related to the statement in vv. 2–3, as it incorporates vv. 4–5. Paul could not exhort the faithful to vigilance without first having allayed their anxieties about the eschatological catastrophe. But having said that, he now urges the faithful not to become complacent.

"Sleep" (v. 6) as well as "keep awake" (v. 6) and "be sober" (v. 6) are here used metaphorically. To sleep means to act like those who belong to the night, hence like the outsiders. Night and sleep go together, as the apostle explains in v. 7. But night is associated with drinking, and day with being sober (v. 8). Thus, both words here have an ethical connotation and are in opposition to each other. The present age is marked by darkness and night and by the corresponding behavior, drinking. The faithful must not succumb to it[49] but must be vigilant (γρηγορῶμεν, grēgorōmen) and sober (νήφωμεν, nēphōmen). In Rom 13:11–14 Paul talks of "laying aside the works of darkness . . . living . . . not in revelling or debauchery or licentiousness."

Vigilance and sobriety are modes of eschatological existence. The call to vigilance occurs in the synoptic apocalyptic passages Matt 24:42, 25:13; Mark 13:35, 37; and Luke 12:35–40 and is echoed also in Rev 3:2–3, 16:15 and 1 Pet 5:8. According to Schlier, this motif concerns knowledge of the "critical future of the Lord," readiness for it, perseverance in the face of the delay, and the resolve to encounter it with the Lord. Vigilance is the first step toward that encounter. But it also concerns accepting the immediate tasks as the legacy of the Lord; above all, it means praying.[50]

---

[49] Schlier (ibid., 89) points to Eph 5:14, which contains a traditional fragment from a baptismal song: "Sleeper, awake! Rise from the dead, and Christ will shine on you."

[50] Ibid. But this comprehensive meaning of vigilance, affirmed by Schlier, can only be drawn from the entire letter.

According to Schlier, sobriety is another form of the end-time existence. It involves a clear assessment of hope-filled reality because of the Lord's coming. Those who are sober entertain no illusions, do not boast, resist the desires arising from the selfish self, and steer clear of the pitfalls ahead.[51]

What this figurative language really means in 1 Thess 5 is indicated in the exhortation in v. 8: "But since we belong to the day, let us be sober (νήφωμεν), and put on the breastplate of faith and love, and for a helmet the hope of salvation (ἐλπίδα σωτηρίας, *elpida sōtērias*)."[52] This means that the way to anticipate the future completion is through faith, love, and hope. These three are eschatological existentials, the way believers put into effect their eschatological orientation.

The putting on of defensive armor represents another shift in Paul's imagery. Most commentators agree that this is an allusion to Isa 59:17, where we find the expression περικεφαλαίαν σωτηρίου, *perikephalaian sōtēriou*. The Isaian text is alluded to also in Wis 5:17–20, in rabbinic literature, and in Eph 6:13. According to Isa 59:17 Yahweh appears as a warrior and dons his armor in order to come in power to bring salvation to his people and destruction to their enemies.

But in NT allusions, people put on the armor. In Eph 6:13 the author exhorts the community to take up "the whole armor of God" so that they "may be able to withstand the evil day." They are to put on the belt of truth, the breastplate of righteousness, the shield of faith, the helmet of salvation, and they are to seize the sword of the word of God (vv. 14–17). In Rom 13:11–14, a parallel to 1 Thess 5:8, Paul exhorts the faithful to lay aside the works of darkness and put on the armor of light, living honorably rather than indulging in debauchery or licentiousness. They are to "put on the Lord Jesus Christ, and make no provisions for the flesh, to gratify its desires."

But in 1 Thess 5:8 Paul simply urges the community to have faith, love, and hope. He can scarcely say, as in Rom 13:11–14, that they must put away the works of darkness, having reassured them in vv. 4–5 that they do not belong to the darkness. Besides, he has

---

[51] Ibid., 90.

[52] Schlier (ibid.) regards the participial constructions as having a causal meaning: "because we are armed with . . . "

already reminded them in 4:2–3 that they are sanctified and must therefore abstain from immorality. Yet the danger is not over, and the temptations and trials of this world of darkness still beset the faithful.[53] The weapons[54] for the day of the Lord are thus faith, love, and hope. The apostle has praised the community in 1:3 for its faith, love, and steadfast hope. Here he exhorts them to continue what they were doing.

This, however, does not mean that they may disregard their daily tasks. In 4:10–11 Paul says, "We urge you . . . to aspire to live quietly, to mind your own affairs, and to work with your own hands, as we directed you, so that you may behave properly toward outsiders and be dependent on no one." And this does not suggest that the faithful can stand on their own: Paul prays that they may be found blameless at the Lord's coming (3:13; 5:23). He knows that certain things in the community are wrong (4:3–6) and thus urges the congregation to be holy (4:7) and to practice love toward one another. Although they are already doing it, they should strive to do it even better (4:10).

Accordingly, faith, love, and hope are necessary and sufficient for properly awaiting the day of the Lord. Those who live in faith, love, and hope will reach their destination. The triad is not new to the Thessalonians, since in 1:3 the apostle thanks God for these things in the community. Whether Paul himself formulated these components of Christian existence, however, is not certain (cf. 1 Pet 4:1). That this triad expresses his own thinking is clear from 1 Cor 13:13. In this hymn love is placed in the emphatic final position and given the greatest and most abiding value, while faith and hope are relegated to the initial position. Love imbues faith and hope with meaning: without love, faith and hope become empty and sterile. But in 1 Thess 1:3 and 5:8 the apostle places the word "hope" in the emphatic final position. This does not belittle love, as the exhortation in this letter indicates (cf. 4:9–12); it does, however, reflect the intensity of hope present in this letter, which is

---

[53] Lövestam (*Wakefulness*, 57) suggests that the weapons are protection against the powers of darkness.

[54] Von Dobschütz (*Thessalonicher-Briefe*, 210) and Frame (*Thessalonians*, 187) hold that this imagery refers to an armed sentry on duty. Rigaux (*Thessaloniciens*, 567) suggests that the armor is a protection against "*coups de la colère.*" According to Schlier (*Apostel*, 91), the armor indicates a dangerous situation, and the apostle unintentionally depicts the *militia Christi*.

focused on the Lord's coming. Paul's concern here is to allay anxiety and to shore up hope. Besides, this end position leads to the final reassurance in vv. 9–10.

E. THE FOUNDATION OF HOPE, 1 THESSALONIANS 5:9–10

The emphatic position of hope in the triad faith, love, and hope in v. 8 leads to the final reassurance in vv. 9–10. This reassurance differs from that in vv. 4–6a, which states that the Thessalonians are believers in good standing. Verses 9–10 ground hope in God's deed for those who believe in Jesus Christ. Paul declares, "For (ὅτι, hoti) God has destined us (ἔθετο, etheto) not for wrath (εἰς ὀργήν, eis orgēn) but for obtaining salvation (εἰς περιποίησιν σωτηρίας, eis peripoiēsin sōtērias) through our Lord Jesus Christ, who died for us (ὑπὲρ ἡμῶν, hyper hēmōn), so that whether we are awake or asleep we may live with him." This reassurance concerns the decision of God, the intention of God, and the faithfulness of God. It interprets God's action in Jesus Christ as an irrevocable step toward realizing our salvation. The reassurance has a negative and a positive component: God has not destined us for wrath; God has destined us to attain salvation. The reason for this confidence is that the Lord Jesus Christ died for us.

According to Rigaux, ἔθετο εἰς, etheto eis, has a Semitic flavor. The expression occurs in Paul only here but is found frequently in the LXX (Isa 48:7; Gen 17:5).[55] When applied to God's action toward the faithful, it means a decision—not an abstract decision to be implemented but a concrete act that determines their entire future. In 1 Thess 5:9 the decision refers to God's deed in Christ's saving death. In that act God has chosen us and destined us for salvation. Hence, the believers are οἱ σῳζόμενοι, hoi sōzomenoi (1 Cor 1:18). This comes close to the meaning of ἐκλογήν, eklogēn, in 1:4, a reference to God's choice of the Thessalonians at the moment of their accepting the gospel from Paul. In 5:9 Paul includes himself among the destined.

God has not destined believers for wrath (εἰς ὀργήν, eis orgēn). The word "wrath" here refers to the calamity depicted in vv. 2–3. In 1:10 Paul describes the Christian existence as waiting for God's Son

---

[55] See Rigaux, Thessaloniciens, 570.

from heaven, who will "rescue us from the wrath to come." That text thus discloses that God's wrath will indeed come but also that Jesus saves believers from that wrath.

Verse 1:10 indicates that wrath is a motif in Paul's missionary sermon. This motif is fully developed in Rom 1:18–32. According to 1 Thess 5:2–3, God's wrath will be poured out on those who live in darkness. But God would never change his mind and pour his wrath on those whom he has destined for salvation. In the death of his own Son for us, God has given us his eternal love. He has committed himself to us. Thus, neither the Lord, who died for us, nor the Father, who sacrificed his own Son for us, could ever go back on this saving purpose. God's love for us is irrevocable.

Paul brings this out in Rom 5:5–10, a passage that resembles 1 Thess 5:9–10 in subject matter. He reassures the Romans, "God proves his love for us in that while we still were sinners Christ died for us. Much more surely then, now that we have been justified by his blood, will we be saved through him from the wrath of God. For if while we were enemies, we were reconciled to God through the death of his Son, much more surely, having been reconciled, will we be saved by his life" (5:8–10). The same reassurance is given also in Rom 8:31–32: "If God is for us, who is against us? He who did not withhold his own Son, but gave him up for all of us, will he not with him also give us everything else?" God's giving up his own Son for us is the unsurpassable proof of God's love for us. The faithful can therefore rest assured of the Father's and the Son's love; the day of the Lord will therefore be the day of salvation for them, a day for which they have been destined by God himself. Salvation is their inheritance through Christ.

The expression περιποίησιν σωτηρίας in 1 Thess 5:9 can mean either the gaining or the possession of salvation.[56] Rigaux opts for the first meaning,[57] while Schlier sees both meanings implied. According to Schlier, God has destined us for the possession of salvation, which is our inheritance in faith, hope, and love. But God has also destined the faithful to inherit salvation in order that it may become their possession.[58]

---

[56] Ibid.; Schlier, *Apostel*, 92.
[57] Rigaux, *Thessaloniciens*, 571.
[58] Schlier, *Apostel*, 92.

With a shift in metaphorical meaning of "awake" and "asleep," Paul now indicates that both the living and the dead are destined by God for salvation (v. 10). In v. 7 the words "sleep" and "wake" are used metaphorically to express two ways of existing, one irresponsible and unprepared, the other responsible and ready for the coming of the Lord. Here, however, these words apply to the living and the dead. But vv. 1–11 do not call for this inclusion of the dead; Paul is here reaching back to 4:13–18,[59] especially to v. 17b, to make a conclusion of the entire section.[60]

The words "we may live with him" (ἅμα σὺν αὐτῷ ζήσωμεν, *hama syn autō zēsōmen*, 1 Thess 5:10) echo πάντοτε σὺν κυρίῳ ἐσόμεθα, *pantote syn kyriō esometha* in 4:17, as the exhortation to comfort one another with this assurance (v. 11) echoes 4:18. To be with the Lord is the inheritance that God has set up for us. The Easter event is thus the concrete foundation of hope set by God himself. And life with Christ forever is the divinely wrought completion of the present life "in Christ." Christian hope is raised by God through his deed in Jesus Christ, is kept alive in the present by God's placing us in Christ (1:1; 2:14; 4:8; 5:18), and is realized by God's placing us with Jesus Christ. The fulfillment is centered on being with Christ and is something very personal. By mentioning the deceased here ("whether we are asleep"), Paul allays once again the anxiety of the Thessalonians about the deceased faithful: death is no obstacle to God's carrying out his saving purpose.

The final exhortation, "Therefore comfort one another and build up each other, as indeed you are doing," in v. 11 echoes that of 4:18. It is, however, stated more broadly, befitting the conclusion for the entire passage 4:13–5:11. What the apostle has said is for the comfort of the faithful; hence, they should build up one another by sharing this comfort. And those who have been comforted must comfort one another (2 Cor 1:4). With the observation "as indeed you are doing," Paul affirms the building up of hope in the community. To build one another up in hope is to build the community of hope, love, and faith.

---

[59] Ibid.; Rigaux, *Thessaloniciens*, 572.
[60] Holtz, *1 Thessalonicher*, 182.

F. PRE-PAULINE TRADITION IN 1 THESSALONIANS 5:1–11

The pre-Pauline tradition, to the extent that it can be brought out in this passage, is most clearly visible in vv. 2–3, where Paul reminds the Thessalonians of what they already know perfectly well: "The day of the Lord will come like a thief in the night. When they say, 'There is peace and security,' then sudden destruction will come upon them, as labor pains come upon a pregnant woman, and there will be no escape!" The expression γὰρ ἀκριβῶς, οἴδατε ὅτι, *gar akribōs, oidate hoti* (v. 2) is Paul's own introduction; it is thus not part of a tradition. The content of that knowledge, however, which Paul recalls, may well be traditional. This is evident from the vocabulary employed in this section. Such expressions as "thief in the night" and "peace and security" (εἰρήνη καὶ ἀσφάλεια, *eirēnē kai asphaleia*) in conjunction with sudden destruction (αἰφνίδιος αὐτοῖς ἐφίσταται ὄλεθρος, *aiphnidios autois ephistatai olethros*), the comparison with a woman in travail, and such seldom-used words as ὠδίν, *ōdin*, ἐκφεύγω, *ekpheugō*, αἰφνίδιος, *aiphnidios*, ἡ ἡμέρα ἐκείνη, ἐφίστημι, *ephistēmi* and ἀσφάλεια, *asphaleia* indicate the presence of a tradition.[61] The cluster of these non-Pauline expressions here and the resemblance of this vocabulary to that in Luke and "Q" and elsewhere in the NT suggest the likelihood of a tradition.[62]

The expression "thief in the night" is significant. It occurs in Paul only here. The closest parallel to this expression is in 2 Pet 3:10, ἥξει δὲ ἡμέρα κυρίου ὡς κλέπτης, *hēxei de hēmera kyriou hōs kleptēs*,[63] but this text may draw either on the synoptic tradition[64]—Matt 24:43 (par Luke 12:39), which speaks of the thief's coming at night—or on 1 Thess 5:3. The latter possibility is entertained by Harnisch.[65] Other, more distant parallels, such as Rev 3:3b and *Gos. Thom.* 21, are derivatives of the synoptic tradition. Many exegetes hold that this phrase alludes to a non-Pauline tradition.[66]

---

[61] Rigaux, "Tradition," 323–25; Plevnik, "Authenticity," 81–84.

[62] For reservations about the presence of a synoptic tradition here, see Tuckett, "Synoptic Tradition," 168–76.

[63] Other parallels mentioned are Luke 12:39–40 par Matt 24:43–44 (Q); Rev 3:3, 16:15; and *Gos. Thom.*, 21b.

[64] Käsemann, "Eine Apologie," 138. Also Pesch, *Entdeckung*, 108.

[65] Harnisch, *Eschatologische Existenz*, 110–11. Harnisch suggests that both 1 Thess 5:2b and 2 Pet 3:10 draw not on a logion of Jesus but on Jewish apocalyptic.

[66] See Plevnik, "Authenticity," 81 n. 28.

Rigaux points out that in the OT this expression is never applied to the coming of Yahweh. Its use in Matt 24:43 (par Luke 12:39) for the Lord's coming may go back to Jesus himself;[67] it is, at any rate, pre-Pauline.[68]

The image of the woman with child is also traditional. It is found frequently in prophetic and Jewish apocalyptic literature, although with somewhat different meanings. Here it brings out the danger, the intense pain, the inevitability, and the suddenness of the action.[69]

According to Rigaux, ἀσφάλεια also is drawn from tradition. The closeness of this text to Luke 21:34–36 and 17:26–27, pointed out by J. B. Lightfoot and A. Plummer, suggests this.[70] Rigaux also points out that the cluster of the words ἐφίστημι, αἰφνίδιος, ἡ ἡμέρα ἐκείνη, and ἐκφεύγω occurs also in Luke 21:34, 36.[71] In addition, much of the vocabulary in 1 Thess 5:3—εἰρήνη, in the sense of security, ἀσφάλεια, αἰφνίδιος,[72] ἐφίστημι,[73] and ὠδίν[74]— is non-Pauline. It appears that both Luke and Paul draw on a common tradition.

Paul, however, does not simply take over a tradition; he also redacts it in order to make it fit the particular circumstances. Rigaux mentions here the rhetorical formula of *praeteritio*, which the apostle already employed in 4:12.[75] According to him, the word ἀκριβῶς (v. 2a) is a flattery,[76] οὕτως, *houtōs* (v. 2b) is a Pauline

---

[67] Rigaux, "Tradition," 324. The pejorative connotation of the word "thief" for the Lord's coming would tend to support Rigaux's suggestion. Harnisch (*Eschatologische Existenz*, 84–116), denies that the image goes back to Jesus. Bultmann (*Synoptic Tradition*, 171), Kümmel (*Promise and Fulfilment*, 55), and Conzelmann ("Gegenwart und Zukunft," 286) leave open the possibility that the saying goes back to Jesus.

[68] Harnisch (*Eschatologische Existenz*, 94–95) suggests that the expression derives from Jewish apocalyptic, but does not give any parallels to it (69–75).

[69] Rigaux, "Tradition," 235.

[70] Rigaux, "Tradition," 324–25. See also Plevnik, "Authenticity," 84 n. 48. The motif of "peace and security" has its equivalent in the picture language in Luke 17:27 par Matt 24:38 and in Luke 17:34–35 par Matt 24:40–41.

[71] See Hartman, *Prophecy Interpreted*, 192–93. Cf. also Plevnik, "Authenticity," 84.

[72] These two words occur only here in Pauline literature.

[73] This word occurs only here and in 2 Tim 4:2, 6.

[74] This word occurs only here in Pauline literature. Moreover, it elsewhere has the plural form.

[75] Rigaux, "Tradition," 326, where Rigaux mentions the observations made by Harnisch (*Eschatologische Existenz*, 53).

[76] According to Hartman (*Prophecy Interpreted*, 191), this phrase is common in Paul's writings. The apostle employs it to introduce well-known facts, passages from the Scriptures, or basic Christian truths. It belongs to Paul's introduction of the content and should not be treated as Paul's redaction of the tradition.

word, and ὅταν λέγουσιν, *hotan legousin* (v. 3) and καὶ οὐ μὴ ἐκφύγωσιν, *kai ou mē ekphygōsin* (v. 3) have a rhetorical tone. But 5:2a, being Paul's introduction, is scarcely a redaction of a tradition.[77] For Paul, the "day of the Lord" now applies to Christ and draws its meaning from the preceding passage, which speaks about being with the Lord forever (4:13–18).[78]

The fact that a definite cluster of words in 5:2b–3 points to Luke 21:24, 36, while another cluster of non-Pauline words echoes Luke 12:39–40, Luke 12:36–38, or Luke 12:42–46, should alert us to the possibility that there may be no single source or version of the synoptic eschatological discourse capable of explaining all the non-Pauline features in this section.[79] Paul's dependence in vocabulary and thought on the synoptic tradition is at best a loose dependence, for 1 Thess 5:2–3 indicates his own paraphrasing.[80]

The presence of synoptic tradition in vv. 4–10 is doubtful at best, since in vv. 4–6 Paul is obviously modifying the threatening character of his statement in vv. 2b–3.[81] The images of "breastplate" and "helmet" in v. 8 may be an allusion to Isa 59:17, although the apostle has creatively appropriated this imagery by transferring the weapons from God to the faithful.[82] Echoes of a tradition may, however, be present in vv. 9–10. As evidence for this, Harnisch mentions the introductory particle ὅτι (v. 9), the prepositional phrase διὰ τοῦ κυρίου ἡμῶν Ἰησοῦ Χριστοῦ, *dia tou kyriou hēmōn Iēsou Christou* (v. 9), περὶ ἡμῶν, *peri hēmōn*, and the participial construction (v. 10).[83] But περὶ ἡμῶν is textually uncertain; this prepositional phrase in v. 9 has become a commonplace in Paul and need not always indicate his direct dependence on a tradition.[84]

---

[77] So also Tuckett, "Synoptic Tradition," 174.

[78] Rigaux, "Tradition," 326. For a discussion of other solutions, see Plevnik, "Authenticity," 83–84.

[79] So Tuckett, "Synoptic Tradition," 60–82, esp. 169.

[80] That Paul was the source of Luke 21:34–36 is maintained by Aejmelaeus (*Wachen*, 99–139); Tuckett ("Synoptic Tradition," 175) is inclined to agree.

[81] See Plevnik, "Authenticity," 85–86.

[82] Ibid., 86.

[83] Harnisch, *Eschatologische Existenz*, 122–23. See Plevnik, "Authenticity," 86–87.

[84] Plevnik, "Authenticity," 86–87. The phrase διὰ τοῦ κυρίου ἡμῶν Ἰησοῦ Χριστοῦ occurs in Rom 5: 1, 11, 21, 7:25, 15:30; 1 Cor 15:57; and 1 Thess 4:2. Περί is read by א* B 33. NA[27] reads ὑπέρ on the basis of 𝔓[30] א[2] A D F G Ψ 0278 𝔐.

CONCLUSION

In 1 Thess 5:1–11 Paul sidesteps the quest for the date of the Lord's coming and thereby indicates that such knowledge is not necessary for authentic Christian existence. The moment of completion belongs to the inscrutable mystery of God. Curiosity about it may be an attempt to manipulate God and can only end in disaster. What the community must know is that to those who are not ready, the Lord will come without warning, when they least expect him, and with dire consequences. The apostle highlights the incalculable, the over-whelming, the uncontrollable, and the threatening character of the day of the Lord. He talks of a catastrophe. Instead of revealing "the times and the seasons," Paul here dispels false security.

But the apostle does not want the community to be unnecessarily anxious or discouraged about the ultimate completion. Through a play on words he gives to his warning a nuance. The talk of wrath and calamity is really meant for the outsiders, not for the community. Paul makes it clear that the community in Thessalonica is in good standing before the Lord. They do not belong to darkness; hence, they are not under this threat of disaster. He restates this several times in a variety of ways. He would not leave the congregation in fear and terror of the Lord's coming.

Yet it remains true that the day of the Lord will come suddenly and as a disaster upon the world in darkness. With a glance at the outsiders, Paul warns and exhorts the community not to be like them (5:6a). They must be vigilant and sober. He appeals to their present Christian existence and to their destiny: "Since we belong to the day, let us be sober" (v. 8). The destiny can be meaningfully awaited only in faith, love, and hope. These are necessary but also sufficient to bring their present existence to its goal. But hope is emphasized here, and the apostle grounds it anew in God's deed for us in Jesus Christ.

The ground of hope in vv. 9–10 echoes 4:14. It is not in what the faithful do but in God's deed in his Son. In the Easter event, above all in Christ's death for us, God has opened for the believer a future with his Son and a sure salvation. The Christian be with the Lord forever. This reassurance builds on the knowledge of who Christ is with respect to God.[85]

---

[85] So also Wanamaker, *1 & 2 Thessalonians*, 18.

As in 4:13–18, so also here the hope expresses the desire to be with Christ and is motivated by the love of God for humanity and by our love for Christ. Christian hope is personal—it is centered on the person of Christ, on being united with Christ. But the ultimate referent of hope is God, the Father of Jesus Christ and the giver of hope through his Son. And the ultimate ground of hope is God's love manifested in the giving of his Son.

In this way Paul first removes false security (vv. 2–3), then the insecurity of the faithful (vv. 4–5), in order to reach a synthesis of the two in his call to vigilance (vv. 6–8). The mystery of completion is thus presented to the faithful as a threat and as a promise. As a threat, the day of the Lord calls for vigilance; as a promise, the day of the Lord is the object of fervent hope.

The extensive and repeated reassurances in this passage, however, indicate that Paul's real message here is hope rather than judgment or threat. He keeps this hope alive by repeating his reassurances in this regard, assuring the community of its good standing in the Lord and of God's faithfulness to his promise of salvation. The Thessalonian community is not under judgment, as is the world outside; but it must not slip back into the world of darkness. In 3:13 and 5:23 Paul prays that the faithful be found blameless at the parousia of the Lord.

5

THE RESURRECTION AT CHRIST'S COMING, 1 CORINTHIANS 15:23–28

First Corinthians 15:23–28 is another key passage dealing with the parousia of Christ. This text occurs within the general theme of the resurrection of the dead, which governs that chapter, and is subordinated to it. Christ's coming thus does not have an independent interest here for Paul: it is appealed to in his argumentation for the resurrection of the dead at the end time. The apostle refers to the parousia in order to situate the resurrection in the unfinished history of salvation. For him the future of the present life "in Christ" is not open-ended but will be concluded at the Lord's coming, which is also the beginning of the kingdom of God.

A. THE CONTEXT

The theme of 1 Cor 15, as is commonly recognized, is the future resurrection from the dead. Yet the apostle begins his argument not with this topic but with a restatement of the gospel that he preached to the Corinthian community when he first brought the faith to them (vv. 3b–5)—the gospel of the salvific death of Christ and of his resurrection from the dead. A right understanding of this gospel includes the promise of the resurrection of the dead. In the credal formula (vv. 3b–5) the reality of Christ's death is supported by a statement about Christ's burial, and the reality of Christ's resurrection by the mention of the appearance of Christ to Peter and to the Twelve. Paul strengthens the latter by listing additional appearances of the risen Lord (vv. 6–11), then argues that denial of the resurrection of the dead necessarily implies denial of Christ's resurrection (vv. 12–19).

In vv. 20–22 the apostle affirms the resurrection of Christ together with its power of giving life.[1] He states, "But in fact Christ has been raised from the dead, the first fruits of those who have died. . . . For as all die in Adam, so all will be made alive in Christ." Christ's resurrection thus has a universal effect: in its wake all will be brought to life, just as in the wake of Adam all have tasted death.

Then come vv. 23–28, the subject of this investigation. The apostle points out a sequence in the implementation of the resurrection: "But each in his own order: Christ the first fruits, then, at his coming (ἐν τῇ παρουσίᾳ αὐτοῦ, *en tē parousia autou*), those who belong to him" (v. 23). The resurrection of the faithful, accordingly, does not occur until the coming of Christ. The parousia, expected in the end time, is mentioned here not for its own sake but as a referent for the resurrection; it anchors the latter in the end-time drama. In vv. 24–28 the apostle then explains in a parenthetical fashion why this must be so: Christ's reign is not completed until all powers hostile to God, including the power of death, are annihilated. The passage ends with the presentation of the ultimate goal, the kingdom of God, when God will be "all in all" (v. 28).

In vv. 29–34, Paul once again brings out the necessity of belief and hope in the resurrection of the dead, making, even more than in vv. 12–19, an ad hominem argument.[2] He points out the futility of faith if there is no resurrection from the dead: the Corinthians' acceptance of baptism on behalf of the dead becomes a contradiction, while his own preaching of the gospel at such cost to himself becomes nonsense. With no resurrection to live for, only one thing matters: to live for the day. Beginning with v. 35 the apostle explains that the resurrection is not a return to the present mortal body.

Verses 23–28 are thus flanked by Paul's arguments for the resurrection of the dead. Verse 23 mentions the resurrection and the parousia—more precisely, the resurrection at the parousia—

---

[1] Here Paul supplies the salvific purpose of Christ's resurrection, which the credal formula in vv. 3b–5 did not make explicit.

[2] The ad hominem character of this section is brought out by Fee, *1 Corinthians*, 760–75.

but vv. 24–28 do not seem to deal with the resurrection, for they do
not mention it. On closer examination, however, vv. 24–28 reveal
why the resurrection has not yet taken place (v. 23): the power of
death has not yet been conquered. The conquest of death is the
effect and the meaning of the general resurrection. In vv. 54–55 the
apostle states that the power of death will finally be broken with
the resurrection/transformation, expected at the coming of the
Lord in the end time—"at the last trumpet."[3] And this links the
conquest of death with the resurrection of the dead and with the
parousia of Christ. It is part of the comprehensive victory of
Christ. The text states that Christ's rule[4] implies the subjugation of
all powers hostile to God. Death, presented here as a power hostile
to God and as the ultimate enemy to Christ's rule, must also be
subjugated. Christ must subjugate death. Thus, in vv. 24–28 Paul
does talk about the resurrection of the dead—as the conquest of
death. The resurrection of the dead implies the conquest of death,
and the conquest of death implies the resurrection of the dead.
The apostle employs here the imagery suggested by Ps 110:1: he
speaks in terms of conflict and subjugation.

Why, precisely, some Corinthians deny the resurrection of
the dead is not stated by Paul and can only be guessed from his own
response in this chapter.[5] It is evident, however, that the apostle
regards the resurrection of the dead as an essential component of the Easter faith. In his answer he affirms the reality
of the general resurrection (vv. 12–22), the not-yet of the
resurrection (vv. 23–28), and the transformation of the body
(vv. 50–55). The last two affirmations remove the mistaken notions

---

[3]The full conquest of death entails the bestowal of eternal life in the body,
which includes the resurrection of the dead and the transformation of the living.
According to Paul, all of this would happen in an instant.

[4]For Paul, Christ's rule is a present reality; see Phil 2:9–11.

[5]On the various positions in this regard, see Sellin, *Streit*, 261–69. According
to Sellin, there are basically two solutions offered by the exegetes:

1. Christ's resurrection is still an exception. Against the enthusiasts, Paul states in
   v. 23 that the resurrection of the Christians will not take place until Christ's
   parousia: Kümmel (*Korinther I/II*, 192–94); Käsemann ("Primitive Christian
   Apocalyptic," 118–33); Güttgemanns (*Apostel*, 67–68); Becker (*Auferstehung*,
   74–82); Wilcke (*Zwischenreich*, 60–62); Robinson and Koester (*Trajectories*, 30–34).

2. There is a necessary link between Christ's resurrection and the resurrection of
   the faithful: Luz (*Geschichtsverständnis*, 332–37). In vv. 24–28 Paul gives a time
   limit to Christ's subjugation of powers. But see Lambrecht, "Christological Use,"
   505–11; Doughty, "Salvation in Corinth," 80–85.

that the resurrection has already taken place in the resurrection of Christ and that the resurrection means a return to the present body. Our text, vv. 23–28, deals with the reason for the not-yet of the general resurrection.

The clue to the nature of the Corinthians' difficulty[6] may well be in Paul's explanation from v. 35 on, that the resurrection of the dead implies a different body from the present one.[7] The apostle is emphasizing the spiritual nature of the risen body, conformity with the heavenly man, and total freedom from death. He talks of the immortality and incorruptibility of the transformed body. In our section, vv. 23–28, however, Paul is still talking about the reality of the resurrection; he is emphasizing Christ's conquest of death. The point he makes here is that the completion is not until after the last enemy, death, is conquered. This is the saving implication of Christ's resurrection.

B. THE MARKS OF THE END

Verses 23–28 belong together, as the sequence ἀπαρχή, *aparchē,* ἔπειτα, *epeita,* and εἶτα, *eita,* suggests, although we may posit a small pause between vv. 23 and 24,[8] since εἶτα does not indicate another, later event or another phase between the resurrection and the completion but, rather, the beginning of the completion (τέλος, *telos*). In v. 23 Paul, having just stated that "all will be made alive in Christ" (v. 22), separates the resurrection of Christ and the resurrection of the rest, asserting, "But each in his own order: Christ the

---

[6] Schmithals (*Gnosticism in Corinth,* 148–50) suggested that the Corinthians were infected with a Gnostic belief. Schmithals's hypothesis, however, did not receive scholarly consensus. According to Lietzmann (Kümmel, *Korinther I/II,* 79) and Cerfaux (*Christ,* 77), the immortality of the soul, held by the Corinthians, made the resurrection unnecessary or undesirable. But as Conzelmann (*1 Corinthians,* 261) points out, Paul is emphasizing not the resurrection of the body but the fact of the resurrection and of the transformation of the present body.

[7] See Fee, *1 Corinthians,* 741.

[8] This view is held by Schnackenburg (*God's Rule,* 292–94), Allo (*1 Corinthiens,* 40), Guntermann (*Eschatologie,* 314), Kümmel (*Korinther I/II,* 193), Héring (*1 Corinthiens,* 140), and Barrett (*1 Corinthians,* 356). See Luz, *Geschichtsverständnis,* 364. On the link between v. 23 and vv. 24–28, see Lambrecht, "Structure," 145–46. Lambrecht points out that the sequence ἀπαρχή, ἔπειτα, and εἶτα bridges vv. 23 and 24, that the two ὅταν, *hotan,* clauses clarify τὸ τέλος, *to telos* (v. 24), and that v. 28 returns to the τέλος idea; γάρ in v. 25 begins the explanation of what the kingdom involves.

first fruits, then at his coming those who belong to Christ." Verses 24–28, explaining what is involved in the completion, supply the reason why the resurrection of the rest does not occur until the coming of Christ: "Then (εἶτα) comes the end, when he hands over the kingdom to God the Father. . . . For he must destroy every ruler. . . . The last enemy to be destroyed is death." The kingdom of Christ, as v. 26 indicates, is not over until Christ annihilates death.

The annihilation of death is here a metaphor for the resurrection of the dead and is associated with the parousia of Christ (vv. 54–55). Hence, the completion includes the resurrection of the dead. Verse 24 associates the completion with the conclusion of Christ's reign, with Christ's handing over the kingdom to the Father after he has subjugated all enemy powers. Verse 28 concludes by identifying the completion with the onset of the kingdom of God. Verses 25–27 point out that the subjugation of enemy powers must include the subjugation of death. Death is the ultimate power. This indicates that vv. 24–28 form, in a way, a unit by itself and that these verses, after all, deal with the resurrection of the dead mentioned in v. 23.[9]

The difficulty in interpreting this sequence in vv. 23–24 concerns the meaning of εἶτα in v. 24: does it mean "afterwards," as in vv. 5 and 7, or "then"? In vv. 5 and 7 εἶτα is employed in the enumeration of the resurrection appearances and brings out the repetition of appearances of the risen Jesus. Every item enumerated here is an event of the same kind. In vv. 23–24, however, the enumeration occurs only in the first two instances—the resurrection of Christ, presented as the ἀπαρχή, and the resurrection of the faithful—which are clearly separated by ἔπειτα; the "order" (τάγμα, tagma) of the resurrection thus extends only to these two events. The εἶτα that links τὸ τέλος[10] to the second event does not add another, third instance of the same—it does not imply that after those who belong to Christ have been raised, the "rest" would be raised—but, rather, terminates the sequence.[11] This εἶτα introduces a comment on the

---

[9] On the chiastic structure of vv. 24–28, see Hill, "Christ's Kingdom," 299. See also Lambrecht, "Structure," 504 n. 10.

[10] Lietzmann (Korinther I/II, 80) tries to interpret τὸ τέλος as "the rest." But Luz (Geschichtsverständnis, 339) points out that no Greek dictionary lists such a meaning for τὸ τέλος. Cf. Sellin, Streit, 272.

[11] According to the dictionaries, εἶτα does not always denote a true temporal succession but is also used in enumeration when two or more things are juxtaposed, with only a blurred awareness of a time sequence. According to Liddell and

second phase of the resurrection; it emphasizes that the completion
will not come until the resurrection of the faithful.[12] Only the
context can disclose whether τὸ τέλος[13] comes after or at the same
time as the resurrection of the dead.

In what follows, the completion is associated with the moment
"when he [Christ] hands over the kingdom to God the Father," and
it presupposes the destruction "of every ruler and every authority
and power," including death. This moment is associated with the
culmination of the reign of Christ. The assertion in v. 25, "He must
reign until he has put all his enemies under his feet," depicts this
event as the subjugation of the enemies of Christ. It implies that
this is also the purpose of the present reign of Christ—that this
purpose is not achieved until all this takes place.[14] Verse 26 then
singles out the ultimate enemy: "The last enemy to be destroyed is
death." Thus, the end and the culmination of the reign of Christ
coincide with the destruction of the last enemy—death.[15]

The language employed here is therefore about the reign of
Christ, the powers, the conflict, the subjugation, and the annihilation. It contains war imagery, probably in association with Ps 110:1,
alluded to in v. 25. This psalm is here interpreted by Paul metaphorically from a christological perspective. It interprets the reign of
Christ (βασιλεύειν, basileuein), mentioned in v. 24 (βασιλείαν,
basileian), as an active enforcement of Christ's rule over the powers
in the cosmos, as an ongoing conflict in which Christ is subjugating
and annihilating these powers. In v. 26 Paul points out that this
includes the subjugation of death. The last act required of the reign
of Christ is the annihilation of the ultimate enemy, death. But what

---

Scott, Lexicon, εἶτα can also mean "and so" or "accordingly," although this is
usually found in questions or in exclamations of surprise or indignation. Cf. Hill,
"Christ's Kingdom," 308.

[12] In verse 24c, the phrase ὅταν καταργήσῃ, hotan katargēsē (aorist) has a future
perfect meaning: Christ will deliver his kingdom when he will have destroyed all
his enemies. Cf. Lambrecht, "Structure," 146.

[13] The expression τὸ τέλος is best taken as "the end." Lietzmann's (Kümmel,
Korinther I/II, 80) interpretation of τὸ τέλος as "the rest" lacks support in Greek
usage; see Hill, "Christ's Kingdom," 308–10.

[14] On the present reign of Christ, see Hill, "Christ's Kingdom," 313–14.

[15] Kreitzer (Jesus and God, 139), however, insists, on the basis of 4 Ezra and
2 Bar., that the messianic reign precedes the eternal age. But these traditions are
later than 1 Cor. Besides, in this explanation, 1 Cor 15:23–28 becomes anticlimactic.
In vv. 54–55 Paul associates the annihilation of death with the resurrection of the
dead and the parousia.

is this reign of Christ that is to culminate in the destruction of
death? And what does this last act, singled out here by Paul, mean
in our context?

The reign of Christ is, for Paul, the reign of the risen Lord. The
beginning of that reign is the resurrection and exaltation of Christ.
The credal formula in Rom 1:3–4 clearly shows that the resurrection
was the moment when Christ became the Son of God "in power" (cf.
Phil 2:9–11). And Phil 3:21 brings out that at his parousia Christ
"will transform the body of our humiliation that it may be conformed to the body of his glory by the power that also enables him
to make all things subject to him." This passage in Philippians is
important in that it clearly affirms that Christ is subjugating
everything to himself. It also affirms, as does 1 Cor 15:35–57, the
transformation of our lowly earthly condition. Christ's subjugation
of the hostile powers and his raising of the dead are thus part of
Paul's understanding of the lordship of the risen Christ.

Paul regards the resurrection/transformation as victory over
death. In 1 Cor 15:54–55, having resumed the discussion of the
parousia and the resurrection, the apostle exclaims, "When this
perishable body puts on imperishability, and this mortal body puts
on immortality, then the saying that is written will be fulfilled:
'Death has been swallowed up in victory. Where, O death, is your
victory? Where, O death, is your sting?' " Paul is talking about the
transformation of the body at the coming of Christ, when the dead
will be raised and all believers will be changed. It will entail a
change from mortality to immortality and from corruptibility to
incorruptibility. This is not something accidental but is required for
entry into the kingdom of God, for only the body that has shed its
mortality and corruptibility is fitting for the kingdom of God (v. 50).
In the kingdom of God there is no place for death or dying.[16]

All this discloses that Paul understands the conquest of death
to take place at the resurrection of the dead, when the dead rise
imperishable and mortals put on immortality. The annihilation of
death is but a metaphor for the resurrection of the dead and the
transformation. In vv. 24–28 Paul speaks of the annihilation of
death[17] as the ultimate conquest of Christ the king, while in vv. 50–55

---

[16] Paul is here in agreement with Jewish apocalyptic, although he presents the
annihilation of death in stronger terms and ascribes it to Christ.

[17] The personification of death has the function of a universal statement: there
will be no more dying, and the dead will be brought to life again. Cf. Sellin, *Streit*, 275.

he focuses on the effect of the resurrection/transformation at the Lord's coming: endowment with immortality and incorruptibility. In both texts he asserts the necessity of the destruction of death (vv. 25–26, 50) before the onset of the kingdom of God.

Thus, the interpretation that would posit a period of time between the resurrection of the faithful and the completion is not supported by the context of 1 Cor 15. The culmination of Christ's reign is envisaged here as the destruction of death and as the resurrection/transformation, both expected to occur at Christ's coming in the end time. The parousia and the completion coincide.[18]

Moreover, there is no hard evidence that Paul spoke of a millennial reign of Christ after the resurrection of the faithful.[19] The imposition of this schema here would place the climax not on the resurrection of the dead, which is the theme of the entire ch. 15, but in a subsequent act of the risen Christ directed against death. But what would this annihilation of death then be? We have seen that vv. 54–55 associate the annihilation of death, presented as the ultimate act of the risen Christ, with the resurrection/transformation in the end time.

The conclusion of Christ's reign is thus at the resurrection/transformation in the end time. But the beginning of Christ's reign, according to Phil 2:9–11, has taken place at the exaltation of Christ: "Therefore God . . . gave him the name which is above every other name, so that at the name of Jesus every knee should bend . . . and every tongue confess that Jesus is Lord." The implication is that Christ has begun to reign with his resurrection from the dead (Rom 8:34; cf. 1 Pet 3:22). Col 1:13 and Eph 1:20 also indicate the existence of a tradition about Christ's present reign, although the word "reign" is not used. If this is so, then there is no need to posit here successive apocalyptic periods.[20]

---

[18] So also Carrez, "Résurrection," 132.

[19] Wilcke, *Zwischenreich,* 156. The millennial reign is documented only in 4 Ezra, *2 Bar.,* and Rev. In Rev. it is related to the privileged status of Christian martyrs: these will be raised and will reign with the Messiah. Cf. also Hill, "Christ's Kingdom," 312.

[20] Luz (*Geschichtsverständnis,* 347), who maintains that τὸ τέλος implies a third period, suggests that the kingdom of Christ begins with the resurrection of the dead and culminates in the annihilation of death. But what would be the function of death during the kingdom of Christ, when all the dead have been raised and the living have been transformed (1 Cor 15:55–56)?

C. THE END

What the end, associated with the Lord's coming, entails is then stated in two parallel clauses in v. 24, each beginning with ὅταν, hotan: "When (ὅταν) he hands over (παραδιδῷ, paradidō)[21] the kingdom to God the Father, when (ὅταν) he has destroyed (καταργήσῃ, katagēsē) every ruler and every authority and power."[22] Verse 25 then gives the reason (γάρ) for this condition: Christ has to (δεῖ, dei) rule "until he has put all his enemies under his feet," while v. 26 points out that death is the last enemy to be destroyed. Accordingly, Christ has to rule until he has conquered death. And v. 27 then supplies the reason (γάρ) for the conquest of death: "For (γάρ) God has placed all things in subjection under his feet."

The rest of v. 27 is an apologetic aside. It removes a possible wrong implication of this understanding of Christ's rule: "It is plain that this does not include the one who subjected all things under him"—it does not mean that God thereby became subject to Christ! In v. 28 Paul recapitulates the thought in vv. 26–27 and brings it to a resounding finale: "When all things are subjected to him, then the Son himself will also be subjected to him who put all things in subjection under him, so that God may be all in all (πάντα ἐν πᾶσιν, panta en pasin)."[23]

The difficulty here is in determining the subject of θῇ, thē (v. 25) and ὑπέταξεν, hypetaxen (v. 27a), the two verbs in parallel statements that appear to be scriptural quotations or allusions. Is the subject the same for both? Is the subject God, inferred retrospectively from the quotation of Ps 8:7 in v. 27a? Is the subject Christ, as in v. 24? Or is there a shift in the subject between v. 25 and v. 27a?

Those who argue that the subject is the same in both statements take v. 25 (ἄχρι . . . αὐτοῦ, achri . . . autou) to be a quotation

---

[21] The United Bible Societies edition of *The Greek New Testament* and Nestle-Aland, *Novum Testamentum*, have παραδιδῷ, attested by 𝔓⁴⁶ ℵ A (b) D (F G) Ψ etc.; παραδῷ in contrast, is attested only by 𝔐 latt; Epiph.

[22] The RSV has, "after he has destroyed," suggesting a temporal or logical priority of this act of Christ to the consummation of his rule. Cf. Luz, *Geschichtsverständnis*, 240 n. 8.

[23] The apostle here makes a play on words, using the verb "to subject" (ὑποτάσσω, hypotassō) with different meanings. For another play on words, see 1 Thess 5:4–6, 10.

of LXX Ps 109:1, and v. 27a as a quotation from Ps 8:7.[24] The function of Ps 8:7 here is to give support for the word πάντας, *pantas,* in v. 25, which is inserted into the quotation of Ps 110:1. The identical ending ὑπὸ τοὺς πόδας αὐτοῦ, *hypo tous podas autou,* found in vv. 25 and 27, indicates that the apostle regarded the two quotations as expressing the same thought. Since the subject in v. 27 is clearly God, then the subject in v. 25 must also be God.[25] But v. 25 contains at best a compound quotation, a mixture of LXX Pss 109:1 and 8:7: ἄχρι οὗ θῇ πάντας τοὺς ἐχθροὺς ὑπὸ τοὺς πόδας αὐτοῦ.[26] The text is not clearly marked as a quotation[27] and shows many changes dictated by the present context. It appears to be an allusion rather than a quotation[28] and as such alludes to two texts and anticipates ὑπο τοὺς πόδας αὐτοῦ in v. 27a, which is an

---

[24]Maier, "Ps 110,1." According to Maier, Paul here quotes Pss 109:1 and 8:7 as two well-known proof texts, interpreting them in the same way. Ps 8:7 was anticipated in v. 25.

[25]Ibid., 155–56.

[26]LXX Ps 8:7 states, πάντα ὑπέτα-ξας ὑποκάτω τῶν ποδῶν αὐτοῦ but 1 Cor 15:25 has, ἄχρι οὗ θῇ πάντας τοὺς ἐχθροὺς ὑπὸ τοὺς πόδας αὐτου

LXX Ps 109:1 reads, ἕως ἂν θῶ τοὺς ἐχθρούς σου ὑποπόδιον τῶν ποδῶν σου and 1 Cor 15:27a affirms, πάντα γὰρ ὑπέταξεν ὑπὸ τοὺς πόδας αὐτοῦ

If 1 Cor 15:25 quotes LXX Ps 109:1, then Paul has: (1) replaced ἕως ἂν with ἄχρι οὗ; (2) changed θῶ (aorist subjunctive, first person singular) to θῇ (aorist subjunctive, third person singular); (3) inserted πάντας; (4) deleted σου after ἐχθρούς; (5) replaced ὑποπόδιον τῶν ποδῶν σου with ὑπὸ τοὺς πόδας αὐτου, in agreement with 1 Cor 15:27a and in partial agreement with Ps 8:7.

The word πάντας (3) is clearly Paul's ad hoc addition, in agreement with the two πᾶσαν in v. 24 (and with πάντα in v. 27a, which agrees with Ps 8:7); and the fifth change appears to be his ad hoc adjustment to v. 27a. In view of these changes it is better to speak here of an allusion rather than a quotation.

If 1 Cor 15:27a quotes LXX Ps 8:7, then Paul has: (1) added γάρ; (2) changed ὑπέταξας (aorist indicative, third person singular); (3) changed ὑποκάτω to ὑπό, with the requisite adjustment to the following words.

These changes are minor compared with those in v. 25.

[27]According to Maier ("Ps 110,1," 139 n. 3), γὰρ may be taken as a possible introduction of a quotation, as in 1 Cor 2:16; 10:5, 26; 2 Cor 9:7; and Rom 10:13; but see Lambrecht, "Christological Use," 522 n. 46. In the examples accepted by Lambrecht, γὰρ is each time inserted into the quotation, while in 1 Cor 15:25 it is removed from the text.

[28]Lambrecht, "Christological Use," 522.

adaptation of LXX Ps 8:7. The last four words of the two texts are identical; in addition, there is a partial agreement between the emphatic πάντας and πάντα. Here Ps 109:1 is paraphrased and adapted to the context. To a lesser extent, this holds true also for Ps 8:7.

In LXX Ps 109:1 it is the Lord God, the Κύριος, who speaks to the κύριος, the king, and subjects everything to him. According to Ps 8:7, God subjects everything to man (Adam). But in 1 Cor 15:25 Paul transposes direct speech into indirect speech, changing thereby θῷ to θῇ and σου to αὐτοῦ. In addition, he replaces ἕως ἄν with ἄχρι οὗ and inserts πάντας (perhaps from LXX Ps 8:7). As a result, there is here barely an echo of Ps 109:1. The second half—ὑπὸ τοὺς πόδας αὐτοῦ—may echo Ps 8:7 (the Hebrew text).[29] The apostle repeats these four words in v. 27a, to affirm again, πάντα γὰρ ὑπέταξεν ὑπὸ τοὺς πόδας αὐτοῦ.[30]

These changes indicate that Paul is here formulating rather freely. Although he alludes to the Scriptures,[31] he integrates these references in his thought in vv. 24–25. The smooth continuity between vv. 24 and 25, but above all the clause δεῖ γὰρ αὐτὸν βασιλεύειν, *dei gar auton basileuein*, suggests that the subject here is Christ: he is the one who delivers (παραδιδῷ) the kingdom to God the Father, he has destroyed (καταργήσῃ)[32] every rule, he is the one who reigns (βασιλεύειν).[33] The latter verb, especially, calls for Christ as the subject. The reader would naturally assume that Christ is the subject of θῇ and that "under his feet" here refers to Christ's feet.[34]

A more explicit allusion to Ps 8:7[35] in v. 27 is indicated by ὅταν δὲ εἴπῃ, *hotan de eipē*,[36] which follows the quotation and

---

[29] The Hebrew text here is תַּחַת-רַגְלָיו, *taḥat raglāyw*.

[30] With the exception of γάρ, all the words here are from a quotation.

[31] Lambrecht, "Christological Use," 506–7. See also Hill, "Christ's Kingdom," 312. On the pre-Pauline use of these psalms, see Callan, "Psalm 110:1," 624–26.

[32] The verb flanks our text, for it comes up again in v. 26 (καταργεῖται, *katargeitai*).

[33] Conzelmann, *1 Corinthians*, 273.

[34] According to Maier ("Ps 110,1," 139–56) and Aono (*Entwicklung*, 26–28), God is the subject of θῇ in 1 Cor 15:25. Luz (*Geschichtsverständnis*, 340, 344) posits behind Paul's references to Pss 110:1 and 8:7 a liturgical tradition that affirmed the victory over the enemy powers at Christ's resurrection/exaltation. But see Lambrecht, "Christological Use," 508.

[35] This is not introduced as a scriptural quotation, in contrast to 1 Cor 1:19, 31; 2:2; 3:19, 20; 9:9; 10:7; 14:21; and 15:45, 54–55. Examples of implicit quotations in 1 Cor occur in 2:16, 5:13, 6:16, 10:26, and 15:32.

[36] Lambrecht ("Christological Use," 510) brings out the likelihood that ὅταν

takes up the word ὑπέταξεν. Yet v. 27a is not an exact quotation of Ps 8:7, and ὅταν δὲ εἴπη most likely refers to a future perfect affirmation, with Christ as the subject;[37] the subject of ὑπέταξεν in v. 27a appears to be Christ, as in the preceding affirmations,[38] although many exegetes hold that the subject here is God.[39] The allusions in vv. 25 and 27a seem to interpret each other,[40] as is indicated by their fusion.[41] Here it is Christ who subjects everything to himself. In fact, the reservation in v. 27bc can only be understood if Christ is the subject in v. 27a: only then is it necessary to hedge the statement in v. 27a by explaining that this does not mean that God becomes subject to Christ, to whom he had subjected everything.[42]

In the subsequent explanation of this statement in v. 27bc,[43] however, Paul employs the same verb (ὑποτάσσω, hypotassō) in order to make it clear that it is really God who is subjugating everything to Christ. Here God is indeed the subject of ὑποτάξαν-τος, hypotaxantos, and ὑποτάξαντι, hypotaxanti. The apostle's thought has shifted, much as in 1 Thess 4:14.[44] Thus, although it is true that Christ must put all things under his own feet, it is also true that it is God who puts all things under Christ's feet. In v. 28 Paul again affirms that God is the one who is subjugating everything to Christ and that ultimately the Son himself will submit to God "so that God may be all in all." The ultimate

εἴπη with its future meaning has Christ as subject: "When Christ shall have said: all things are subjected (to me)."

[37] Morissette, "Psaume VIII,7b," 323 n. 8; also Lambrecht, "Christological Use," 510. Luz (Geschichtsverständnis, 340), however, understands this as "Wenn es heisst" ("When it is said").

[38] Conzelmann, 1 Corinthians, 273; Ellis, Paul's Use, 104–5; Lambrecht, "Christological Use," 510. For further literature, see ibid., 522 n. 49.

[39] See Lambrecht, "Christological Use," 522 n. 48. Lately, Kreitzer (Jesus and God, 150) argues that while in 1 Cor 15:24c, 25b Christ is the subject, in v. 27a the subject is God, in parallelism with v. 28. But this ignores the transitional nature of verse 27b and the shift in v. 27c.

[40] Hay, Glory, 37 n. 19.

[41] Maier, "Ps 110,1," 139–56.

[42] With God as the subject in 1 Cor 15:27a, such a reservation is scarcely necessary. For an argumentation in favor of Christ being the subject in 1 Cor 15:27a, see Lambrecht, "Christological Use," 510–11.

[43] "But when it says, 'All things are in subjection,' it is plain that this does not include the one who put all things in subjection under him."

[44] In 1 Thess 4:14 Paul first states that Christ "rose from the dead," and then that "God raised him from the dead."

completion is God himself; Christ's reign is meant to bring about the kingdom of God and the sovereignty of God.

The passage thus first focuses on the activity of Christ before the end, then on God's activity through Christ, and then on the kingdom of God as the ultimate goal. That Christ has been given all authority and that he shall come in that power is also clear from Phil 3:21 (cf. also Matt 28:19; Luke 22:29, 69).

Hence, the Father's and the Son's actions are not separated. The Son does not act independently of the Father but, rather, in the power the Father gave him. As God is subjugating all things to Christ, establishing the dominion of Christ, Christ is destroying all powers that are hostile to God, thus establishing the dominion of God. This reign of Christ is reflected in the Scriptures—in God's plan of creation that man subjugate all things in the world, and in God's plan that his Messiah bring everything to God. The two scriptural texts are here interpreted in light of the Easter event and in its implication for his future coming. Psalm 109:1 supplies the imagery of contest and conflict: just as God subjugates to the king all his enemies, making him Lord, so also God subjugates to his Son all the hostile powers in the world. The point that Paul makes here is that even death is subject to the sovereign power of the risen Christ, for Christ's resurrection carries within it the power and the promise of life for all (vv. 20–22). God raised Christ to life and thereby made him the bringer of life to all.

The present situation, however, is not yet the completion. The resurrection of Christ lies in the past, while the resurrection of the faithful is yet to come, at Christ's parousia. It will be then, at the resurrection wrought at Christ's coming, that death will be finally annihilated: there will be no more dying, and those who have died will be raised to life. For there is no place for death and dying in the kingdom of God (v. 50).

Then only will the commission entrusted to the Son be fulfilled. Then he will hand over to the Father the power that he received to carry out this purpose. Then he will have brought to the Father all things, the renewed creation, but above all those who belong to him by faith. And then God will become all things in all: the fullness of God will fill everyone and everything, and the whole creation will be fully alive to God forever.

D. THE POWERS

According to v. 24, Christ will have destroyed "every ruler and every authority and power"[45] before he hands over his reign to the Father. The context makes it clear that rulers, authorities, and powers here are hostile, for according to v. 26 death, an enemy power, is to be annihilated together with these powers. The hostility of these powers is also indicated by the allusion to LXX Ps 109:1. According to the psalm, God has subjected to the king all his enemies: "The Lord said to my Lord, 'Sit on my right hand, until I make your enemies your footstool . . . rule in the midst of your enemies' " (vv. 1–3). According to vv. 5–6, the enemies are the nations and kings: "The Lord at your right hand has dashed in pieces kings in the day of his wrath. He shall judge among the nations."[46]

But in 1 Cor 15:24 the enemy powers are not kings but cosmic forces. Their subjugation by Christ occurs during his reign and is to be completed at his coming.[47] This antagonistic motif here is linked to Paul's Christology and eschatology. The apostle understands Christ's lordship in the wake of the resurrection and exaltation to entail the subjugation of certain superhuman powers responsible for the present disorder in the cosmos.[48]

M. de Boer has brought out that OT depictions of the day of the Lord include punishment of the hosts of heaven and of the kings of the earth. According to Isa 24:21–22:

On that day the Lord will punish
the hosts of heaven in heaven,

---

[45] In Eph 1:21 are mentioned the same three powers and, in addition, the κυριότης, kyriotēs, and the ὄνομα, onoma. But this text refers to the exaltation of Christ at his resurrection. Here as well, it is God who has raised Christ from the dead and exalted him. And here also occurs the phrase πάντα ὑπέταξεν ὑπὸ τοὺς πόδας αὐτοῦ. A similar depiction occurs also in 1 Pet 3:22. For a different interpretation of Eph 1:21, see Black, "ἐξουσίαι," 74.

[46] This is alluded to in a variety of contexts in Mark, Acts, the Pauline epistles, Heb, and 1 Pet. According to Black ("ἐξουσίαι," 79–82), the psalm provides the "sub-structure of a fundamental piece of Christian doctrine, the session of Christ at God's right hand and the prediction of the parousia."

[47] Perhaps it is for these reasons that Paul alludes only to the portion ἕως ἂν θῶ τοὺς ἐχθρούς σου ὑποπόδιον τῶν ποδῶν σου. Does δεῖ γὰρ αὐτὸν βασιλεύειν, dei gar auton basileuein, in 1 Cor 15:25 paraphrase Κάθου ἐκ δεξιῶν μου, Kathou ek dexiōn mou, in Ps 109:1?

[48] Baumgarten (Apokalyptik, 157–58) speaks here of a diminished transcendence of God.

and on earth the kings of the earth.
They will be gathered together like prisoners in a pit;
they will be shut up in a prison,
and after many days they will be punished.

References to this occur also in 1 Enoch 1:5, 6:1–10:17, and
21:1–10, which speak of the angels who have brought corruption
into the world. But why does the apostle here associate death
with them?

The words ἀρχή, archē,[49] and δύναμις, dynamis,[50] are employed
in Rom 8:38, where Paul asserts, "For I am convinced that neither
death, nor life, nor angels, nor rulers (ἀρχαί, archai), nor things
present, nor things to come, nor powers (δυνάμεις, dynameis), nor
height, nor depth . . . will be able to separate us from the love of
God in Christ Jesus our Lord." But not every pair mentioned here
refers to a personified power.[51] Angels, rulers, and powers are
mentioned together with certain conditions affecting human existence, such as life, death, things present, things to come, height,
and depth. But death here is no more personified than life. All
these factors in human life may be an obstacle to the relationship
between Christ and the faithful. But Paul asserts that Christ's love
for us will not be thwarted by any created power in the cosmos.
The word ἐξουσία, exousia, is employed for a personified power
only here in Pauline letters.[52]

The best parallels to the trio of powers mentioned in 1 Cor
15:24 occur in Ephesians and Colossians. In Eph 1:21 God seats
Christ at his right hand in heavenly places, "far above all rule and
authority and power and dominion, and above every name that is
named." The text depicts the exalted Christ's peaceful reign in
heaven. But 2:2 speaks of the ruler of the power of the air (τὸν
ἄρχοντα τῆς ἐξουσίας τοῦ ἀέρος, ton archonta tēs exousias tou

---

[49]The same meaning of ἀρχή is found also in Eph 1:21, 3:10, 6:12; Col 1:16,
2:10, 15; and Titus 3:1. A related term is ἄρχων, archōn. Both Paul and John use it
in the sense of the leader of this world (1 Cor 2:6; Eph 2:2; John 12:31; 14:30; 16:11).

[50]The term δύναμις, employed in the sense of personified power, occurs in the
letters commonly attributed to Paul only in 1 Cor 15:24 and Rom 8:38; it is also
found, however, in Eph 1:21 and 1 Pet 3:22.

[51]Here we find the following contrasting pairs: death–life, things present–
things to come, and height–depth. Personification is only weakly present in the first
pair.

[52]It also occurs, however, in Eph 1:21, 2:2, 3:10, 6:12; Col 1:16, 2:10, 15; Titus
3:1; and 1 Pet 3:22.

aeros), a spiritual (τοῦ πνεύματος, *tou pneumatos*) power now at work among the unbelievers. The spiritual nature and hostility of these powers is emphasized in 6:12, where the author exhorts the community to put on the armor of God so that they may "stand against the wiles of the devil. For our struggle is not against enemies of blood and flesh, but against the rulers (ἀρχάς, *archas*), against the authorities (ἐξουσίας, *exousias*), against the cosmic powers of this present darkness, against the spiritual forces of evil in the heavenly places." Ephesians thus affirms Christ's superiority over all the powers in creation, especially over the spiritual powers associated with Satan. There is an ongoing struggle of the faithful against spiritual forces of evil.

A similar picture is portrayed in Colossians. Colossians 1:16 acclaims Christ as the firstborn of all creation. In Christ "were created all things in heaven and on earth . . . whether thrones or dominions or rulers or powers." In 2:10 Christ is said to be "the head of every power and authority," including the elemental spirits of the universe, which are still seducing people of the world. And in 2:15 the author reminds the community that God has "disarmed the rulers and authorities, and made a public example of them."[53] In 1 Pet 3:22 the author mentions the resurrection and exaltation of Christ, "who has gone into heaven and is at the right hand of God with angels, authorities, and powers made subject to him." Revelation 11:18 associates the destruction of destroyers, of Satan and his associates, with the beginning of the reign of God. The twenty-four elders praise God for having taken up his power and "for destroying those who destroy (διαφθείροντας, *diaphtheirontas*) the earth."

Thus, this cluster of words occurs in the early church tradition in connection with the (cross and) exaltation of Christ.[54] This agrees with Phil 2:11, which situates the exaltation of Christ at his resurrection.

Pauline tradition, therefore, knows of hostile powers. This may explain why in 1 Cor 15:24–28 Paul depicts the risen Christ's rule in

---

[53] According to 1 Pet 3:22, at his resurrection Christ "has gone into heaven and is at the right hand of God with angels, authorities, and powers made subject to him."

[54] Luz (*Geschichtsverständnis*, 347–48), positing the reign of Christ after the parousia, denies that 1 Cor 15:24 implies the present reign of the exalted Lord. According to him, 1 Cor 15:24 represents the period from the Hellenistic acclamation of Christ's exaltation at his resurrection to the future completion, in dependence on Jewish apocalyptic.

antagonistic terms: there is a power struggle. The rule of Christ
includes the subjugation of the powers hostile to God. But Paul,
who is interested here in the resurrection of the dead, focuses on
the conquest of death. When, in the wake of Christ's resurrection,
the dead will be raised to life, the power of death will also be
annihilated: death will then lose its hold on human beings. As
vv. 52–55 indicate, total annihilation of death implies the transformation from mortality to immortality and from corruptibility to
incorruptibility. The change at the parousia of Christ involves the
dead as well as the living.[55] But Paul's concern here is not so much
with the resurrection of individual Christians as with the power of
Christ's resurrection.[56] He is affirming the future and the ultimate
dimension of the resurrection of Christ.[57]

Those who see here three orders (τάγματα, tagmata)—the resurrection of Christ, the universal resurrection, and the conquest of
enemy powers—make a distinction between the parousia of Christ
and Christ's ultimate victory over these powers.[58] The two are
separated by the reign of Christ. According to these scholars, Paul is
here importing an apocalyptic schema of periods. In this pattern,
death, which is conquered at the consummation of Christ's reign, is
a real apocalyptic antagonist of Christ, as in the Book of Revelation.
But what does the annihilation of death here, then, really mean?

Other scholars[59] insist that the notion of an "interregnum" is
documented only after the destruction of the second temple, 70 CE.
It is mentioned in the Book of Revelation, but also in 4 Ezra and
2 Baruch. After the thousand-year reign come the general resurrection and the final judgment. According to Rev 20:6, the devil
will then be thrown into the lake of fire. Death and hades will
give up the dead and will be thrown into the lake of fire (v. 14).

---

[55] The text here incorporates the statement in v. 26 but goes beyond it by
insisting on immortality and incorruptibility.

[56] Luz, Geschichtsverständnis, 349.

[57] Because of this, Luz (ibid., 350) calls Paul an "apocalyptic theologian."

[58] Luz (ibid., 347) distinguishes between the pre-Pauline (or non-Pauline)
tradition and Paul's interpretation of that tradition. In the former, the reign of
Christ takes place either in the future or in the present. Luz also distinguishes
between the lordship (κυριότης) of Christ and the reign of Christ. According to
him, Phil 2:9–11, Rom 8:34, and Col 1:13 deal with the lordship of Christ and cannot
be adduced to support the reign of Christ. But is this Paul's distinction?

[59] Wilcke, Zwischenreich, 48.

The Book of Revelation thus distinguishes between the different acts of the completion, in order to emphasize the reward of the faithful witnesses. It presents the first resurrection as a privilege granted to these alone. But this is not the situation in 1 Cor 15:23–28. Here Paul does not deal with a general persecution and with the problem of perseverance in tribulations. He does not give to the faithful witnesses a preferential status in the order of completion. His one sustained concern here is to show that the general resurrection will indeed happen and that it will occur at Christ's coming. It is presented as a component part of Christ's victory.

E. THE CONQUEST OF DEATH

Christ's coming means ultimate victory over death. Then all opposition to God will be overcome forever, and Christ will truly become Lord over all things. Paul's Christology and eschatology include the subjugation of death.

Thus, death is here personified as a power, in association with the other powers mentioned in this section.[60] Paul refers to death as a personified power also in Rom 5:12, 14, 17; 6:9; and 8:2.[61] In fact, personification is characteristic of Paul's thought, occurring abundantly in Romans. According to W. Foerster, such personification is found also in profane Greek.[62]

According to Isa 25:7–8, which Paul quotes in 1 Cor 15:54, when the Lord of hosts establishes on Zion a feast for all peoples, he will destroy death forever. "He will destroy on this mountain the shroud that is cast over all peoples . . . he will swallow up death (בִּלַּע הַמָּוֶת, billa‛ hammāwet) forever.[63] Then the Lord God will wipe

---

[60] In contrast to Eph 1:20 and 1 Pet 3:22, Christ here annihilates these powers.
[61] On death as a personified power, see Rev 6:8 and 20:13, 14.
[62] W. Foerster, "ἐξουσία," 571–73.
[63] De Boer (Defeat, 127) notes that the LXX rendition, κατέπιεν ὁ θάνατος ἰσχύσας, katepien ho thanatos ischysas ("death in his strength has devoured"), reverses the meaning of the MT. But Aquila has, καταποντίσει τὸν θάνατον εἰς νῖκος, katapontisei ton thanaton eis nikos ("he will draw death in victory"), and Symmachus has, καταποθῆναι ποιῆσαι τὸν θάνατον εἰς τέλος, katapothēnai poiēsai ton thanaton eis telos ("he will cause death to be swallowed up to the uttermost"). It appears that Aquila, Symmachus, and Paul are closer to the MT than is the LXX. Cf. Conzelmann, 1 Corinthians, 292.

away the tears from all faces, and the disgrace of his people he will take away from all the earth."

This feast, which here inaugurates the new age, contains joy and peace "for all peoples" and is linked with Yahweh's eschatological reign on Zion. The swallowing up of death means the end of dying—the end of tears and shame. Von Rad establishes that here death is for the first time "objectified . . . and made independent as a reality hostile to Yahweh."[64] In Hos 13:14 and Job 28:22 as well, Abaddon and death are personified (cf. Job 26:6; 31:12; Prov 15:11; 27:20). Personification of death is thus a feature in the OT,[65] in Jewish apocalyptic, and in the NT. In 4 Ezra 8:53–54 death is personified in connection with the turn of the ages: "The root of evil is sealed up from you, illness is banished from you, and death is hidden, hell has fled and corruption has been forgotten; sorrows have passed away, and in the end the treasure of immortality is made manifest." Here, as in 1 Cor 15:26, 54–55, the bestowal of immortality is linked to the banishment of death. Illness, death, hell, corruption, and sorrows are associated with evil that has been annihilated. Death and hades are personified.

In Rev 20:13–14, when the earth and the heaven were abolished and the book of life was opened, "the sea gave up the dead that were in it," and "Death and Hades gave up the dead that were in them." Then "Death and Hades were thrown into the lake of fire," and the dead were then judged according to their works (cf. 1:18; 6:8; 18:8). Moreover, the eschatological and universal resurrection of the dead and the annihilation of death go together.

Paul's words ποῦ σου, θάνατε, τὸ νῖκος; ποῦ σου, θάνατε, τὸ κέντρον; (pou sou, thanate, to nikos? pou sou, thanate, to kentron?) in 1 Cor 15:55 are a loose quotation from LXX Hos 13:14: ποῦ ἡ δίκη σου, θάνατε; ποῦ τὸ κέντρον σου, ᾅδη; (pou hē dikē sou, thanate? pou to kentron sou, hadē? Hebrew: אֱהִי דְבָרֶיךָ מָוֶת אֱהִי קָטָבְךָ שְׁאוֹל, ᵓehî deḇārêḵā māwet ᵓehî qāṭāḇeḵā šeᵓôl)—"O death, where are your plagues? O death, where is your sting?" Again death is personified. That the apostle uses personification for death elsewhere is clear from Rom 5:12, 14, 17, 21; 6:9; 8:2, 38 and 1 Cor 3:33.[66]

---

[64] Von Rad, Theology, 1.390.

[65] De Boer, Defeat, 83–91.

[66] The following metaphors are associated with the annihilation of death: death is "swallowed up"; the "plagues" and the "sting" of death are no more; death is "thrown into the fire"; death is "destroyed"; death "gives up" those who are

F. THE RESURRECTION OF THE DEAD
AND CHRIST'S PAROUSIA

All of 1 Cor 15 deals with the resurrection of the faithful, and vv. 23–28 are no exception to this, although the word for resurrection does not occur here. In v. 23 Paul asserts that the resurrection takes place in two installments (τάγματα, *tagmata*). First comes the resurrection of Christ, then the resurrection of those who belong to Christ. The sequence is indicated with the words ἀπαρχή, *aparchē* and ἔπειτα οἱ τοῦ Χριστοῦ, *epeita hoi tou Christou*: Christ is the ἀπαρχή, the first of the many and the promise for the rest.

The words ἀπαρχή and ἔπειτα suggest a temporal separation between the resurrection of Christ and the resurrection of the others. Although all will be brought to life "in Christ," the resurrection of Christ and the resurrection of the rest do not coincide. The resurrection of Christ is a fact of the past; the resurrection of the rest, however, is yet to come, as the future tense in ζωοποιηθήσονται, *zōopoiēthēsontai*, indicates. It has not yet occurred, but it is promised and is therefore the object of hope. The phrase "those who belong to Christ" states the condition for sharing in this resurrection.[67] The verse thus clarifies as well as restricts the affirmation in v. 22 that "all will be made alive (ζωοποιηθήσονται) in Christ."[68]

Verses 24–28 then relate the conditions for the consummation to the expected resurrection.[69] Although this section is introduced with εἶτα, it does not indicate another installment, for there is no third resurrection. It does not continue the sequence of v. 23 but,

---

in its hold; death "reigns" (ἐβασίλευσεν, *ebasileusen*); and death "dominates" (κυριεύει, *kyrieuei*). This imagery should be distinguished from death as an angelic minister of God ("the angel of death," 2 *Bar.* 21:23). Cf. de Boer, *Defeat*, 90–91.

[67] Although in vv. 20–22 Paul clearly has the universality of the resurrection in mind, as the typological comparison between Christ and Adam and the repeated πάντες, *pantes* indicates, in v. 23 he restricts his remarks to those who belong to Christ. Verses 50–57 indicate that the resurrection is a salvific event. Cf. de Boer, *Defeat*, 112–13.

[68] According to de Boer (ibid., 114), "What is at stake is the question of the relation of God to the world as this finds expression in the gospel of the Christ who *has been raised from the dead.*"

[69] But see ibid., 113: "Since the point at issue is the fate of those who have physically died, Paul would hardly have needed to insist that they are not raised in the present but only the future. The fact that the physically dead are not raised from the dead now would be obvious to the Corinthians as it is to us."

rather, specifies what must take place in order that the completion occur. This will not and cannot come until the dead are raised. The priority of conditions is stated, but not necessarily an interval between the parousia and the completion. The word εἶτα does not separate the two, for when death has been conquered, all are brought to life. And it does not suggest a third resurrection in addition to the resurrection of those who belong to Christ.

Verses 24–28 are thus an explanation of the second installment of the resurrection—why there is no completion until this happens, and what must happen first. The annihilation of death here is associated with the resurrection of the dead. Only those who totally neglect the connection between v. 26 and vv. 25–27 maintain that there is a third order. But then they have to posit a third installment of the resurrection, in addition to the resurrection of those who "belong to Christ." They have to explain what the annihilation of death means here[70] and how this third order, the annihilation of powers and the resurrection of the rest, fulfills the "raising to life in Christ" affirmed in v. 22. If τὸ τέλος comes after the resurrection, then the entire passage becomes anticlimactic, locating as it does the resurrection at an intermediate stage. This sequence imports an apocalyptic millennium in order to explain the continuing struggle between Christ and the powers after the general resurrection.

According to de Boer, the central issue in 1 Cor 15 is death.[71] But the focal issue is really the resurrection from the dead, which in vv. 24–28 is expressed as the end of death. The passage addresses two things: the destruction of principalities and powers (vv. 24, 25, 26, 27), and the goal of Christ's rule (vv. 24, 25, 28). What is at stake is the relation of God to the world in the resurrection of Christ and the subsequent lordship of Christ. The temporal limitation of Christ's reign sets the limits to the present situation in the cosmos, in which death is still a reality. Death, the ultimate enemy of God, is irreconcilable with God's kingdom and will be annihilated. The very

---

[70] Paul seems to have only one future resurrection in mind. The phrase "those who belong to Christ" indicates that he is thinking here of the resurrection of the faithful. Rev, however, mentions two resurrections, the resurrection of the martyrs and the general resurrection. The first resurrection is really a return of the martyrs to this life in order to reign with Christ for a thousand years. Rev thus assures the persecuted Christians of their special place in the completion. This, however, is not Paul's intention in 1 Cor 15.

[71] De Boer, *Defeat*, 114.

purpose of Christ's lordship, linked as it is to his resurrection, is to bring about the annihilation of death. By divine decree Christ must rule until he has subjugated all God's enemies, including death. The subjugation is total, as the repeated πάντα indicates. But de Boer[72] rightly observes that while the Corinthian position is based on anthropology and experience, Paul's answer is based on Christology. It involves the correct understanding of Christ's resurrection in God's plan of salvation.

It appears that in v. 24 powers are mentioned only in anticipation of the scriptural allusions in vv. 25 and 27. Paul here adopts the imagery of the scriptural passages, above all of LXX Ps 109:1,[73] to state that Christ will annihilate the ultimate power, death. And while the scriptural passages are theocentric, Paul's use of them here appears to be christocentric.[74] It is this feature that explains the cautionary explanation in v. 27bc: "But when it says, 'All things are put into subjection,' it is plain that this does not include the one who put all things in subjection under him."

The annihilation of death means that the faithful will then be freed from death and dying. According to the apostle, the faithful will be changed into the likeness of the heavenly man, the risen Christ (v. 49); they will become immortal and incorruptible (vv. 52–57). The victory over death thus embraces the resurrection of the dead and the transformation of the living at the Lord's coming. Then the dead will be raised into a life that is free of death and corruption, and the living will be endowed with immortality and incorruptibility.

But the parousia of Christ is that event in the future which will bring about this change. At Christ's coming only, and not before, will the faithful be raised from the dead. Verse 26 states that the last enemy, death, must be conquered by Christ; the implication is that the end time resurrection/transformation will be the victory of Christ. He will at last vanquish death forever. According to Phil 3:20–21, the risen Lord has been given the power to change our present lowly body into a body like his own resurrected body.

---

[72] Ibid., 120.

[73] De Boer (ibid., 118–19) makes a strong argument that Paul is here drawing on a tradition.

[74] De Boer (ibid., 116–17) defends the theocentric explanation on the basis of v. 27a by working backward. But Paul might have made a shift, as he does in 1 Thess 4:14. At any rate, the reader would assume the same subject as in v. 24 until v. 27b.

CONCLUSION

In 1 Cor 15:23–28 Paul mentions the parousia as the culminating event in the future at which the dead will be raised to life. The εἶτα τὸ τέλος, *eita to telos*, is not a third "order," or τάγμα; Paul is here contrasting only two orders: the resurrection of Christ and the resurrection of the rest, the latter being the completion of the former. The point he makes here is that apart from Christ, the resurrection has not yet taken place.

In agreement with the imagery of Pss 110:1 and 8:7, the apostle depicts the reign of Christ as the subjugation—annihilation—of hostile powers in the cosmos. The present reign of Christ includes this subjugation (v. 25). It is the working out of the empowerment Christ has received from the Father (v. 27), who placed everything under his authority. This reign will not be completed until all these powers are annihilated and all disorder removed from creation. In contrast to Pss 110:1 and 8:7, Paul thinks here of spiritual powers, and since the passage deals with the resurrection, he speaks of the power of death. The annihilation of death belongs to the comprehensive victory of the risen Lord—he must subjugate all (πάντα, *panta*) his enemies. It is the ultimate (ἔσχατος, *eschatos*) conquest. Verses 54–56 indicate that Christ will subjugate death by raising the dead to life and by removing corruption and dying from the world. The activity of the risen Christ is depicted in antagonistic terms, as a struggle and a victory.

The parousia is here referred to not for its own sake but as the anchor for the expected resurrection of the dead, which is the topic of ch. 15. Paul states that the resurrection of the dead will not take place until the parousia of Christ, which means that the coming of Christ extends to others the victory over death wrought at Easter. First Corinthians 15:23–28 thus locates the resurrection in the history of salvation, at the future coming of Christ. It speaks of the parousia as the completion of the dominion of the risen Lord and the beginning of the kingdom of God. But the kingdom of God entails a profound change in the world.

6

⬦

THE TRANSFORMATION AT CHRIST'S COMING, 1 CORINTHIANS 15:50–55

First Corinthians 15:50–55 concludes Paul's second argument in 1 Cor 15, which begins in v. 35 and deals with the resurrected body. In the first argument, in vv. 1–34, the apostle affirms the reality of the resurrection of the dead and its occurrence at the Lord's parousia; in this section he points out the difference between the present human body and the resurrection body, as well as the latter's conformity with that of the risen Christ. In v. 35 he raises the questions "How are the dead raised? With what kind of body do they come?"[1] In vv. 50–55 Paul asserts that the bodies of those who inherit the kingdom of God must conform to the conditions of the kingdom, which does not allow any corruptibility and mortality. He stresses that "at the last trumpet"—at the parousia—the dead will be raised with a body that is incorruptible and the living will exchange their mortal bodies for an immortal one. Here also the parousia situates the end-time resurrection and transformation: it will happen "at the last trumpet."

A. THE CONTEXT

The larger context is 1 Cor 15 with its theme of the resurrection of the dead. The narrower context is vv. 35–49, which deals with the resurrection body. Using the example of the seed that sprouts in

---

[1] The second question specifies the first. See K. Müller, "Leiblichkeit," 178–84.

the soil and becomes a plant, Paul points out in vv. 35–41 that the
seed must first die in order to come to life, that what comes to life and
grows from the seed is not another seed of the same kind that was
sown but the plant that corresponds to this kind of seed. In vv. 42–49
he then applies this analogy to the resurrection of the dead. In vv. 42–
44a he states, "What is sown is perishable, what is raised is imperishable. It is sown in dishonor, it is raised in glory. It is sown in
weakness, it is raised in power. It is sown a physical body, it is raised
a spiritual body." In v. 44b, taking up the last statement, he affirms
the reality of the spiritual body, stating, "If there is a physical body,
there is also a spiritual body." In vv. 45–48 the apostle then contrasts
the first and the last Adams, and their effects on human existence,
while in v. 49 he affirms the future conformation of human beings
with the heavenly man: "Just as we have borne the image of the
man of dust, we will also bear the image of the man of heaven."

Having asserted the spiritual reality of the resurrection life and
its conformity to the second, heavenly Adam, Paul then points out
the change that must take place in our present human condition in
order that we may enter into this existence. In v. 50 he states that
what is perishable and mortal cannot enter the kingdom of God:
"What I am saying, brothers and sisters, is this: flesh and blood
cannot inherit the kingdom of God, nor does the perishable inherit
the imperishable." In vv. 51–53 he then unveils the mystery of the
completion, the change that will qualify those who are now mortal
and perishable to enter the kingdom of God: "We will not all die, but
we will all be changed, in a moment, in the twinkling of an eye, at
the last trumpet. For the trumpet will sound, and the dead will be
raised imperishable, and we will be changed. For this perishable body
must put on imperishability, and this mortal body must put on immortality." In vv. 54–55 he brings his argument to a close with a quotation
from Isa 25:8 and Hos 13:14, exulting over the conquest of death.

The word παρουσία, parousia, is not mentioned in 1 Cor
15:50–55, but there can be no doubt that Paul alludes to the Lord's
coming when he says in v. 52, " . . . at the last trumpet. For the
trumpet will sound, and the dead will be raised." "The last trumpet" refers to the parousia, as does the trumpet of God in 1 Thess
4:16.[2] It is the trumpet sound that signals the completion, the

---

[2]Cf. Rev 11:15, where, at the seventh—the last—trumpet sound, the kingdom
of the world becomes the kingdom of God and his Messiah.

passing of this world and the beginning of the kingdom of God (1 Cor 15:50; cf. Rev 11:15). The latter is associated in 15:23-28 with the parousia of Christ and the victory over death.

Just as vv. 23-28 conclude Paul's argument for the occurrence of the resurrection at Christ's coming, so vv. 50-55 conclude his argument for the transformation at Christ's parousia. Both texts mention the conquest of death (vv. 26, 54-55) and the kingdom of God (vv. 28, 50). The Lord's coming thus marks the transition from the present human existence to the ultimate, heavenly form of existence.

B. THE NECESSITY OF TRANSFORMATION

In v. 50 Paul asserts, "What I am saying (τοῦτο δέ φημι, *touto de phēmi*), brothers, is this: flesh and blood cannot inherit the kingdom of God, nor does the perishable (ἡ φθορά, *hē phthora*) inherit the imperishable (τὴν ἀφθαρσίαν, *tēn aphtharsian*)." In v. 51 he explains, "Listen (ἰδού, *idou*), I tell you a mystery (μυστήριον, *mystērion*)! We will not all die, but we will all be changed." With three prepositional (ἐν, *en*) phrases he describes the nature and the occasion of that change: it will happen "in (ἐν) a moment, in (ἐν) the twinkling of an eye, at (ἐν) the last trumpet" (v. 52a). By way of a parenthesis he asserts the reality of the latter, saying, "For the trumpet will sound" (v. 52b). He continues, "And the dead will be raised imperishable, and we will be changed" (v. 52c). In v. 53 he supplies the reason for this: "For this perishable body must put on imperishability, and this mortal body must put on immortality." Verses 54 and 55 conclude this assertion with a victory song over death in the words of Isa 25:8 and Hos 13:14. These verses are also the conclusion of the entire chapter, taking up the imagery in v. 26, where death is presented as the ultimate enemy to be annihilated.

Verse 50, as most exegetes now agree, begins a new paragraph.[3] This is indicated by the adversative conjunction δέ, *de*, the vocative αδελφοί, *adelphoi*, and the kindred words ἄφθαρτοι, *aphthartoi*, φθαρτόν, *phtharton*, and ἀφθαρσίαν, *aphtharsian* in vv. 53-54, echoing φθορά and ἀφθαρσίαν in v. 50.[4] But v. 50 does not by itself

---

[3] See Conzelmann, *1 Corinthians*, 289-90; K. Müller, "Leiblichkeit," 227. Schweizer ("σάρξ") still links v. 50 with the preceding section.

[4] See Fee, *1 Corinthians*, 798; Conzelmann, *1 Corinthians*, 289; K. Müller, "Leiblichkeit," 227.

conclude the preceding section; the entire passage introduced by this verse is a resounding conclusion of Paul's argumentation of vv. 35–49 and, indeed, of the entire chapter.

Verses 50–53 retain the contrast, explained by the list of differences in vv. 42–49,[5] between the present body and the resurrection body, and they disclose the mode of transition from the one to the other. Paul's point ever since v. 37 has been that the resurrection body will be different from the present body, which is determined by the flesh (σάρξ, sarx). In vv. 50–55 he asserts the incompatibility of the two: the present body carries the mark of death; it is either a dead body or mortal. In either case, it cannot inherit the kingdom of God, in which there is no death or corruptibility.

The metaphor κληρονομέω, klēronomeō, meaning "to inherit" (v. 50), occurs often in an eschatological context for the inheritance of the ultimate reality. It is used in Mark 10:17 (cf. Luke 10:25; 18:18; Matt 19:29) in the sense of gaining eternal life. Paul employs it in the phrase "to inherit the kingdom of God" in 1 Cor 6:9, 10; Gal 5:21; and here.[6] It occurs also in Jewish apocalyptic literature (2 Bar. 44:13). The word κληρονομέω occurs in the OT usually in the phrase "to inherit the earth."

The phrase "the kingdom of God" occurs 7 times in Pauline epistles—5 times in 1 Corinthians. It is used also frequently in the Synoptic Gospels.[7] Thus, both κληρονομέω and βασιλεία τοῦ θεοῦ, basileia tou theou, occur relatively frequently in 1 Corinthians. The apostle uses the expression "to inherit the kingdom of God" as a warning: those who do such things will not inherit the kingdom of God (1 Cor 6:9, 10; Gal 5:21). But in 1 Cor 15:50 he does not warn; he asserts the incompatibility (οὐ δύναται, ou dynatai) when he

---

[5] K. Müller, "Leiblichkeit," 227–28 n. 189.

[6] The noun κληρονομία, klēronomia, is used for the inheritance of the eschatological reality in Acts 7:5; Gal 3:18; Eph 1:14, 18, 5:5; Col 3:24; Heb 9:15; and 1 Pet 1:4. See also κληρονόμος, klēronomos, in Rom 8:17; Gal 3:29, 4:7; Titus 3:7; Heb 6:17; and Jas 2:5. The verb κληρονομέω , klēronomeō, is employed by Paul in 1 Cor 6:9, 10; 15:50 and Gal 4:30; 5:21. With the exception of Gal 4:30, it is used for inheriting the kingdom of God (cf. Matt 25:34). The verb has this eschatological meaning elsewhere in the NT. In Matt 19:29; Mark 10:17; and Luke 10:25, 18:18 it refers to "eternal life"; in Heb it refers in 1:14 to "salvation," in 6:12 to "the promises," and in 12:17 to "the blessing."

[7] It is a characteristic expression in Mark and Luke–Acts, while Matthew has the equivalent phrase βασιλεία τῶν οὐρανῶν, basileia tōn ouranōn. In John it occurs only twice.

says, "Flesh and blood cannot inherit the kingdom of God." Here it is not a transgression that excludes one from entering the ultimate reality; it is the present physical condition of human beings that makes them unworthy to enter God's kingdom.

The phrase "flesh and blood" (σὰρξ καὶ αἷμα, sarx kai haima)[8] occurs also in Gal 1:16. The entire statement, "Flesh and blood cannot inherit the kingdom of God," sounds Semitic, although Paul is here scarcely drawing on a tradition, since he has employed every element of this clause in other contexts. According to J. Jeremias, since σὰρξ καὶ αἷμα (cf. Sir 14:18; 17:31) originally referred only to the living, it must have this sense also here. The clause "Flesh and blood cannot inherit the kingdom of God" refers to the living, while the parallel clause, "nor does the perishable (φθορά) inherit the imperishable," refers to the dead. The parallelism here is synthetic, the second member complementing[9] rather than merely restating the first. This dichotomy of the living/the dead then governs the rest of the passage.

But this interpretation has not met with wide agreement. As G. D. Fee points out, its main difficulty lies in identifying the abstract noun φθορά[10] with the dead.[11] E. Schweizer notes that vv. 53–54, which take up v. 50 and restate the necessity of change,

---

[8] This phrase occurs also in Matt 16:17, Gal 1:16, Eph 6:12, and Heb 2:14. The Hebrew turn of phrase is וְדָם בָּשָׂר, bāśār wādām. See Billerbeck, Kommentar, 1.730; Meyer, "σάρξ," 116.

[9] J. Jeremias, "Flesh and Blood," 155.

[10] The word φθορά and its derivatives διαφθορά, diaphthora, and καταφθορά, kataphthora, in the LXX usually translate the Hebrew שַׁחַת, šaḥat, "the pit." The word is thus a synonym for hades, the place of the dead. In the Hebrew way of thinking, this sphere also extends to the sick.

In the Dead Sea Scrolls, שַׁחַת means "the pit" as well as "perdition." 1QH 2:21 and CD 14:2 speak of "the snares of the pit" (Maier translates "perdition"), while 1QH 3:12 mentions "the pangs of the pit" (Mansoor's translation) and "the waves of the pit" (cf. 1QH 3:16; 1QS 9:16, 22; 10:19). Cf. Harder, "φθείρω"; Usami, " 'The Dead Raised,' " 489–90.

In Jewish Hellenistic writings, καταφθορά signifies "death" (Sir 28:6), often with a moral connotation. Josephus uses φθορά for a "crushing defeat" (J.W. 2.559), a massacre (J.W. 2.477), a physical degradation through sickness (Ant. 9.101), or moral corruption (Ant. 4.216). He employs the antithesis φθαρτός-ἄφθαρτος, phthartos-aphthartos, for the opposition between material bodies and the soul. For Philo, φθορά signifies "perishable" and is applied to the body or to the soul. It is used also in an ethical sense (Harder, "φθείρω," 100–101).

[11] Fee, 1 Corinthians, 798 n. 11. According to J. Gillman ("Future Life," 320–22), quoted by Fee, the chiastic structure to which Jeremias appeals in support of his thesis is not present here; the structure is, rather, A-B-A′.

do not maintain the synthetic parallelism.[12] While K. Müller agrees with Jeremias that "flesh and blood" had been understood in Judaism to refer to the living only,[13] Fee points out that in 1 Cor 15:50 the phrase refers to the body in its present form, "composed of flesh and blood, to be sure, but subject to weakness, decay, and death, and as such ill-suited for the life in the future."[14]

The clause οὐδὲ ἡ φθορὰ τὴν ἀφθαρσίαν κληρονομεῖ, *oude hē phthora tēn aphtharsian klēronomei*, asserts the incompatibility. Here ἀφθαρσίαν is the object of κληρονομεῖ and is the mark of the ultimate existence. Fourth Ezra and *2 Baruch* provide the apocalyptic background for this formulation. There the incorruptibility is identified with the future, never-ending age of promise, when "what was corruptible shall perish" (4 Ezra 7:31; cf. 7:112; *2 Bar.* 44:9). In apocalyptic thought this means a transformation, rather than the removal, of the present physical component of human beings. In 4 Ezra 7:31–32 God reveals to Ezra the following mystery: after the messianic kingdom everyone, including the Messiah, will die; the world will be turned back to primeval silence for seven days "so that no one shall be left." In 7:88–97 the angel-interpreter informs Ezra of the seven orders of the souls of the just that have been separated from their mortal body and are joyfully waiting for the completion. "They understand . . . the glory which awaits them in the last days . . . they rejoice that they have now escaped what is mortal, and shall inherit what is to come . . . they see the spacious liberty which they are to receive and enjoy in immortality . . . it is shown to them how their face will shine like the sun, and how they are to be made like the light of the stars, being incorruptible from then on." In 8:53–54 Ezra is given the final divine answer on the world to come: "The world which is not yet awake shall be roused, and that which is corruptible shall perish. And the earth shall give up those who sleep in it, and the chambers shall give up the souls which have been committed to them." In that age to come "illness is banished . . . death is hidden, hell has fled and corruption has been forgotten, sorrows have passed away . . . the treasure of immortality is made manifest." Ezra thus expects the resurrection

---

[12] Schweizer, "σάρξ."
[13] K. Müller, "Leiblichkeit," 229 n. 195.
[14] Fee, *1 Corinthians*, 799.

and the transformation. What is now in the clutches of death and corruption will become immortal and incorruptible.

In *2 Bar.* 74:2 Baruch is told by the angel interpreter about the completion: "That time is the end of that which is corruptible and the beginning of that which is incorruptible." Baruch himself, in his parting speech to the people in 44:9, asserts, "For everything will pass away which is corruptible, and everything that dies will go away." The new world that is coming "does not carry back to corruption those who enter into its beginning." The incorruption here refers to the physical constitution of human beings. Both 4 Ezra and *2 Baruch* use the metaphor "to inherit" or "inheritance" for the acquisition of this state of bliss (4 Ezra 7:9, 17, 96; *2 Bar.* 44:13.

This is also the thought of Paul. Throughout this comparison the apostle deals with the corporeal reality of human existence in the present and in the beyond; but he does not argue, as in 2 Cor 5:1–10, against those who maintain that the completion involves only the spirit.[15] He simply takes it for granted that the body will be involved in the ultimate reality. Paul's model is the somatic reality of the risen Christ.

Christ is the model of the future existence. In 1 Cor 15 Paul has been presenting the resurrection of the faithful as the universal extension of Christ's resurrection. Christ is "the heavenly man," and the risen believers are "those who belong to heaven," who will "bear the image of the heavenly man" (vv. 48–49; cf. Rom 8:29).

The apostle's point is that the resurrected body will be a transformed body—πάντες δὲ ἀλλαγησόμεθα, *pantes de allagēsometha.* Did the opponents in Corinth express their reservation against a resurrection that is a return to this life?[16] Paul asserts that the dead will not return to the present body, for such a body would still be subject to death and dying; they will be raised with a different body, one that is totally free of death. But by the same token, the survivors at the parousia will also shed from their bodies mortality

---

[15] According to Fee (ibid., 800), the Corinthians "would have been plumping for a nonsomatic immortality."

[16] According to Lietzmann (*Korinther I/II*, 86), v. 50 establishes that the Jewish notion of a resurrection of this physical body is to be rejected. Conzelmann (*1 Corinthians*, 290) suggests that this may have been the original point of the thesis that Paul makes here.

and assume immortality—through a bodily transformation. Both the survivors and those raised from the dead will in this regard become conformed to the heavenly man. The resurrection/transformation is the ultimate redemption (ἀπολύτρωσις, *apolytrōsis*) of the body from the slavery of decay (cf. Rom 8:21–23).

Thus, the phrase "flesh and blood" here indicates the constitution of the present body as described in 1 Cor 15:42–44. This human body is perishable, in dishonor, weak, physical, and earthly. As such, it is not fit for the kingdom of God, for in the wake of Adam's sin it lacks the original perfection. It does not have the glory that God originally bestowed on it and intended for it. Paul does not think of the loss of righteousness, as in Rom 3:23,[17] but of the loss of a quality of life affecting the body (cf. Rom 8:23): because of sin, the body became θνητόν, *thnēton*, mortal. The body that is fit for the kingdom of God must be imperishable, glorious, powerful, and spiritual—as is the resurrection body. Life in the kingdom of God is eternal life *in the body*, and the eschatological expectation of Paul includes the desire for the glory and honor and immortality (Rom 2:6, 10; 8:20–25) that affect the body. In Rom 8:23 he speaks of the ἀπολύτρωσιν τοῦ σώματος ἡμῶν, *apolytrōsin tou sōmatos hēmōn* ("the redemption of our bodies"). Thus, in 1 Cor 15:50 the immortality and the incorruptibility refer to the body.

Against J. Jeremias's suggestion that "flesh and blood" implies that the living, in contrast to the dead, cannot enter the kingdom of God,[18] K. Müller points out that Paul is here not interested in the privileged status of one group or another. The apostle is not contrasting the living with the dead; in v. 51 he asserts categorically, "We will all be changed."[19] The apostle thus refers here to the survivors in order to make an inclusive statement: all, dead or alive, must change.

Transcendence of ultimate existence in the resurrection body comes into view in the image of the second, the heavenly man, presented here as the model for the risen life. Those who will be raised to life in the end time will belong to heaven, will be οἱ

---

[17] According to Schlier (*Römerbrief*, 106), the clause "since all have sinned and have fallen short of the glory of God" (Rom 3:23) refers to the loss of the original glory and perfection of human beings. Adam was once clad in such a glory.

[18] Jeremias refers to Schlatter as the first one to suggest this, but Fee (*1 Corinthians*, 799) points out that this view had been advocated by Godet (*1 Corinthians*).

[19] K. Müller, "Leiblichkeit," 230 n. 199.

ἐπουράνιοι, *hoi epouranioi*, as is the second man (v. 47). This dimension of the completion is affirmed also in 2 Cor 5:1, where Paul states, "For we know that if the earthly tent we live in is destroyed, we have a building from God, a house not made with hands, eternal in the heavens." The apostle's desire is to be clad (with a body) rather than naked (without a body), "so that what is mortal may be swallowed up by life" (5:4).

The ultimate existence is life in the kingdom of God. In the OT, the kingdom of God is not presented as an otherworldly reality in the way it is for Paul and Jewish apocalyptic. *Second Baruch* depicts the kingdom of God taking place after the last judgment (73:1; 83:7). The sequence of events is the messianic rule (30:1), the resurrection of the righteous, the last judgment (30:1–5). Yet even here the kingdom of God somehow includes life on earth, albeit a transformed earth. This holds true also for Rev 21:1–4, where the holy city, the new Jerusalem, comes down from the new heaven to the new earth and becomes the home of God among mortals. On this earth "death will be no more; mourning and crying and pain will be no more, for the first things have passed away" (v. 4). But in Dan 12:3 we read, "Many of those who sleep in the dust of the earth shall awake, some to everlasting life, and some to shame and everlasting contempt. Those who are wise shall shine like the brightness of the sky, and those who led many to righteousness, like the stars forever and ever."[20] In Daniel the resurrection is still not truly universal, although it involves the good and the bad.

The resurrection of the dead and the transformation are clearly stated in 4 Ezra 8:53–54 and *2 Bar.* 50:2. According to the latter, the transformation occurs after the resurrection. But there is no mention in these texts of any conformity to the glory of the Son of man or the Messiah.[21] Jewish apocalyptic, to be sure, knows of a messianic reign in the end time in which sin, death,

---

[20] See also Matt 13:43: "Then the righteous will shine like the sun in the kingdom of their Father." The righteous here are the "children of the kingdom" (οἱ υἱοὶ τῆς βασιλείας, *hoi huioi tēs basileias*). There is no place for the wicked in the kingdom of God.

[21] *1 Enoch* 90:37–38 contains the following animal imagery of the end-time transformation: "Then I saw that a snow-white cow was born, with huge horns; all the beasts of the field and all the birds of the sky feared him and made petition to him all the time. I went on seeing until all their kindred were transformed, and became snow-white cows; and the first among them became something, and that something became a great beast with huge black horns on its head."

illness, and hostility will have no place; but this is envisioned as a prolonged and intensified life of bliss on the transformed earth. This life is brought about by God. The Messiah sometimes plays a role in it, usually in liberating the elect ones and ruling over them. In 4 Ezra 7:29–30 we are told that at the end even the Messiah will die.

In 1 Thess 4:17 Paul talks about being with the Lord forever: the faithful taken up by the clouds to meet the Lord "will be with the Lord forever." But this life "with the Lord" (cf. 5:10), sustained by the power of God (4:16–17; 2 Cor 4:14; Phil 3:21), differs from the present life on earth (4:17),[22] for the whole glory and joy here consist in being with the Lord.

This motif occurs also elsewhere in Paul. Thus in 1 Cor 1:7–9 the apostle states, "By him [God] you were called into the fellowship (εἰς κοινωνίαν, eis koinōnian) of his Son, Jesus Christ our Lord." While the κοινωνία here no doubt applies to the present fellowship with Christ, usually expressed as "belonging to Christ" or being "in Christ," or even being "with Christ," which extends till the parousia,[23] the ultimate completion will be the perfect κοινωνία.[24]

The end-time existence is usually expressed as being "with Christ," or sharing life with Christ, or being conformed to Christ. Romans 8:16–17 speaks of the "heirs of God and joint heirs with Christ." The completion, according to this text, will be a sharing in the sonship, in the inheritance with Christ. Verse 23 indicates that the expected completion includes the redemption (ἀπολύτρωσιν) of our bodies.

Philippians 3:21 talks of the end-time conformity to the Lord: "He [the Lord Jesus Christ] will transform our body of humiliation that it may be conformed to the body of his glory, by the power that also enables him to make all things subject to him." This conformity to the Lord is thus a glorification (cf. Rom 8:30). The text also clearly states that it will be the risen Lord himself who will bring about this conformity.

---

[22] The desire to be with the Lord is mentioned also in 2 Cor 5:6–8, where Paul states, "We would rather be away from the body and at home with the Lord." Here being "at home with the Lord" still means life in a heavenly body (2 Cor 5:1).

[23] Conzelmann, 1 Corinthians, 29.

[24] Dupont, L'Union, 81.

Our passage, 1 Cor 15:50–55, also says that the inheritance of the kingdom of God will include a transformation of the present human body. The context, provided by vv. 42–49, indicates that this entails conformity with the heavenly man. Paul is interested not in the eschatological glory for its own sake but in sharing the glory with the risen Lord.

All this awaits those who belong to Christ (v. 23), who are led by the Spirit of God, who are children of God (Rom 8:14–17, 23). Paul has in mind here the resurrection of the believers, for in his presentation the resurrection is also a glorification.[25] The resurrection is thus salvific. In Rom 8:21 he talks about the "freedom of the glory of the children of God,"[26] and in v. 23 about the υἱοθεσίαν, huiothesian, which includes the redemption (ἀπολύτρωσιν) of our bodies.

C. THE MYSTERY OF THE END TIME

The introduction, ἰδοὺ μυστήριον ὑμῖν λέγω, idou mystērion hymin legō (1 Cor 15:51), resembles the introduction in 1 Thess 4:15: τοῦτο γὰρ ὑμῖν λέγομεν ἐν λόγῳ κυρίου, touto gar hymin legomen en logō kyriou. But in 1 Cor 15:51 Paul does not appeal to the Lord, and the affirmation that follows is not a quotation. The "mystery" in 1 Cor 15:51 indicates the heavenly nature of this disclosure. It means that this knowledge is not derived from this world.[27]

---

[25] In somewhat different language, the author of Col says, "When Christ who is your life is revealed, then you also will be revealed with him in glory" (3:4). The revealing of Christ mentioned here refers to his coming in the end time.

[26] Another image for the end-time completion is the reigning with Christ. See Dupont, L'Union, 84–87.

[27] On the Jewish background of this usage of μυστήριον, see Brown, " 'Mystery.' " According to Brown, this background is provided by סוֹד, sôd, which carries the idea of divine council deliberating on the government of the world. The prophets were admitted to these secret deliberations in heaven. סוֹד also came to mean decisions rendered by these councils. In Prov and Sir and in Qumran, סוֹד refers to secrets or mysteries.

In the LXX μυστήριον occurs only in the postexilic books, together with the synonyms κρυπτά and ἀπόκρυφα, apokrypha, but it translates רָז, rāz, not סוֹד, (ibid., 417–18). In Dan 2:27–29 it refers to the contents of the dream symbols.

In the Pseudepigrapha, mysteries (1 Enoch 6–11) involve charms, cosmic mysteries (stars, sun, moon, etc.), and God (1 Enoch 63:3). Mystery often relates to the future, especially to God's judgment. The term is applied also to the Elect One, the Son of man (1 Enoch 48:6–7; 62:1; 69:14). In 4 Ezra the visionary receives the revelation of the mysteries of God (6:32–33).

Perhaps the closest parallel to the mystery in v. 51 is in 1 Cor 2:7.[28] There Paul speaks of the wisdom "of this age or of the rulers of this age, who are doomed to perish," and of the "wisdom" of God, which he is proclaiming. The latter is a secret (ἐν μυστηρίῳ, en mystēriō), hidden (ἀποκεκρυμμένην, apokekrymmenēn) from the beginning of the world until the moment chosen by God. The secret is that salvation is through the crucified Christ. The apostle is the proclaimer of this secret of God, which is not comprehended by the rulers of this world. In v. 9 he states, "What no eye has seen, nor ear heard, nor the human heart conceived . . . God has prepared for those who love him." Yet God has revealed this mystery "through the Spirit" (v. 10). In v. 12 the apostle states, "Now we have received . . . the Spirit that is from God, so that we may understand the gifts bestowed on us by God. And we speak of these things . . . in words . . . taught by the Spirit" (v. 13). Paul was thus the privileged receiver of this revelation through the Spirit.

The mystery in 1 Cor 2 refers to a decree of God concerning the ultimate reality. The revelation discloses that the end-time completion will be a sharing in the glory of God beyond all present human experience and knowledge. The faithful are assured that it will happen, but they do not have firsthand experience of it. Hence, the mystery, though disclosed, remains a mystery. The revealer of the mystery is the Spirit of God.[29]

First Corinthians 2:6–13 may thus be an important text for interpreting the "mystery" in 15:51. In 2:6–13 also the apostle speaks of a disclosure of a mystery. He mentions a mystery (μυστήρίῳ, v. 7), which God "has revealed to us" (ἀπεκάλυψεν ὁ θεός, apekalypsen ho theos, v. 10) through the Spirit. This mystery concerns the end-time glorification of the faithful (εἰς δόξαν ἡμῶν, eis doxan hēmōn, v. 7)—"what God has prepared for those who love him" (v. 9). In the context Paul asserts that he has prophetic power. He claims to have received "the Spirit that is from God," which enables him to "understand the gifts bestowed on us by God" (v. 12). He speaks in words taught by the Spirit; he interprets spiritual things

---

[28] The term "mystery" seldom occurs in the Gospels (Matt once, Mark once, Luke once) and always in the phrase τὰ μυστήρια τῆς βασιλείας τοῦ θεοῦ (or τῶν οὐρανῶν), ta mystēria tēs basileias tou theou (or tōn ouranōn). It occurs twice in Rom, 6 times in 1 Cor, 6 times in Eph, 4 times in Col, and 4 times in Rev.

[29] All this points to a mystical experience of Paul; see also 2 Cor 12:1–4 and Acts 22:17–21.

(v. 13); and he has "the mind of Christ" (v. 16), so that he can instruct others.[30] In 13:2 he associates prophetic powers with the understanding of mysteries and with having knowledge. Paul regards himself as the interpreter of God's mysteries. In 4:1 he tells the Corinthians that they should regard him and his companions "as servants of Christ and stewards of God's mystery (οἰκονόμους μυστηρίων τοῦ θεοῦ, oikonomous mystērion theou)."[31] And in 2 Cor 12:7 he talks of "the exceptional character of revelations (τῇ ὑπερβολῇ τῶν ἀποκαλύψεων, tē hyperbolē tōn apokalypseōn). There is thus no doubt that Paul himself has been granted revelations concerning the final completion in order that he may raise the hope of the faithful and instruct them concerning their future.

The μυστήριον in 1 Cor 15:51 concerns God's plan for the quality of the resurrected body. It will not be like the present body. The weight of the pronouncement in v. 52b—"We will not all die, but we will all be changed (πάντες δὲ ἀλλαγησόμεθα)"—is on the last part, "we will all be changed." The universal scope ("all") of this is made clearer, in contrast to the first statement, which is restrictive: "We will not all die (κοιμηθησόμεθα, koimēthesometha)."[32] The sense of these two statements is that both the living and the dead will be transformed. The necessity of this has been stated in v. 50: no one can enter the kingdom of God in the present physical condition, which is marked by mortality and corruptibility. While elsewhere Paul asserts that it is sin that prevents entry into the presence of God, here he speaks of the lack of glory and perfection in our present physical constitution. Human beings, to the extent that they are subject to death and dying, are not fit for the glory of God's kingdom.

Here (cf. also 2 Cor 5:1–2) Paul is in tune with Jewish apocalyptic thinking of the time. The vision of the end-time condition of the just in 4 Ezra and especially 2 Baruch provides the apocalyptic background for this imagery. In these writings, composed soon after

---

[30] Some scholars do not hesitate to attribute to community prophets important revelations, although very little is known about them, but they are reluctant to ascribe to Paul such power, although he mentions it several times.

[31] In 1 Cor 2:1 the term "mystery" refers to the gospel of God, which Paul proclaims. This is clear from his apology: "When I came to you . . . I did not proclaim the mystery of God to you in lofty words of wisdom."

[32] The unusual word order πάντες οὐ may anticipate the next clause beginning with πάντες δέ. The first clause is probably concessive: even though we will not all sleep, we will all be changed. Cf. Fee, 1 Corinthians, 800.

the destruction of the second temple,[33] we find metaphorical language for the end of death and dying: illness is "banished"; death is "hidden"; hades "flies away"; and corruption has been "forgotten" (4 Ezra 8:53; cf. 4 Ezra 6:28; 7:31–32; 2 Bar. 44:9). The present age of corruption will pass away (2 Bar. 74:2; cf. 4 Ezra 7:96), and everything that is corruptible shall vanish (2 Bar. 22:9). Then will begin "that which is incorruptible" (2 Bar. 74:2; 85:5), a "time that does not pass away," a "new world which does not carry back to corruption those who enter into its beginning. . . . For those are the ones who will inherit this time . . . and to these is the heritage of the promised time" (44:11–13). The expectation here is that the completion will come soon (4 Ezra 8:61), that everybody will die (7:78), and that after this the just will be raised. A similar expectation is found also in Rev 20:13–15.

D. THE NEARNESS OF THE PAROUSIA

Paul expects the Lord to come soon; his statement that "we shall not all die" suggests this. And he clearly states in 1 Cor 7:29, 31 that "the appointed time has grown short" and that "the present form of this world is passing away." The inclusive "we" in 15:51 indicates that he himself expects to live to see that day. The transformation of the living, asserted here, also suggests or is congruent with this.

That the apostle includes the living in the end-time change is clear from the assertion "We will not all die but we will all be changed." This idea is absent in 4 Ezra (and in 2 Baruch), which expects that the whole corruptible world will come to an end. Only after that will the dead be raised. This is probably also the scenario in Rev 20:11–15, which speaks only of the resurrection of the dead, and of the old world passing away (21:1). In 1 Cor 15:52 and 1 Thess 4:13–18 Paul hints that he expects to be alive at this completion.[34] In 2 Cor 4:14 as well, he presumes that the Corinthians will also then be alive.[35] As 1 Cor 7:25–31 clearly

---

[33] The thinking and the imagery found in 4 Ezra and 2 Bar. may be older than the composition of these writings.

[34] Fee, 1 Corinthians, 800.

[35] But Paul expects that he himself will not be alive then. He talks here about his own resurrection.

shows, Paul is convinced that he is living in the last generation on earth.[36]

With the three prepositional phrases in v. 52, Paul indicates the nature and the occasion of the transformation. The phrases resemble the three prepositional phrases in 1 Thess 4:16. But while the latter depict the Lord's coming from heaven in awesome power and glory, the former refer to the transformation. The first two of these phrases in 1 Cor 15:52 indicate its instantaneous quality: the change will happen in a split second, in the twinkling of an eye.[37] The third, "at the last trumpet," is an allusion to the Lord's coming: it will happen at the parousia.

Suddenness is a common motif in NT apocalyptic.[38] It occurs in 1 Thess 5:2 and also in Luke 17:24 and Matt 24:27 (Q). But while the eschatological parables and 1 Thess 5:2–3 mention, by means of the suddenness, the unpredictability of the Lord's coming and hence the need to be ready for it, the phrases ἐν ἀτόμῳ, ἐν ῥιπῇ ὀφθαλμοῦ, en atomō, en rhipē ophthalmou,[39] according to Daube, suggest "the hope which will materialize in an instant when God so decrees."[40] It does not suggest the wonder of the happening. Still, this is not a natural event, or something that can be derived from creation: it is God's action of elevating the human being to the glory of the kingdom of God. And it does not suggest that the parousia is very close.

But to Paul's thinking, the parousia has not receded into the distant future; he keeps on talking about the near approach of the end. In Phil 4:5 he asserts, "The Lord is near (ὁ κύριος ἐγγύς, ho kyrios engys)," and in Rom 13:11–12 he states, "Salvation is nearer to us now than when we became believers; the night is far gone,

---

[36] In view of the impending crisis, Paul counsels the virgins not to get married (see 1 Cor 7:29, 31).

[37] The Greek phrase ἐν ἀτόμῳ occurs only in Symmachus's translation of Isa 54:8, where it seems to translate רֶגַע, rega‏ᶜ. According to Daube (Sudden, 76), ἐν ἀτόμῳ translates רֶגַע rather than הֶרֶף, herep.

[38] Daube, Sudden, 76–78.

[39] The first phrase, ἐν ἀτόμῳ, is good Greek usage, although it is a hapax legomenon in the Bible. The second phrase, ἐν ῥιπῇ ὀφθαλμοῦ, which is a hapax legomenon in the Bible and in extant Greek writing, echoes the Semitic phrase עַיִן הֶרֶף, herep ᶜayin (cf. Daube, Sudden, 76–78). For a similar employment of two synonyms, see 1 Thess 5:5, where Paul first employs the Semitic υἱοὶ φωτός, hyioi phōtos and υἱοὶ ἡμέρας, hyioi hēmeras then the corresponding Greek οὐκ ἐσμὲν νυκτὸς οὐδὲ σκότους, ouk esmen nyktos oude skotous.

[40] Daube, Sudden, 76.

the day is near." Rather, the apostle is becoming aware that the end ⌄ of his own life has come closer. But his own death does not spell for him the end of his present relationship with the risen Lord but, rather, an intensification of that union. It is clear that he here thinks of a continuity of life beyond death, although he does not reflect on the interim state beyond asserting that he will then be closer to the Lord.

That in 1 Cor 15:50–55 Paul implies that his is the last generation is evident also from the early textual emendations. This was also understood by the early transcribers of the text. In the history of textual transmission of the statement, πάντες οὐ κοιμηθησόμεθα, πάντες δὲ ἀλλαγησόμεθα, *pantes ou koimēthēsometha, pantes de allagēsometha* caused difficulties to transcribers who lived several generations after Paul. They had problems with both parts of this pronouncement. By that time it was becoming clearer and clearer that people were dying before the Lord's coming. Paul himself had died. Death came to be expected, despite the awaiting of the parousia. This led to the following changes in the first part: πάντες οὖν κοιμηθησόμεθα, *pantes oun koimēthēsometha;* πάντες κοιμηθησόμεθα, *pantes koimēthēsometha;* and ἀναστησόμεθα, *anastēsometha.* The first includes the change from οὐ, *ou,* to οὖν, *oun,* which is easy to make. The second omits οὐ, and the third substitutes ἀναστησόμεθα for the entire clause.

The second part of the pronouncement, dealing with the change, was also corrected. If the transformation, according to vv. 48–49, includes conformity with Christ, then only those who belong to Christ will be changed into the likeness of the heavenly man. Only these will be endowed with immortality and incorruptibility—the requisites for entering the kingdom of God. The others will not enter the kingdom of God. This led to οὐ πάντες δὲ ἀλλαγησόμεθα, *ou pantes de allagēsometha,* found in all other readings.[41]

---

[41] 1. πάντες οὐ κοιμηθησόμεθα, πάντες δὲ ἀλλαγησόμεθα;
   2. πάντες οὐ κοιμηθησόμεθα, οὐ πάντες δὲ ἀλλαγησόμεθα;
   3. πάντες οὖν κοιμηθησόμεθα, οὐ πάντες δὲ ἀλλαγησόμεθα;
   4. πάντες κοιμηθησόμεθα, οὐ πάντες δὲ ἀλλαγησόμεθα;
   5. ἀναστησόμεθα, οὐ πάντες δὲ ἀλλαγησόμεθα.
No. 1 has a good textual support and is the more difficult reading for transcribers. All other readings are made easier by the changes in the second part, and in nos. 3–5 also by the changes in the first part. Critical editions agree that no. 1 is the original reading. The Bible Societies' third edition gives the first reading the highest grade of certainty, {A}.

E. RESURRECTION OR IMMORTALITY

The corporeal aspect of the resurrection is indicated in the second question asked in v. 35: "With what kind of body do they come (ποίῳ δὲ σώματι ἔρχονται, *poiō de sōmati erchontai*)?" This is not a new question but a specification of the preceding question, "How are the dead raised?"[42] As H.-H. Schade has observed, the somatic character of the resurrection is here taken for granted.[43] The entire argumentation that follows deals with the *difference* in the body—between the present body and the resurrection body. The question concerns the kind of body, not whether there will be a body at the resurrection of the dead.

The example from nature, of the seed that, put in the ground, dies, sprouts, and produces a plant, illustrates a change from one body to another, from seed to plant. Paul emphasizes that the first body, the grain, dies and that it differs from the body that arises out of it. The rising of the new kind of body, the plant, is regarded as God's doing: it occurs just as "God gives," although it corresponds to the seed from which it arose.[44]

The listing of different heavenly bodies (vv. 40–41), distinguished by their different perfections, anticipates the resurrection body of those who "belong to heaven" (v. 48). The transition that Paul wants to explain will be not from one earthly body to another but from the earthly body to the heavenly body. There is a variety of heavenly bodies, but the transition that Paul has in mind here will not be to any heavenly body but to the body like that of the second Adam, the man from heaven. This is the body of God's choice, one that corresponds to the present body on earth, as the wheat plant corresponds to the grain of wheat.

But why does the apostle talk of the resurrection of the body as a transformation? It is true that the resurrection of the body is a traditional expectation, upheld by the Pharisees and in apocalyptic

---

[42] This is now generally accepted by the exegetes. See K. Müller, "Leiblichkeit," 178–84.

[43] Schade, *Apokalyptische Christologie*, 204. For a different view, see Dahl, *Resurrection*, 17–19.

[44] This does not exclude the regularity of nature, as Bultmann (*Glauben und Verstehen*, 59) would have it, for Paul regards the working of nature as proceeding according to the plan of the Creator. He does not here oppose nature to God or regard nature as being independent of God. Cf. Sider, "Resurrection Body," 431–35.

circles. This is clear from Dan 12:2; *1 Enoch* 62:15–16; 2 Bar. 49–51; 4 Ezra 7:95–98, 8:51–54; Mark 12:18; and Acts 23:6–8. Jewish writings, however, are not unanimous in this regard; they speak of the immortality without the resurrection of the body (Philo, Wisdom) and also of the resurrection as the return into the present body.

In *2 Bar.* 51, for instance, the transformation takes place after the judgment: the earth gives back the dead as it has received them (v. 3), then the judgment follows, and then the transformation. The change affects the just and the bad: the just are transformed into the splendor of angels and the stars (v. 5), or into any shape they desire, "from beauty to loveliness, and from light to the splendor of the glory" (v. 10); the wicked are changed into horrible shapes in which they waste away.

Some scholars have suggested that in 1 Cor 15 Paul is interested in the continuity between the present body and the resurrection body. Parables of Jesus like the Mustard Seed[45] or the parable of the Sower show that such continuity exists in the world of vegetation. Others point out that even in the example of the seed and the plant growing from it, there is no continuity: it is God who sovereignly chooses the body to come out of the seed.[46] The resurrection body is wholly other, with no relation to the present body. But this is an overstatement, for the sower sows grains of wheat in expectation of the wheat harvest. The seed sprouts and grows into the corresponding plant. Paul is probably thinking of the order that God has established at creation[47] and is observed by everyone. He has scarcely in mind a new and arbitrary act of creation for every sowing. The sower does not determine the outcome, but the sower sows wheat in expectation of a wheat harvest.

Paul's point is not that there is a somatic continuity; he takes it for granted, as the repeated "this" in v. 53 indicates:[48] "For this perishable body must put on imperishability, and this mortal body must put on immortality." His point, rather, is that there will not be a return to the present kind of body. He has already estab-

---

[45]Dahl, "Parables of Growth," 148; see also *Resurrection*, 31–36.

[46]This is maintained by Craig ("1 Corinthians") and Conzelmann (*1 Corinthians*, 281). For Conzelmann, the new life is "a *new* creation."

[47]Sider, "Resurrection Body," 432. This is implied also by K. Müller ("Leiblichkeit," 193).

[48]Conzelmann, *1 Corinthians*, 280. According to K. Müller ("Leiblichkeit," 182), however, the aim of Paul in this section is the physical nature of the resurrection body; cf. also Dahl, *Resurrection*, 28. But this is not indicated in the text.

lished the difference among the various earthly bodies, among the various heavenly bodies, and between the earthly and the heavenly bodies. He uses σάρξ for the living things on earth, and σῶμα, *soma*, for the heavenly things.[49] The contrast pertains only to the undesirable properties of the present body, such as dying, death, and lowliness. Σάρξ (flesh) is what living organisms have in common and what also makes them different from one another. There is a variety of σάρξ. First Corinthians 15 contains no hint that the apostle regards the present body from the moral perspective, as a sinful body.[50] In 2 Cor 4:16–18 he states that there is an ongoing spiritual renewal in the present while our physical body is experiencing dying, illness, humiliations, etc. But in that context the apostle still expects to be raised from the dead at the Lord's coming (4:14).[51]

The resurrection body is thus not a new creation.[52] The apostle talks in 1 Cor 15:51–54 about "change" (ἀλλαγησόμεθα, *allagēsometha*) and the transformation, rather than about a "creation." Besides, the repeated "this" links the present body to the resurrection body. Yet the resurrection and transformation are very much an act of God: it happens in a moment, in the twinkling of an eye, at the last trumpet. It is not a natural or gradual transition from one state to a higher state. The change lies not in assuming the likeness of Adam but in being assimilated into the second Adam, the man from heaven. It undoes the loss of life that the first Adam has incurred for all human beings.

---

[49] Conzelmann (*1 Corinthians*, 282) argues that despite appearances Paul does not use σάρξ and σῶμα in 1 Cor 15:39–41 synonymously: σάρξ is the stuff of which the body consists; it stands on its own, while σῶμα is combined with δόξα. Accordingly, σῶμα is not the stuff of the body but the form, and δόξα is its state. But against Conzelmann's position speaks the fact that σάρξ is specified by Paul as σάρξ of beasts, of birds, of fish, of men. And in 1 Cor 15:40 Paul uses δόξα for the heavenly as well as for the earthly things. K. Müller ("Leiblichkeit," 202–5 n. 114) suggests for δόξα here the Hebrew כָּבוֹד, *kābôd* in the sense of "appearance." According to him, Paul is here drawing on Gen 1:14–19.

[50] Although Paul relates Adam's sin to the mortality of the human race, he is here not thinking of the sinfulness (Sider, "Resurrection Body," 432–33), as in Gal 5:21, but of the mortality and corruptibility of the present body. The bondage here is the bondage to death. But see Dahl, *Resurrection*, 82–83. In 1 Cor 15:53–54 Paul does not exhort to holiness of life, as in Gal 5:21.

[51] Conzelmann, *1 Corinthians*, 281.

[52] K. Müller ("Leiblichkeit," 187–227), speaks of new creation to emphasize the otherness of the resurrected body.

The word δεῖ, *dei* ("must") in v. 53 echoes the δεῖ in v. 25: death must be subjected to Christ; death must be eliminated.

Schade,[53] following L. Schottroff,[54] suggests that the answer to Paul's insistence on the risen body is rooted in Christ as the prototype of the faithful. Just as Christ was raised in body, albeit in a different body, so also will those who belong to him be raised in a body that resembles the risen Christ's body. Their body also will be suffused by the Spirit. But there is a difference between Christ and Christians: Christ is the "life-giving Spirit." In light of Gen 2:7, he is the protagonist of creation. He is not only endowed by life and Spirit; he endows others with life and Spirit.

The resurrection thus also represents God's victory—the conquest of death and sin (vv. 54–57). God's design for human beings cannot be undone by sin: God will not only restore human beings to the original glory but also allow them to share in the glory of his Son.

F. THE LIVING AT THE PAROUSIA

Against the objection that the resurrection of the body means a return to the present body, Paul emphasizes the otherness of the resurrection body. With v. 50 he asserts, "Flesh and blood cannot inherit the kingdom of God, nor does the perishable inherit the imperishable." The resurrected body will not be "flesh and blood," nor will it be mortal and corruptible. This means the necessity of change in the living human beings. There is an incompatibility between mortal human beings and the kingdom of God. The incompatibility, involving as it does the very constitution of human beings, is no accident. Paul links it to the salvific purpose of Christ: Christ must reign until he has put death under his feet (v. 27). Only with the removal of death will God be all things to all. Only then will the mission of Christ be fulfilled.

The apostle thus makes in v. 50 a statement whose truth goes beyond the resurrection of the dead, the subject matter of this chapter. The living, such as they are, cannot inherit the kingdom of God. They must first be changed. The statement in v. 51, "We will not all die, but we will all be changed," hence implies two

---

[53] Schade, *Apokalyptische Christologie,* 206.
[54] Schottroff, *Der Glaubende,* 133–34.

things: that the parousia will come before everybody will die and that Paul himself expects to live to see it.

Paul does not assert that he himself will in fact be alive when the Lord will come, but he clearly expects to be alive then. He does not think that everyone will die or that everyone must first die before the Lord comes. In 2 Cor 4:14, however, he expects to be raised up; it seems that by this point he has come to terms with the likelihood that he will die before the Lord comes.

In Phil 1:21–23 Paul is even more definite: he wants to die so that he will be with the Lord. Death will not be an end but will bring him home, where the Lord is. He expects to be with the Lord immediately upon his death; that is why he would like to depart: he wants to be with the Lord.

Yet the awareness of people dying is present in 1 Cor 15, just as it is in 1 Thess 4:13–5:11. But in 1 Thess 4:13–18 dying before the Lord's coming was still regarded as an exception, and Paul provided an assurance that God will look after these exceptions. In 1 Cor 15, however, dying is no longer regarded as an exception; Paul's entire discussion in this chapter has been about the resurrection of the dead at the end time. Still it is not the rule for all, since the parousia is expected to take place soon.[55]

Yet in ch. 15 the apostle does not deal with the problem of the near or delayed parousia. His focus in vv. 50–56 is on the transformation, his main assertion being, "We will all be changed." The statement "We will not all die" suggests that some, Paul among them, will live to see the Lord's coming.[56]

Thus, those who will be alive at the parousia will also be changed. They are flesh and blood, and must undergo a change. Paul presents that change as a miraculous event effected by the power of God and his Christ. Christ is the life-giving Spirit who will reconstitute our present body into a spiritual body like his own.

G. 1 CORINTHIANS 15:50–55 AND 1 THESSALONIANS 4:13–18

The differences between 1 Thess 4:13–18 and 1 Cor 15:50–55 have been noted earlier. They reflect the different questions that Paul is answering in each instance. In 1 Thess 4:13–18 he assures

---

[55] Cf. 1 Cor 7:29, 31.
[56] This is a concessive clause: "Although we will not all die."

the community that the deceased believers will share with the living in the Lord's coming. For this reason he presents the resurrection as a return to this life, so that those brought to life again can qualify for the taking up. The ultimate reality here is life with the Lord forever. In 1 Cor 15:50–55 he asserts that life in the risen body does not mean a return to the present body. The kingdom of God calls for a change, and that change will affect the dead as well as the living. The dead will be raised to possess a glorified body, and the living will be transformed. All will be endowed with immortality and incorruptibility at the Lord's coming. Thus, in 1 Thess 4:13–18 he portrays the parousia, while in 1 Cor 15:50–56 he depicts the end-time transformation. In 1 Thess 4:13–18 the dead return to this life, but in 1 Cor 15:50–56 they are raised into an immortal and incorruptible life. Here the parousia is the occasion for the transformation.

There are also notable similarities in the structure of the two texts. Paul's introductory clause, ἰδοὺ μυστήριον ὑμῖν λέγω, *idou mystērion hymin legō* in 1 Cor 15:51 corresponds to ἐν λόγῳ κυρίου, *en logō kyriou* in 1 Thess 4:16. The description ἐν ἀτόμῳ, ἐν ῥιπῇ ὀφθαλμοῦ, ἐν τῇ ἐσχάτῃ σάλπιγγι, *en atomō, en rhipē ophthalmou, en tē eschatē salpingi*, in 1 Cor 15:52 corresponds to ἐν κελεύσματι, ἐν φωνῇ ἀρχαγγέλου καὶ ἐν σάλπιγγι θεοῦ, *en keleusmati, en phōnē archangelou, en salpingi theou*, in 1 Thess 4:16. "The dead will rise incorruptible" (1 Cor 15:51) echoes "*the dead* in Christ *will rise* first" (1 Thess 4:16); and "*we* will all be changed" (1 Cor 15:52) corresponds to "after that *we*, who are alive, who are left" (1 Thess 4:17). The suggestion has been made that 1 Cor 15:50–55 draws on 1 Thess 4:13–18.

The correspondence is impressive but to be expected, for the apostle deals in both instances with the Lord's parousia and the events associated with it. There is correspondence in the general structure, rather than in the individual items and in the meaning of these items. The word ἀλλαγησόμεθα, for instance, is the key word in 1 Cor 15:50–56. It is used in this sense by Paul only here, although he employs it also in Gal 4:30 and Rom 1:23. This usage also differs from the apocalyptic references to transformation in the end time. *Second Baruch* 49–51, which comes closest to Paul in its description of end-time events, mentions the resurrection and the transformation. In *2 Baruch* 49–51 the transformation follows the resurrection. Through the resurrection, human beings are restored to the former body and are subsequently transformed.[57] But according to 1 Cor 15:50–55, the dead are raised directly into a spiritual body.

Jewish apocalyptic also insists that in paradise there will be no place for death, dying, sickness, sin, etc. In this regard, Paul in 1 Cor 15 does not differ significantly from this view. He goes, however, deeper, in vv. 50–53, when he insists on the impossibility of corruption and death in the kingdom of God and when he telescopes the resurrection and the transformation into one instantaneous and miraculous act. *Second Baruch* seems to agree more with 1 Thess 4 than with 1 Cor 15. And Paul still envisions the parousia in the near future, indefinite as that may be; hence he envisions a transformation of the living. In this respect, he differs from Jewish apocalyptic thought in *2 Baruch*, *4 Ezra*, and even *1 Enoch*.

The apostle mentions the living and the dead in 1 Cor 15:50–55 in order to bring out the universality of the ultimate change: whoever would enter the kingdom of God must be changed. The idea of equality is not his concern here. In 1 Thess 4:16–17, however, that idea is very much present in his entire depiction of the ultimate fulfillment. There he insists that the dead will share equally and together with the living in the Lord's coming. He introduces that entire depiction by saying, "We who are alive, who are left until the coming of the Lord, will by no means precede those who have died" (v. 15). Hence, comparing these two texts from this point of view is misleading: Paul is answering two quite different questions.[58]

In 2 Cor 4:14, however, the apostle does emphasize the equality. The situation there, however, is quite different. What he asserts is that he himself, who is experiencing suffering in the present and who may die, will not be any worse off for that than they will be in the end-time fulfillment. He states, "We also . . . know that the one who raised the Lord Jesus will raise us also with Jesus, and will bring us with you into his presence." Paul

---

[57] This difference has been usually neglected by the exegetes, including K. Müller. It is often assumed that the resurrection in 1 Cor 15 is also the model for that in 1 Thess 4, which is scarcely the case; cf. Klein, "Naherwartung," 255–56.

[58] Nor is Paul here presenting the resurrection as an equally acceptable fulfilment to the transformation, as Hoffmann (*Toten*, 247) suggests. According to K. Müller ("Leiblichkeit," 235 n. 220), this does not agree with the apostle's emphasis here on the end-time change. Only a resurrection that is at the same time also a transformation makes the dead fit for the kingdom of God.

places himself among those who will be dead at the parousia of the Lord; he lets the Corinthians believe, however, that they will still be alive at that time.

CONCLUSION

In 1 Cor 15:50–55 Paul brings to a close the argument that he began in v. 35: "How are the dead raised? With what kind of body do they come?" According to him, it is foolish to expect that the dead will be raised with the same body that they had before they died. Christ has, through his resurrection, become the heavenly man; as a result, the faithful will also become heavenly. The kingdom of God has no place for death and corruption; therefore the faithful, as they are now, deceased or alive, are not fit for the kingdom of God. The dead must be raised and become immortal, and the living must become imperishable and incorruptible. Everyone must change.

Paul talks here of physical existence; he does not have in mind the imperishable and immortal soul. He thus differs in this respect from Hellenistic eschatology, although he employs words such as "incorruptibility" and "immortality." He speaks of an incorruptible and immortal body, as does Jewish apocalyptic. The resurrection that he envisages is the resurrection of the body or the resurrection into the body. It is not merely that the souls of the dead are released from the place of the dead. And the change in the living includes the change in the body. It is this universal restoration that he regards as God's victory over death. But the restoration is not a return to the present life in the body, for that body would still be subject to death and that life would still not be like the life of the heavenly man.

The parousia is not mentioned here explicitly. Rather, it is implied in the phrase "at the last trumpet" (v. 52) (cf. 1 Thess 4:16). In fact the parousia is not the focus here, as it is in 1 Thess 4:13–18. The Lord's coming is the occasion for the resurrection of the dead; it serves as the anchor for the latter. Hence, Paul does not describe the parousia; he only asserts the reality of it when he states, "For the trumpet will sound" (v. 52).

Compared with 1 Cor 15:23–28, vv. 50–55 have a wider horizon: they deal not only with the resurrection but also with the end-time transformation. Here the resurrection is subsumed under the transformation, which includes the living and the dead. But the living do not have to die first in order to be transformed. And the dead do not have to be restored to this life first in order to be transformed.

Whereas 1 Thess 4:13–18 emphasizes union with the Lord, 1 Cor 15:50–55 stresses transformation into the likeness of the risen Lord, the "man from heaven." The resurrection therefore has different functions in these two texts. In 1 Thess 4:13 the return to this life qualifies the risen for the taking up. This "resurrection" provides the starting point, the terminus a quo, of the translation to the Lord. It is the link that connects the dead with the taking up. This resurrection must therefore take place before the taking up.

But in 1 Cor 15:50–56 there is no translation and no before or after. Here Paul talks of instantaneous transformation. Everything takes place "in the twinkling of an eye." The resurrection here entails a transformation of the dead directly into the somatic life like that of the risen Lord. In the scheme of 1 Thess 4:13–18, it involves not only the terminus a quo—the living and the dead—but also the shift from this mode of existence to the terminus ad quem. While 1 Thess 4:13–18 deals with life with the Lord, 1 Cor 15:50–56 concerns life resembling that of the risen Lord—being conformed to the Lord. It is therefore intrinsically salvific. Although 1 Cor 15 deals with the resurrection of the dead, Paul still thinks of the living at the parousia and speaks of their transformation. As 7:29–31 indicates, the apostle still hopes to live to see the Lord's coming.

The ethical component of 15:56–58 gives the impression of being an appendix. Ethical concerns occur also in 1 Thess 4:16, which speaks of the dead "in Christ," and in 1 Cor 15:23, which envisions the resurrection of those "who belong to Christ." The ethical component is a strong feature in 1 Thess 5:1–11, which contains a warning to those living in darkness, a reassurance to those who belong to the light and the day, and an exhortation to vigilance and sobriety. The next section to be investigated, Phil 3:20–21, also contains a strong ethical dimension.

7

THE FINAL DESTINATION,
PHILIPPIANS 3:20–21

In agreement with 1 Thess 4:16, Phil 3:20–21 states that the Lord will come from heaven, although it does not employ the term παρουσία. Paul asserts, "But our citizenship is in heaven, and it is from there that we are expecting a Savior, the Lord Jesus Christ. He will transform the body of our humiliation that it may be conformed to the body of his glory, by the power that also enables him to make all things subject to himself." The statement is in antithesis to the sad observation of the preceding verses that "many live as enemies of the cross of Christ." Since the Lord is expected to come from heaven and since he will change our lowly bodies, the faithful should strive for the things of heaven, rather than for earthly satisfactions. The parousia is here a referent of Paul's ethical exhortation.

This text contains some of the motifs that were found in 1 Thess 4:13–18, 5:1–11 and 1 Cor 15:23–28, 15:50–55. It mentions the coming of the Savior from heaven, the transformation of our present bodies, the conformation to the risen Lord, and the power of the exalted Lord to subject all things to himself. Most important, Phil 3:20–21 contains a clear assertion that at his coming the exalted Christ himself will transform our bodies.

A. THE SITUATION

The immediate context of Phil 3:20–21 is the exhortation in which Paul is urging the faithful in Philippi to set their eyes on the ultimate completion that comes from heaven, rather than on the fulfillment that the world gives (vv. 17–19). In vv. 20–21 he gives the reason (γάρ) why they should imitate him rather than those he mentioned in vv. 17–19—the enemies of the cross of Christ, whose god is their belly, whose glory is in their shame, and whose minds are set on earthly things. The believers must set their sights on the reality beyond this life, that is, on heaven: it is from there that the Savior will come who will transform their present lowly body into the likeness of his own glorious body.

It has been observed that Phil 3, in which our text is located, stands in sharp contrast to the preceding chapters. In v. 2 Paul suddenly warns the community against certain Christians whom he calls "dogs" and "evil workers." The vehemence of this language resembles that of 2 Cor 11:13, where he is encountering his slanderers in Corinth.[1] And there as well the language is in sharp contrast with that found in the preceding chapters.

Although the apostle mentioned in Phil 1:15–17 that some preach Christ "from envy and rivalry," from a selfish motive and out of spite, he managed to put a good meaning on their preaching: Christ is proclaimed in every way, whether out of false or true motives (v. 18). Assured that the proclamation of his competitors is basically acceptable, Paul remained serene and calm as he wrote to the Philippians, willing to be upstaged. He did not feel a "divine jealousy" (cf. 2 Cor 11:2) for the community; he did not warn it of deceivers, and he did not defend his apostolic status before them, although he called them "opponents" (ἀντικειμένων, antikeimenōn, 1:28).

In 3:2–4, however, the apostle suddenly turns on one group of people with such words as "dogs," "evil workers," and "those who mutilate the flesh (κατατομήν, katatomēn)." The pent-up vehemence of his language indicates that here the threat is perceived as real. Paul feels that he has to counter this threat. Some scholars suggest that Paul is speaking against the itinerant Christian missionaries of Judaizing stamp.[2] It seems that they were putting emphasis on circumcision (mutilation of the flesh), tradi-

---

[1] Paul calls his opponents here "false apostles, deceitful workers, disguising themselves as apostles of Christ" while they are really ministers of Satan. He warns that "their end will match their deeds" (2 Cor 11:13–15).

[2] Byrne, "Philippians," 791–92. Here, however, Paul does not talk as he does in 2 Cor 11:13–15. The missionary component of their identity is thus not clear.

tional worship, and belonging to the chosen race. The apostle warns the Philippians against them, as the triple βλέπετε, *blepete*, in v. 2 indicates.

These opponents, it is asserted, can scarcely be the same as those mentioned in ch. 1, unless in the meantime, before Paul wrote ch. 3, something changed his mind about their teaching. To account for this discrepancy, many scholars have resorted to the compilation hypothesis.[3] Schmithals suggests that the present letter to the Philippians is a conflation of three letters written at intervals to the Philippian community. In his scheme, 3:2–4:3, 8–9, in which our text is imbedded, belongs to Letter C.[4] Schmithals's hypothesis has been adopted with minor variations by a great number of scholars.[5] According to Schmithals[6] and J. Müller-Bardorff,[7] Paul now makes a more accurate assessment of the same situation, regarding the intruders as a real threat to the community's standing in the faith, and is dealing with the same group of opponents as in ch. 1.[8]

While Schmithals considers the objective situation in Philippi to have been the same during Paul's writing of these letters—that only Paul's judgment of it has changed—Gnilka asserts that the situation itself has changed in the meantime. According to him, since Paul's writing of chs. 1–2, a mission took place in Philippi in which the missionaries infected the community with wrong notions.[9] Gnilka identifies them as the heralds of the θεῖος ἀνήρ, *theios anēr*, doctrine.[10] But it is best not to label these opponents too

---

[3] For a survey of opinions, see Garland, "Composition," 141–42.

[4] Schmithals suggests the following division of Phil: A: 4:10–23; B: 1:1–3:1, 4:4–7; C: 3:2–4:3, 8–9. This division has been adopted with minor variations by Koester ("Purpose," 317), Bornkamm ("Philipperbrief," 193–95), Marxsen (*Introduction*, 61–62), Rahtjen ("Three Letters of Paul," 167), Beare (*Commentary*, 4–5, 101–2), Benoit (*Les Epîtres*, 19), Friedrich (*Briefe*, 126–28), Murphy-O'Connor, "Philippiens," 1211–12), Gnilka (*Philipperbrief*, 5–11), Schenk (*Philipperbriefe*, 6–9), and others. Kümmel (*Introduction*, 333) and many others still defend the unity of the epistle; see Garland, "Composition," 142–43.

[5] The unity of Phil has been discussed since the seventeenth century. See Gnilka, *Philipperbrief*, 6; Schmithals, "Irrlehrer."

[6] Schmithals, "Irrlehrer," 300–306.

[7] Müller-Bardorff, "Einheit des Philipperbriefes."

[8] Schmithals regards these opponents as Gnostics.

[9] Gnilka, "Antipaulinische Mission"; see also *Philipperbrief*, 8.

[10] Gnilka, *Philipperbrief*, 211–18. According to him, the Philippian opponents were Hellenistic Jewish Christians who regarded Jesus as a θεῖος ἀνήρ and themselves as sharers of his power and glory through the Spirit. The θεῖος ἀνήρ

strictly or settle the discussion about their doctrine. For one thing, there is considerable doubt that Paul is here fighting a well-defined Gnostic sect.[11] For another, there is no hard evidence in ch. 3 that the opponents are missionaries, like those in 2 Cor 11:13.

In Phil 3 itself W. D. Lütgert sees two groups of opponents, the Jewish persecutors of Christians (vv. 2–11) and the opponents of the cross in the community (vv. 12–21).[12] Schmithals, Koester, and Gnilka, however, regard the opponents mentioned in vv. 2–4 and 17–19 as a single front, although they identify it somewhat differently. But is the group mentioned in vv. 17–19 the same as that in vv. 2–4? And does the conceptual unity of ch. 3 rule out a shift in Paul's response in v. 17? In contrast to v. 2, the apostle in vv. 17–19 repeats his earlier warnings against the enemies of the cross of Christ, who are dangerous because of their denial of the cross in their lives. It is in antithesis to vv. 17–19 that in vv. 20–21 he sets before the Philippians the true goal for which they should strive.

The compilation theory, however, is convincingly challenged by W. J. Dalton,[13] D. E. Garland,[14] and L. G. Bloomquist.[15] Dalton points out "a regular pattern of words and ideas" repeated throughout Philippians in a manner that indicates "the inner movement and meaning of the text."[16] Garland brings out the pattern of inclusion between 1:27 and 4:3 and disputes the basis of the division in 3:1–2, which is the hinge of all compilation theories. According to him, those who defend the compilation of Philippians agree that there is a shift in 3:1–2 but disagree about the boundaries in 4:1–10 and 1:1–3.[17]

---

notion, Gnilka asserts, is found in Philo's writings and comes through in the Moses midrash in 2 Cor 3:12–18. The reflection of divine light on the face of Moses is a sign of his being given divine glory, which is passed on to his followers through the Spirit. With this outlook, the opponents mentioned in Phil 3:17–19 embraced a realized eschatology in which a sharing in the passion of Christ played no role.

[11] Most scholars regard Schmithals's theory as an overstatement.

[12] Lütgert, *Die Vollkommenen*, 10–32. Gnilka, however, denies that there is a shift in Phil 3:12 (*Philipperbrief*, 196–98). Against Dibelius (*Thessalonicher I/II, Philipper*, 59, 92), Beare (*Commentary*, 133), and Betz (*Nachfolge und Nachahmung*, 151), who locate this change at v. 17, Gnilka asserts the unity of the chapter.

[13] Dalton, "Integrity of Philippians."

[14] Garland, "Composition."

[15] Bloomquist, *Suffering*, 101–3. Bloomquist bases his argument on lexical and thematic parallels found throughout Phil.

[16] Ibid., 99; also 101–3. Hooker ("Interchange in Christ," 356–57) also points to the agreement in vocabulary between Phil 3 and the earlier chapters.

[17] See Garland ("Composition," 155) for the list of attempts to divide the letter.

The identification of the shift in 3:1–2 is, however, based on a questionable translation of the word βλέπετε as "beware": "Beware of the dogs, beware of the evil workers, beware of those who mutilate the flesh!"[18] As G. D. Kilpatrick points out,[19] the βλέπετε here does not have its object clause introduced by μή, mē, or by the preposition ἀπό, apo, as is the case when it means "beware." It is followed by a direct object and should be translated as "consider." Garland concludes from this that here Paul is not warning the community against a Jewish menace but "is holding the Jews up for consideration as a cautionary example."[20]

In his counterposition the apostle gives two negative examples: the boasts of superiority and the rejection of the cross. To the first he opposes his own abandonment of his former grounds for superiority. For him now the supreme value is Christ, with whom he wants to be conformed in the acceptance of the cross and in the resurrection. He therefore presses forward beyond the present to the goal (vv. 12–15). To those who are engrossed in the enjoyment of life, he opposes the end-time destruction (v. 19).

According to Garland, "The community is not being warned about the gathering cloud of antagonists of Paul who would imperil their spiritual welfare."[21] The apostle does not explain here precisely what the community should guard against. "There are no external opponents in view, and all quests for their identity and party line are red herrings."[22] Garland's suggestion about the thrust of Paul's thought in ch. 3, however, while right in many respects, does not sufficiently embed vv. 20–21 in Paul's train of thought. What links Paul's response is the reversal of values: what he himself once valued highly as a Jew he now regards as rubbish, because of the supreme value, Christ Jesus (vv. 7–8). Those who glory in this world will see that glory destroyed. Hence, the believer should seek the glory of heaven.[23]

---

[18] NRSV; NEB; NAB; *Einheitsübersetzung der Heiligen Schrift: Das Neue Testament; Traduction oecuménique de la bible. Edition intégrale: Nouveau Testament.*

[19] See Kilpatrick, "ΒΛΕΠΕΤΕ."

[20] Garland, "Composition," 166. Garland is quoting Caird, *Paul's Letters,* 131. Baumbach ("Zukunftserwartung," 444–45) points to the absence of concrete data about these opponents and the absence of information on the concrete situation in which they worked. On Phil 3:1 see also Reed, "Hesitation Formulas," 65.

[21] Garland, "Composition," 166.

[22] Ibid.

[23] Ibid., 167–71.

In addition, there is Paul's determination to press forward to the goal. In v. 14 he states, "I press on toward the goal for the prize of the heavenly call of God in Christ Jesus." And in v. 20 he asserts, "But our citizenship is in heaven, and it is from there that we are expecting a Savior, the Lord Jesus." The response in v. 14 is personal, but in v. 20 it is communal: it turns into an exhortation.

According to Garland, ch. 3 therefore is not only a unity but also fully integrated with the rest of the epistle. Paul achieves this by means of the structural device of inclusion. This device makes 1:27–4:3 into a literary unit with its own coherence.[24] In 3:1 the apostle repeats what "he has already spoken of before in his ministry among the Philippians, namely his condemnation of Jewish boasts of superiority, his reminiscences about his life as a devout Pharisee, and the nature of righteousness through faith in Christ as opposed to righteousness based on the law."[25] Paul repeats as well his condemnation of Christians who have abandoned the cross. Garland points out the recurrence in 3:20, 4:1, and 4:3 of rare words that appeared first in 1:27, which would "seem to mark out 1:27–4:3 as a unit."[26] Paul employs in 1:27 the verbs πολιτεύεσθε, politeuesthe, στήκετε, stēkete, and συναθλοῦντες, synathlountes. These verbs are echoed respectively by πολίτευμα, politeuma (3:20), στήκετε (4:1), and συνήθλησαν, synēthlēsan (4:3). The fact that πολιτεύομαι, politeuomai, and πολίτευμα occur only here in Paul's writings, and συναθλέω, synathleō, only in 1:27 and 4:3 in the NT, increases the significance of this agreement.[27] It appears that Philippians is a unified composition, after all. Thus, the entire letter is the larger context of our passage.

B. THE EXPECTATION OF THE LORD'S COMING FROM HEAVEN

With the emphatic ἡμῶν γάρ, hēmōn gar in v. 20 Paul takes up πολλοὶ γάρ, polloi gar, in v. 18. He contrasts the shameful life and

---

[24] Garland (ibid., 159–60) singles out 1:12–26, 27–30 and 2:1–18, 19–24, 25–30 as such units.

[25] Ibid., 164–65.

[26] Ibid., 169.

[27] Garland (ibid., 161) mentions also σωτηρία, sōtēria (1:28), ἀπώλεια, apōleia (1:28; 3:19), σωτήρ, sōtēr (3:20), παράκλησις, paraklēsis (2:1), παρακαλῶ, parakalō (4:2), τὸ αὐτὸ φρονῆτε, to auto fronēte (2:2), τὸ αὐτὸ φρονεῖν, to auto fronein (4:2).

end of the opponents of the cross (vv. 18–19) with the community's goal. The community's home country (πολίτευμα) is heaven: it is from heaven that they expect their Savior Jesus Christ. The ultimate reality is not the pleasures of this world but heaven. It is from heaven that Christ will come. The horizon of his expectation thus includes existence beyond the life on earth. Paul here presents to the community the vision of salvation that is associated with the coming of the Lord Jesus Christ.

Some scholars have suggested that πολίτευμα here is an allusion to the status of Philippi as a Roman military colony. According to K. L. Schmidt, Paul is implying that the believers here on earth are like a colony consisting of a group of emigrants whose privileges are preserved in their home country, heaven.[28] P. Bonnard suggests that πολίτευμα here refers to heaven as the capital city from which the Savior will come to deliver the faithful on earth; it does not denote the heavenly refuge of the faithful after death but, rather, the sovereign authority of the Savior.[29] For M. Dibelius[30] πολίτευμα implies that the Philippian community is an image of the heavenly πολιτεία, politeia, their home country, just as an earthly πολίτευμα is a miniature of the native πολιτεία and carries its name.[31] To E. Güttgemanns, πολίτευμα suggests that the Philippian Christian community is a transcendent entity.[32]

But Gnilka dismisses these suggestions as too elaborate. According to him, Paul here tries to make it clear to the Philippians that they are sojourners and strangers on earth, since their city and their citizenship are in heaven.[33] They are destined for the heavenly homeland. The apostle is confronting the "realized eschatology" of his opponents. In contrast to the attitude castigated in vv. 17–19, he indicates that the home country of the community is not on earth; neither is it now in their possession; it is in heaven and yet to be reached. The contrast between τὰ ἐπίγεια, ta epigeia, and ἐν οὐρανοῖς, en ouranois, corresponds to the contrast between the claims of fulfillment in the present and the expectation of the

---

[28] Schmidt, Christianisme primitive, 90–91.

[29] Bonnard, Philippiens, 71–72.

[30] Dibelius, Thessalonicher I/II, Philipper , 93.

[31] For further literature on this, see Gnilka, Philipperbrief, 206.

[32] Güttgemanns, Apostle, 243 n. 19.

[33] Gnilka (Philipperbrief, 206) points out that in Hellenistic Greek the term πολίτευμα refers also to the state and to citizenship.

completion in the future. It reflects the opposition between the realized eschatology and the apocalyptic expectation.[34] The spatial imagery here brings out the fact that the believers are only strangers and pilgrims on earth and that their true home is in heaven.

The prepositional clause ἐξ οὗ[35] καὶ σωτῆρα ἀπεκδεχόμεθα κύριον Ἰησοῦν Χριστόν, *ex hou kai sōtēra apekdechometha kyrion Iēsoun Christon*, contains three marks of the Christian fulfillment: it will be heavenly; it will take place in the future (ἀπεκδεχόμεθα); and it will be accomplished by Jesus Christ. Paul's constant expectation is that the risen Lord will come from heaven. We find this in 1 Thess 1:10, 4:16; 1 Cor 15:47; 2 Cor 5:2; and Gal 1:8; and it is also implied elsewhere (1 Thess 3:13; 1 Cor 1:7). Against the realized eschatology of the opponents and their boasting, the apostle stresses the unredeemed state of the present Christian existence, at least in respect to lowly corporeal existence.

Jesus Christ is referred to as the Savior. Although Paul uses this designation for Christ only here, he does ascribe to him a saving function elsewhere. In his view, salvation is through Jesus Christ, although it is ultimately God's doing. Usually, it is Christ's act in the past, his death for us and his resurrection, that is regarded as salvific. But in 1 Thess 1:10 it is the risen Christ, awaited at the end time, who is said to be ῥυόμενον ἡμᾶς, *rhyomenon hēmas*, saving us from the coming wrath. In 5:9 the apostle reassures the community that "God has destined us not for wrath but for obtaining salvation through our Lord Jesus Christ." In that context, salvation is guaranteed by Christ's death for us and delivered at the end time, when he comes as Lord. In 1 Cor 15:20–28, 45–55 Christ is presented as the second Adam, the life-giving heavenly man. At his coming, the dead will be raised imperishable and the living will be transformed. And in Rom 8:20–25 Paul speaks of the ultimate υἱοθεσία, *huiothesia*, that is still to be revealed. The future glory consists in the revelation of this υἱοθεσία, when the faithful will be manifested as "the children of God." There the full glory implies "the redemption (ἀπολύτρωσιν) of our bodies," expected at Christ's coming. In the

---

[34] See Koester, "Purpose," 330.

[35] The phrase ἐξ οὗ refers to οὐρανοῖς rather than to πολίτευμα despite the plural, "heavens." Paul referred to the expectation of Christ ἐκ τῶν οὐρανῶν, *ek tōn ouranōn* (1 Thess 1:10); he described his coming as ἀπ᾽ οὐρανοῦ, *ap' ouranou* (1 Thess 4:16; cf. 2 Thess 1:7); and he referred to the expected dwelling ἐξ οὐρανοῦ, *ex ouranou* (2 Cor 5:2).

present condition, the believers still "groan inwardly" as they await this completion.

Thus, Christ's coming in the end time is regarded by the apostle as a saving act. Usually, he ascribes salvation to the liberation from death, entailing the resurrection and the transformation. In Phil 3:20–21 the word σωτῆρα, sōtēra, refers to the transformation of our humble physical existence. The present existence of the believers still lacks the δόξα for which they are destined (cf. Rom 8:21–23). The realization of this glory is here attributed to the power of Christ to subject all things to himself. It is the subjugation of death, although the apostle does not state this explicitly. It is the establishment of the ultimate order of creation, in which the present lowly body will have no place. Yet the ultimate order involves the body.

Thus, what the faithful expect is salvation through Jesus Christ at his coming. The saving action at the end time is the implementation of Christ's rightful lordship over the cosmos, which has been his prerogative since the resurrection. He has been given the power to subject all things to himself (v. 21). We find here an echo of 1 Cor 15:25, 27, 52–55 and of Phil 2:11. The transformation of our bodies is thus a component of Christ's taking up his eschatological lordship at his coming. But whereas in 1 Cor 15:25–27 Paul talks about the annihilation of death, of the resurrection of the dead, and of the transformation of the survivors, here he simply asserts the end-time transformation of the present lowly body. Phil 2:11 focused on the living body, but in that context Paul talked about the resurrection. His own hope in Phil 3:20–21 is to share in the power of the Lord's resurrection and, hence, for his dead body to be raised and changed into a body like that of the risen Lord.

The contrast to vv. 18–19, implied in ἡμῶν γάρ, restricts this expectation to the faithful. Since the transformation implies conformity to the glory of the risen Christ, it can scarcely be the destiny of those who have denied Christ here on earth or refused to share in the cross of Christ. It is faith in Jesus Christ that counts now, and the righteousness that comes from God based on faith (v. 9). He states in vv. 8–11, "For his sake I have suffered the loss of all things, and I regard them as rubbish, in order that I may gain Christ and be found in him. . . . I want to know Christ and the power of his resurrection and the sharing of his sufferings by becoming like him in his death, if somehow I may attain the resurrection from the dead." In v. 17 he calls on the Philippians to imitate his own example of sharing in the sufferings and death of Christ (cf. v. 10). What he regards here as the cross of Christ is a manner of life that denies worldly values. It is a manner of life attuned to Christ. It is a conformity with the sufferings of Christ (v. 10), an experience of the power of Christ's resurrection, and the hope of the ultimate conformity with Christ through the resurrection. What the apostle wants is to be found in Christ now and in the end time.

Thus, although in vv. 20–21 the apostle does not mention the resurrection, the entire discussion in ch. 3 presupposes it. The ultimate transformation is inclusive, and it includes Paul. He asserts that he himself hopes to share in the power of Christ's resurrection, having also shared in Christ's death. He therefore hopes to be raised from the dead.

The relative clause ὃς μετασχηματίσει τὸ σῶμα τῆς ταπει-νώσεως ἡμῶν, *hos metaschēmatisei to sōma tēs tapeinōseōs hēmōn* ("who will transform the body of our humiliation") then describes the particular effect of the Lord's parousia on the believers with whom the apostle identifies himself—the transformation of our present earthly existence. This is the salvific meaning of Christ's coming. Verse 21b specifies this change as Christ's act of conforming us to himself (σύμμορφον, *symmorphon*), while v. 21c roots this act in Christ's power to subject all things to himself.

Paul is here clearly referring to the Lord's parousia. This is suggested by the verb ἀπεκδεχόμεθα and by the reference to heaven as the place from which the Savior will come (cf. 1 Thess 4:16). According to Gnilka, the apostle employs ἀπεκδέχομαι, *apekdechomai*, for the awaiting of the end-time fulfillment (Rom 8:19, 25; 1 Cor 1:7; Gal 5:5).[36] Normally, the verb refers to an eschatological feature associated with the Lord's coming, such as the υἱοθεσία, *huiothesia* (Rom 8:23), the revelation of the sons of God (8:19), the hope of justification (Gal 5:5). But here and in 1 Cor 1:7 it refers to the awaiting of Christ himself.

In 1 Cor 1:7 the present Christian existence is described as "waiting (ἀπεκδεχομένους, *apekdechomenous*) for the revealing of our Lord Jesus Christ." The apostle points out to the Corinthians that God has bestowed on them an abundance of spiritual gifts and

---

[36] Gnilka, *Philipperbrief,* 207.

will continue to sustain them to the end, so that they will be "blameless (ἀνεγκλήτους, *anenklētous*) on the day of our Lord Jesus Christ" (v. 8). He assures them of God's faithfulness in calling them to the fellowship (κοινωνίαν, *koinōnian*) of his Son.

The expectation of a fulfillment in the future thus means that the present life on earth is not yet the ultimate goal. Paul's point in Phil 3:8–21 is that present existence in the faith is governed by the cross of Christ as well as by our human condition. Mortality and lowliness are part of our physical makeup. The faithful must be conformed to the cross of Christ in order to become conformed to Christ in glory. What they do now will affect their ultimate completion. Those who reject the cross of Christ in their lives will end in destruction. Their present shameful existence will bring them the shame of the end time. Hence, the apostle calls on the Philippians to direct their lives toward the ultimate fulfillment rather than to the shallow offers of this world.

The object of this awaiting is the Savior (σωτῆρα), who is then specified with the appositional title κύριον Ἰησοῦν Χριστόν. The fulfillment is therefore centered on Jesus Christ: he is the goal of all the desires of the faithful. The completion does not consist in belonging to the people of salvation whom Christ will establish in freedom and life, as in Jewish apocalyptic, but in being with Christ forever, in sharing in his resurrection, in becoming like him.

C. THE TRANSFORMATION

The saving activity attributed to the Lord in the end time is indicated here by two expressions, μετασχηματίσει and σύμμορφον: the Lord awaited from heaven will transform (μετασχηματίσει) our lowly bodies, conformed (σύμμορφον) to his own glorious body. The emphasis is on the assimilation. All this will bring the faithful to perfect fellowship (κοινωνία) with the Lord forever. That the fulfillment includes change and conformation to Christ is affirmed by Paul in 1 Cor 15:47–52; in v. 51 he states that "we will all be changed," and in v. 49 that we will bear the image of the heavenly man.

The word μετασχηματίζω, *metaschēmatizō*, occurs in the NT only in Pauline epistles. In 1 Cor 4:6 it has the meaning of "adapt" or "apply": he is applying the foregoing to himself and Apollo. And in 2 Cor 11:13, 14, 15 it means a change of outward appearance, a pretense: false apostles pose as the apostles of Christ. In neither case does it describe an eschatological change.

Philo[37] employs the verb μετασχηματίζω in association with the changing of clothes. When Gaius ambitiously tried to become a demigod, he put on the insignia of a demigod. By changing into the robes of different demigods, "he performed a feat . . . by remodeling and recasting what was nothing but a single body into manifold forms (ἑνὸς σώματος οὐσίαν μετασχηματίζων καὶ μεταχαράττων εἰς πολυτρόπους μορφάς, *henos sōmatos ousian metaschēmatizōn kai metacharattōn eis polytropous morphas*)." It is possible that Paul has borrowed μετασχηματίζω from the vocabulary of Hellenistic mystery cults.

In *T. Rub.* 5:6 this word is used for the transformation of the heavenly Watchers: allured by the beautiful women on earth, these Watchers changed (μετασχηματίζοντο, *metaschēmatizonto*) their heavenly appearance and assumed the form of man. Here the very mode of existence is involved—angelic and human. The reverse transformation, from the earthly to a heavenly form, is suggested in 4 Macc 9:22: The oldest of the Maccabees endured torture by fire as if he were being transformed into incorruptibility (ἐν πυρὶ μετασχηματιζόμενος εἰς τὴν ἀφθαρσίαν, *en pyri metaschēmatizomenos eis aphtharsian*).

The idea of transformation is a commonplace in Paul's eschatological passages. In 1 Cor 15:52–55 the apostle emphasizes the necessity of change for all who enter the kingdom of God. He employs the word ἀλλαγησόμεθα, *allagēsometha* and the imagery of "putting on" a vestment: the perishable body will "put on" imperishability, and the mortal body will "put on" immortality. The same imagery is employed also in 2 Cor 5:2, 4 in conjunction with the imagery of a change of habitation. The present tent will be replaced by a heavenly house; Paul's desire is to be "clothed" with a heavenly "dwelling."

The imagery of transformation occurs often in the descriptions of the ultimate reality in Jewish apocalyptic writings, especially in connection with the acquisition of the ultimate reality. According to *2 Bar.* 51:5–10, the just will be transformed into the splendor of angels and stars. In addition, they can change into any form they

---

[37] *Legat.* 80.

like.[38] The imagery of the change of robes is employed in *1 Enoch* 62:15–16, where the righteous and the elect shall rise from the earth and "shall wear the garments of glory. These garments . . . shall become the garments of life from the Lord of the Spirits." The context indicates that these are the garments of immortality: the garments shall not wear out.

The second word for the eschatological change employed in Phil 3:21 is the adjective σύμμορφον. It indicates the conformation with Christ: in the end time, Christ will make our bodies resemble (σύμμορφον) his own glorified body. While the word μετασχη-ματίσει applies to the starting point, our lowly body, the σύμμορ-φον relates to the finish, to the glorious body of the Lord (τῷ σώματι τῆς δόξης αὐτοῦ, *tō sōmati tēs doxēs autou*). But while the former occurs also in Jewish apocalyptic writings, the latter is unique to the NT and characteristic of Pauline writings.

Paul uses "conformity" to express also our present assimilation to Christ. In Phil 3:10 he employs the verb συμμορφίζω, *symmorphizō*, for the sharing in the death of Christ: he wants to resemble Christ in his death (συμμορφιζόμενος τῷ θανάτῳ αὐτοῦ, *symmorphizomenos tō thanatō autou*). The word σύμμορ-φος, *symmorphos*, is used in Rom 8:29 for the eschatological conformity: "For those whom he foreknew he also predestined to be conformed (συμμόρφους, *symmorphous*) to the image (τῆς εἰκόνος, *tēs eikonos*) of his Son." This eschatological statement resembles that of 1 Cor 15:49, where Paul asserts, "Just as we have borne the image of the man of dust, we will also bear the image of the man of heaven" (cf. Rom 6:8). The eschatological conformation to Christ presumes the exaltation of Christ. But as Phil 3:10 indicates, in v. 21 the apostle has in mind a present sharing in the likeness of Christ as well as the future one. The present sharing is directed to the death of Christ, the future one to the glory of Christ. Christ is thus in everything the πρωτότοκος, *prōtotokos*, the first in a family. What happened to him will happen to those who belong to him.

---

[38] According to *2 Bar.* 51:1–6, the transformation affects the evil and the just. Those who are found guilty at the last judgment will be made more evil "so that they shall suffer torment" (v. 2). They shall be changed into horrible shapes. But the splendor of the righteous will be like that of the angels and the stars: "And they will be changed into any shape which they wished, from beauty to loveliness, and from light to the splendor of glory" (v. 10).

The phrase τὸ σῶμα τῆς ταπεινώσεως ἡμῶν (v. 21) does not signify the body as opposed to the soul or the spirit of man, as in Greek dualistic thinking, but rather the whole corporeal existence of a human being. As Gnilka insists, τὸ σῶμα τῆς ταπεινώσεως is the finite and mortal human existence on earth.[39] Paul, describing in 1 Cor 15:42–44 the contrast between the body that dies and the resurrection body, lists the characteristics of the present physical existence of human beings: the present body is perishable, weak, lacking in honor, and physical. In 2 Cor 5:1 he refers to this earthly existence as the "earthly tent." "The body of our humiliation" in Phil 3:21 thus refers to our present humble existence.[40] Paul here emphasizes the lowliness of this existence, since some have made it their ultimate desire (vv. 17–19). He raises the vision of the Philippians from the present existence to the glory that is to come, to sharing in the glory of Christ.

D. CHRIST THE SAVIOR

The title σωτήρ, applied to Christ, is a unique feature in Phil 3:20–21. This is the earliest written designation of Christ as Savior in the NT,[41] although Paul associates salvation (σωτηρία) with Jesus Christ all along. He ascribes the saving action in a variety of ways to the Christ-event in the past[42] (1 Thess 5:10; 1 Cor 11:24; 15:3b; 2 Cor 5:14, 15; Gal 1:1; 2:20; 3:13; Rom 5:6, 8), to the proclamation of the gospel in the present (2 Cor 6:2; Rom 1:16; cf. Eph 1:13), and to the end-time coming of Jesus (1 Thess 5:8, 9; Rom 13:11).

In Phil 3:20–21 the apostle states that it is from heaven that "we are expecting a Savior (σωτῆρα), the Lord Jesus Christ." A similar statement occurs in 2 Tim 1:9–10: "This grace . . . has now been revealed through the appearing of our Savior (τοῦ σωτῆρος, *tou sōtēros*) Christ Jesus, who abolished death and brought life and immortality to light through the gospel." But there the reference is

---

[39] Gnilka, *Philipperbrief,* 207.

[40] In Phil 2:6–7 Paul speaks of Christ's self-abasement in assuming our human form.

[41] The title occurs 24 times in the NT. It is used 8 times with θεός and 16 times with Jesus Christ (Luke 2:11; John 4:42; Acts 5:31; 13:23; Eph 5:23; Phil 3:20; 2 Tim 1:10; Titus 1:3, 4; 2:10, 13; 3:4, 6; 2 Pet 1:1, 11; 2:20; 3:18; 1 John 4:14). In the letters commonly accepted as Pauline it occurs only in Phil 3:20.

[42] The salvific action is usually made in references to Christ's death for us.

to Christ's coming (revealing) in the past: it was in that event that Christ abolished death, and it is through the proclamation of the gospel that he is bringing about life and immortality.

The act of salvation is ascribed to Christ's future coming in Rom 5:9, 10:13 and 1 Cor 5:5. Thus in Rom 5:10 Paul contrasts the justification wrought at Christ's death with salvation "by his life"—a reference to the risen Christ's future coming. In v. 9 he states, "Much more surely then, now that we have been justified by his blood, will we be saved (σωθησόμεθα, sōthēsometha) through him from the wrath of God." The wrath of God here is the end-time wrath, as in 1 Thess 1:10 and 5:2–3. The faithful who live by the gospel are οἱ σωζόμενοι, hoi sōzomenoi, those destined for salvation (1 Cor 1:18; 2 Cor 2:15).

In the Hellenistic world, the title "Savior" was employed for gods and men.[43] Gods who rule over human beings are saviors from the dangers of life. They are protectors of cities and of their inhabitants.[44] The title "Savior" was also applied to the Ptolemies and Seleucids who, as emperors, were called θεοὶ σωτῆρες, theoi sōtēres.[45] The Roman emperor cult also employed the title "Savior": the emperor who is ushering in the golden era is hailed as the "savior of the world."[46] But Paul here is scarcely comparing Christ with the Hellenistic gods or emperors.

In pseudepigraphical literature the title is reserved for God. While the messianic figures in 1 Enoch are empowered by God to judge, salvation belongs to God alone (the Lord of the Spirits). The righteous are saved "in his name" (48:7). According to 50:3, on the day when the righteous will be given honor, glory, and victory, the sinners will suffer affliction, "yet through his [the Lord of the Spirit's] name they shall be saved." In the Greek fragments of 1 Enoch, σῴζω, sōzō (106:16) and σωτηρία (99:10; 102:7; 98:10, 14; 99:1) are used in the eschatological sense for God's universal saving action, which includes freedom from oppression, sin, and death as well as endowment with life, glory, peace, and grace.

---

[43] See Foerster, "σῴζω, σωτηρία," 104–12.

[44] Ibid., 1004–9.

[45] Ibid., 1009.

[46] According to Foerster (ibid., 1010–12), this designation has no connection with the oriental idea of the beginning and end of time.

In the LXX the title σωτήρ translates מוֹשִׁיעַ, môšî‘a. It is given to humans—the judges (cf. Judg 3:9, 15)—and to God. The tendency, however, is to reserve it for God (Judg 2:18; Neh 9:27): it is not the judge but God who saves Israel.

In the *Testaments of the Twelve Patriarchs* we find the words σῴζω, σωτήριος, *sōtērios*, σωτηρία (*T. Levi* 10:2; 14:2; *T. Dan* 6:7, 9; *T. Gad* 8:1; *T. Jos.* 1:6; *T. Benj.* 3:8; etc.) for God's help to the God-fearing in their struggle against Belial as well as for the eschatological salvation that God will bring about through the tribes of Levi and Judah. But the word σωτήρ is rare; it occurs only in passages that are likely Christian interpolations (*T. Levi* 10:2; 14:2; *T. Dan* 6:9; *T. Benj.* 3:8).[47] In *T. Levi* 2:10–12[48] the angel tells Levi concerning the future redemption (περὶ λυτρώσεως [Aᵝ], *peri lytrōseōs*; τοῦ μέλλοντος λυτροῦσθαι, *tou mellontos lytrousthai*), "By you and Judah[49] shall the Lord appear among men, saving (σῴζων, *sōzōn*) every race of men."[50]

In the Levi-Judah passage in *T. Napht.* 8:2, the patriarch, having shown to his children the last times, states, "Command your children that they may be in unity with Levi and Judah, for through Judah will salvation arise in Israel, and in him will Jacob be blessed." Instead of "salvation," MSS e f have here σωτήρ. Charles[51] and M. de Jonge[52] regard this text as a Christian interpolation, while Kee seems to accept its authenticity. In *T. Judah* 22:2 the term τὸ σωτήριον, *to sōtērion*, refers to God's intervention that will end foreign rule over Judah. The rule of Judah will be terminated "until the salvation (τὸ σωτήριον) of Israel comes, until the coming

---

[47] In his translation, Kee ("Testaments," 775–828), following Charles (*APOT*, 291), marks all these texts as Christian interpolations.

[48] ß, Aᵝ, s¹. See also *T. Dan* 6:79 (ß); *T. Gad* 8:1 (ß-bg); *T. Jos.* 1:6.

[49] According to de Jonge ("Christian Influence"; "Once More"), the present Levi-Judah passages indicate a Christian redaction at a later stage of the composition of the *Testament of Twelve Patriarchs*. While de Jonge considers *T. Levi* 2:11 as a Christian interpolation, Charles regards the phrase "saving every race" to be genuine.

Charles (*APOT*, 289–90) regards *T. 12 Patr.* to be essentially a Jewish composition written between 109 and 107 BCE but considers now some Christian interpolations. Since the discovery of the Dead Sea Scrolls, opinions on this issue have become polarized. Philonenko (*Interpolations*, 1–66), Dupont-Sommer (*Qumran and the Essenes* and *Essene Writings*), and van der Woude (*Die messianischen Vorstellungen*) accept sections and passages that Charles regards as interpolations, while de Jonge (*Testaments*, 52) takes the entire work to be a Christian composition. Philonenko, van der Woude, and de Jonge regard *T. Levi* as the original nucleus of, and as an example for, the other testaments. Cf. also Russell, *Method*, 55–57; Charlesworth, *OTP*, 1.781.

[50] The phrase "saving every race of men" is omitted in the A version; cf. Charles, *APOT*, 286.

[51] Charles, *Testaments*, 155.

[52] De Jonge, *Testaments*, 87.

(παρουσίας) of God's righteousness." In the Levi-Judah passage T. Gad 8:1, the patriarch exhorts his children to obey Judah and Levi, "because from them the Lord will raise up a Savior (ἐξ αὐτῶν ἀνατελεῖ κύριος σωτῆρα, ex autōn anatelei kyrios sōtēra) for Israel."[53]

The Levi-Judah passage in T. Dan 5:10–11, foretelling the return of the exiles, speaks of God's mercy and peace: "And there shall arise for you from the tribe of Judah and [the tribe of] Levi the Lord's salvation. . . . And he will take from Beliar the captives, the souls of the saints." According to the Levi-Judah passage as found in T. Sim. 7:2,[54] the salvation (τὸ σωτήριον) will arise, "for the Lord shall raise up from Levi as it were a High-priest, and from Judah as it were a King [God and man], He shall save (σώσει, sōsei) all [the Gentiles and] the race of Israel."[55]

Similarly, T. Asher 7:3 states that final salvation will be brought about by the Most High when he will "visit the earth." He will crush the dragon in the water and save Israel and the nations. In T. Benj. 10:5–11 the patriarch exhorts his children to keep the commandments of God "until the Lord reveals his salvation (τὸ σωτήριον) to all the nations." This text contains the eschatological order of the resurrection, followed by the transformation.

We also find a reference to the order of the resurrection in T. Judah 24–25. After the rising of "the Star from Jacob" (24:1), a man from Judah's posterity will come. He will be the "shoot of God" (v. 5), the "fountain for the life of all humanity" (v. 5), and the "rod of righteousness for the nations, to judge and to save all that call on the Lord" (v. 6). Then, says the patriarch, "Abraham, Isaac, and Jacob will be resurrected to life and I and my brothers will be chiefs" (25:1).

In Pss. Sol. 10:8 and 12:6 the term σωτηρία is employed for Israel's end-time salvation. In 17:3 God is said to be σωτήρ for sending his Messiah. In 4 Ezra 6:25–26 we also read, "It shall be that

---

[53] The parallel passage, T. Jos. 19:11, has, "for from them shall arise the salvation (σωτηρία) of Israel." This text is taken from the Armenian version. The text in c ß has at this place an obvious Christian interpolation: "Because from their seed will arise the Lamb of God who will take away the sins of the world, and will save all the nations, as well as Israel."

[54] The following is from Charles's restored reading, since the variants are widely divergent at this point.

[55] Kee ("Testaments," 787) translates this text as follows: "Do not exalt yourselves above these tribes [because from them will arise the Savior come from God]. For the Lord will raise up from Levi someone as high priest and from Judah someone as king [God and man]. He will save all the gentiles and the tribes of Israel." De Jonge (Testaments, 88) regards this as a Christian interpolation.

whoever remains after all that . . . shall be saved and shall see my salvation and the end of the world. And they shall see the men who were taken up, who from their births have not tasted death."

In all these texts, however, it is God who is said to be the Savior. He brings about salvation even though he works through the tribes of Levi and Judah or through the figures associated with these tribes. Salvation consists basically in liberation from foreign oppression, in the kingship of Judah, and in the spiritual rule and integrity of Levi. In the final salvation there will be no more disobedience among the sons of Israel.

Thus, the end-time saving action of Jesus, as envisaged by Paul in Phil 3:20–21, his transforming our lowly physical existence on earth, is clearly different from the messianic expectations in the Jewish apocalyptic writings or from the "Savior" designations in Hellenism. The messianic figure in *1 Enoch* (the Messiah, the Elect one, the Son of man) comes closest to the NT messianic designation, but even here there are essential differences. Paul affirms that at his coming Christ will conquer death by transforming our physical makeup. There is no mention of Christ annihilating or subjugating the enemies of the people of the faithful. The salvific action of Christ is spiritual, somatic, and cosmic.

Philippians 3:20–21 also differs from the Hellenistic savior gods. While these intervene in isolated dangers in this life, they do not transform the present human existence or establish a universal salvation. Nor is the savior concept in Phil 3:20–21 to be associated with the Roman emperor cult or with the Gnostic savior figure. Philippians 3:20–21 is closer to the OT depiction of God's coming on earth to establish his rule and kingdom. But what was in the OT attributed to God alone is here ascribed to Christ, who comes from heaven empowered with the fullest authority over everything in creation. His coming means the end of physical existence as we know it now and the beginning of life that is free from mortality and corruptibility.

E. TRADITION AND APOCALYPTIC

The solemn tone of Phil 3:20–21 has led some scholars to believe that the text contains a hymn. E. Lohmeyer[56] sees in these

---

[56] Lohmeyer, *Philipper, Kolosser, Philemon,* 157.

verses a hymn of six lines that Paul himself composed, while
N. Flanagan,[57] Güttgemanns,[58] and G. Strecker[59] regard them as a
non-Pauline hymn but related in thought and vocabulary to 2:6–11,
another non-Pauline hymn. The following correspondence has
been pointed out:

μορφῇ (2:6)	σύμμορφον (3:21)
ὑπάρχων (2:6)	ὑπάρχει (3:20)
σχήματι (2:7)	μετασχηματίσει (3:21)
πᾶν γόνυ κάμψῃ (2:10)	τοῦ δύνασθαι αὐτόν (3:21)
κύριος Ἰησοῦς Χριστός (2:11)	κύριον Ἰησοῦν Χριστόν (3:20).[60]

This vocabulary correspondence and the presence of relative
clauses, which are characteristic of hymn material, suggest that
3:20–21 likewise is a non-Pauline hymn.

But the vocabulary in 3:20–21 has an echo beyond Phil 2:6–11.
Gnilka[61] points out that ὑπάρχω, hyparchō,[62] as well as the title
κύριος Ἰησοῦς Χριστός[63] are found frequently in Pauline writings
and should not be counted as non-Pauline vocabulary. And Garland[64] observes that the "distinctive" vocabulary of 2:6–11 in fact
pervades all of ch. 3. Besides, there is a significant difference in
content between the two texts: 2:6–11 mentions Jesus Christ's
preexistence in God, whereas Christ's preexistence is not in the
picture in 3:20–21; in 2:6–11 the return to God is presented as

---

[57] Flanagan, "A Note," 8–9.

[58] Güttgemanns, Apostel, 240–47.

[59] Strecker, "Redaktion," 75–76.

[60] Güttgemanns, Apostel, 241; cf. Gnilka, Philipperbrief, 208–9; Garland, "Composition," 158.

[61] Gnilka, Philipperbrief, 209.

[62] The word ὑπάρχω is characteristic of Luke–Acts vocabulary, occurring in the
Gospel 15 times and in Acts 25 times. Matt uses this word only 3 times, and Mark
and John not at all. It occurs in Paul 12 times—once in Rom, 5 times in 1 Cor, and
2 times each in 2 Cor, Gal, and Phil.

[63] Strecker ("Redaktion," 76 n. 50) notes that the phrase κύριος Ἰησοῦς
Χριστός occurs in Paul only in two texts, Phil 2:11 and 1 Cor 8:6, which are both
non-Pauline. But Strecker disregards Paul's practice of varying the order of these
words and inserting ἡμῶν between them. Counting all these occurrences, Paul uses
this combination at least 25 times, in greetings, introductory prayers, hymns, and
the body of his letters (Rom 1:4, 7; 5:1, 11, 21; 6:23; 7:25; 8:39; 15:6, 30; 1 Cor 1:2,
3, 8, 9; 15:57; 2 Cor 4:5; 8:9; Gal 1:3; 6:14, 18; Phil 1:2; 2:11; 3:20; 4:23; 1 Thess 1:1,
3; 5:9, 23, 28). Cf. also Gnilka, Philipperbrief, 209 n. 138.

[64] Garland, "Composition," 159.

Christ's exaltation, while 3:20–21 speaks of the believer's transformation; and the constitutive thought of 3:20–21, salvation and the sharing in Christ's life through the glorification of the body, is missing in 2:6–11.[65] But Gnilka's objection that the content in the two texts differs only points out that the two texts deal with two different events. The different contents call for different motifs or different employment of the same motifs.

According to Gnilka,[66] in Phil 3:20–21 Paul employs traditional material and stereotyped expressions. He draws on a credal formula dealing with the coming of Christ the Savior from heaven. This credal fragment, which cannot be reproduced, is meant to refute the opponents. But the notion of "re-creation"—Gnilka refers here to the expression μετασχηματίσει—Paul takes over from his opponents in order to correct their views: the present life on earth is not the ultimate reality; the completion is still to come with the parousia of the Lord.

According to Gnilka, Paul is here correcting the θεῖος ἀνήρ idea, which clad the present existence with the robes of the ultimate reality and denied the cross and the future completion. The opponents are locating the occurrence of salvation in the earthly life of Jesus and in the believers' present sharing in that existence. They deny the cross and the expectation of the resurrection; hence, the apostle here emphasizes the sharing in the cross and in the power of Christ's resurrection.[67]

Against this interpretation is the fact that the apostle's language in Phil 3:20–21 occurs elsewhere in his epistles. The verb μετασχηματίζω occurs also in 1 Cor 4:6 and 2 Cor 11:13, 14, 15, and the μετασχηματίζω motif is restated in the expression σύμμορφον τῷ σώματι τῆς δόξης αὐτοῦ (Phil 3:21). Paul has already used this language in Phil 3:10, where he talks about being conformed to his death (συμμορφιζόμενος τῷ θανάτῳ αὐτοῦ). The latter has nothing in common with the θεῖος ἀνήρ doctrine. In Rom 8:29, which resembles Phil 3:20–21 in language

---

[65] For a similar refutation of Güttgemanns's arguments that Phil 3:20–21 replicates the hymn in 2:6–11, see Gundry, *Sōma in Biblical Theology*, 177–83. According to Gundry, while the vocabularies in 2:6–11 and 3:20–21 are similar, they occur in different order and with different applications. Besides, many important terms in one are missing in the other.

[66] Gnilka, *Philipperbrief*, 209–10.

[67] Ibid., 211–18.

and content, we find συμμόρφους τῆς εἰκόνος τοῦ υἱοῦ αὐτοῦ, *symmorphous tēs eikonos tou huiou autou*. And in 1 Cor 15:49 Paul states that we will "bear the image of the man of heaven" (φορέσομεν καὶ τὴν εἰκόνα τοῦ ἐπουρανίου, *phoresomen kai tēn eikona tou epouraniou*).

As mentioned earlier, the term πολίτευμα occurs only once in the NT.[68] It may reflect the political situation in Philippi as a Roman colony.[69] It may be one of the many ad hoc formulations used by Paul in responding to the situation in Philippi. But what does πολίτευμα here mean? Is heaven the home country of the faithful because Christ is expected from heaven or because the faithful will be taken up to heaven? If the latter is the case, then our text reflects the thought of 1 Thess 4:13–18. It therefore appears that the main thought in these verses is Paul's own, but generously sprinkled with traditional and stereotyped phrases and images. The apostle has creatively refashioned the existing language in order to make his special point here. In this he is true to form.

The specific point that Paul makes here concerns the glorious refashioning of the present human existence, expected at the Lord's coming and effected by the Lord. But it is a moot question whether he is thinking of the resurrection of the dead or of the transformation of the living.[70] The apostle is not excluding either group from this glorious completion, although he leaves the reader with the impression that he is thinking primarily of the living.

This passage thus cannot be taken in isolation from its immediate context in Phil 3. In this chapter the apostle mentions sharing in the cross of Christ and in the power of Christ's resurrection. He expresses hope that he will be raised from the dead. He makes it clear that the present life is not the completion and that he strains forward toward the ultimate prize. The passage, however, is firmly fixed in the apocalyptic framework adopted by the early church.[71] Heaven is the transcendent place above, whence Christ the Lord

---

[68] The verb πολιτεύομαι, however, occurs in Acts 23:1 and Phil 1:27. On the occurrence of πολίτευμα elsewhere in Greek literature, see Gnilka, *Philipperbrief*, 206 n. 120.

[69] Ibid., 206.

[70] Ibid., 208.

[71] The presence of apocalyptic imagery here is admitted also by Gnilka (ibid., 210), who regards Strecker's ("Redaktion," 76) and Koester's ("Purpose," 330–32) descriptions of it as exaggerations.

will come in power, and it is the place of the awaited completion.[72]
The fulfillment will come in the future, and entails a transformation. Christ will come as the Lord in the fullness of power, which
includes the power to transform present human existence.

Yet despite this framework in 3:20–21, the apocalyptic descriptions and imagery have been drastically reduced. Perhaps the
reason for this is that in 3:20–21 Paul is not depicting the parousia
as such, as he does in 1 Thess 4:16, but is only asserting that the
Lord's coming is being awaited (ἀπεκδεχόμεθα) by the community.
No doubt the Philippians can supply the imagery from what Paul
taught them earlier about the Lord's coming. The union with the
coming Lord, depicted in 1 Thess 4:16–18 with another cluster of
apocalyptic images, is here not presented as a taking up, which
effects togetherness, or as being "away from the body and at home
with the Lord," as in 2 Cor 5:8, but as a conformation (σύμμορφον)
to the glorious body of the risen Lord (cf. 1 Cor 15:47–49). And the
transformation (μετασχηματίσει) is not depicted with the imagery
of putting on clothes, as in 1 Cor 15:53–55 and 2 Cor 5:2–4, or as a
change from a lowly habitation to a heavenly habitation, as in
2 Cor 5:1. In Phil 3:20–21 the apostle is not correcting false ideas
about the resurrected body, as he does in 1 Cor 15:50–55 and 2 Cor
5:1–10; he is employing the parousia and the transformation to
correct a way of life centered on this world. He is raising the
expectations of the faithful by highlighting the glorious completion
that will change our present physical constitution. As in all previous instances, the completion here is centered on the exalted
Lord. The motifs of this depiction are found in 1 Cor 15:23–27,
47–49, 52 and 1 Thess 4:16.

CONCLUSION

The above investigation has shown that Phil 3:20–21, firmly
embedded in ch. 3, has as its immediate context vv. 18–19, to which
it is related antithetically. It has also brought out that the vocabulary and the motifs in vv. 20–21 reflect the development of thought
of other chapters in this letter, as well as of other letters of Paul.
Thus the noun πολίτευμα echoes the verb πολιτεύεσθε of 1:27,

---

[72] In Phil 3:14 the apostle talks of the upward call in Jesus Christ.

and the terminology in 3:20–21 resembles that in 2:6–11; hence, in every respect, the passage belongs to the letter to the Philippians as we know it. The σύμμορφον motif and the μετασχηματίσει motif echo Paul's statements in 1 Cor 15:47–48 and 1 Cor 15:53–54, 2 Cor 5:2–4 respectively.

Christ, expected from heaven, is presented in Phil 3:20–21 as savior (σωτῆρα), perhaps to counter the realized eschatology of those mentioned in vv. 17–19. While this title occurs here for the first time in Pauline correspondence, the notions of salvation at Christ's coming and of Christ's active role in effecting the end-time salvation occur in 1 Thess 1:10, 5:9–10 and 1 Cor 15:24–27. The notion of salvation of the body, implied in Phil 3:20–21, is mentioned in Rom 8:23 (ἀπολύτρωσιν) and implied in 1 Cor 15:26, 50, 54–55 and 2 Cor 5:4. In Phil 3:20–21 salvation is related to the transformation of the body, presented as an exaltation. While in 1 Cor 15:50–55 the transformation effects a change from the present mortality and corruptibility of a human body, in Phil 3:20–21 it effects a change from the present lowly state of a human body. The end results are correspondingly different. In 1 Cor 15:50–55 the end term is an immortal and incorruptible body; in Phil 3:20–21 it is life in a glorious body (τῷ σώματι τῆς δόξης). Sharing in the likeness of the risen Lord is asserted in 1 Cor 15:47–48 and in Phil 3:21. But in Phil 3:20–21 the emphasis is on the sharing of Christ's glory, while in 1 Cor 15:47–49 it is on Christ's immortality and incorruptibility. The δόξα of the risen Lord, however, implies incorruptibility and immortality. The transformation brings about a conformity (σύμμορφον) to the risen Christ's body.

The transformation refers, in the first place, to the living, since Paul is talking here about the transformation of the present body. This is suggested also by the antithesis between Phil 3:20–21 and vv. 17–19. The latter presents enjoyment of the satisfactions of this world (of the "belly") as the ultimate reality. But the resurrection of the dead is implied in the context (v. 10) and is an essential component of Christian hope mentioned by Paul. The apostle himself expects it (v. 10). Still, the resurrection is not the reason here for Paul's mentioning the transformation or the Lord's coming. In this regard Phil 3:20–21 differs from 1 Cor 15.

Whereas in 1 Cor 15:23, 52 the parousia serves as the anchor for the resurrection of the dead, in Phil 3:20–21 it anchors the ultimate completion. But here Paul is not making the point, as in

1 Cor 15, that the resurrection has not yet taken place. Nor is he assuring his readers, as in 1 Thess 4:13–18, that the dead Christians will share equally with the living in the Lord's coming. His point here, rather, is that the present life on earth is not the ultimate fulfillment: it lacks the glory of heaven, for which the faithful are destined. That glory will be bestowed on the faithful at the Lord's coming; hence, they should make heaven their goal.

Philippians 3:20–21, more clearly than other texts, ascribes the transformation to Christ himself, although the theocentric dimension is still present, as it is in 1 Cor 15:24–28: Christ has been endowed by the Father with the fullness of power (Phil 2:9–11). But 3:20–21 states more clearly than 1 Cor 15:50–55 that Christ himself will transform our lowly existence. The text suggests that heaven is the ultimate goal: Christ comes from heaven, and those who belong to Christ will share in his heavenly existence. They will bear the image of the heavenly man (1 Cor 15:48). But the text does not depict the acquisition of this existence as a translation from the earth to heaven.

The faithful should therefore make heaven their true goal, rather than the present life on earth. This is the ethical dimension of this passage, in antithesis to vv. 17–19. In this they should imitate the apostle, who is striving to reach the ultimate goal and shares in the cross of Christ. Like Paul, they must share in the cross of Christ (συμμορφιζόμενος τῷ θανάτῳ αὐτοῦ, v. 10) in the hope of sharing also in the power of Christ's resurrection.

PART TWO

THEOLOGICAL INVESTIGATION

The first part of this investigation examined the background of ideas and images Paul employed in his depictions of the Lord's coming, and it took up the soundings of his own thought on the coming by examining key passages dealing with the parousia. This provided us with a fairly good idea of the movement of the apostle's thought on this topic.

In the second part, the investigation extends to other passages in Paul's letters. More synthetic than analytical, it locates the parousia in wider streams of Paul's eschatology and seeks the theological framework of the statements investigated in the first section. This part entails a thematic investigation of such topics as hope, judgment, the conflict motif, "with Christ," the church in Pauline eschatology, the development of Pauline eschatology, and Pauline apocalyptic. It concludes with suggestions for contemporary proclamation.

8

⊛

HOPE

The awaiting of the Lord's coming is of necessity related to the future as presented by faith and hope. It deals with what is yet to come through Christ and is part and parcel of Paul's understanding of God and of Paul's Christology.

Although in his epistles Paul also discusses the future of outsiders, and of the Christians who live like outsiders, his thought is not focused on judgment but on the joyful completion that awaits those who live by faith, love, and hope. This is the hope that he himself cherishes and that he raises in his communities. It is filled with his very personal desire to be ultimately with the Lord whom he loves so dearly and whom he serves. It explains his efforts to bring his communities unblemished to the Lord on the last day.

Hope[1] provides a comprehensive horizon for Paul's statements dealing with salvation and eschatology. It is not an explicit theme as such in Pauline writings, but it pervades all his epistles. It is employed in this investigation as a convenient tool with which to gather Paul's disparate statements concerning the future of the believers.

A. THE LANGUAGE OF HOPE

A glance at a concordance for the NT use of the Greek words ἐλπίς, *elpis* (hope) and ἐλπίζω, *elpizō* (to hope) is revealing.[2] The

---

[1] On hope in biblical and extrabiblical literature, see Woschitz, *Elpis, Hoffnung,* 63–214.

[2] For a lexical study of hope and its synonyms in Pauline writings, see Nebe, *"Hoffnung,"* 19–35.

verb ἐλπίζω occurs in the Gospels and Acts only 7 times, mostly in Luke–Acts,[3] but only 4 times does it deal with Christian hope. In the Pauline epistles ἐλπίζω occurs 13 times—7 times in connection with Christian hope. The noun ἐλπίς is not found in the Gospels but only in Acts and in the NT epistles (44 times).[4] Of the 8 times that it occurs in Acts, it is found 6 times on the lips of Paul. The author of Acts has thus caught a main characteristic of Pauline theology. In the Pauline epistles ἐλπίς occurs 25 times, mostly in 1 Thessalonians and Romans, and always in the context of Christian existence. This is a significant finding.

The message of hope, however, is more pervasive than this vocabulary. It occurs also in texts where Paul does not make use of the Greek words for "hope" or "to hope." It is present when he speaks of the resurrection, the coming of the Lord, and the establishment of the kingdom of God. When he speaks of these realities, he speaks of hope. The apostle also associates with "hope" expressions for awaiting (ἀναμένω, anamenō), expecting (ἐκδέχομαι, ekdechomai; ἀπεκδέχομαι), and looking forward to (ἀποκαραδοκία, apokaradokia, Rom 8:19; Phil 1:20).[5] He also speaks of yearning (Phil 1:23), groaning (2 Cor 5:2, 4), striving (Phil 3:12–14), patience (1 Thess 1:3; Rom 8:24, 25), endurance (Rom 5:4–5), joy (1 Thess 2:19; Rom 5:2), confidence (2 Cor 5:6), and the like. These words bring out the subjective side of hope: the intense joy at the thought of the fulfillment; the deep desire to be with Christ; the pain of separation; the faithfulness and persistence in long awaiting; and endurance in struggles and sufferings.

The combination of all these expressions associated with hope indicates that hope is indeed a "comprehensive framework of

---

[3] The verb occurs in Matt 12:21 in a quotation from Isa 42:1–4, which is applied to Christ in the Gospel, and in John 5:45, where Moses is the object of hope. It is employed 3 times in Luke, but only in 24:21 does it deal with the hope in Christ. It also occurs twice in Acts, but only in 26:7 does it refer to the hope of Israel and of Paul.

[4] It occurs mostly in Paul (25 times) and in Pauline tradition (11 times).

[5] On the meaning of these synonyms, see Nebe, "Hoffnung," 25–29. Nebe mentions other expressions that are semantically close to these words but are not properly synonyms, such as ἐπιμένειν, epimenein, καταμένειν, katamenein, γρηγορεῖν, grēgorein, διώκειν, diōkein, ἐπιποθεῖν, epipothein, θέλειν, thelein, ζητεῖν, zētein, πεποιθῆναι, pepoithēnai, πιστεύειν, pisteuein, γινώσκειν, ginōskein, εἰδέναι, eidenai (p. 29).

Pauline theology."[6] According to G. Bornkamm, without eschatology—and hope deals with eschatology—Paul's "teaching on the Law, his doctrine of justification and salvation, and all else he has to say on the word of the cross, on baptism and the Lord's Supper, on the working of the Spirit and the nature of the church," would be inconceivable.[7]

In his letters the apostle talks about hope from a variety of perspectives and in a variety of contexts. He keeps this hope before the eyes of his congregations; he nurtures this hope in the faithful; he corrects false ideas that undermine hope; and he encourages and strengthens existing hope. He understands his own apostolic existence, which he calls a sharing in the death of Christ, within this horizon of hope.

In order to bring out the structure of hope, we shall focus on the object, the basis, and the subject of hope. This is not the division that Paul himself made but a convenient way of organizing his thought without doing much violence to it.[8]

B. HOPE IN CHRISTIAN EXISTENCE

The scope of salvation in the good news of Jesus Christ, of which Paul is a herald, embraces the past, the present, and the future as they touch Christ and as they touch the believer. The Christ-event itself embraces the past, the present, and the future. The past centers on the death and resurrection of Christ; the present includes the lordship of the risen Christ as the effect of his resurrection; and the future concerns the culmination and completion of that lordship at the parousia.

All these aspects of Christ also touch the hope of the faithful. The event in the past—the Easter event—is the objective foundation of salvation, in which the believer in the present participates and which is directed toward the future completion. It makes possible the present life in faith and hope and the present salvific sharing in Christ's death and resurrection. And it opens the future envisaged in the resurrection of the faithful and their union with the exalted Lord.

---

[6] Plevnik, *What Are They Saying?* 91.

[7] Bornkamm, *Paul*, 197.

[8] This division is not an imposition of a pattern foreign to Paul's thought but a way of bringing out the components of hope present in his own thought.

The present lordship of the risen Christ provides the dominion in which the faithful live. It is, as it were, their living space and their safety zone. The exalted Lord is actively involved in the present Christian existence, maintaining it and protecting it. And this is another reason for hope and confidence. Those who are in Christ now will be with Christ at his coming.

And the future parousia provides the direction and the goal of Christian striving in the present. It is a vector drawing Paul and the believers forward toward the completion (1 Thess 2:19; Phil 3:13–14). The present is not the ultimate completion; Paul makes this clear by distinguishing between Christ's resurrection and the resurrection of the faithful (1 Cor 15:23) and by insisting on the future transformation (v. 51). The present, however, is a partial realization of the promise and a payment toward the possession of what is yet to come (1 Thess 5:9–10).

Hope is thus related to salvation, but salvation is not yet a secured possession. In fact, the apostle tends to use the word "salvation" for the completion expected in the end time.[9] For the present life of faith he prefers to employ such words as "justification," "reconciliation," "new creation," "participation in Christ," and the like. Believers, who are justified by faith and have in them the Holy Spirit, "eagerly wait for the hope of righteousness" (Gal 5:5; cf. Rom 5:5). Those who are justified, or who are reconciled with God, boast in the hope of sharing the glory of God (Rom 5:2). The present life of faith is imbued with hope, whereas hope ceases with the attainment of the goal, the vision of God face-to-face (1 Cor 13:1–13).

The structure of the present Christian existence can thus be described as a combination of the "already" and the "not yet." The present condition is the effect of Christ's death and resurrection. It already contains salvific realities. In the present, the believer appropriates Christ's death and, in a way, Christ's resurrection (Rom 6:1–14). The believer is said to be "in Christ" and takes on a new meaning and identity. In Gal 2:19–20 Paul states, "I have been crucified with Christ; and it is no longer I who live, but it is Christ who lives in me." Yet the full sharing in Christ's resurrection is yet to come (1 Cor 15:23). It is not here.

---

[9]Bultmann, *Theology*, 1.319–24.

All this marks the present Christian existence as a life of hope,[10] as a pilgrimage toward the ultimate goal. Believers are not the "saved" but those who are "being saved" (1 Cor 1:18). When he does use the word "salvation" for the present Christian experience, Paul often adds the word "hope" to it. Thus in Rom 8:24 he states, "For in hope we were saved." The present existence is hence not a peaceful and secure enjoyment of salvation but, rather, a sharing in the cross of Christ, which entails dying to the values of the world and of the old self. It means straining forward to the goal (Phil 3:12), to the union with Christ, to sharing in the glory of God, and to inheriting the kingdom of God.

The hope of Christians is essentially the effect of God's salvific work through Christ. It should not be limited to the life of faith. As Beker brings out against Bultmann,[11] hope is more than a "believing posture" in which the past Christ-event is significant only as a factor of faith, with no objective reality of its own, or in which the future Christ-event is completely fused with the present life of faith,[12] being nothing else but a factor of faith—the believer's openness to God, who is always coming. For Paul, the past event is an objective salvific happening and as such the foundation of faith and hope. The resurrection of Christ is real and essential for the realization of Christian hope: without it there is no resurrection of the faithful and no parousia of Christ. And for Paul, the future Christ-event holds the objective completion. The parousia of Christ is real, and the resurrection and life with Christ are real. And this brings us to the object of hope.

C. THE OBJECT OF HOPE

According to Bultmann, hope expresses the possibility of an open future of faith in God, "who always comes to us from the future."[13] This, however, is an abstraction and an unwarranted

---

[10] On hope and eschatology, see Nebe, *"Hoffnung,"* 81–168.

[11] Beker, *Paul the Apostle,* 147.

[12] On Bultmann's notion of hope, see his *Theology,* 1.319–24. For Bultmann, faith is also hope. The righteousness attained by faith has an eschatological dimension, being both here and to come as the future of the believer. "Hope is the freedom for the future and openness toward it which the man of faith has because he has turned over his anxiety about himself and his future to God in obedience" (p. 320).

[13] Beker, *Paul the Apostle,* 147, referring to Bultmann, *Primitive Christianity,* 186.

reduction. It prescinds from the concrete ways in which God raises
and sustains hope and in which he promises to fulfill hope. And it
disregards the concrete ways in which Paul presents the fulfillment
of hope. Against Bultmann Beker insists[14] that, for Paul, hope has a
specific content: the parousia of Christ, the resurrection of the
dead, the redemption of the body, life with Christ forever, etc. Hope
is concrete and focused.

The ultimate reality as the object of hope is the kingdom of God,
or the rule of God (1 Cor 6:10; 15:50; Gal 5:21). This traditional term
is used only occasionally in Paul's letters, but the notion of God's
kingdom is present in other ways, and is an important element of,
Pauline theology. In 1 Cor 15:28, for instance, Paul speaks of God's
being everything to everyone. What he means is the experience of
the ultimate fullness of God and the triumph of God through Christ.
Christ will triumph over the powers of the cosmos and over death.
According to Beker, this is the center of Paul's theology.[15]

The notion of the kingdom of God is rooted in OT hope[16] and in
the language of Jesus, as the Synoptic Gospels indicate. In Mark's
Gospel, Jesus introduces his message with the words "The time is
fulfilled, and the kingdom of God has come near" (Mark 1:15). Paul,
however, uses this term for the reality that will take place when
Christ's work of salvation has been completed, hence for the reality
after the parousia of Christ. His notion of the kingdom of God
presumes the apocalyptic horizon of the future, the end time, and
the heavenly kingdom of God.

In 1 Cor 15:50 Paul asserts, "Flesh and blood cannot inherit
the kingdom of God, nor does the perishable inherit the imperishable." The kingdom of God has no room for death and dying. It
therefore implies the resurrection of the dead and the transformation of the living.

The apostle employs the phrase "the kingdom of God"[17] also
in warnings. Thus in Gal 5:21 he states, "I am warning you, as I
warned you before: those who do such things will not inherit the

---

[14] Beker, *Paul the Apostle*, 147.

[15] Ibid., 355–67.

[16] See von Rad, "βασιλεύς." On the OT hope see Woschitz, *Hoffnung*, 219–315.

[17] The phrase occurs in Paul 8 times: Rom 14:17; 1 Cor 4:20; 6:9, 10; 15:24, 50;
Gal 5:21; and 1 Thess 2:12. According to Beker (*Paul the Apostle*, 146), Paul uses
this term in "clearly traditional contexts, borrowed from the Jewish-Hellenistic
church." But this is not obvious for Rom 14:17; 1 Cor 4:20; 15:24, 50; and 1 Thess 2:12.

kingdom of God." And in 1 Cor 6:9–10 he asks, "Do you not know that wrongdoers will not inherit the kingdom of God? Do not be deceived! Fornicators, idolaters . . . none of these will inherit the kingdom of God." The kingdom of God here is the ultimate goal and the object of hope. But in 1 Thess 2:12 the apostle associates δόξα, doxa with the kingdom of God. He asserts that God calls the faithful "into his own kingdom and glory (δόξαν)." According to Rom 5:2, the justified are rejoicing in the "hope of sharing the glory of God." And in Rom 8:18 Paul asserts, "I consider that the sufferings of this present time are not worth comparing with the glory about to be revealed." But the glory of God is not shared fully at present. In vv. 23–24 he speaks of the adoption and the redemption (ἀπολύτρωσιν, apolytrōsin) of our bodies, and of the hope that is not seen (v. 25). In 2 Cor 4:17–18, comparing the present sufferings and the glorious future in store for him, Paul speaks of "an eternal weight of glory beyond all measure, be-cause we look not at what can be seen but at what cannot be seen; for what can be seen is temporal, but what cannot be seen is eternal."

Paul had a glimpse of what is to come in a revelation that he mentions in 1 Cor 2:9–13. Quoting Isa 64:4, 52:15 and Sir 1:10, he describes it as follows: "What no eye has seen, nor ear heard, nor the human heart conceived, what God has prepared for those who love him." In 13:9–12 also he talks of the completion expected in the end time, comparing it with the present reality: "For we know only in part, and we prophesy only in part; but when the complete comes, the partial will come to an end." In v. 12 he resumes his thought, saying, "For now we see in a mirror, dimly, but then we will see face to face. Now I know only in part; then I will know fully, even as I have been fully known."

The completion entails the Lord's coming; hence, the latter also becomes an object of hope. Paul talks about the parousia of Christ in 1 Thess 1:3, 2:19, 3:13, 4:13–18, 5:23; 1 Cor 15:23, 52, 16:22; Phil 3:20–21; and elsewhere. First Thessalonians especially is filled with this hope. In the introductory section of the letter he praises the Thessalonians' "steadfastness of hope in our Lord Jesus Christ" (1:3). In 2:19 he professes his cherished hope of finding them, the fruit of his apostolic labor, with the Lord at his coming: "For what is our hope or joy or crown of boasting before our Lord Jesus at his coming? Is it not you?" And in 4:13–18 he assures them that the

deceased faithful will share equally with the living in the glory of
Christ's coming and Christ's company.

The parousia of Christ is thus the means of bringing the
faithful into the presence of God (cf. 1 Thess 4:14). It is God who
through Christ brings the faithful into his presence. The parousia is
a joyful event in its own right, for then the faithful will be united
with the Lord, to whom they belong and for whom they yearn. In
vv. 13–18 Paul presents the ultimate completion as being "with the
Lord forever" (v. 17; cf. 5:10).

Christ's coming is associated with the resurrection of the dead,
the transformation of the living (cf. 1 Cor 15:23, 52; 2 Cor 4:14; Phil
3:20–21), and the entry into the kingdom of God. Hence, these
realities likewise become an object of hope. There is no place for
death or mortality in the kingdom of God. Transformation of the
dead and of the living is thus a necessary condition for inheriting
the kingdom of God. That transformation will be wrought through
Christ (Phil 3:20–21) at his coming. In 2 Cor 4:14 Paul points to the
parousia of Christ as the source of his own resurrection and of his
own admission into the presence of God. He declares, "We know
that the one who raised the Lord Jesus will raise us also with Jesus,
and will bring us . . . into his presence."

Whereas in 1 Thess 4:16–18 the dead are raised so as to
qualify for the taking up, in 1 Cor 15:23–27, 50–55 the resurrection itself is the focus. Through the resurrection and the transformation, the faithful become conformed to the exalted Lord and
are made ready for entry into the kingdom of God. They are
endowed with immortality and incorruptibility. Again, according
to Rom 8:23, the present physical existence still needs to be
redeemed, for it is still subject to death; but the ultimate reality
will redress all this. Then existence in the body will be reconsti-
tuted, made glorious and imbued with the Spirit like that of the
risen Christ (1 Cor 15:46–49). According to Phil 3:20–21, the Lord
himself will come and change our lowly physical existence and
conform it to his glorious existence.

The apostle's own hope and yearning for the resurrection and
transformation are clear in 2 Cor 5:1–10. He groans not because he
is afraid to die but because he wants to be further clothed, "so that
what is mortal may be swallowed up by life" (v. 4). But he groans
also because at present he is not with the Lord. His desire is to be
"at home with the Lord" (vv. 7–8).

Thus, the future coming of Christ, the resurrection from the dead, the transformation, and the union with the risen Lord all have a salvific significance. The apostle himself fervently awaits the resurrection and the transformation, but above all union with the Lord in God's presence. For him, the resurrection and the transformation are not neutral happenings: they mean conformity to Christ and fellowship with Christ. Through the resurrection the believer becomes heavenly, like the heavenly man.

Paul's hope is filled with an intense personal desire to be with the Lord (2 Cor 5:7; Phil 1:21), to share in the Lord's resurrection (Phil 3:10–11), and to behold him (2 Cor 5:7). It is not merely a desire to enter the joys of paradise (1 Cor 2:9); it is directed to the person of Christ, in whom all God's promises are centered and whose love has touched Paul so deeply. This explains his fervent expectation of the completion in the near future. It is characteristic of human hope that it experiences distance and separation as painful and intolerable. The greater the love is between two persons, the more they desire to be together, the more they in their hearts foreshorten the expected reunion. The heart leaps over the distance in space and time to be united with the beloved.

D. THE BASIS OF HOPE

Just as the object of hope in the Pauline letters is God and his Son, so also are they the foundation of hope. Paul bases his hope on the Christ-event of the past, on God's saving deed through Jesus Christ (1 Thess 4:14; 2 Cor 4:14). In that event he came to understand deeper than before God's saving intention, power, faithfulness, and love. Not only Easter but also the present Christian existence, as a partial fulfillment of Easter promises, have become a basis for hope.

1. God's Faithfulness, Love, and Power

According to the OT, God revealed himself to Israel as the God of Abraham, Isaac, and Jacob, as the one who chose his people, rescued them from the bondage of Egypt, and stood faithfully by them even when Israel disobeyed him. Bultmann summarizes this relationship by saying that in the OT, God is the hope of Israel.[18] This is true, but too abstract and too subjective as it stands. Hope prescinds from God's self-communication to Israel. Israel placed its hope in God because it came to know him through his concrete self-revelation and through his mighty acts on Israel's behalf. It came to know God as mighty, faithful, and loving.

Isaiah 43:1b–4 presents a divine assurance in which all these components are present.

> Do not fear, for I have redeemed you;
>   I have called you by name, you are mine.
> When you pass through the waters, I will be with you;
>   and through the rivers, they shall not overwhelm you;
> when you walk through fire you shall not be burned,
>   and the flame shall not consume you.
> For I am the LORD your God,
>   the Holy One of Israel, your Savior . . .
> you are precious in my sight,
>   and honored, and I love you.

Here it is God the creator, the Almighty—"he who created you, O Jacob" (v. 1)—who speaks and raises Israel's hope. He is pointing to himself as the creator of Jacob, to his redemptive acts on Israel's behalf and his continuing protection of Israel as proof of his faithfulness, and to his love for them. He discloses that he has called Israel by name, that it belongs to him, that it is precious and honored in his sight, that it is loved; Israel should therefore not fear. He then gives Israel a promise that he will gather the people together from the four corners of the world (vv. 6–7). Although the word "hope" is not employed here, the entire passage clearly deals with it.[19] What is still missing here from the Christian perspective is the christological component.

---

[18] Bultmann, "ἐλπίς," 523.

[19] For the vocabulary of hope in the OT, see Nebe, "Hoffnung," 46–47. This vocabulary is found above all in the prophets, with Second Isaiah as the prophet of hope par excellence. In these writings we find a vague anticipation of a new and definitive intervention of God, a break between the present and the future, the judgment of God separating the two. But depictions of this future are not uniform.

In Jewish apocalyptic, the break between the present and the future, the earthly and the heavenly is definite. Certain figures, such as the Son of man, the Elect One, and the Messiah are mentioned in connection with the completion. The resurrection of the dead is expected, as well as the transformation effecting life in the end time.

Paul's hope is likewise based on God's power, faithfulness, and love. The apostle speaks of the "power (δύναμις, *dynamis*) of God" (Rom 1:16), of the "God of steadfastness and encouragement" (τῆς ὑπομονῆς καὶ τῆς παρακλήσεως, *tēs hypomonēs kai tēs paraklēseōs*, 15:5), and of the "God of love" (θεὸς τῆς ἀγάπης, *theos tēs agapēs*, 2 Cor 13:11). Paul understands God from the christological viewpoint, for Christ is God's supreme self-revelation. Hence, his statements about God have a christological referent. It is through Christ that God reveals his power, his faithfulness (saving intention), and his love. God is the Father of Jesus Christ, the Lord. God sent his Son into the world for our salvation (Gal 4:4; Rom 8:3). And God showed his supreme love for us in sending his Son into death for us (Rom 5:8).

In accordance with this perspective, Paul assures the faithful in Corinth that God will strengthen (βεβαιώσει, *bebaiōsei*) them to the end, so that they "may be blameless on the day of our Lord Jesus Christ." He asserts, "God is faithful (πιστός, *pistos*); by him you were called into the fellowship of his Son, Jesus Christ our Lord" (1 Cor 1:8–9). God will not let them be tested beyond their strength (10:13). The apostle's parting prayer for the Corinthians is, "And the God of love (θεὸς τῆς ἀγάπης) and peace will be with you" (2 Cor 13:11). When he writes to the Roman community, Paul prays, "May the God of hope fill you with all joy and peace in believing, so that you may abound in hope by the power of the Holy Spirit" (Rom 15:13).

Often the love of God is expressed through the activity of the Holy Spirit in believers. Thus in Rom 5:5 Paul affirms, "And hope [of sharing the glory of God] does not disappoint us, because God's love has been poured into our hearts through the Holy Spirit that has been given to us" (cf. also 2 Cor 5:5). But this does not eliminate the christological referent, for God's Spirit is also the Spirit of Christ. In v. 2 the apostle states that the present peace with God has been given "through our Lord Jesus Christ, through whom we have obtained access to this grace." And in vv. 6–10 he speaks of God's love for us in Jesus Christ. The presence of the Spirit is the affirmation that those who believe in Christ and have been redeemed by Christ's death are loved by God and will share in God's promises.

In Rom 8:9–11 he talks in the same breath of the Spirit of God and the Spirit of Christ: those who have the Spirit of God in them also have the Spirit of Christ. It is because of the presence in them of this Spirit, through whom God raised Jesus from the dead, that Paul assures the Romans God "will give life to your mortal bodies also through his Spirit that dwells in you" (v. 11). The Spirit also bears witness that the faithful are children of God, heirs of God, and joint heirs with Christ (vv. 16–17). Those who belong to Christ live by the Spirit (v. 25), and conversely, those who live by the Spirit have the Spirit of Christ in them—they have Christ living in them (8:9–10).

2. The Death and the Resurrection of Christ

In Pauline writings, the Christ-event of the past is condensed into Christ's death and resurrection; hence, these two events become the basis of hope. For Paul, it is the death of Christ, above all, that manifests God's love for us, as is clear in Rom 5:5–10, where he assures the Romans of God's faithfulness to the end. In v. 6 he points out Christ's love for us: "While we were still weak, at the right time Christ died for the ungodly." The apostle shifts in v. 8 to the love of God: "But God proves his love for us in that while we still were sinners Christ died for us." This becomes in v. 10 the hope of salvation: "For if while we were enemies, we were reconciled to God through the death of his Son,[20] much more surely, having been reconciled, will we be saved by his life." The argument here assumes Christ's special status and claim to God's love as God's beloved Son. It is this bond of love proper between the Father and the Son that makes the death of the Son, willed by the Father, the highest revelation of God's love.[21] But at the end of this passage the referent is not merely Christ's death but also Christ's resurrection: "Much more surely . . . will we be saved by his life."

This argument is resumed and expanded in 8:31–32, where the apostle asks, "If God is for us, who is against us? He who did not withhold his own Son, but gave him up for all of us, will he not with him also give us everything else?" Here God's love for us in the

---

[20] Both justification and reconciliation are ascribed by Paul to God's own action through Christ—see Rom 3:22–26; 2 Cor 5:18–19. In the latter passage the apostle states, "All this is from God, who reconciled us to himself through Christ, . . . not counting their trespasses against them." On reconciliation, see Blank, *Paulus und Jesus,* 285.

[21] Blank, *Paulus und Jesus,* 285.

death of his Son serves as the absolute assurance that we are
destined for salvation. But in the verses that follow, Paul points to
the death and resurrection of Christ as evidence of God's love for
the faithful. It is God and his Son, the crucified and the exalted
Lord, who are presented as taking our side. The apostle asks and
answers his own questions, saying,

> Who will bring any charge against God's elect? It is God who justifies.[22] Who
> is to condemn? It is Christ Jesus, who died, yes, who was raised, who is at the
> right hand of God, who indeed intercedes for us. Who will separate us from
> the love of Christ? . . . No, in all these things we are more than conquerors
> through him who loved us. For I am convinced that neither death, nor life,
> nor angels, nor rulers, nor things present, nor things to come, nor powers,
> nor height, nor depth, nor anything else in all creation, will be able to
> separate us from the love of God in Christ Jesus our Lord (Rom 8:33–39).

This passage indicates that the real reason for hope is in God
and his Son: no charge against us can prevail when God justifies
us; no condemnation can touch us when Jesus is interceding for us;
and no one can separate us from God's love for us in Christ's death.
Hence, nothing in creation can stop that love or sever God from us.
But the referent here is Christ's death, resurrection, and exaltation:
Christ's death as the guarantee of the Father's love for us, the risen
and exalted Christ's present intercession as the proof of his love
for us.

But Christ's resurrection can also be appealed to directly as a
reason for hope. Thus in Rom 4:25 Paul states that Jesus "was
handed over to death for our trespasses and was raised for our
justification." Here the resurrection of Christ is a salvific event,
effecting our justification and the hope of salvation, which it
sustains. According to the apostle, justification is effected in the
hope of salvation yet to come (5:1–2). More frequently, however, the
resurrection of Christ is presented as the ground of hope for the
future resurrection. Christ is the "first fruits" of the dead. Through
and because of Christ's resurrection, all will come to life: "For as
all die in Adam, so all will be made alive in Christ" (1 Cor 15:22).[23]

---

[22] In Rom 3:24–25 the apostle ascribes justification to God's action in Christ:
"They [the sinners] are now justified by his [God's] grace as a gift, through the
redemption that is in Christ Jesus, whom God put forward as a sacrifice of
atonement by his blood."

[23] Although in v. 23 the apostle then speaks of the resurrection of those who
belong to Christ.

The resurrection of Christ is here seen as God's promise to us. As P. Ricoeur states, "The resurrection, interpreted within a theology of promise, is not an event which closes, by fulfilling the promise, but an event which opens, because it adds to the promise by confirming it."[24]

Paul often appeals to Christ's resurrection when he talks of the future completion. We have seen that this argument is employed in 2 Cor 4:13–14 for Paul's own resurrection: "We know that the one who raised the Lord Jesus will raise us also with Jesus, and will bring us with you into his presence." The same argument occurs also in 1 Thess 4:14, where the apostle assures the Thessalonians, "For since we believe that Jesus died and rose again, even so, God will bring with him those who have died with him."[25] Here as well the weight of the argument is on the resurrection of Christ.

But usually it is the twofold event of Christ's death and resurrection that serves as the pattern for believers. A typical Pauline principle, according to Schnackenburg, is "That which happened to Christ happens also to Christians; dying and rising with him becomes a rule in the Christian life, which works itself out in all areas and in every aspect of life."[26] This principle is often presented as a pattern for the eschatological fulfillment (1 Thess 4:14; 1 Cor 15:3–5, 20–28; 2 Cor 4:14; Rom 6:8; 8:17).

3. The Present Fulfillment

Paul looks not only to the Christ-event in the past but also to the effect of that event in the present for the source of hope: he finds assurance in the present fulfillment, which confirms God's promise. The action of God in Christ extends into the present, implementing the Easter event. According to the apostle, God has placed the faithful "in Christ" (2 Cor 1:21; 1 Cor 1:30); he has justified them through Christ's death (Rom 3:21–26); he has reconciled them to himself (Rom 5:10; 2 Cor 5:18); he has re-created them (2 Cor 7:17); and he has poured into them his Holy Spirit, through which they have the hope that belongs to sons and

---

[24] Ricoeur, *Essays*, 159.

[25] The argument holds no matter whether we relate διὰ τοῦ Ἰησοῦ, *dia tou Iēsou* to the preceding κοιμηθέντας, *koimēthentas* or to ἄξει, *axei*. Our translation here differs from that in the NRSV.

[26] Schnackenburg, *Baptism*, 157.

daughters (Rom 5:5; 8:9–11, 26–27; 2 Cor 5:5), the inheritance with Christ. As Ricoeur notes, "Each fulfilment is perceived as confirmation, pledge, and repetition of the promise."[27] Each fulfillment is an installment toward the ultimate completion.

But each fulfillment is understood as the pledge of what is yet to come. Those who are "in Christ" now will be with Christ at his coming (1 Thess 4:16; 1 Cor 15:23; Rom 6:1–8). Those who have been justified and have peace with God boast in the hope of sharing the glory of God (Rom 5:1–2). This hope does not disappoint us because "God's love has been poured into our hearts through the Holy Spirit that has been given to us" (v. 5). This is taken up again in 8:9–39, where Paul talks of the present Christian existence as a life "in the Spirit," as having "the Spirit of Christ," as "belonging to Christ," and as "Christ living in them" (vv. 9–10). In v. 11 he then states, "If the Spirit of him who raised Jesus from the dead dwells in you, he who raised Jesus from the dead will give life to your mortal bodies also through his Spirit that dwells in you." Those who have the Spirit of God in them are children of God (8:16). "And if children, then heirs, heirs of God and joint heirs with Christ" (v. 17).

The fulfillment in the present is but an initial fulfillment. The apostle never stops with the present but raises the vision of the faithful to what is yet to come. The present is marked by the cross of Christ (1 Cor 1:18–31), by sufferings (2 Cor 1:8–9; 4:7–12; 11:23–29), dying, humiliations, etc. It is also marked by the ongoing spiritual struggle in which the faithful "crucify the flesh with its passions and desires" and live by the Spirit (Gal 5:16–26). The cross and the present struggle are the reason why Paul often encourages the faithful in their present existence and points to the gifts—the life in Christ, the Spirit—that they have received and that carry the promise of further gifts.

These gifts of God through Christ thus have end-time significance. They do not merely express the believers' openness to God, who is always coming. They can only be understood in the framework of the objective completion. God has begun to realize his promise. The present fulfillment thus provides a ground of hope. Moreover, the risen Lord is not thought of as being in the distant heaven, enjoying the exaltation at God's right hand and being unconcerned with events in the world below. He is, rather,

---

[27] Ricoeur, *Essays*, 158.

effectively carrying out his salvific role by the power of God. He is subjugating hostile powers (1 Cor 15:24–27). He is establishing his dominion, in which Satan and sin have no power.

The faithful are thus placed in the domain of salvation, the domain of Christ. In 1 Cor 1:18 Paul addresses the Corinthians who follow the cross as those who are being saved (σῳζομένοις, sōzomenois). The believers are "children of light and children of the day" (1 Thess 5:5), destined for the glorious day of Christ and not for the wrath of God (v. 9). They are awaiting the coming of God's Son, who will rescue them from the coming wrath (1:10).

E. THE SUBJECT OF HOPE

The basis and the goal of hope effectively delimit the subject of hope. According to Paul, hope springs from the knowledge, given in faith, of the mystery of salvation wrought by God in Jesus Christ. Since God's saving action, both in its inception and in its completion, is centered on Christ, it is those who believe in Christ and belong to him who have the well-founded hope of salvation. This, of course, presupposes faith in the one God, who is the Father of Jesus Christ. Faith is the presupposition for attaining the ultimate completion. For the apostle, God is "the Father, from whom are all things and for whom we exist," and Jesus is the Lord, "through whom are all things and through whom we exist" (1 Cor 8:6). The Lord is also the one in whom the believer exists and with whom the believer hopes to live forever.

This means that the proper subject of hope is a committed believer (1 Thess 4:13; 5:4–11), the one who shares Christ's death and resurrection (Rom 6:1–14). The sharing in Christ's death means not only accepting sufferings in the present life but also dying to the old, sinful self. The committed believer walks by the Spirit and does not gratify the desires of the flesh. The apostle lists the works of the flesh as follows: "fornication, impurity, licentiousness, idolatry, sorcery, enmities." He writes the Galatians, "I am warning you . . . those who do such things will not inherit the kingdom of God" (Gal 5:19–21). This is a recurring theme in Paul's letters (see 1 Cor 6:9–11; 1 Thess 2:12; Phil 2:1–5; 3:17–19; Rom 1:18–2:29; 12:1–2, 9–21; 13:8–14). Those who walk by the Spirit do not gratify the desires of the flesh (Gal 5:16–17). The Spirit is associated with "joy, peace, love, patience, kindness, generosity, faithfulness, gentleness, and self-control" (vv. 22–23). Paul states, "Those who belong to Christ Jesus have crucified the flesh with its passions and desires" (v. 24). He exhorts, "If we live by the Spirit, let us also be guided by the Spirit" (v. 25). The faithful are to put on the mind of Christ, which means to love one another. Hope is mentioned together with faith and love in 1 Thess 1:3 and 5:8.

Hence, Paul exhorts, encourages (1 Thess 4:18; 5:11), and warns (Phil 3:17–19) the faithful. Others are treated only marginally. Sometimes he states that the outsiders "have no hope," as in 1 Thess 4:13. Yet in Rom 2 he acknowledges that pagans who live good lives have hope, for God repays in accordance with each one's deed: "To those who by patiently doing good seek for glory and honor and immortality, he [God] will give eternal life" (v. 7). These people follow the law of their conscience. In 8:18–27 he ascribes hope to the entire creation,[28] asserting that the entire cosmos wants to share in the glory of the children of God.

F. CHRIST, THE HOPE OF CHRISTIANS

What distinguishes Paul's hope from the OT hope or from that in Jewish apocalyptic is its centeredness on Christ: it is through Christ that God is bringing about salvation. It is through Christ's death and resurrection that God opened the way to salvation. It is through placing the believer in Christ that God enables the faithful to share in the effects of Easter. It will be through Christ that God will bring about the ultimate fulfillment. Thus, neither the love of God nor the gift of the Spirit, on which hope is based, can be explained in Pauline theology apart from Christ.

But Christ is for Paul the preexistent Son of God (Phil 2:6–11) and Lord. The Christ-event is regarded as the eschatological coming of God's Son into the world to change the existing human condition (Gal 4:6; Rom 8:15; Phil 2:6–11). Only this explains for Paul the redemption of the whole world, and only this makes Christ into the second Adam (Rom 5:12–21), the comprehensive principle of salvation. The highest proof of God's love for us is seen in God's giving his Son for us. And the highest possible proof of Christ's love for us is seen in his dying for us.

---

[28] See Bindemann, *Hoffnung*, 118–69.

The risen Lord in his present activity is seen as effecting the promise of Easter. The faithful are made to share in the death of Christ in the hope of sharing in his glory as well. The faithful are "in Christ," for only those who are "in Christ" have a legitimate hope of being eventually "with Christ."

Christ is also the goal of our hope. The deepest desire of the faithful, and of Paul himself, is to be with Christ, to be at home with him (2 Cor 5:6–8; 1 Thess 4:18; 5:10). The ultimate reality entails a conformity to Christ (1 Cor 15:49; Phil 3:21), and Christ himself is expected to come and to change our lowly bodies (Phil 3:21). Christ is thus truly the hope of Christians. As Nebe notes,[29] Christ in the past, in the present, and in the future is an essential component of Christian eschatology. Pauline hope arises from the Christ-event in the past and extends to the coming of Christ in the end time. For Paul, the centering on Christ is essential for hope, for this centering indicates his love for Christ. It is because of this love that he wants to be with Christ forever (Phil 1:21–23).

G. THROUGH CHRIST IN GOD

Yet, for all the centering on Christ, God, the Father of Jesus Christ, remains the ultimate ground and goal of hope. This is the framework of Paul's soteriology, Christology, and eschatology.[30] It is the Father's love, above all, that is revealed in his sending his Son to die for us. It is God who is placing us "in Christ." It is God's love that is poured into the faithful through the Holy Spirit. And it is God who, through Christ, is bringing the faithful into his presence (1 Thess 4:14; 2 Cor 4:14).

But God is the Father of Jesus Christ, and Jesus is God's Son. Paul appeals to this relationship, which involves the deepest communion of love, in order to assure the faithful of God's faithfulness to the end. Jesus is not an agent independent from God (1 Cor 15:28) but is the Son whom the Father sent into the world in the fullness of time to redeem human beings (Gal 4:4) and whom the

---

[29] Nebe, "Hoffnung," 172.

[30] According to Nebe (ibid., 51, 172), in Pauline eschatology God is in the background and Jesus Christ in the foreground of hope. But there is scarcely an eschatological statement in Paul in which God is not mentioned as the ultimate agent and goal.

Father has endowed with supreme authority and power (1 Cor 15:24–27).

Correspondingly, Jesus' sole aim is the glory of God the Father. The hymn in Philippians, stating that God himself exalted Jesus after his death on the cross, ends on this note: "Every tongue should confess that Jesus is Lord, to the glory of God the Father" (2:11). Jesus' present lordship is God's own doing and redounds to God's glory. When his work is completed, the Son will surrender his commission to the Father so that God may be everything to everyone (1 Cor 15:28).

The Father is thus the principle and the end of everything. As the confessional formula in 1 Cor 8:6 states, "Yet for us there is one God, the Father, from whom are all things and for whom we exist, and one Lord, Jesus Christ, through whom are all things and through whom we exist." The path of redemption and salvation is thus through Christ to God. In Rom 11:33–36 Paul ends on the wonder of the ways of God, in particular on God's ways with Israel: "O the depth of the riches and wisdom and knowledge of God! How unsearchable are his judgments and how inscrutable his ways! . . . For from him and through him and to him are all things. To him be the glory forever. Amen."

H. THE APPROPRIATION OF HOPE

In Paul's vocabulary, associated with hope are words that mark the subjective appropriation of hope. Paul speaks of joy (καυχήσεως, kauchēseōs, 1 Thess 2:19; καυχώμεθα, kauchōmetha, Rom 5:2), yearning (ἐπιθυμίαν ἔχων, epithymian echōn, Phil 1:23), striving (διώκω, diōkō, Phil 3:12, 14), groaning (στενάζομεν, stenazomen, 2 Cor 5:2, 4; Rom 8:23), confidence (θαρροῦντες, tharrountes, 2 Cor 5:6), patience/endurance (ὑπομονή, hypomonē, 1 Thess 1:3; Rom 5:4–5; 8:25), and the like.[31] The spectrum of these expressions brings out the many aspects of Christian existence in hope.

Just as faith is not only the acceptance of the saving act of God in Christ but also obedience, as Bultmann brings out,[32] so also hope, rooted in faith, is not only the expectation of the fulfillment

---

[31] Nebe, focusing on the vocabulary of hope, fails to draw on these expressions for his assessment of Pauline hope.

[32] Bultmann, *Theology*, 1.314–19.

but also a commitment to, and openness toward, the future. The apostle can speak of "steadfastness of hope in our Lord Jesus Christ" (1 Thess 1:3), of patient endurance of trials (Rom 5:4–5; 8:25), and of making heaven our home country (Phil 3:20). References to steadfastness occur in the context of persecution or tribulation, when the believer may become discouraged.

The words "joy," "desire," and "encouragement" indicate that hope is not an endurance contest or an obligation. The element of joy here expresses delight and enthusiasm at the thought of the completion that awaits the believer (1 Thess 2:19); the assurance of sharing in the completion gives comfort and encouragement (4:18; 5:11); and the yearning and groaning reveal a heart that is restless until it rests in the Lord (Phil 1:23). To be with the Lord forever (4:17) is not an obligation but the deepest desire of the heart, greater than the desire for life and survival. It springs from the believer's love of Christ. The ultimate motive for hope is the love of God for us in Jesus Christ, which in turn evokes in the believer the love for Christ and the Father, as well as full trust and confidence (Rom 8:31–39). It is only when assured of God's and Christ's love that the believer, beset by physical and spiritual dangers, can trust.

The yearning to be with Christ turns into a groaning because of the separation. The believer yearns for the eschatological existence that will be "a building from God, a house not made with hands, eternal in the heavens" (2 Cor 5:1). This is not simply a desire for life (vv. 2, 4) but a desire to be close to the Lord. According to Paul, "while we are at home in the body we are away from the Lord" (v. 6). While we are on earth, we are "walking by faith, not by sight" (v. 7).[33] Thus, groaning here is not related to the fear of death but to the burden of separation (cf. Phil 1:23). The whole creation, according to Rom 8:22–23, has been until now "groaning (συστενάζει, systenazei) in labor pains" with the believers.[34] The

---

[33] Walking "by faith" is contrasted with walking "by sight," expected at the completion. The completion "cannot be seen" as long as we are in the present physical condition (2 Cor 4:18). In Rom 8:24 Paul states categorically, "Now hope that is seen is not hope. For who hopes for what is seen?" The present state of Christian existence is depicted as something incomplete in 1 Cor 13:8–12.

[34] On Rom 8:18–25 see Nebe, "Hoffnung," 82–94; Bindemann, Hoffnung, 67–95. The creation is here thought of as a complement to the believers (Nebe, "Hoffnung," 86–87). It, too, is suffering from the effects of the fall. Paul extends to the creation the language he employs for the believers: the creation actively participates in hope; it perceives, groans, and desires.

present situation of the creation is described as "subjection in futility" (v. 20) in the hope of obtaining freedom "from the bondage of decay," the "freedom of the glory of the children of God"—the redemption (ἀπολύτρωσιν) of our bodies (v. 23).[35] The present Christian existence is described as endowment with the "first fruits of the Spirit" (v. 23) and as a groaning (στενάζομεν) for the redemption of the body.

Thus, hope brings joy to the present Christian existence as it anticipates the fulfillment. The apostle himself is filled with this joy, and he communicates it to his communities. In 1 Thess 2:19 he is rejoicing in anticipation of the glory in which he will share when the Thessalonian Christians will be brought before the Lord at his coming: "For what is our hope or joy or crown of boasting before our Lord Jesus at his coming? Is it not you?" In 1 Cor 16:22 Paul concludes his letter with the cry "Our Lord, come!"

And hope helps the believer to endure the hardships of the present life with confidence. In Rom 8:18 Paul declares, "I consider that the sufferings of this present time are not worth comparing with the glory about to be revealed to us." In 2 Cor 4:17 he says, "This slight momentary affliction is preparing us for an eternal weight of glory beyond all measure." The apostle here takes personal comfort from the thought of the glorious completion. For all its pain, the present affliction is minor in comparison with the glory to come. Although pain seems to stretch time into eternity, the present pain is but a moment compared with the bliss and joy to come.

Hence hope, as Paul presents it, is scarcely an escape from the trials and duties of life. It is, rather, a call to responsibility (1 Thess 5:6, 8)[36] in view of the judgment to come (2 Cor 5:10). It makes life bearable and meaningful. But it is not a hope against hope. It is grounded in the knowledge of God. It is not primarily a desire for the joys of paradise but, rather, a desire to be with Christ. Hope is very personal.

---

[35] Here we find an expansion of the Pauline horizon: what will happen to the believers will happen also to the whole of creation. The entire order of creation will be restored if not transformed.

[36] The call to social responsibility as the implication of Christian hope is developed by Moltmann (*Theology of Hope*, 283–338) in reaction to the Marxist's appropriation of Christian hope.

Yet hope needs to be nourished. Any misunderstanding of the sharing in the ultimate fulfillment must be removed. The faithful must not grieve as the outsiders do (1 Thess 4:13), for death is no obstacle to God's purpose. To the Corinthians Paul affirms the reality of the future union with Christ through the resurrection: "If for this life only we have hoped in Christ, we are of all people most to be pitied" (1 Cor 15:19). In Phil 3:17–21 he raises the sight of the congregation to the completion that comes with Christ. Elsewhere he urges the believers "to encourage one another" (1 Thess 4:18; 5:11), to "build each other up" (5:11). He assures the faithful, "The one who calls you is faithful, and he will do this" (v. 24).

Finally, hope needs to be supported by prayers. The apostle prays that the believers may be strengthened in holiness in the present so that they "may be blameless before our God and Father at the coming of our Lord Jesus Christ with all his saints" (1 Thess 3:13). He concludes 1 Thessalonians saying, "May the God of peace himself sanctify you entirely; and may your spirit and soul and body be kept sound and blameless at the coming of our Lord Jesus Christ" (5:23). Paul prays that hope may increase and that the Roman community may be rich (περισσεύειν, *perisseuein*) in it, stating, "May the God of hope fill you with joy and peace in believing so that you may abound in hope by the power of the Holy Spirit" (Rom 15:13).

CONCLUSION

The Lord's coming is thus deeply rooted in the hope that Paul and the early church draw from their faith in, and knowledge of, God, above all from God's deed for us in Jesus Christ, his Son. The faithful and Paul draw courage also from their present experience of living "in Christ," which implements and confirms God's saving intention toward them and affirms their share in God's plan of salvation. The knowledge that faith provides—the meaning of God's salvific deeds in the past and in the present—thus gives rise to hope. Paul speaks out of his faith (1 Thess 4:14; 2 Cor 4:13–14) when he assures the believers of their share in the parousia or of his own share in the resurrection. The present life of faith, which is an imperfect sharing in the Christ-event, is therefore a life of hope—hope of sharing fully in the Christ-event. Paul's expectations reach beyond faith to vision, to the experience of "the eternal weight of glory beyond all measure" (2 Cor 4:17), prepared for those who love God (1 Cor 2:9). The hope that Paul preaches thus extends beyond this life.

The basis of this hope is ultimately God—God's love, faithfulness, and power. Paul was raised in this hope before he became a Christian, and kept it ever since. The specifically Christian hope, presented by the apostle, locates its basis in God's deed in Jesus Christ. What the exodus was for the OT hope, Easter is for Paul, and more—for in the Easter event God gave up his beloved Son for us. The exodus is not abandoned but surpassed in the greatest testimony to God's love. Thus, God's giving up his Son for us has become the surest ground of hope (Rom 8:31–33). And the power of God and of his Christ prevails over all the obstacles of the cosmos (vv. 37–39). Nothing can therefore "separate us from the love of God in Christ Jesus our Lord" (v. 8:39). And God is faithful. Paul states in 1 Thess 5:9–10, "For God has not destined us for wrath but for obtaining salvation through our Lord Jesus Christ, who died for us, so that whether we are awake or asleep we may live with him."

In addition, this hope has a basis in the present Christian existence, which is the initial fulfillment and an installment toward the final completion. Those who believe are now "in Christ," and those who belong to Christ are justified. At their death (Phil 1:21–23) and, ultimately, at the Lord's coming (1 Thess 4:18; 5:10) they will be "with Christ." The believers have also been given the Holy Spirit, and since "God's love has been poured into our hearts through the Holy Spirit," this hope cannot fail (Rom 5:5). The Holy Spirit is indeed the guarantee of God's intention to give us our inheritance in Jesus Christ (2 Cor 5:5; Rom 8:11, 15–17).

While the foundation of hope is God's past deed in Jesus Christ, the completion of hope is in God's future deed through Jesus Christ. Paul looks forward to the Lord's coming from heaven, when the Lord will bring us into God's kingdom. In 1 Thess 4:14 he states that God will bring us through Jesus into his presence. In 1 Cor 15:23–28 he asserts that the Father has endowed his Son with the fullness of power to bring about on earth the conditions necessary for the kingdom of God: the annihilation of death and of other powers that do not belong in the kingdom of God. According to Phil 3:20–21, the Savior, expected at the end time, will conform our bodies to his own glorious body. The hope of salvation is therefore bound up with hope in the resurrection and the transformation (1 Cor 15:50–55). But it is centered on Jesus Christ—on being with him, on being conformed to his glorious life, and on sharing in his glory. And this personal component is responsible for the foreshortening of perspective, for the intense desire to be with the Lord tends to bridge the distance to the completion.

Hence, for Paul, the legitimate subject of hope is a believer who is truly living "in Christ" and has abandoned the ways of this world, which are under God's condemnation (1 Thess 1:10; 1 Cor 1:18; Rom 1:17–32; 2:1–29). And this entails the acceptance of the cross (1 Cor 1:18–31; Phil 3:10) and a life according to the Spirit that has been given to the believer (Gal 5:16–24). Thus, the apostle exhorts the faithful to be vigilant and sober (1 Thess 5:6–8; Rom 13:11–14) and to share in the cross of Christ. This means a responsible Christian existence, which Paul interprets as a life of faith, love, and hope. Christian hope is therefore not an escape from the duties and burdens of this life but involves responsibility, preparedness, patience in sufferings, and perseverance in trials (1 Thess 1:3; 5:6–8; Rom 5:1–4).

Thus, Christ is the object of hope. Paul, however, never isolates Christ from the Father but links the two, as the language of Father and Son indicates. Paul assures the Roman believers that: He who gave up his Son for us cannot be against us (Rom 8:31–32). And he who raised the Lord Jesus will raise us also through Jesus. What happened to Christ will happen to those who belong to Christ (1 Thess 4:14; 2 Cor 4:14). The fulfillment of hope will be in the Son's coming at the end time in the fullness of power that the Father gave him. Christ leads us to God and the Father brings us though his Son into his kingdom.

The faithful should therefore be confident. They should grow in hope, rejoice in it, and persevere in it through trials. But this hope must be supported and built up; hence, Paul exhorts the Thessalonians to "encourage one another, and build up each other" (1 Thess 5:11). The faithful, then, should share with one another in their consolation, in their faith, and in their hope. And they should pray that they may all be found blameless at the coming of the Lord "with all his saints" (3:13). What the believer does in this life will be subject to judgment (2 Cor 5:10; Rom 14:10–12).

9

THE PAROUSIA OF CHRIST
AND JUDGMENT

The Lord's coming in the end time is a saving event and the object of hope; this is the main thrust of Paul's references to the Lord's coming in the passages examined so far. But the Lord's coming, according to the apostle, will also entail giving an account of all that one has done in this life (cf. 2 Cor 5:10). First Thessalonians 5:2–3 contains a depiction of the end-time disaster. In 3:13 and 5:23 Paul prays that the community be blameless in holiness at the Lord's coming. This brings us to the subject of judgment in connection with the Lord's coming.

Judgment is an essential component of the OT depictions of the day of the Lord and of apocalyptic depictions of the end-time completion. In apocalyptic, judgment concludes the present age and inaugurates the age to come. The final judgment determines who will enter into the bliss of the completion and who will be punished for the evil done in this life. The wicked will be condemned, while the just will be approved and saved. Judgment is thus understood within the horizon that embraces life beyond this life on earth.

The last judgment is also a firmly established component of the NT eschatology, as the Gospels,[1] the epistles,[2] and above all the Book of Revelation[3] disclose. It is certainly a part of Jesus' teaching, as

---

[1] Matt 11:20–24; Luke 10:13–15; Matt 24:45–51; Luke 12:35–46; Luke 13:1–5; Matt 7:13–14, 22–23; Luke 13:22–30; Matt 24:23–44; Luke 17:22–37; Mark 9:42–50; Matt 18:6–9; Luke 17:1–2; Matt 25:14–30; Luke 19:11–27; Matt 25:31–46.

[2] 2 Thess 1:5–12; Heb 10:26–39; 12:25–29; Jas 2:8–13; 2 Pet 3:8–10.

[3] Rev 20:11–15 and the many disasters preceding the opening of the seventh seal; see also chs. 15–19.

the numerous passages dealing with the completion and the numerous parables about vigilance and readiness indicate. The Gospels link this event with the coming of the Son of man. Paul likewise expects this event at the Lord's parousia; he refers to it as "the day of the Lord," which has judicial overtones.[4]

A. THE LANGUAGE OF JUDGMENT

Although Paul talks about judgment, the forensic setting may not always be present. Nor are the words "judgment" and "to judge" (κρίσις, krisis, κρίνω, krinō) used consistently in these contexts. In fact, there are three images for judgment: a dynamic image of the Lord's coming in power to enforce God's rule (1 Thess 4:16–18; 3:13; 5:23; cf. Mark 9:38; 13:24–27); the image of a sudden disaster that resembles the flood or Sodom and Gomorrah (1 Thess 5:2–3; cf. Luke 17:26–29); and the image of the throne of judgment (cf. 2 Cor 5:10; Rom 14:10; cf. Matt 25:31–46).[5]

The act of judging is expressed as "judging" (κρίνω, 1 Cor 6:2, 3), or "judgment" (κρίμα, krima, Rom 5:16), or by metaphors that bring out the hidden truth, such as "make visible" (δηλώσει, dēlōsei, 1 Cor 3:13), "reveal" (ἀποκαλύπτεται, apokalyptetai, 1 Cor 3:13), "bring to light" (φωτίσει, phōtisei, 1 Cor 4:5), "disclose" (φανερώσει, phanerōsei, 1 Cor 3:13[adj.]; 4:5), and "test" (δοκιμάσει, dokimasei, 1 Cor 3:13).

Paul makes use of traditional imagery for judgment. He speaks of "wrath" (ὀργή, orgē, Rom 3:5; 4:15; 5:9; 9:22; 1 Thess 1:10; 5:9), of "the wrath of God" (ὀργὴ θεοῦ, orgē theou, Rom 1:18; [3:5]), of "the day of wrath" (ημερα οργης, hēmera orgēs, Rom 2:5), of "wrath and fury" (ὀργὴ καὶ θυμός, orgē kai thymos, Rom 2:8), of "the revelation of God's just judgment" (ἀποκαλύψεως δικαιοκρισίας τοῦ θεοῦ, apokalypseōs dikaiokrisias tou theou, Rom 2:5), and of "fury" (θυμός,

---

[4]The phrase ἡμέρα κυρίου, hēmera kyriou and its variants occur in 1 Cor 1:8; 5:5; 2 Cor 1:14; Phil 1:6, 10 (Χριστοῦ); 2:16 (Χριστοῦ); 1 Thess 5:2. It is implied in 1 Cor 3:13; 4:4–5. Beyond the commonly accepted Pauline epistles we find this expression also in 2 Thess 2:2; 2 Tim 1:12 (ἐκείνην, ekeinēn); 4:8 (ἐκείνην); Heb 10:25 (ἡμέραν, hēmeran, alone); 1 Pet 2:12 (ἐπισκοπῆς, episkopēs); 2 Pet 2:9 (κρίσεως, kriseōs); 3:7 (κρίσεως); 3:12 (τοῦ θεοῦ, tou theou); 3:18 (αἰῶνος, aiōnos); 1 John 4:17 (κρίσεως); Jude 6 (μεγάλης, megalēs); Rev 6:17; 16:14.

[5]All three images are found also in the rest of the NT (cf. Mark 13 par Luke 17:22–37; Matt 25:31–46) and reflect the OT imagery.

Rom 2:8). The terms κατάκρισις, katakrisis (2 Cor 3:9; 7:3), κατακρίνω, katakrinō (Rom 2:1; 8:34; 14:23; 1 Cor 11:32), and κατάκριμα, katakrima (Rom 5:16, 18; 8:1) denote the sentencing.

For reward or punishment Paul employs such terms as "reward" (μισθόν, misthon, 1 Cor 3:14), "calamity" (ὄλεθρος, olethros, 1 Thess 5:3), "loss" (ζημιωθήσεται, zēmiōthēsetai, 1 Cor 3:15), "destruction" (ἀπώλεια, apōleia, Rom 9:22; Phil 1:28; 3:19), "death" (θάνατος, thanatos, Rom 1:32; 6:21, 23), "praise" (ἔπαινος, epainos, Rom 2:29; 13:3; 1 Cor 4:5), "boast" (καύχημα, kauchēma, Rom 4:2; Phil 2:16), "glory" (δόξα, Rom 2:7, 10; 8:18; 2 Cor 3:9; 4:17; Phil 3:21; 1 Thess 2:12, 14, 20), "joy" (χαρά, chara, Rom 14:4; 1 Thess 2:19, 20), "life" (ζωήν, zōēn, Rom 2:7), "honor" (τιμή, timē, Rom 2:7, 10), "immortality" (ἀφθαρσίαν, aphtharsian, Rom 2:7), "peace" (εἰρήνη, Rom 2:10), "freedom" (ἐλευθερίαν, eleutherian, Rom 8:21), "be saved" (σώζομαι, sōzomai, Rom 5:9, 10; 8:24; 9:27; 10:9, 13; 11:26; 1 Cor 1:18, 21; 3:15; 10:33; 15:2; 1 Thess 2:16), "salvation" (σωτηρία, sōtēria, Rom 1:16; 10:10; 11:11; 13:11; 2 Cor 1:6; 6:2; 7:10; Phil 1:28; 2:12; 1 Thess 5:9), and "kingdom" (βασιλεία, basileia, 1 Thess 2:12; 1 Cor 6:10; 15:50; Gal 5:21).

B. JUDGMENT OF THE NONBELIEVERS

Paul's gospel is a message of salvation (1 Thess 1:3; 2:19; 4:13–18; 5:9–10; 5:23). In 1 Thess 5:9–10 he assured the Thessalonians, "God has destined us not for wrath but to obtain salvation through our Lord Jesus Christ." But the apostle proclaims this message, as did the early church and Jesus, with the warning that the world is under God's judgment, and with a call to repentance.[6] Thus in vv. 9–10 he reminds the Thessalonians how they "turned to God from idols, to serve a living and true God, and to wait for his Son from heaven . . . who rescues us from the wrath that is coming." Here the risen Jesus is said to be the one who rescues (ῥυόμενον, rhyomenon)[7] the faithful from God's wrath (ὀργῆς). The

---

[6] Cf. Christ's warning to the Galilean cities (Luke 10:10–16 par Matt 10:14–15 and 11:20–24) or the warning about the sudden disaster at the coming of the Son of man (Luke 17:26–37). See also Rom 1:18–32.

[7] According to Rigaux (Thessaloniciens, 395–96), ῥύομαι, rhyomai, is a synonym for σώζω, sōzō, but it connotes salvation from, referring to that from which one is rescued. On the OT usage of ῥύομαι, see ibid.

text implies that the world is under God's judgment.[8] The "wrath that is coming" refers to the eschatological judgment, to "the day of judgment." According to Rom 2:5, on the "day of wrath" God's righteous judgment will be revealed.

In 1 Thess 5:2–3 the apostle describes more extensively what the wrath of God will be like: "The day of the Lord will come like a . . . sudden destruction . . . and there will be no escape!" Instead of the parousia, the apostle speaks here of the coming of the day of the Lord: it will sneak up on them; it will strike as a disaster strikes, when the people least expect it, when they feel secure and safe.[9] Its finality is underscored with the emphatic note that there will be no escape. But in the verses that follow, the apostle makes clear that this really is not in store for the Thessalonian Christians.[10] The proper object of God's wrath is not the community in good standing before the Lord (vv. 4–5) but those who live in darkness. Presumably Paul is thinking of the outsiders. God did not destine the believers for wrath but for the attainment of salvation (vv. 9–10).

The image of the day of the Lord, as used here, suggests a catastrophe of universal proportions. It reflects the established Jewish imagery of the flood, which swept away corrupt mankind, living in false security. In 1 Enoch 6–16, 19, 21, 54–55, 83–84, 88–89 the flood is the prototype of the final judgment. Comparable imagery occurs in the apocalyptic sections of the "Q" source, Luke 17:22–37, and Matt 24:23–39, 17–18, 40–41, which describe the calamity at the coming of the Son of man in terms of the flood or of the disaster at Sodom, and in Luke 21:34–36, where Jesus warns against dissipation, drunkenness, and the worries of this life lest the "day catch you unexpectedly, like a trap." Jesus warns that the day will come upon "all who live on the face of the whole earth" (v. 35), and he calls for vigilance.

In Rom 1:18–32 Paul talks about the revelation of God's wrath against the idolaters. According to him, the "wrath of God" is "revealed from heaven" against those who in their wickedness suppress the truth of the one true and living God (vv. 18–23). The

---

[8] This is thematically developed in Rom 1:18–3:20.

[9] The motif of peace and security occurs also in 2 Bar. 48:31–32: "And the time will come . . . which brings affliction. . . . And it will be in those days that the inhabitants of the earth will live in peace with each other because they do not know that my judgment has come near." Cf. ch. 4 above.

[10] See ch. 4 above.

apostle, however, is not talking about the end-time revelation of God's wrath but about the present revelation, as the present perfect παρέδωκεν, paredōken (vv. 24, 26, 28) indicates. The judgment has been pronounced and its effects are visible. The threat of the final judgment, however, is still an overtone that cannot be missed here. That the wicked are also ripe for the eschatological wrath of God is stated in Rom 2, 1 Cor 6:9–10, and Gal 5:19–21. In Rom 2:1–16 Paul points out that God, who is impartial, condemns all evil actions, even the ones done by those who know God and God's law. He asks, "Do you imagine, that . . . you will escape the judgment of God?" (2:3). He then warns, "By your hard and impenitent heart you are storing up wrath for yourself on the day of wrath, when God's righteous judgment (δικαιοκρισίας, dikaiokrisias) will be revealed. For he will repay (ἀποδώσει, apodōsei) according to each one's deeds" (vv. 5–6). God will bring "wrath and fury" to the selfish who live wickedly, and will reward with eternal life those who seek "glory and honor and immortality" (vv. 7–10).

Here, in contrast to Rom 1:18, wrath is clearly associated with the end time. Paul speaks of "the day of wrath" (ἡμέρα ὀργῆς), which is "the revelation of God's righteous judgment" (ἀποκαλύψεως δικαιοκρισίας τοῦ θεοῦ, v. 5). The future tense in the expression "he will repay" (ἀποδώσει, v. 6) looks to the eschatological day on which an account will have to be given by everyone of all the things done in this life. The emphasis that the judgment will be in accordance with what one does (κατὰ τὰ ἔργα, kata ta erga) is echoed in 2 Cor 5:10, but in Rom 2 it indicates, above all, God's impartiality: God will reward the good done by everyone, Jew or pagan, and he will punish sin committed by everyone. The judgment is here presented as a day in court.

C. PUNISHMENT OF THE PERSECUTORS OF CHRISTIANS

In the OT[11] and in Jewish apocalyptic literature,[12] the persecuted look to God for justice and expect the punishment of those who have done wrong to them in this life. In the apocalyptic literature it is the judgment at the end of this age that will even the score and

---

[11] Pss 86:16–17; 91; 94:1–11, 23; 101; 106; 107; etc.
[12] 1 Enoch 103:1–15; 4 Ezra 9:1–13; 2 Bar. 82–83.

reveal God's justice. Then the wicked, the mighty, the powerful, and the Gentiles will be punished for what they have done. Punishment is often linked with the appearance of a heavenly figure such as the Son of man, the Elect One, or the Messiah (1 Enoch 48:1–10; 50:1–5; 60:6; 62:7–16; 63:1–12; 4 Ezra 6:17–28, 32–44, 75–100; 12:31–36; 13:26–50; 14:35–36; 2 Bar. 13:4–12; 48:47–50; 54:20–22; 55:1–8; 59:2; 72:1–6).

Paul does not call down God's judgment upon his persecutors or console his congregations with such thoughts. The closest he comes is in 1 Thess 2:16 and Phil 1:28. But 1 Thess 2:16 is a dubious and much-disputed text. It contains an invective against the Jews who have persecuted the churches of God in Palestine. Paul states that just as the Thessalonians have suffered from their own compatriots, so the Jewish congregations have suffered from "the Jews, who killed both the Lord Jesus and the prophets, and drove us out; they displease God and oppose everyone by hindering us from speaking to the Gentiles so that they may be saved. Thus they have constantly been filling up the measure of their sins; but God's wrath (ὀργή) has overtaken (ἔφθασεν, ephthasen) them at last (εἰς τέλος, eis telos)." While the text speaks of God's wrath, it is not clear when this wrath will be poured out or has been poured out. There is some indication that the statement refers to an event that has already occurred.

The expressions ἔφθασεν and εἰς τέλος here are obscure. Zerwick and Grosvenor[13] translate the latter as "to the full, to the utmost," while the RSV renders it as "at last."[14] The word ἔφθασεν like ἐγγίζειν, eggizein may mean "has come,"[15] or "has approached," as in Matt 12:28. In the latter sense it can refer to the future event expected to happen at any time, as the kingdom of God is expected to occur at any time. This uncertainty in language has led many scholars to posit here a later interpolation.[16] Rigaux, however, suggests that this is an eschatological event in agreement with the eschatological character of this letter: the event, certain to come, is still in the near future but described as

---

[13] Zerwick and Grosvenor, Grammatical Analysis, 2.616.

[14] See Rigaux, Thessaloniciens, 453.

[15] Ibid., 452. Bammel ("Judenverfolgung," 295, 310) and Jewett ("Agitators," 205 n. 5) suggest historical events in the recent past to which Paul could be referring here.

[16] Pearson, "1 Thessalonians 2:13–16."

having already taken place.[17] In Jewish apocalyptic literature are found similar invectives against the Gentiles who have persecuted Israel.[18] Paul's reason here for invoking God's punishment on the Jewish persecutors is that they are displeasing God and hindering or preventing him from spreading the gospel of salvation among the Gentiles. The grudge does not spring from personal antipathy, although, according to his own account, Paul himself was the subject of Jewish persecution (2 Cor 11:24).

A somewhat less controversial text is Phil 1:28. Paul, having encouraged the community to live in harmony and according to the gospel of Christ, says, "And [you] are in no way intimidated by your opponents (ἀντικειμένων, antikeimenōn). For them this (ἥτις, hētis) is evidence (ἔνδειξις, endeixis) of their destruction (ἀπωλείας, apōleias), but of your salvation (σωτηρίας, sōtērias). And this is God's doing." The community is persecuted (cf. 1 Thess 2:2) or facing a determined opposition. The threat is coming from external opposition,[19] which is not further described by the apostle here. The relative clause introduced by ἥτις is loosely linked with the preceding and refers to the entire statement about the community's united and firm front. It is this determination, according to Paul, that indicates the future destruction of the opponents and the salvation of the faithful. The community's constancy is a sign to the opponents (αὐτοῖς, autois), who should see in its united stand a sign that God is with the faithful (cf. v. 13). The opponents should thus realize that they are working against God. Their ultimate defeat is described here as annihilation (ἀπωλείας), and the community's victory as salvation (σωτηρίας).[20]

D. JUDGMENT OF THE BELIEVERS

While Paul assures the faithful that God has not destined them for wrath, he, on occasion, also warns and threatens certain members of the community and calls all to be responsible. The

---

[17] Rigaux, *Thessaloniciens*, 452.

[18] Ibid., 454.

[19] So Gnilka, *Philipperbrief*, 99; Michaelis, *Philipper*, 30; Lohmeyer, *Philipper, Kolosser, Philemon*, 69. It is not clear who the opponents are; exegetes agree that they are outsiders to the community. According to Gnilka, they are Jews or Gentiles, while Bonnard (*Philippiens*, 35) suggests that they are Jews or Judaizers.

[20] When this will happen is not stated, but Paul is expecting the day of the Lord (Phil 1:10, 16; 3:20–21; 4:5) to come soon (4:5).

referent here is the day of the Lord. All of them will have to give an account of their doing before the Lord. In 2 Cor 5:10 he states, "All of us must appear before the judgment seat of Christ, so that each may receive recompense for what has been done in the body, whether good or evil." The apostle at times threatens with destruction, at other times with a loss that does not include damnation. He exhorts the faithful to be ready for the Lord's coming, and he prays that they may be found blameless.

1. The Condemnation of Believers

Paul does not turn a blind eye to sin in the community, and in his letters he warns about the future destruction of a believer guilty of a serious transgression. Those who are not living according to the gospel message they have received are heading for destruction. Those who have abandoned the cross (Phil 3:17–19), or are not living according to the Spirit (Gal 5:16–21; 1 Cor 6:9–10), or are guilty of having destroyed the life of Christ in another believer (1 Thess 4:6; 1 Cor 3:16–17; 8:11; Rom 14:15) are singled out for his warnings. The apostle imposes punishment on a guilty community member in order to bring that person to repentance before the final judgment takes place (1 Cor 5:1–5). He warns the Corinthians that baptism by itself will not save them, no more than the Jews were saved in the desert, although they had been baptized into Moses and had eaten spiritual food in anticipation of the food that is now given to the Christians (10:1–22).

In Phil 3:17–19 Paul unexpectedly calls on the faithful to imitate him rather than those whose behavior is no longer in accordance with the gospel he has preached. He notes with a heavy heart, "Many live as enemies of the cross of Christ; I have often told you of them, and now I tell you even with tears. Their end (τέλος) is destruction (ἀπώλεια); their god is the belly; and their glory is in their shame; their minds are set on earthly things" (vv. 18–19). Who the "many" are that live as "enemies of the cross of Christ" is not entirely clear from the text. It is likely that the apostle has warned the community before in this regard, as his remark "I have often told you of them" suggests. But it is obvious that they are Christians.[21] Paul is thus addressing a

---

[21] See Schmithals, *Paul and the Gnostics*, 204.

persistent problem.[22] When exactly the problem arose or became a threat in the Philippian community is also not clear.[23] Nor is it clear what way of life these opponents propagated. Schmithals maintains that the opponents of the cross here are Gnostic freethinkers;[24] according to Gnilka, they are itinerant Christian preachers advocating a Jewish type of Christianity.[25]

What is clear is that in v. 19 Paul depicts in powerful imagery the destruction of those who have become enemies of the cross. He warns that "their end is destruction." This is scarcely his scornful language against Jewish dietary practices, as some have suggested.[26] Here the apostle uses the eschatological terms "end" (τέλος), "god" (ὁ θεός), and "glory" (δόξα) to express the eschatological reversal that corresponds to the values they chose in their behavior ("their god is their belly"; "they glory in their shame"). This is the end for those who think that they have already reached their completion.[27] The word "destruction" (ἀπώλεια) here indicates the ultimate fate, the painful loss of life.[28] In 1 Cor 1:18 Paul notes that, to those who are perishing (τοῖς ἀπολλυμένοις, tois apollymenois), the gospel of the cross sounds like foolishness. The word "destruction" thus refers to the future condemnation and damnation. But the apostle does not dwell on the nature of this destruction.

---

[22] Gnilka, *Philipperbrief*, 204. A similar warning occurs in Rom 16:17–18: "I urge you . . . to keep an eye on those who cause dissensions and offenses, in opposition to the teaching that you have learned. . . . For such people do not serve our Lord Christ, but their own appetites." Gnilka (p. 204 n. 106) rejects the opinion of Beare, Bonnard, Haupt, and Michaelis, who suggest that the danger occurred only outside the Philippian community.

[23] According to Gnilka (ibid., 204), the problem arose since Paul's visit to the community, which took place between the writing of Letter A and that of Letter B. Gnilka (p. 10) postulates that the present epistle to the Philippians is a compilation of two letters (A = 1:1–3:1a; 4:2–7, 10–23; B = 3:1b–4:1, 8–9). See ch. 7 above.

[24] Although there might have been similar dangers in other communities, they should not be reduced to the common denominator. It may be that Paul has in mind itinerant preachers, but why should this group be singled out here as enemies of the cross of Christ?

[25] Gnilka, *Philipperbrief*, 204, 211–18.

[26] This is held by Bonnard (*Philippiens*, 71) and Behm ("κοιλία," 788). See Gnilka, *Philipperbrief*, 205.

[27] Problems of morality were connected with a particular view on the present state of perfection. See Gnilka, *Philipperbrief*, 206, 211–18.

[28] This word is employed for the end-time destruction in Matt 7:13; John 17:12; Acts 8:20; Rom 9:22; Phil 1:28, 3:19; 1 Tim 6:9; Heb 10:39; 2 Pet 2:1, 3, 3:7, 16; and Rev 17:8, 11.

The word "shame" in Phil 3:19 denotes a behavior that the apostle, from the faith perspective, regards as reprehensible. The glorying in shame suggests that these individuals openly approve and even boast of doing things that the believer, informed and guided by the Spirit, finds shameful and not in accordance with the mind of Christ (Phil 1:9–11; Gal 5:16; cf. Rom 1:32). It is a life in accordance with the sinful flesh and in opposition to the Spirit—the life that the apostle here refers to as "the belly" (κοιλία, koilia). The cross is opposed to the perverse mentality of the world, just as heaven is opposed to the lowliness of the world (see Phil 3:20–21).[29]

In 1 Cor 8:11 and Rom 14:15 Paul addresses another problem—that of giving scandal to the weak in the community, of inducing them to sin. Both texts deal with eating what some in the community may still regard as forbidden (cf. also 1 Cor 10:23–32). In both texts the apostle warns the stronger "brother" not to destroy by his action the life of Christ in a weaker member of the community. First Corinthians 8:1–11 deals with eating food that has been sacrificed to idols. The "stronger" brother, the one who has the "knowledge" (vv. 1–2, 4, 7, 10, 11), who knows that "no idol in the world really exists" and that "there is no God but one" (v. 4), acts inconsiderately when he eats this food regardless of the effect of his action on the community. The apostle is troubled with this cold, haughty, and brazen reasoning that disregards love (v. 1–2). The weak brother, the one who "became so accustomed to idols until now," regards eating such food as a participation in sacrifices to idols (cf. 10:14–22). While Paul agrees with the stronger "brother" that there are no idols, he condemns his action as doing harm in the community. The weak brother, following the example of the stronger brother,[30] also eats such food—against his conscience. The effect is disastrous. The apostle accuses the stronger believer of having caused the destruction of the life of Christ in the weaker believer: "So by your knowledge those weak believers for whom Christ died are destroyed (ἀπόλλυται, apollytai)" (8:11). This is a "sin against members of your family" and a "sin against Christ" (v. 12).[31]

---

[29] 1 Enoch 62:10 notes that at the end-time judgment the faces of the mighty and the rulers "shall be filled with shame, and their countenances shall be crowned with darkness"; cf. 63:11. It is not evident that in Phil 3:18 Paul regards shame as a present experience of punishment, as Gnilka (Philipperbrief, 205) maintains.

[30] On eating food sacrificed to idols, see Conzelmann, 1 Corinthians, 147–48.

[31] A similar situation is mentioned in 1 Cor 10:23–32.

Paul sees here a twofold destruction: that of the weak brother and that of the strong brother. The word "brother" here indicates that the two are members of the community. What is destroyed is the present "life in Christ" of the weak brother, but from the cognate passages, Rom 14:13–15 and 1 Cor 3:16–17, it is clear that the one who has destroyed the life of faith in another will also be destroyed. In 1 Cor 3:16–17 Paul, speaking of an action in the community that destroys Christian existence in a believer, states, "Do you not know that you are God's temple and that God's Spirit dwells in you? If anyone destroys (φθείρει, *phtheirei*) God's temple, God will destroy (φθερεῖ, *phtherei*) that person. For God's temple is holy, and you are that temple." Here also the destroyer of God's temple is another Christian.

Romans 14:1–23 deals with a similar problem, that of following dietary laws. But the problem has to do with following Jewish or non-Jewish dietary practices, with their religious implications of clean and unclean (see v. 14). Likewise, Paul insists that believers should respect one another's conscience. They should be aware of the possible destructive effects of their action on others. Paul exhorts the community to make sure that they all, whether by eating or by abstaining, honor the Lord (vv. 6–9). They are to leave the judgment to God. The apostle cautions, "For we will all stand before the judgment seat of God. For it is written, 'As I live, says the Lord, every knee shall bow to me, and every tongue shall give praise to God.' So then, each of us will be accountable to God" (vv. 10–12). The judgment seat is said to be "of God," in agreement with the quotations from Isa 45:23 and 49:18, but the mode of argumentation resembles that in 1 Cor 8:1–13. Paul first expresses his agreement that before the Lord, everything is clean, then he states his reservation: "But it is unclean for anyone who thinks it unclean" (Rom 14:14). He warns, "If your brother or sister is being injured by what you eat, you are no longer walking in love. Do not let what you eat cause the ruin of one for whom Christ died" (v. 15). In v. 20 he again admonishes, "Do not, for the sake of food, destroy the work of God."[32]

---

[32] Mattern (*Verständnis*, 117) reduces everything to the dichotomy faith–rejection of faith, in order to avoid the difficulty of a justified believer being finally condemned. But see Luz, *Geschichtsverständnis*, 316; Roetzel, *Judgement*, 6–7, 39–40, 140–41, 166–70.

A somewhat less definite threat of the end-time punishment occurs also in 1 Thess 4:6. The passage 4:1–8 deals with the exhortation to a holy life, above all in sexual behavior (vv. 3–5). In this matter, the faithful are to be different from "the Gentiles who do not know God" (v. 5). In v. 6 Paul cites it as the will of God "that no one wrong (ὑπερβαίνειν, hyperbainein) or exploit (πλεονεκτεῖν, pleonektein) a brother or sister in this matter (ἐν τῷ πράγματι, en tō pragmati), because the Lord is an avenger (ἔκδικος, ekdikos) in all these things, just as we have already told you beforehand and solemnly warned you." The matter in question here seems to be "impurity" (ἀκαθαρσίᾳ, akatharsia, v. 7), since this verse is flanked by Paul's condemnation of pagans' sexual excesses (v. 5) and by his reminder that the Lord did not call them "to impurity but in holiness" (v. 7).[33] What, exactly, the crime was is difficult to say, but the apostle reminds the community that God punishes such deeds. The title "Lord" most likely refers to Christ, expected to return at the parousia.[34] The vehemence of Paul's castigation of this deed suggests that ἔκδικος implies damnation.[35]

On several occasions (Gal 5:19–21; 1 Cor 6:9–10; 10:6–11) Paul, in his exhortations, warns the faithful that certain sinful behavior will exclude them from inheriting the kingdom of heaven. He makes it clear that what believers do here and now will affect their ultimate salvation. He warns them not to presume that they stand so firm that they can not fall. But he also assures them that God will support them in their efforts to be holy and irreproachable until the coming of the Lord (1 Thess 3:13; 5:9, 23; Phil 1:5; 2:13; 1 Cor 1:8).

2. The Testing of Believers

Paul, when warning the faithful of the impending judgment, sometimes indicates that eternal salvation is not at stake. In 1 Cor

---

[33] So also Rigaux (Thessaloniciens, 510), Milligan (Thessalonians, 50), Frame (Thessalonians, 152), Neil (Thessalonians, 81), Best (Thessalonians, 166), A. L. Moore (Thessalonians, 63), and R. F. Collins, "1 Thessalonians," 777). But Dibelius (Thessalonicher I/II, Philipper, 21), Dobschütz (Thessalonicherbriefe, 167), and Schürmann (1 Thessalonicher, 75) suggest some sort of business exploitation here.

[34] So R. F. Collins, "1 Thessalonians," 777; Best, 1 Thessalonians, 166; Rigaux, Thessaloniciens, 511.

[35] Paul usually employs the verb ἐκδικέω, ekdikeō (Rom 12:19), the noun ἐκδίκησις, ekdikēsis (Rom 12:19; 2 Cor 7:11; cf. 2 Thess 1:18), and the adjective ἔκδικος (Rom 13:14; 1 Thess 4:6) for condemnation or punishment.

3:12–15 he states explicitly that this judgment will not involve the loss of salvation; in 4:3–5 he points to his own judgment; and in 2 Cor 5:9–10 he exhorts, rather than admonishes, the community to please the Lord, since they will all have to appear before his judgment seat.

First Corinthians 3:12–15 contains the most explicit portrayal of the judgment of believers. The context is divisions in the community occasioned by various missionaries. In vv. 5–9 Paul discusses the contribution of Apollos and of himself, stating that they are merely workers who plant and water while God gives the growth. In v. 8 he asserts that each worker "will receive wages according to the labor" each has done. The assertion is positive. In v. 10, however, the apostle makes a distinction between his work and the work of others,[36] saying, "According to the grace of God given to me . . . I laid a foundation, and someone else is building on it." He warns, "Each builder must choose with care how to build on it." His own laying of the foundation is not under scrutiny, for he laid the one and only foundation, Jesus Christ (v. 11). But what was built on this foundation is not beyond reproach.[37] Verses 12–15 deal with the latter: "Now if anyone builds on the foundation with gold, silver, precious stones, wood, hay, straw—the work of each builder will become visible, for the Day will disclose it, because it will be revealed with fire, and the fire will test what sort of work each has done. If what has been built on the foundation survives, the builder will receive a reward. If the work is burned up, the builder will suffer loss; the builder will be saved, but only as through fire."

Paul is here mixing metaphors—building a house, testing precious metals, burning—but the meaning of his statement is clear. He is speaking of the diverse quality of the work done by other workers in the building up of the community.[38] The building

---

[36] 1 Cor 3:10–15 is not a digression, as Kuck (*Judgment*, 170–71) correctly observes against Bultmann.

[37] Paul himself does not like to build on the foundation laid by someone else, and he watches with a critical eye those who build on his foundation (cf. 2 Cor 10:15).

[38] Paul is not speaking here against those who oppose his gospel: there is agreement in what concerns the fundamentals of the faith. According to Kuck (*Judgment*, 171–72), other workers mentioned here by Paul need not be outsiders. In 1 Cor 12:28–30 he lists apostles, prophets, teachers, and others who are active in the building up of the community. But Paul lets the community guess whom he means. Nor is the community itself being tested here, as Kümmel suggests (see Conzelmann, *1 Corinthians*, 76).

materials employed are of different value; the possibilities are indicated with the list of choices from gold to straw. The last two scarcely qualify as acceptable building material.[39] It could be that the apostle has in mind the building of a temple, since he mentions gold, silver, and precious stones (cf. 1 Cor 3:16).[40] Since Paul is employing the image of building as a metaphor for spiritual input, the quality of this work done on his foundation is not at present evident to the eye. It is not clear whether it is "gold" or "wood" or "straw" or "hay." But the day—the day of the Lord—will reveal it through fire.[41]

Again, Paul is mixing metaphors. He is thinking of fire not as a light that illumines and thus reveals the true worth of the material but as a means of testing (δοκιμάσει, *dokimasei*) precious metals and of purifying them. The prevailing image is still the construction of a building and the use of building materials, although the latter are not all metals and can scarcely be tested for their worth by fire.[42] By fire the precious metal is brought to its melting point, and the impurities, which did not dissolve at that temperature can then be removed. What Paul wants to state by using this imagery is this: the final testing will separate what is authentic from what is inauthentic in the worker's contribution to the community. "The fire will test what sort of work each has done."

The next sentence contains yet another shift in the imagery: "If what has been built on the foundation survives, the builder will receive a reward (μισθὸν λήμψεται, *misthon lēmpsetai*). If the work is burned up (κατακαήσεται, *katakaēsetai*), the builder will suffer loss (ζημιωθήσεται, *zēmiōthēsetai*); the builder will be saved, but only as through fire (ὡς διὰ πυρός, *hōs dia pyros*)" (1 Cor 3:14–15). Here the apostle speaks of a consuming fire and of burning up (κατακαήσεται). The underlying idea is clear: the substandard

---

[39] Kuck (*Judgment*, 172) points out that none of the lists of building materials, either in the Bible or in secular literature, includes hay or straw. Weiss (*Der erste Korintherbrief*, 80) and Strack and Billerbeck (*Kommentar*, 3.334) state that hay was not used as building material.

[40] Kuck, *Judgment*, 177.

[41] Roetzel (*Judgement*, 164) situates this judgment within the framework of the church. According to him, it will be the building—the church—that will be tested. But what is really tested here is not the church but the work done in the church by certain individuals.

[42] See Zech 13:9; Isa 1:25; 4:5; Jer 5:29; Ezek 22:20; 24:11; Prov 5:16–17; Wis 3:6; 1 Pet 1:17; *T. Abr.* 13; *Pss. Sol.* 15:6–8; 1QH 5:16–17. For references to Christian literature on this, see Gnilka, *Schriftzeugnis*, 17.

material, such as hay or straw, will burn up. In this sense fire has three functions: it reveals (φανερὸν γενήσεται, *phaneron genēsetai;* ἀποκαλύπτεται, *apokalyptetai*) what was until then hidden;[43] it also tests (δοκιμάσει) the worth of the material; and it consumes (κατακαήσεται) what is worthless.[44] The latter function indicates that fire is also an instrument of punishment.[45]

In these verses the apostle again mentions reward and loss,[46] reverting from the metaphor of the temple to the builder (v. 12). The builder whose work burned up in the testing will be painfully affected (ζημιωθήσεται) by the loss, but he will not perish (αὐτὸς δὲ σωθήσεται, *autos de sōthēsetai*). Yet he will be saved "only as through fire (ὡς διὰ πυρός)." Paul is thus envisaging a judgment and a punishment, as the experience of loss indicates.[47] The builder's work in the community did not contribute to the building up of a life in Christ—it was worthless, and it burned up. This is Paul's rather circumspect warning to his coworkers to be responsible. At the same time he calls on the community to discern.[48] Fire is the means of testing and discerning, more than of punishment. The outcome of judgment is positive or negative, but judgment is not depicted as a forensic event. While vv. 12–15 do not say who will do the testing and the exposing, in 4:4–5 Paul ascribes this to the Lord. There he employs such expressions as φωτίσει and

---

[43] In the OT, Yahweh is said to uncover Israel's sins in the sight of all; see Mic 1:6; Nah 2:7; Isa 47:2; Jer 13:26. See also *1 Enoch* 98:6; *2 Bar.* 83:3.

[44] Fire as a purifying agent is mentioned in Isa 1:24–26, 4:2–4, 6:6–7; Zech 13:9; Mal 3:2–3; and 1QH 5:15–16 (Kuck, *Judgment,* 180 n. 156).

[45] Fire as a punishing agent is frequently mentioned in the Bible; see Kuck, *Judgment,* 180 n. 155. This function of fire is documented elsewhere in the NT. The presence of this function in 1 Cor 3:12–15 should not be denied out of fear that this would mean accepting the doctrine of purgatory; see Gnilka, *Schriftzeugnis.*

[46] Reward, like punishment, is part of Paul's complex thought here dealing with the present life of faith and the future completion. Paul is not thinking of justification but of what comes after it—life in accordance with the gift received. Mattern (*Verständnis,* 109–11, 176–78) is caught in a false dilemma by constantly asking whether the person has lost faith and, hence, justification. 1 Cor 3:13–15 causes difficulties for Mattern because she is forcing Paul's thought here to conform to her notion of justification by faith. As Kuck (*Judgment,* 185) observes, the apostle does not see any contradiction between his statement in 1 Cor 3:13–15 and his doctrine of justification by faith.

[47] The person suffers a loss; hence the fire is a punishment. Loss is not merely "a loss of potential reward," as Kuck (*Judgment,* 181) maintains.

[48] It is not a warning not to anticipate the judgment, as Mattern (*Verständnis,* 109–10) and Kuck (*Judgment,* 181) maintain; 1 Cor 4:5 is responding to a different situation.

φανερώσει at the coming of the Lord, rather than the image of fire. It is a question of shedding light and of revealing, rather than of testing and of removing the impurities. The Lord is the one who demands an account from his missionaries. He will bring to light what is hidden and expose the true worth of their work in the building up of the community.

First Corinthians 4:3–5 relegates the community's judging of the apostle, as well as the mutual charges in the community, to the future judgment by the Lord. Apparently some Corinthians have questioned and criticized what Paul is doing.[49] The apostle responds by urging the community to regard him as a "servant of Christ and steward of God's mysteries" (v. 1), by whom it is required that he be trustworthy. As such he is accountable to the Lord, not to men. Human judgments do not worry him and are in fact premature.

> But with me it is a very small thing that I should be judged [ἀνακριθῶ, anakrithō] by you or by any human court [ὑπὸ ἀνθρωπίνης ἡμέρας, hypo anthrōpinēs hēmeras]. I do not even judge [ἀνακρίνω, anakrinō] myself. . . . It is the Lord who judges [ἀνακρίνων, anakrinōn] me. Therefore do not pronounce judgment [μὴ κρίνετε, mē krinete] before the time, before the Lord comes [ἔλθη, elthē], who will bring to light [φωτίσει] the things now hidden in darkness and will disclose [φανερώσει, phanerōsei] the purposes of the heart. Then each one will receive commendation [ἔπαινος, epainos] from God (1 Cor 4:3–5).

Unlike 3:12–15, this text concerns Paul's own work for the community.[50] The apostle here acknowledges his responsibility to the Lord, whose "steward" he is. Hence the Lord, not anyone else, is his judge.[51] Paul neither acquits himself, although his conscience is clear, nor accepts the community's judgment of himself. In his opinion it is best to leave judging to the Lord when he comes: only he knows what goes on in the human heart;[52] he can bring to light

---

[49] For the context of this passage, see Fee, 1 Corinthians, 158.

[50] This is especially clear from the use of the first person singular in 4:3–4. For a more social interpretation of the passage, see Kuck, Judgment, 201–10. Kuck reacts to Theissen's (Psychological Aspects, 57–114) psychological interpretation of this passage.

[51] Paul uses the word "day" (ἡμέρας) for the day of judgment, as in 1 Cor 3:15.

[52] God knows and searches human hearts, as is clear from 1 Sam 16:7; Ps 139:1–12; Jer 17:10; Matt 6:4, 6, 18; 1 Thess 2:4; and Rom 2:16. In the Gospels, Jesus knows what is in the heart of another (Luke 5:22; 6:8; 14:1–6; 19:5; 20:23). For Paul, the risen Lord is endowed with knowledge not given to mortals. As Rom 2:16 indicates, God will through Jesus Christ judge the secret thoughts of all.

what is hidden to the human eye. This passage clearly refers to the end-time judgment of believers, including Paul, and it associates the judgment with Christ's coming.[53] The event will disclose what is hidden. But the words φωτίσει and φανερώσει, ascribed to the Lord, are here associated with praise (ἔπαινος; cf. μισθόν, 3:14). The apostle is thus optimistic about the outcome of this exposure, as the reference to ultimate praise indicates (v. 5). He rests his case with the Lord, in whom he trusts, and in the Lord's power to illumine the innermost secrets of the heart.[54]

A positive note is struck also in 2 Cor 5:9–10. Here, having given his assurance of the glorious completion that will include the body (vv. 1–5) and having expressed his desire to be with the Lord (vv. 6–8), Paul urges, "So (διό, dio) whether we are at home or away, we make it our aim to please him. For all of us must appear before the judgment seat of Christ, so that each may receive recompense for what has been done in the body, whether good or evil."

The text clearly deals with the faithful and concerns hope. It is based on the explanation in 2 Cor 5:1–8. What is important now, Paul states, is to please the Lord (εὐάρεστοι αὐτῷ εἶναι, euarestoi autō einai). The clause "whether we are at home (ἐνδημοῦντες, endēmountes) or away (ἐκδημοῦντες, ekdēmountes)" in v. 9, meaning whether we are alive or dead, refers to the antithesis in vv. 6–8.[55] Verse 10 then gives the reason (γάρ) why they must please the Lord: "All of us (πάντες) must appear (φανερωθῆναι, phanerōthēnai) before the judgment seat (ἔμπροσθεν τοῦ βήμα-τος, emprosthen tou bēmatos) of Christ."

Christ is thus the universal judge of the living and of the dead: all must appear before him, although the apostle thinks primarily of the community and of himself (ἡμᾶς) here. The word φανερωθῆναι[56] may suggest complete transparency before the judge (cf. 1 Cor 4:5) as well as "to appear before," as found in Rom 14:10, which asserts, "For we will all stand (παραστησόμεθα, parastēsometha) before the judgment seat of God." The matter

---

[53] Kuck, Judgment, 200–201. The accountability to Christ is not in tension with the accountability to God, as Kuck implies.

[54] According to Kuck (Judgment, 204–205), Paul's point here is not that the unconscious motives are beyond human judgment but that the Lord is the sole judge. This excludes Paul and the Corinthians.

[55] Hoffmann, Toten, 280.

[56] The word φανερόω, phaneroō, occurs 13 times in Paul; it seems to be his favorite word in 2 Cor 2–7, where it occurs 8 times.

that will come under scrutiny is "what has been done in the body" (τὰ διὰ τοῦ σώματος, *ta dia tou sōmatos*, v. 10)—human actions here on earth. The judgment seat suggests a court scene. The positive or negative outcome is indicated by the expression "receive recompense" (κομίσηται, *komisetai*)[57] and by "good or bad" (ἀγαθὸν εἴτε φαῦλον, *agathon eite phaulon*).

The apostle has in mind the end-time judgment,[58] at which all the living and all the deceased will appear before Christ the judge.[59] Unlike Rom 14:10, judgment here is attributed to Christ. But v. 11 indicates that Christ's judgment is not to be separated from God's judgment. Christ is the judge in the end time, judging in God's stead and with divine power.[60]

Does Paul here envision the sinner's damnation? The possibility cannot be excluded, but the context is positive, and the apostle is addressing a believing community. It seems best to interpret this passage in the light of 1 Cor 3:12–15, 4:3–5 and 1 Thess 5:6–10, where the apostle is not threatening the faithful with damnation.

Romans 14:8–12 also deals with the judgment of the believers. Paul exhorts the factions not to recriminate one another for eating clean or unclean food but, rather, to honor the Lord in everything they do, whether they eat or abstain from eating a particular food. He ends with this warning: "Each of us will be accountable (λόγον δώσει, *logon dōsei*) to God" (v. 12). The future tense of the verb, δώσει, refers to the eschatological judgment. The reference to God's throne (τῷ βήματι τοῦ θεοῦ, *tō bēmati tou theou*) in v. 10 is occasioned by the scriptural quotation in v. 11. As in 2 Cor 5:10, the judgment is forensic and universal. Verse 11 indicates that the future and universal judgment by God is the

---

[57] The word κομίζω, *komizō*, is used by Paul only here. It is employed in the eschatological context in Eph 6:8; Col 3:25; Heb 10:36, 11:39; and 1 Pet 1:9; 5:4.

[58] Hoffmann, *Toten*, 285.

[59] Allo (*2 Corinthiens*, 133) thinks of the particular judgment of the soul at the moment of death, but it is not at all certain that Paul has this in mind.

[60] The notion that God will entrust the judgment to his plenipotentiary is found in the entire NT and has its roots in Dan 10:14 and in the nonbiblical apocalyptic literature (*1 Enoch* 45:3; 51:3–4; 55:4; 62; 63:77; 69:27; *2 Bar.* 72). According to *1 Enoch* 69:27, the Son of man or the Elect One is seated "on the throne of his glory" and is given the sum of the judgment. He judges in the name of the Lord of the Spirits (*1 Enoch* 45:3; 62:2; 69:27). His judgment is directed against the kings of the earth (*1 Enoch* 55:4; 62:6, 9; 63), the heavenly Watchers and their associates (*1 Enoch* 55:4), and the nations (4 Ezra 13:37). The righteous faithful are not judged but vindicated.

consequence of God's universal and sovereign lordship. Then every human being will have to acknowledge God's supreme lordship. But in this passage the apostle also emphasizes Christ's lordship over the living and the dead.

Paul can, in addition, refer to the present experience of judgment or punishment in the community, as in 1 Cor 5:3–5 and 11:29–32. In 5:3–5 he himself, armed with apostolic authority, has already "pronounced judgment" in the name of the Lord[61] on the one who is living with his father's wife (v. 1), and he calls on the community to do the same. But this judgment has an eschatological referent: they are to hand the culprit over to Satan "for the destruction of the flesh, so that his spirit may be saved in the day of the Lord" (v. 5).[62] That this is not the ultimate condemnation is evident from the remark "That his spirit may be saved in the day of the Lord." The purpose of this punishment is the salvation of the man's spirit. It is carried out by Paul and the community with the power of the Lord's Spirit.

A similar judgment is mentioned in 11:29–32, where Paul mentions certain sicknesses as the result of the community's unworthy participation in the Eucharist. The eschatological referent is clear in v. 32, where Paul states, "But when we are judged by the Lord, we are disciplined, so that we may not be condemned along with the world." Paul's references to judgment in the community are to individuals in the community. Although the whole community will be judged, the apostle never threatens the whole community with destruction (cf. Rev. 3:1–6).

E. PRAYERS TO BE BLAMELESS AT THE LORD'S COMING

Since the faithful must appear before the Lord's judgment seat, they must pray that they will be blameless on the day of the Lord. Concern about the last judgment thus enters the prayers of both

---

[61] For a discussion of other options of reading this text, see Fee, *1 Corinthians*, 206–7.

[62] It is unlikely that Paul means here the death of the culprit, as Conzelmann (*1 Corinthians*, 97) suggests, for the ultimate purpose of the punishment is still to save the man's spirit. Cf. Fee, *1 Corinthians*, 209–13. The remark in 2 Cor 2:5–11 suggests a community punishment (ἐπιτιμία, *epitimia*), but the culprit is alive and is to be subsequently forgiven by the community for his own spiritual good (cf. also Gal 6:1; 2 Thess 3:14–15).

Paul and the faithful. Such petitions occur in 1 Thess 3:13, 5:23; 1 Cor 1:8; Phil 1:10–11; and elsewhere. They are addressed to God. The apostle begs God to preserve the community blameless or strengthen them in their irreproachable life until the judgment day, until the coming of the Lord Jesus Christ. The prayers appeal to the faithfulness of God and to his salvific will.

Thus in 1 Thess 5:23 the apostle prays, "May the God of peace himself sanctify you entirely; and may your spirit and soul and body be kept sound and blameless at the coming (ἐν τῇ παρουσίᾳ, en tē parousia) of our Lord Jesus Christ." God is the God of peace. Paul begs him to keep the community free from turmoil inside and out and without any inner anxiety.[63] Confusion and anxiety are not part of God's will. Moreover, Paul is aware that there is need of healing (ἁγιάσαι, hagiasai) and strengthening in body, soul, and spirit. This prayer also gives an assurance: "The one who calls you is faithful, and he will do this" (v. 24). To reach the parousia unblemished is the goal of the community as well as the intention of God.

The petition in 1 Thess 3:13 contains a similar prayer of the apostle for the faithful: "And may he [the Lord Jesus][64] so strengthen your hearts in holiness that you may be blameless before our God and Father at the coming (ἐν τῇ παρουσίᾳ) of our Lord Jesus with all his saints."[65] Here also Paul prays that spiritual gifts be used correctly by the faithful.

In the thanksgiving section 1 Cor 1:4–9, Paul assures the Corinthians, "He [God?][66] will also strengthen you to the end, so that you may be blameless on the day of our Lord Jesus Christ. God is faithful; by him you were called into the fellowship of his Son, Jesus Christ our Lord" (v. 8). This prayer resembles 1 Thess 3:13. The apostle not only prays that the faithful be strengthened to the end; he also reassures the community that God will do so, since

---

[63] The apostle is not simply praying for the abundance of spiritual gifts, as Rigaux (*Thessaloniciens*, 595) suggests.

[64] So Rigaux (ibid., 487).

[65] According to Rigaux (ibid., 491–92), "all his saints" probably refers to the risen faithful rather than to the angels, as in Zech 14:5, but Wanamaker (*1 & 2 Thessalonians*, 145) disagrees.

[66] The construction here is unclear; the subject of this clause could be either God or Christ, who is mentioned last in the preceding clause. Conzelmann (*1 Corinthians*, 28) and Barrett (*1 Corinthians*, 39) opt for Christ, while Fee thinks it is God who does the strengthening.

God is faithful: God called them into the fellowship (κοινωνίαν, koinōnian) of his Son through Paul's testimony, and he will complete (ἕως τέλους, heōs telous)[67] what he has begun in them (1 Thess 5:9–11). The phrase "the day of our Lord Jesus Christ" refers to the final judgment. The basis of Paul's confidence is God himself, his faithfulness, not the Corinthians themselves.

A similar prayer occurs in the thanksgiving section Phil 1:9–11: "And this is my prayer, that your love may overflow more and more with knowledge (ἐπιγνώσει, epignōsei) and full insight (αἰσθήσει, aisthēsei) to help you to determine what is best, so that in the day of Christ you may be pure and blameless, having produced the harvest of righteousness that comes through Jesus Christ for the glory and praise of God." Paul's concern here is the love within the community—that the present love may increase more and more (περισσεύῃ, perisseuē). Love is the gift of the Spirit (Rom 5:5), and as such it must be prayed for.[68] But he prays that this love may be informed with spiritual knowledge and insight so that the community may discern (δοκιμάζειν, dokimazein) what is best (τὰ διαφέροντα, ta diapheronta)[69] and appear pure and blameless on the Lord's day. The apostle's prayer is also an exhortation to the community.[70]

CONCLUSION

The eschatological judgment is a component of the Lord's coming: the exalted Christ is the judge of the living and of the dead. In this, Paul agrees with the rest of the NT. Although his central message is salvation, the latter has to be worked out in a life that appropriates faith, hope, and love, above all in a life that accepts the cross (1 Cor 1:18–24) and is guided by the Holy Spirit (Gal 5:16–26). Therefore, the overtones of exhortation, warning, and threat are heard together with the message of hope. The day

---

[67] According to Fee (1 Corinthians, 43), the primary meaning of this phrase is one of time, not of degree.

[68] Gnilka, Philipperbrief, 51.

[69] Although in 1 Thess 4:9–11 Paul states, "Concerning love of the brothers and sisters, you do not need to have anyone write to you, for you yourselves have been taught by God (θεοδίδακτοί ἐστε, theodidaktoi este)," here he calls for a discerning love and prays for the gift of the spirit to discern.

[70] Gnilka, Philipperbrief, 51.

of the Lord is an ambiguous day: it brings judgment and salvation, reward and punishment.

When he talks about condemnation, Paul thinks in the first place of the outsiders whose lives are marked with all kinds of sin that are the result of their denial of the one and true God (Rom 1:18–32). Others who commit such sins, although they believe in God (Rom 2) or accept Christ (1 Cor 3:16–17; Gal 5:19–21), will also be condemned at the final judgment. When he talks about the judgment of the outsiders, Paul distinguishes between the pagans and the Jews. And when he talks of the judgment of the believers, he differentiates between a condemnation (1 Cor 3:16) and a judgment that does not endanger salvation (v. 15). He threatens, warns, exhorts, and prays, as the context demands. The truth he inculcates is that everyone will come before the tribunal of Christ. But even what Paul says about the nonbelievers is meant as a warning to the believers. The latter are to be different from the world and from what they once were, because they now belong to Christ and have the Holy Spirit dwelling in them. They should thus take warning from what happened to the Israelites: they should abstain from idol worshipping. Faith, baptism, and the Eucharist alone will not save them. They should therefore examine themselves—whether they are testing Christ (1 Cor 10:9), or complaining, or indulging in sexual immorality and idolatry.

When he talks to the believers about judgment, Paul also reassures them: God's ultimate intention is salvation, not condemnation (1 Thess 5:9–11; 1 Cor 10:12–13; Rom 5:5–10). His references to judgment occur often in exhortations to the faithful to be constant and holy, and in warnings against transgressions. The emphasis is on works that correspond to their commitment in faith. As Bultmann observes, the apostle preaches a judgment according to works in a seeming contradiction to his doctrine of justification by faith[71] (1 Cor 3:12–15; 5:4; 10:1–22; 2 Cor 5:10; Rom 2:1–29). Paul urges constant vigilance, often pointing out that this is the end of the ages and that time is running out (1 Cor 7:29; 10:11; Rom 13:12). It is important to be faithful to the end. The apostle is concerned that life in Christ of the faithful be protected (1 Cor 3:16) and that they continue to strive to reach the end. Since the believers are constantly tested by the world, which Paul regarded as crooked and

---

[71] Bultmann, *Theology,* 1.75.

perverse (Phil 2:15), he prays that they be holy and irreproachable at the Lord's coming (1 Thess 3:13). And he reassures them that God will not test them beyond their strength (1 Cor 10:13).

The imagery of judgment varies. The event may be presented as a universal and sudden catastrophe, or as the Lord's coming that echoes God's active and powerful intervention on the day of the Lord, or as a court scene. Usually, the end-time judge is Christ, but when the apostle draws on an OT quotation, as in Rom 14:10, the judge is God. The judgment is the ultimate manifestation of God's power and of Christ's lordship.

10

<hr>

CONFLICT AT THE PAROUSIA

According to 1 Cor 15:25, Christ must rule until he has put all his enemies under his feet. This text, in contrast to the parousia texts 1 Thess 4:13–18, 1 Thess 5:1–11, 1 Cor 15:50–55, and Phil 3:20–21, deals with the overpowering and destruction of the sources of opposition to God. The opposition is not necessarily human opposition. The completion of Christ's reign at his parousia envisages also the destruction of certain powers and the end-time victory of Christ: Christ will be the Lord; through that lordship God will be ultimately all things to all (1 Cor 15:28). The Lord's coming will thus mean the end-time victory.

The conflict motif emphasizes this feature of the parousia of Christ. Christ is presented as the protagonist, and the powers as the antagonists. But who are these hostile powers? How does all this relate to the NT view of Christ's salvific activity? How does it relate to Jewish apocalyptic?

The motif of conflict in the present and the end time reflects the situations when Jesus encountered Satan, the demons, and the unclean spirits. And it reflects the post-Easter situation addressed in the Pauline epistles, which is still marked by antagonism between the dominion of Christ and the dominion of these spiritual powers. And we must remember that this conflict motif is a characteristic feature in Jewish and NT apocalyptic. Paul, however, uses war imagery seldom, and then sparingly. The most important passages in his letters containing this motif are 1 Cor 15:23–28 and Rom 16:20, but traces of conflict are found also in 1 Cor 2:6, 8, 15:54–56 and 1 Thess 4:16, 5:8.

A. THE CONFLICT WITH POWERS AND WITH DEATH, 1 CORINTHIANS 15:23–28

We have examined 1 Cor 15:23–28 earlier[1] and have brought out its function in the context of the parousia and the resurrection of the dead—the topic of 1 Cor 15. Now we focus on the conflict motif in this text and what this motif discloses about Paul's understanding of the Lord's coming. How does this motif enter into the picture here? Who are the powers? How do the powers, authorities, and principalities mentioned here fit in with Paul's view expressed elsewhere in his epistles about these forces? How is death a hostile power?

1. The Conflict Motif in 1 Corinthians 15:23–28

Since 1 Cor 15:23–28 has been analyzed earlier, it suffices here merely to point out the presence and function of the conflict motif in this passage. Verse 24 depicts the risen Jesus, expected in the end time, as a Messiah entrusted with God's kingly rule (βασιλείαν, basileian). He has been entrusted with this rule ever since his resurrection and exaltation. But he is not to hand back this rule to God the Father until "after he has destroyed (ὅταν καταργήσῃ, hotan katargēsē) every ruler (πᾶσαν ἀρχήν, pasan archēn) and every authority (πᾶσαν ἐξουσίαν, pasan exousian) and power (δύναμιν, dynamin). The power that Christ has received from the Father thus has a specific purpose: victory over all the hostile powers. The destruction of powers includes the destruction of death. In v. 26 the apostle states, "The last enemy to be destroyed is death." Verse 27a gives a reason for this charge entrusted to Christ by God: "He has put (ὑπέταξεν, hypetaxen) all things in subjection under his feet." Christ is, by God's will, to be the master of the entire creation (v. 27bc).

Paul draws here on the language of Pss 8:6 and 110:1, often quoted in the early church in a variety of contexts. These psalms asserted the rule of God's anointed king in terms of conflict and subjugation. They envisioned the subjugation of the nations. But Paul does not think of Christ as an earthly Jewish king who asserts his dominion in conflict with the nations. For Paul, Christ is Lord

---

[1] See ch. 5.

over all things in heaven, on earth, and under the earth (Phil 2:11). And the apostle thinks primarily of the risen and exalted Christ, the Son of God.

The connection of this passage with the resurrection of the dead and the parousia, affirmed in v. 23, indicates that Paul envisages this conquest at the time of Christ's coming. That coming will be in power and glory (1 Thess 4:16), to which even death will have to submit. The note of hostility, indicated in v. 25, identifies these powers as enemies (τοὺς ἐχθρούς, *tous echthrous*) and suggests that καταργήσῃ and καταργεῖται, *katargeitai*, here mean "destroy." The parousia thus means the annihilation of all opposition to God's order in creation, but above all the end of death's power over human beings.

Unlike Phil 2:9–11, which presents Christ's exaltation after death, Paul here asserts conquest and destruction. He locates this conquest at the parousia of Christ as the outcome of Christ's royal rule ever since his resurrection from the dead. This implies that the kingly rule of Christ in the present, asserted in Phil 2:9–11 and implied in 1 Cor 15:24, is opposed to the rule of these powers in the cosmos. These powers have not yet been destroyed; they are, however, to be destroyed (καταργούμενοι, *katargoumenoi*; see, e.g., 1 Cor 2:6; 2 Cor 3:7, 11, 13). In their present rule they are being overpowered by the rule of the risen Lord. The antagonism is present now, for the kingdom of Christ is taking place now. The opposition between these powers and the rule of Christ is total: the New Testament speaks of hostility and annihilation. While sinners are οἱ ἀπολλύμενοι, *hoi apollymenoi* (those on the road to perdition) the powers are οἱ καταργούμενοι—those destined for destruction (e.g., 1 Cor 1:18; 2 Cor 2:15; 4:9; 2 Thess 2:10).

But the text does not dwell on the leaders of the opposition or why there is such an opposition, how these powers affect the world and the faithful, or how Christ can reign while these forces are still operating in the cosmos. For all this, we must draw on the notions current in Judaism and reflected in the NT writings.

2. Conflict Motif in Apocalyptic Writings

The conflict motif is part of the OT presentation of the day of the Lord; in it Yahweh appears as the leader of the heavenly armies.[2] Some of its features are observed in the "holy war" tradition and are echoed in Jewish apocalyptic—for example, in *1 Enoch* 1:3–9, which at present introduces the entire *1 Enoch* collection: "The Holy Great One will come forth from his dwelling and . . . march upon Mount Sinai and appear in his camp emerging from heaven with a mighty power . . . and the Watchers shall tremble." The Holy Great One, according to this depiction, comes with his mighty heavenly army—hence in full force—in order to subdue the foe, the Watchers. The Watchers are the fallen angels who have brought hostility to God on earth and are responsible for all kinds of evil in the world. They are at the root of idolatry. In the following chapters Enoch describes God's decree to eliminate these sources of evil and destruction on earth. The Watchers and their leaders[3] are bound and imprisoned by the archangels from heaven,[4] at the end to be thrown into the eternal fire (10:4–17; 19:1),[5] while the children of the Watchers are expelled from among the people and destroyed (10:9–10; 16). Thus, all injustice on earth is rooted out (v. 16). Here Enoch describes the cleansing of the earth from the superhuman evil that swept down on and corrupted the world and its dwellers before the flood (Gen 6:1–4). This future event, revealed to Enoch before the flood, was God's action at the time of Noah—an action that will be concluded at the end of time with the total destruction of these spiritual forces.

In 54:3–6 the seer is shown the ultimate fate prepared for the armies of Azaz'el, the messengers of Satan: on the great day of judgment they will be bound and cast into the "abyss of complete condemnation."[6] According to 55:3–4 the Son of man will judge the fallen angels and their progeny. The Lord of the Spirits says, "When I would give consent so that they should be seized by the hands of the angels of tribulation and pain . . . kings and potentates, dwellers of the earth . . . would have to see my Elect One, how he sits in the throne of glory and judges Azaz'el and all his

---

[2] See ch. 1.

[3] *1 Enoch* 6:7 mentions the leader Semyaz and the leaders of ten. In 10:4 and 13:1 the seer mentions Azaz'el, the corrupter.

[4] *1 Enoch* 10 mentions Raphael, Gabriel, and Michael

[5] *1 Enoch* 13 states that God's decree is final and no intercession can prevail.

[6] Although Enoch here also mentions "the kings and potentates" (54:1), these are clearly distinguished from the fallen angels, although they also are being destroyed.

248 PAUL AND THE PAROUSIA

company, and his army, in the name of the Lord of the Spirits!"
Here the Almighty has relegated the judgment of these superhuman
spirits to the Elect One (cf. 54:6; 69:2, 28). But everything still
depends on the power of the Lord of the Spirits, who sends his
angels to seize the destroyers and contaminators of the earth.
Chapter 56 mentions an army of angels of punishment sent to
catch the elect of the Watchers. The condemned here are not
merely imprisoned: they have been brought from the prison in
order to be destroyed.

An exhaustive enumeration of elemental spirits occurs in
1 Enoch 60:11–21 and *Jub.* 2:2. The passages mention the "angels
of power," the "angels of principalities," and other powers. Both
the heavens and the earth are filled with these powers,[7] but some
of them are identified with the fallen world. They have destroyed
the right order of seasons and induced people to worship them
(*1 Enoch* 75:1–2; 80:6–7). The spirits set over the nations have
usurped their power and led the nations astray (*Jub.* 15:31; *1 Enoch*
90:22). They are regarded as the corrupters of mankind, the
source of evil in the present world. The demons, who are corrupt-
ing and oppressing the people, are the progeny of these angelic
powers and of the women on earth.

In Jewish apocalyptic writings, spiritual forces have been given
certain roles in the administration of creation.[8] The ἄρχοντες, *archon-
tes*, regulate the movements of the heavenly bodies. These "leaders of
the chiefs of the thousands" are the regents of seasons, months, and
days and have caused the people to err in this regard (*1 Enoch* 75:1–2;
82:4, 8, 10). *First Enoch* 80:6–7 mentions the perversion among these
heavenly leaders, who induce the people to honor them as gods. In
18:13–16 and 21:1–3 are mentioned the stars that have transgressed
God's command and are now being punished for it.

In the vision in 4 Ezra 13, the man from the sea came upon the
clouds, carved for himself a great mountain, and sat upon it
(vv. 1–4). When "an innumerable multitude of men" gathered to
make war against him (v. 5), "he neither lifted his hand nor held a
spear or any weapon of war." Ezra recounts, "But I saw only how
he sent forth from his mouth as it were a stream of fire, and from

[7] According to Jewish apocalyptic writings, God is wholly sovereign over these
forces: they were all created by God and were allotted certain roles by God.
[8] See G. F. Moore, *Judaism*, 1.400–413.

his lips a flaming breath, and from his tongue he shot forth a storm of sparks . . . and burned them, so that suddenly nothing was seen of the innumerable multitude but only the dust of ashes and the smell of smoke" (vv. 9–11).

Here the conflict motif is evident. The man from the sea is the Son of the Most High (v. 32), who delivers creation. The opponents are not the watchers or the demons or Satan but the nations. Standing on top of Mount Zion, he "will reprove the nations for their ungodliness, reproach them . . . with their evil thoughts and with the torments with which they are to be tortured . . . and . . . destroy them without effort by the law" (v. 37).[9]

In the *War Scroll* of the Dead Sea documents, the conflict motif occurs in the end-time war. In this event human beings and spirits engage in the battle, which lasts for forty years (1QM 1:13). The Qumran warriors, the elect ones, fight alongside "the Prince of Light" (13:10), the "princely angel of the kingdom of Michael" (17:7). The opponents are Satan and "all the spirits of his company" (13:4), "the angels of destruction" (13:12), the prince of the kingdom of wickedness (17:5), and the hostile nations. Chapter 12 mentions that God will muster his elect with his "Holy Ones" and his "angels," that "they may be mighty in battle, [and may smite] the rebels of the earth . . . and that [they may triumph] together with the elect of heaven" (v. 4).[10] Verses 10–11 speak of the angelic host and of the Hero of war joining the congregation in the battle.

The Qumran writings mention two created spirits who are ruling the people in this aeon "till the time of visitation" (1QS 3:17–18; cf. 4:16–17, 19–20). The "angel of darkness" (1QS 3:21) rules over "the children of falsehood" who "walk in the way of darkness." This angel, with the help of other spirits, is responsible for the aberrations among the "children of righteousness" and tries to trip them up with chastisements and persecutions (1QS 3:23–24). *War Scroll* 13:4 mentions Belial[11] and all the spirits of his company, who exercise their "wicked rule" and have an "ungodly purpose." In v. 2 these spirits are called "angels of destruction." But God sustains the righteous in their trials

---

[9] On the punishment of the nations that have trodden down Israel, see *2 Bar.* 72.
[10] Translated by Vermes (*Dead Sea Scrolls*).
[11] Beliar is a corrupt form of Belial; see Burrows, *More Light*, 288.

(14:8–10) and has set "an end for falsehood"; at the "time of his visitation He will destroy it forever" (1QS 4:18–19). The end-time battle will take place amid "the clamour of gods and men" (1QM 1:11); the army of Belial and all the "angels of his kingdom" will then be destroyed (vv. 14–15).

The Book of Revelation as well uses the conflict motif in its depiction of Christ's coming. A striking example of this occurs in 19:11–21. The Lord comes on a white horse (v. 11), accompanied by the heavenly armies (v. 14), to judge in righteousness and to make war (πολεμεῖ, *polemei*, v. 11). From his mouth issues a sharp sword with which he will strike the nations (v. 15) and then impose his rule of iron on them. He is the "King of kings and Lord of lords" (v. 16), pouring the fury of God's wrath on his opponents, the captains, the mighty, the kings with their armies, the beast, and the false prophet. In the ensuing battle, the opponents are defeated and the beast and the false prophet are captured. The latter two are then thrown alive into the lake of fire, while the rest are killed by his sword (vv. 20–21).

Revelation 11:15–18 speaks about what happened when the seventh seal was broken and the seventh trumpet sounded. Voices in heaven acclaimed this moment as the inauguration of the ultimate reality: "The kingdom of the world has become the kingdom of our Lord and of his Messiah, and he will reign forever and ever" (v. 15). This is the moment of God's wrath against nations. It is also the moment for the judgment of the dead and for "destroying those who destroy the earth" (v. 18). The Book of Revelation is filled with war imagery and often depicts the final battle between heaven's agents and their opponents. It mentions the dragon, or Satan (12:7–9), the first beast (13:1–9), and the second beast (vv. 11–19). They are united in their opposition to the Lamb and make war against him; but the Lamb will conquer them (17:14). In 20:1–3 an angel from heaven seizes the dragon and throws him into the bottomless pit. Satan, together with death, will at the end be destroyed (vv. 8–10).[12] It suggests that the enmity directed against God includes superhuman agents. In fact, they are regarded as the principal opponents to God. Ultimate reality has no place for this opposition to God.

---

[12] See Ernst, *Gegenspieler.*

3. Hostile Powers in Pauline Writings and in Pauline Tradition

It is no surprise to find echoes of this fundamental opposition to God also in Paul's letters. First Corinthians 15:24 mentions the rulers, the authorities, and the powers. It is only here that Paul refers to them with such emphasis, using synonyms of power (authorities, rulers, principalities) to identify them. As the plural indicates, there are whole sets of powerful opponents.[13] According to Schlier, their very being is the wielding of power.[14] The dominion of Christ and the dominion of these powers are in total opposition.[15]

According to 2 Thess 2:6–8,[16] the Lord's coming will take place after the rebellion inspired by the lawless one. In this present time the mystery of lawlessness is already at work, although it is restrained. But "the lawless one" must still be revealed, and then the "Lord Jesus will destroy [him] with the breath of his mouth, annihilating him by the manifestation of his coming." The verses that follow associate the coming of the lawless one with the working of Satan.

The best parallel to 1 Cor 15:24 is found in Eph 1:21. The text mentions ἀρχή, ἐξουσία, δύναμις, as well as κυριότης and "every name that is named not only in this age but also in the age to come." But this passage does not look ahead to the Lord's coming, as does 1 Cor 15:24, but back to the exaltation of Christ at his resurrection. It was then that "God put this power to work in Christ when he raised him from the dead and seated him at his right hand in the heavenly places, far above all rule and authority and power and dominion" (Eph 1:20–21). The allusion of "has put all things under his feet" to LXX Ps 8:6 (109:1) is here interpreted as God's making Christ "the head over all things" (Eph 1:22), rather than Christ's annihilation of these powers. In content, v. 21 agrees with Phil 2:11 rather than with 1 Cor 15:23–28.

---

[13] On the presence of these powers and the various names by which they are called in the NT, see Schlier, *Principalities*, 11–12.

[14] Ibid., 19.

[15] Ibid., 40–52.

[16] In the wake of Trilling's *(Untersuchungen)* linguistic analysis, 2 Thess is regarded by many scholars as a non-Pauline epistle, although many still maintain its Pauline authorship. The letter, at any rate, is close to 1 Thess. This passage is an instance of the use of the conflict motif in depicting the coming of the Lord.

Some of these terms occur also in Eph 3:10[17] and 6:12. According to 3:10, the mystery of God is made known through the church "to the rulers and authorities in the heavenly places." Ephesians 6:12 makes it clear that these powers are opposed to the believers' life in Christ, and associates them with the devil and the cosmic powers of darkness—the spiritual host of wickedness in heavenly places. The author exhorts the community to "put on the whole armour of God, so that you may be able to stand against the wiles of the devil (τοῦ διαβόλου, tou diabolou)" (v. 11). He explains the seriousness of this conflict, saying, "For our struggle is not against enemies of blood and flesh, but against the rulers (τὰς ἀρχάς, tas archas), against the authorities (τὰς ἐξουσίας, tas exousias), against the cosmic powers (τοὺς κοσμοκράτορας, tous kosmokratoras) of this present darkness, against the spiritual forces of evil (τὰ πνευματικὰ τῆς πονηρίας, ta pneumatika tēs ponērias) in the heavenly places" (vv. 11–12). The author warns the community to brace itself for the coming evil day.[18]

The hymn in Col 1:12–20 also contains some of these terms; but this hymn asserts Christ's dominion over these powers from the beginning of creation. Christ is "the firstborn of all creation"; "in him all things . . . were created, things visible and invisible, whether thrones (θρόνοι, thronoi) or dominions (κυριότητες, kyriotētes) or rulers (ἀρχαί) or powers (ἐξουσίαι)—all things have been created through him and for him" (v. 16). Christ is therefore Lord over all these powers. The hymn thus celebrates the universal lordship of Christ—even his authority over evil powers—and locates the origin of this lordship not at the moment of exaltation that is connected with his resurrection, as is done in Eph 1:21, but at the time of creation. These powers were "created through him and for him."[19]

In Col 2:8–10[20] the author warns the faithful, "See to it that no one takes you captive through philosophy and empty deceit, according to human tradition, according to the elemental spirits of

[17] In Eph 3:10 the author mentions rulers and authorities (ἀρχαί, ἐξουσίαι, exousiai) to whom the mystery of God's making in Christ one people of Jews and Gentiles has been revealed (cf. 3:6).
[18] According to Schlier (Principalities, 58–68), the "evil day" refers to the conflict before the parousia of Christ, although the battle has already begun.
[19] Ibid., 37.
[20] Col 2:10 is similar to Eph 3:10.

the universe, and not according to Christ." In v. 10 he asserts that Christ is "the head of every ruler (ἀρχῆς, *archēs*) and authority (ἐξουσίας)," and in v. 15 he assures the Colossians that God has, through Christ's cross, erased the record against them and "disarmed the rulers and authorities and made a public example of them, triumphing over them in it." The author points to the lordship of Christ over these powers and asks, "If with Christ you died to the elemental spirits of the universe, why do you live as if you still belonged to the world?" (v. 20). According to this text, Christ has already triumphed over these powers.

Clearly, these texts in Pauline tradition are our closest parallels to 1 Cor 15:24. They give us a horizon within which to interpret these spiritual phenomena, even though they occur in a different context and in a different eschatology. The hostility of these powers is clear, although it is not stated in every text. But it is also evident that these powers are mentioned in connection with the lordship of Christ. Christ's superiority is here rooted either in his parousia or in his resurrection or in his work at the moment of creation. While Ephesians and Colossians only affirm Christ's superiority over these powers, 1 Cor 15:24 asserts Christ's annihilation of them. Hence, it locates this event at the parousia.

Some of the names for these powers occur also in Rom 8:38. The passage contains an extensive list of personified situations and powers that could come between the love of God and the believer. The apostle mentions death (θάνατος), life, angels, rulers (ἀρχαί), things present, things to come, powers (δυνάμεις), height, and depth. The list does not contain, however, isomorphic items but a variety of possibilities that a believer may encounter in this life or in the next. For Paul, these things come from the created universe, but God is the creator of, and master over, the universe; hence, his love for us cannot be severed by anything in creation.

In 2 Cor 4:3–4 Paul speaks of the continued opposition to the gospel among the unbelievers as being inspired by certain powers. The apostle's gospel is veiled to the unbelievers whom the "god of this world"[21] has blinded so that they cannot see "the light of the gospel of the glory of Christ, who is the image of God." Most

---

[21] In Eph 2:2 we find "the ruler (ἄρχοντα, *archonta*) of the power of the air," and John 12:31, 14:30, and 16:11 mention the "ruler (ἄρχων) of this world." Cf. Allo, *2 Corinthiens*, 99–100; Schlier, *Principalities*, 11–12.

commentators take the "god of this world" (v. 4) to be a reference to the devil. In Pauline writings and in the entire NT, the devil is pictured in active opposition to Christ and the gospel (Matt 4:1–11; 12:26; Mark 3:26; Luke 4:1–13; 11:18; John 13:27; Acts 5:3; 26:18; 1 Cor 5:5; 2 Cor 6:15; 11:13; 12:7; Gal 4:3; 1 Thess 2:18; 3:5; etc.). Thus, both "the rulers of this world" (Gal 4:3; Col 2:8, 20) and the "god of this world" (2 Cor 4:4) are behind the rejection of the gospel.

In Gal 4:3–10 (cf. Col 2:8, 20) the apostle reminds the Galatians that when we were minors, we were enslaved to the "the elemental spirits of the world" (τὰ στοιχεῖα τοῦ κόσμου, *ta stoicheia tou kosmou*, v. 3),[22] "beings that by nature are not gods" (v. 8), that are beggarly and weak (v. 9). This situation has changed with the coming of God's Son, who gave them adoption as sons. Thus, the world before Christ was enslaved to these forces, but the faithful who are "children of God" (4:7) are free. The Galatians, however, are in danger of falling back into slavery to these elements by observing special days, months, seasons, and years (v. 10). According to Schlier,[23] the context of the passage suggests that the στοιχεῖα are endowed with the authority of angelic powers, demanding worship from the people. They are closely associated with the ruling elements of nature and exert their influence through these. The demands that the στοιχεῖα make on the pagan world are a voice of the fallen world.[24] N. Kehl's[25] suggestion, however, that στοιχεῖα stands for the whole created order diminishes the personal and spiritual character of this opposition seen by Paul in 4:3.

In 1 Cor 2:6, 8 Paul mentions the "rulers (ἀρχόντων, *archontōn*) of this age," who are "doomed to perish." They have failed to understand God's secret wisdom. "None of the rulers of this age (τῶν ἀρχόντων τοῦ αἰῶνος τούτου, *tōn archontōn tou aiōnos toutou*) understood this; for if they had, they would not have crucified the Lord of glory." Paul thus sees the death of Jesus as the result of a

---

[22] The expression στοιχεῖα τοῦ κόσμου occurs in Gal 4:3, 9 and Col 2:8, 20.
[23] Schlier, *Galater,* 191.
[24] Ibid., 194.
[25] Kehl, *Der Christushymnus,* 137–61. According to Kehl, the στοιχεῖα are the ultimate constitutive elements of the cosmos—the stars, the moon, the sun, water, air, fire, spirits, etc. Lohse (*Kolosser und Philemon,* 147) points to the use of this term in Greek philosophy and in Hellenistic Judaism (4 Macc 12:13; Philo, *Cher.* 127; Josephus, *Ant.* 3.183). See also Gnilka, *Kolosserbrief,* 123–27.

conspiracy of these leaders. And he sees the present world and its wisdom as being under these leaders, who have never understood the salvific mystery of the crucified Christ or God's plan for those who love him (vv. 2, 9).[26]

The Corinthian correspondence indicates that Paul is aware of certain spiritual forces linked to idol worship. These forces have usurped the honor that rightly belongs to God and his Christ. They are the antagonists of Christ. Although Christ is above them, they still exist and operate in the world. Christ's rule is incomplete until they are annihilated. Here it is not a question of converting these powers but of conquering them.

In 1 Cor 8:5 Paul concedes that there are such beings in the cosmos when he states, "Indeed, even though there may be so-called gods in heaven or on earth—as in fact there are many gods and many lords . . . " He is earnest about the demons and their opposition to God. According to him, the demons have lured the nonbelievers to worship idols (10:20–21), usurping for themselves the sacrifice that should have been offered to God: "What pagans sacrifice, they sacrifice to demons and not to God" (v. 20). Paul looks upon any association with demons (through worship) as a denial of Christ. Christians must therefore abstain from idol worshipping, for they cannot "partake of the table of the Lord and the table of demons" (v. 21). In 2 Cor 4:4 he mentions "the god of this world" (ὁ θεὸς τοῦ αἰῶνος τούτου, *ho theos tou aiōnos toutou*) blinding the minds of the nonbelievers in order "to keep them from seeing the light of the gospel of the glory of Christ, who is the image of God" (cf. 2 Cor 6:14–16).

But the picture in Paul and in Pauline tradition is not entirely coherent. Both Paul and the tradition admit the existence of spiritual forces hostile to God. According to Ephesians, all these forces were subordinated to Christ at his resurrection and exaltation. But according to Colossians, Christ was set above these forces at the creation of the world. Yet both Ephesians and Colossians suggest that these powers are still operating in the cosmos. Paul

---

[26] These leaders can scarcely be secular, political authorities. Conzelmann (*1 Corinthians*, 61 n. 47) asks here, "What should earthly powers have to do with supernatural wisdom?" See also Feuillet, "Les 'chefs de ce siècle,' " 1.383–93. For the opposite view, see Fee, *1 Corinthians*, 104; Carr, *Angels and Principalities*, 118–20; Miller, "ἀρχόντων."

himself sees Christ's resurrection as the moment of his exaltation over these forces, and Christ's parousia as their annihilation.

Thus, the conflict between the risen Lord and these powers is taking place in the present and is to be completed at the coming of the Lord in the end time. The parousia of Christ is presented as the victory of Christ over all these enemies. The victory is total, entailing their destruction, even though the destruction is not depicted. In the kingdom of God there is no place for these hostile powers.

The present rule of Christ is thus marked with a conflict, for idol worshipping is still going on and death is still taking place. Christ's endowment with the highest power does not signify solely a peaceful possession of heavenly honors; his messianic commission (δεῖ, 1 Cor 15:25) means the universal liberation of the human spirit and body. Hence, the goal of Christ's exaltation is victory over all hostile spiritual powers, and that includes death. With the power given to him, Christ will subjugate all of them. The scriptural quotation of Pss 110:1 (LXX, 109:1) and 8:6 in 1 Cor 15:23–28) is used to bring this out.[27]

4. Death as a Hostile Power

The main topic of 1 Cor 15:23–28 is the resurrection of the faithful, hence liberation from death. "The last enemy to be destroyed is death." Just as the kingdom of God has no place for the ἀρχαί, ἐξουσίαι, and δυνάμεις, dynameis, so also it has no place for death. Christ's rule therefore entails the conquest of death: death is totally incompatible with the eternal life bestowed by the risen Lord at his parousia.

The conquest of death here is a metaphor for the resurrection/transformation in the end time, to be wrought by the parousia of Christ. The personification of death also occurrs in the OT. In fact, Paul relies on this language in v. 54, where he quotes from Isa 25:8 and Hos 13:14:

Death has been swallowed up in victory.
Where, O death, is your victory?
Where, O death, is your sting?

---

[27] War imagery is not used in this depiction of Christ. There is a minimal resemblance between this picture of Christ and that portrayed in Rev 19:11–21.

The immediate context of the quotation from Isa 25:8 portrays a vision of Yahweh's bringing about the eschatological salvation of his people: he will remove the veil of spiritual blindness from the nations, he will swallow up death forever, and he will wipe away all tears. Yahweh reveals himself in this act as the Lord, the savior, and the giver of life. And the context of Hos 13:14 gives a picture of Yahweh deliberating whether to ransom Ephraim from destruction. In a synonymous parallelism death is presented as the power of Sheol. The Lord asks, "Shall I ransom them from the power of Sheol? Shall I redeem them from Death?" (Hos 13:14).

In Jewish apocalyptic, statements about the annihilation of death occur in connection with the universal resurrection. Thus *Apoc. Elijah* 5:38 speaks about the millennial reign, "No deadly devil will exist in them."[28] In 4 Ezra 8:52–54 God assures the visionary that when the paradise is opened, the "tree of life" will be planted, illness will be banished, death will be hidden, hell will flee, and corruption will be forgotten. Ezra and the righteous like him will be spared death in the last age, although death will still work among the evil. Death and hell (hades) are personified.

In *2 Bar.* 21:23 the seer begs God, "Therefore, reprove the angel of death, and let your glory appear, and let the greatness of your beauty be known, and let the realm of death be sealed so that it may not receive the dead from this time, and let the treasuries of the souls restore those who are enclosed in them." These treasuries are the places in which are kept the souls of those who have passed away. This text speaks of the "angel of death" as an agent of God.[29] God himself is to reprove this minister, stop all dying in the world, and restore the dead to life by opening the stores of the spirits.[30]

The Dead Sea Scrolls associate Satan and death. In 1QM 14:9–10, the author praises God for helping him against Belial's spirits: "Thou hast driven (גִּעֲרְתָּ, *gāʿartā*) his spirits (of destruction) far from (Thine elect), Thou hast preserved the soul of Thy redeemed (from the snares) of his dominion." According to this reconstruction of the original text, Belial and his helping spirits cause destruction—death—in the world. The culmination of the

---

[28] See Wintermute, "Apocalypse of Elijah," 753. According to Wintermute, *Apoc. Elijah* was written between the first and the fourth centuries CE (p. 730).

[29] On the "angel of death" being God's minister, see *T. Abr.* 8:12; *Asc. Isa.* 9:16. All these texts belong to later apocalyptic writings.

[30] See also *2 Bar.* 42:7–8; 44:12–13.

redemptive plan of God will be the overcoming of the Prince of Destruction controlling the world. According to 1:10–11, God made Belial for destruction, and in the end Belial will be destroyed "when the great hand of God is raised against Belial and against the whole army of his dominion."

In Heb 2:14 Satan is said to have "the power of death" (τὸ κράτος ἔχοντα τοῦ θανάτου, *to kratos echonta tou thanatou*). According to this text, Jesus has become man and died in order to "destroy the one who has the power of death, that is, the devil, and free those who all their lives were held in slavery by the fear of death." We find the twofold image of death/hades in Rev 20:13–14.[31] Freedom from death, as well as from Satan, is here affirmed for the thousand-year reign of the Messiah. But this is only a partial freedom. The Devil and Satan are bound, but not annihilated (vv. 2–3), until the thousand years are ended. Only the martyrs for the faith are here brought back to life to live in freedom from the wiles of the Devil. But death has not been eliminated; the nonbelievers are still in hades, in the power of death.[32] But at the final judgment the sea, death, and hades give up the dead; death and hades are then thrown into the lake of fire. Here death is the ultimate enemy to be destroyed before the inauguration of the kingdom of God. Then God "will dwell with them" and "death will be no more" (21:3–4).

What, then, is the meaning of Christ's victory over death mentioned in 1 Cor 15:26? First of all, as it has been noted earlier, the context here is the resurrection of the faithful. The statement in v. 26 is resumed in v. 54—the depiction of the eschatological transformation through which mortality and corruptibility will be abolished. Paul is thus talking about the eschatological endowment of life, after which death, sickness, and dying will be abolished forever.

Whereas in much of the OT the overcoming of death often means a prolongation of life on earth rather than life beyond death untouched by death[33] (cf. Ps 18:8–20), in the Isaian apocalypse (Isa 26:19) and in Dan 12:1–3 we find the notion of life after death. The pious faithful have begun to hope that at their death

---

[31] These apocalyptic writings come from the same period.

[32] Rev 20:6 asserts that the martyrs who have been brought back to life will not be subject to "the second death." This death is for those who were condemned at the final judgment.

[33] See Hoffmann, *Toten*, 73.

Yahweh will snatch them from hades.[34] The notion that there will be a resurrection at the final judgment is also documented in *1 Enoch*, *4 Ezra*, and *2 Baruch*. At that event death will be annihilated. Jewish apocalyptic around NT times (*4 Ezra*, *2 Baruch*) associates death with the principles of opposition to God in this age. Thus, the inauguration of the new and eschatological life by God entails the annihilation of death (*2 Bar.* 21:22). God's triumph over death means the resurrection of the dead and the abolition of mortality, sickness, and suffering in the world (*4 Ezra* 7:48; 7:144; 8:52; *2 Bar.* 21:22).

Paul's view in 1 Cor 15:23–28 comes close to these ideas. But, for the apostle, death is conquered through the risen Christ: it is the ultimate effect of Christ's resurrection. It is, in fact, the universal implementation of the Christ-event, for in Christ's death and resurrection the power of death and sin over human beings has been broken in principle. At his resurrection, Christ has been exalted above all powers in creation. He is at present actively establishing his reign of grace and life in the faithful, who are in the dominion of Christ, where they are alive to God and destined to be with Christ. Sin and death have lost their firm hold. Death still has some hold on them as long as they are in the mortal and corruptible body, but death will finally be broken when their bodies also will rise from the dead and/or be transformed.

B. THE CONFLICT MOTIF ELSEWHERE IN PAULINE LETTERS

In 1 Cor 15:23–28 Paul talks about the parousia of Christ in terms of a conflict. There are other passages in Paul that contain an echo of this motif in connection with the Lord's parousia, such as Rom 16:20a; 1 Cor 2:6, 8, 15:54–56; and 1 Thess 4:14, 5:8.

1. Romans 16:20a

In his concluding encouragement to the Roman community, Rom 16:17–20, Paul writes, "The God of peace will shortly crush (συντρίψει, *syntripsei*) Satan under your feet" (v. 20a). In a way, this statement resembles that in 1 Cor 15:24–27, which deals with

---

[34] Ibid., 76. On the development of presentations of afterlife in intertestamental Judaism, see also Nickelsburg, *Resurrection*, 170–76.

God's putting everything under the feet of Christ. But here it is the community that will triumph, and it is Satan who is put under their feet. The triumph is expected to take place soon, but is this the eschatological victory? It is God who will bring this about, but the link with Christ is clear in the next sentence: "The grace of our Lord Jesus Christ be with you" (v. 20b). O. Michel calls this reassurance a prophecy in apocalyptic language.[35]

This reassurance comes on the heels of a warning by Paul that they are to keep an eye on those who are causing dissensions and are opposing the teachings they have received. Such people "do not serve our Lord Christ" but, rather, their own appetites. That they are associated with Satan is implied by the juxtaposition of these instructions and Rom 16:20a. For Paul, Satan is a total opponent of God, trying to prevent the word of salvation from being heard (1 Cor 7:5; 1 Thess 2:18; 2 Cor 11:14) or from being kept. Satan is a disturber of peace and a deceiver.

The words "Satan" and "crush" (συντρίψει) thus suggest antagonism. The word συντρίβω, syntribō, is used in Hellenistic Greek and in the LXX (1 Macc 3:22) for the crushing of the enemy,[36] and it may here correspond to καταργεῖται, katargeitai in 1 Cor 15:26, where it interprets the ὑπέταξεν, hypetaxen of Ps 110:1, quoted in v. 27. Although most commentators see in Rom 16:20a an allusion to Gen 3:15, Schlier disputes it.[37] While the real antagonism is between Satan and God, the text indicates that the battle rages over the community.[38] Schlier holds that Satan is a reality, but Fitzmyer[39] attempts to demythologize this figure.

According to Rom 16:20, this struggle is not permanent but will come to an end soon (ἐν τάχει, en tachei). Most commentators see here an allusion to the parousia of Christ,[40] although Schlier

---

[35] Michel, Römer, 385.

[36] Schlier, Römerbrief, 450.

[37] Ibid., 449. Recently Dunn (Romans 9–16, 907) again affirms this allusion to Gen 3:15.

[38] The preceding verses suggest that Satan does not have a direct hold on the community but only through the guile and deceit of his human agents, whom he uses in order to disturb the community's harmony.

[39] According to Fitzmyer ("Romans," 868), "Satan is to be understood as the personification of all disorder, dissension, and scandal in the community."

[40] For literature on this, see Schlier, Römerbrief, 450. Käsemann (Romans, 418–19) likewise leans to the view that the text refers to the near parousia, but suggests that then the passage should not be included in Paul's epistle to the Romans. Dunn (Romans 9–16, 907) also implies that the text refers to the parousia.

suggests that the conflict refers to a struggle internal to the Roman community.[41] According to J. D. G. Dunn, the statement in Rom 16:20a "effectively ties together the whole sweep of salvation-history: God's purpose is nothing less than the complete destruction of all evil which has grown like a large malignant cancer within the body of humankind and the restoration of his creation to the peace and well-being he originally designed for it."[42] Käsemann, Schlier, and others regard the saying "God of peace will shortly crush Satan under your feet" (Rom 16:20a) as a reflection of the view expressed in *Jub.* 23:29, *T. Levi* 18:11–12, *T. Sim.* 6:6, *T. Mos.* 10:1, and the imprecation of the twelfth benediction in שְׁמֹנֶה עֶשְׂרֵה, *Šᵉmōneh ᶜEśrēh*. According to *Jub.* 23:29, at the completion "there will be no Satan and no evil (one) who will destroy." *Testament of Levi* 18:10–11 speaks of the paradise when the sword will be removed, the saints will receive eternal life, Beliar will be bound, and "wicked spirits" trampled upon. *Testament of Simeon* 6:6 asserts that then the spirits of error will be "trampled underfoot" by the people (cf. *As. Mos.* 10:1).[43]

In the NT, Rev 20:10 likewise depicts the battle at the end of the thousand-year reign. When the fire devoured the host of enemies who besieged the camp of the saints, "The devil who had deceived them was thrown into the lake of fire and sulphur, where the beast and the false prophet were."

All these texts clearly witness to the annihilation of Satan at the beginning of God's kingdom and also mention the community's involvement in that act. If the date of origin of the *Testaments of the Twelve Patriarchs* suggested by Kee[44] is correct, then this view was held in Jewish apocalyptic prior to the NT and could have influenced Paul's formulation here.[45]

---

[41] According to Schlier (*Römerbrief,* 449), Paul is here referring to the short battle with Satan, who is behind the divisions in the community, but not necessarily to the end-time parousia of Christ. Fitzmyer ("Romans," 868) does not mention the parousia here.

[42] Dunn, *Romans 9–16,* 907. Dunn holds that the text refers to Gen 3:15. The allusion to Gen 3:15 is held also by Käsemann (*Romans,* 418) and Fitzmyer ("Romans," 868). Yet if Rom 16:20 has vv. 17–19 as its context, Paul's focus here is on the Roman community's victory over Satan.

[43] Also known as the *Testament of Moses.* The *Assumption of Moses* is dated to the first century CE by Priest ("Testament of Moses," esp. 919).

[44] Kee ("Testaments," 777–78) suggests the Maccabean period as the date of composition of *T. 12 Patr.*

[45] In 1 Cor 6:2–3 Paul asks, "Do you not know that the saints will judge the world? . . . Do you not know that we are to judge angels?"

2. 1 Corinthians 2:6, 8; 15:54–56; 1 Thessalonians 5:8

The expectation of the forthcoming destruction of evil spirits is present also in 1 Cor 2:6, 8. The text states that the "rulers of this age, who are doomed to perish," control the wisdom of this age. Paul accuses them of having caused the death of Christ. Since the reference is to the whole present age, it can scarcely be that the apostle is referring to the political rulers who were responsible for Christ's death and who will therefore die. Not they but the spiritual rulers of this age are controlling the wisdom of this age.[46] The text does not mention when this destruction will take place, but the conviction in 1 Cor 1:8, 7:26, 29, and 10:11 is that the present time is "the end of the ages."

First Corinthians 15:54–56, in a composite quotation from Isa 25:8 and Hos 13:14, mentions that death has been swallowed up. The text contains a personification of death and speaks about the bestowal of immortality and incorruptibility at the resurrection/ transformation, which will occur at the coming of Christ. The next verse associates death with sin and the law: "The sting of death is sin, and the power of sin is the law." We have seen that this text complements the thought expressed in 15:26.[47]

In 1 Thess 5:8 the apostle urges the faithful to put on "the breastplate" of faith and love and "the helmet" of salvation. The terms "breastplate" and "helmet" suggest conflict and danger. The faithful must protect themselves, but not against physical violence. The allusion here and in Eph 6:11 is to Isa 59. But Eph 6:11 specifies the source of danger: the faithful are to put on "the whole armor of God" in order to withstand the wiles of the devil. The eschatological confrontation is clearly expressed in vv. 12–13: "For our struggle is not against enemies of blood and flesh, but against the rulers, against the authorities, against the cosmic powers of this present darkness, against the spiritual forces of evil in the heavenly places. Therefore take up the whole armor of God, so that you may

---

[46] Luke 22:3, 31 and John 13:2, 37 speak of Satan's plot to remove Jesus from the world.

[47] 1 Thess 4:16 does not mention explicitly the end-time struggle between the Lord and the hostile forces. The coming of Jesus produces the restoration of life for the deceased faithful and the taking up of all the faithful by the cloud. But the κέλευσμα motif, as we have suggested above, reflects the Hebrew גָּעַר, gāʿar, which was traditionally employed for God's subjugation of hostile powers.

be able to withstand on that evil day, and having done everything, to stand firm."

CONCLUSION

The antagonistic aspect of the parousia presumes a conflict between Christ and hostile powers. Paul asserts that the parousia of Christ entails the final destruction of the powers that have seduced human beings to idolatry, for the parousia implies the restoration of the cosmic order that corresponds to the truth of God and his creation. In the new order there will be no place for sin, death, Satan, rulers, dominions, and authorities.

In 1 Cor 15:24–27 Paul talks about the antagonism between life and death in the wake of Christ's resurrection, the subject of all of ch. 15. The power of death will be broken at the resurrection of the dead, which will occur at Christ's parousia. The apostle is speaking of physical death, which has been the fate of mankind since the fall of Adam. But the roots of this death are spiritual: it was after Adam's transgression that all human beings became subject to death.

In a metaphorical sense, death is presented in 1 Cor 15:26 as a personified power opposed to God. Paul envisages the conquest of death in the resurrection of the dead and the transformation of the living. Christ has been entrusted with this authority and power by the Father. The apostle depicts the conquest with a reference to Pss 8:6 and 110:1, hence as part of the messianic function, affirming thereby Christ's conquest of these powers as well as the Father's subjugation of everything to Christ. God has made death subject to Christ.

This conflict affects also the faithful, for the apostle talks about the resurrection of those who belong to Christ. Although they are now in the dominion of the risen Lord and are alive in Christ, they have not yet reached the final salvation. They are still dying, and the dead are still awaiting the resurrection day. The parousia will put an end to this situation by bringing about the resurrection of the dead and the transformation of the living.

The text also indicates that the risen Lord is at present exercising power on earth by pushing back the powers hostile to God and God's intended order in creation. The risen Christ, constituted by the Father as Lord, is not in peaceful possession of the ultimate reality but is establishing in the present his kingdom on earth. The conflict indicates that Christ's rule is not yet complete and that God is not yet all things to all (1 Cor 15:28). Christ's function in history is to annihilate this spiritual and superhuman opposition to God through the resurrection of the dead and the transformation of the living. Only when our lowly bodies have been redeemed will Christ's messianic function be completed.

11

❋

LIVING WITH CHRIST FOREVER

Paul speaks of the end-time union of the faithful with the Lord in a variety of ways. In 1 Thess 4:17, concluding the depiction of the faithful's meeting with the Lord, he says, "And so we will be with the Lord forever"; in 1 Cor 15:49 he talks about bearing "the image of the man of heaven"; in Phil 3:21 he mentions conformation to the glorious body of Christ; and in Phil 1:23 he expresses his great desire "to depart and be with Christ."

The completion thus entails eternal life close to the Lord and the sharing in his mode of existence—in his risen life. Dupont[1] suggests that the phrase "with the Lord" is the earlier Pauline formulation[2] (1 Thess 4:13–18; 1 Cor 15:50–56; 2 Cor 5:1–5), retaining the Christian and Jewish flavor, while the notion of sharing in the Lord's life is a later formulation (2 Cor 5:6–10; Phil 1:21–26), showing the influence of the Hellenistic distinction between the soul and the body.[3] According to Dupont, being "with Christ" in 1 Thess 4:13–18 is devoid of any mystical and personal connotations[4] and deals only with collective experience of the Lord's coming, whereas 2 Cor 5:6–10 and Phil 1:23 refer to the union with Christ after one's death and reflect a deep personal and religious experience.[5] This

---

[1] Dupont, *L'Union*, 79–113. According to Dupont, this union takes place at the parousia of Christ, which includes the resurrection of the dead.

[2] Ibid., 112, 184.

[3] Ibid., 186–87.

[4] Ibid., 186.

[5] Ibid.

calls for a new investigation of the Pauline eschatological notion of being with the Lord.

A. WITH THE LORD AT THE PAROUSIA

In 1 Thess 4:17b Paul draws this conclusion from the preceding portrayal of the taking up of the faithful to meet the Lord: "And so we will be with the Lord forever" (οὕτως πάντοτε σὺν κυρίῳ ἐσόμεθα, houtōs pantote syn kyriō esometha). This is the hoped-for outcome of this event. In 5:10 he states that Christ "died for us, so that whether we are awake or asleep we may live with him (ἅμα σὺν αὐτῷ ζήσωμεν, hama syn autō zēsōmen)." The two texts indicate that the whole purpose of the Christ-event is to make it possible for the faithful to be with Christ and to share in his life. Both times the apostle employs the preposition σύν to depict this ultimate union with the Lord, which is the fervent hope of the faithful. The σὺν αὐτῷ, syn autō in 1 Thess 4:17b differs from that employed in v. 14, where Paul states that God will bring the deceased faithful with him (ἄξει σὺν αὐτῷ, axei syn autō), that is, with Christ. The latter text indicates that the faithful will be brought by God: it deals with the mode of transition from the grave to God's presence. Whoever belongs to Christ now will be brought with Christ into the ultimate reality. The σὺν αὐτῷ in 4:17 and 5:10, in contrast, refers to the destination, the arrival. Here the Lord is not the means of translation but the goal; the text deals with life with the Lord (σὺν αὐτῷ ζήσωμεν). Ultimate happiness is experienced in being with him or living with him forever. It is something intensely personal—an intimate attachment to the Lord, a love for him, and the fulfillment of the deepest longing. Living with the Lord, effected by the taking up, is not merely a change of location, or a collective gathering around the Lord in which the individual is lost in the crowd. It is, rather, a union of life and thus a sharing in life, involving a total personal presence to each other that was not there before. It is granted to those who already belong to the Lord here, who are "in Christ," and it involves an elevation of life from the present mode on earth to that of the risen Christ.

This yearning to be with the Lord is expressed forcefully in Phil 1:23, although the text does not deal with the Lord's coming. There Paul himself expresses his deepest longing for the Lord, saying,

"My desire is to depart and be with Christ (σὺν Χριστῷ εἶναι, *syn Christō einai*), for that is far better." It is a confession of his overwhelming love for the Lord, which is greater than his love for his own life here on earth. It is a response to the love that finds his present life a painful separation from the Lord. It is as if the apostle could not bear any longer to be away from the Lord, for being in the body here and now means being away from the Lord. Hence, he regards the departure from this life not as a burden but as a blessing: it will bring him close to the Lord, where his heart is and wants to be.

The same yearning to be with the Lord is expressed also in 2 Cor 5:8, which most likely does not refer to dying before the parousia but to the parousia, which includes resurrection and transformation.[6] Having stated in the preceding verse that "while we are at home in the body we are away from the Lord," Paul declares in v. 8, "We would rather be away from the body and at home with the Lord." According to the apostle, the departure from this life will bring him close to the risen Lord; he will then be at home with the Lord. Because of this, death is seen not as a burden or a threat but as the avenue to the Lord. It is the present life in the body, rather, that is a burden, since it keeps him away from the Lord. But the text speaks of a transformation of the body and of the resurrection of the dead (4:14).

All these texts bring to light the intensely personal character of this hope focused on the Lord.[7] They disclose a deep yearning to be with the Lord, a longing greater than the desire for life here on earth. This yearning is fed by the springs of deep love that the apostle has for the Lord, a love that finds it intolerable to be separated in space and time from the Lord. It is the longing of the one who can say: "For to me, living is Christ and dying is gain" (Phil 1:21). And it is nourished by Paul's knowledge of Christ's overwhelming love for him. To the apostle, Christ is the one "who loved me and gave himself for me" (Gal 2:20). Hence, Paul can desire the Lord's coming (1 Cor 16:21), the sharing in the power of Christ's resurrection (Phil 3:10–11), the conformation with the heavenly man (1 Cor 15:49), and the union with Christ at death (Phil 1:21–23). But this personal and "mystical" desire to be with

---

[6] Hoffmann, *Toten*, 281–85.

[7] This is recognized by Hoffmann (*Toten*, 302) and Gnilka (*Philipperbrief*, 78).

the Lord is by no means present only in Phil 1:23, which refers to
dying before the parousia. It belongs also to Paul's eschatology.

This intensely personal character of hope distinguishes the
apostle's vision of the future from that of Jewish apocalyptic
literature, no matter how much he draws on it for language and
pattern of thought. Apocalyptic literature does picture the coming
of the Messiah in the end time, but the picture it provides is that of
a mighty leader, judge, and vindicator. And while the elect are
gathered by the Elect One, the element of deep personal love, of the
kind we find in Paul's depiction of the relationship between Christ
and the faithful, seems to be missing there. Christians, however,
look back on the Christ-event, seeing in Christ's death for us the
greatest expression of love (Rom 5:8). They are, as Paul is, over-
whelmed by Christ's love for them. In 2 Cor 5:14–15 the apostle
confesses, "For the love of Christ urges us on, because we are
convinced that one has died for all. . . . And he died for all, so that
those who live might live no longer for themselves, but for him who
died and was raised for them." Moreover, Christians understand the
present life of faith as a life already closely united with Christ. The
faithful are "in Christ," sharing in his death (and resurrection).
Thus, Paul can declare to the Galatians, "It is no longer I who live,
but it is Christ who lives in me. And the life I now live in the flesh I
live by faith in the Son of God, who loved me and gave himself for
me" (Gal 2:20).

Some scholars have described this as the mysticism of Paul,[8] but
this is inaccurate, for mystical experience appears to be a privilege
and an exception. This attachment to the Lord, of which the apostle
speaks, however, is not something reserved for the apostle alone: it
is what the apostle wants to bring about in all the faithful. And this
"mysticism" of Paul does not begin with 2 Cor 5:1–10.

B. CONFORMED TO THE RISEN LORD

For the ultimate reality, Paul also employs the image of
sharing in the Lord's life, of being conformed to the Lord.
Composite expressions—verbs or adjectives joined with the preposition "with" (σύν)—are one of the ways in which he expresses

---

[8] Cf. Schweitzer, *Mysticism of Paul*, 101–40, 205–396; Wikenhauser, *Pauline Mysticism*, 163–242.

this. Thus in Rom 6:8 the apostle writes, "If we have died with Christ, we believe that we will also live with him (συζήσομεν αὐτῷ, syzēsomen autō)." In 8:17 he speaks of the faithful being "joint heirs (συγκληρονόμοι, synklēronomoi) with Christ," while in 8:29 he affirms that those whom God foreknew he also predestined "to be conformed (συμμόρφους, symmorphous) to the image of his Son, in order that he might be the firstborn within a large family." This sharing with Christ is the ultimate communion of life, surpassing the present life of faith (Gal 2:20; 2 Cor 4:17–18; 5:7): the faithful will participate in it by being conformed to his life and glory (δόξα). It involves a change in the present mode of existing—the resurrection from the dead and the transformation—at the Lord's coming (1 Cor 15:52–55). And it is not limited to the union with Christ immediately upon one's death.

The end-time sharing with Christ is a consequence of the present sharing in Christ's death (and resurrection). The believer is now "in Christ," sharing in Christ's death, which Paul interprets as an existential change and an objective transfer from the world and dominion of sin to the present dominion of the risen Lord.[9] It entails an interior liberation from the power of sin, a renunciation of the values of the world and of the old self, and the adoption of the values communicated through the cross. The baptismal incorporation into Christ's death bears the imprint of this objective change. It puts into effect the death and resurrection of Christ and signifies a life for God patterned on the life of Christ and in union with Christ. Thus, Paul exhorts the Romans on the basis of their present sharing in Christ's death and resurrection, "So you also must consider yourselves dead to sin and alive to God in Christ Jesus" (Rom 6:11). In vv. 12–14 he then urges them not to let sin any longer control their lives but to live as those who have been brought from death to life.

The ultimate completion of this life will involve the full sharing in the resurrection of Christ: the resurrection of the dead. The apostle assures the Romans, "For if we have been united with him (σύμφυτοι, symphytoi) in a death like his, we will certainly be united with him in a resurrection like his" (6:5). Here the expression σύμφυτοι means to grow together into one, inseparable living

---

[9] Cf. Tannehill, *Dying and Rising*, 7–43.

reality.[10] He repeats this in v. 8: "But if we have died with Christ, we believe that we will also live with (συζήσομεν) him."

Here "living with him" means a sharing with Christ that includes conformity. The latter comes up clearly in 8:29, where Paul assures the Romans, "For those whom he foreknew he also predestined to be conformed (συμμόρφους) to the image of his Son." The next verse indicates that this means a sharing in the glory of the risen Lord: "Those whom he justified he also glorified." This idea and this imagery occur also in Phil 3:21. According to this text, at his coming Christ will "transform (μετασχηματίσει, *metaschēmatisei*) the body of our humiliation that it may be conformed (σύμμορφον, *symmorphon*) to the body of his glory." The "body of his glory" is here presented as a future and heavenly reality, rather than the present existence. Paul emphasizes here the transformation, principally the transformation of the present life in the body.

This conformity to Christ can also be expressed in other ways, without using a noun or an adjective with the preposition σύν. Thus in 1 Cor 15:48–49 Paul states, "As is the man of heaven, so are those who are of heaven. Just as we have borne the image of the man of dust, we will also bear the image of the man of heaven." The context here is the resurrection of the dead and the transformation, or rather the shape of the things to come. Paul insists that the ultimate reality is not a return to the present human existence, patterned on the first Adam, but the assumption into the life of the risen Lord, the last Adam. The resurrection of Christ is the model of the life to come.

Still another way of expressing this is through the notion of the "sonship of God." In Gal 4:4–7 Paul states, "But when the fullness of time had come, God sent his Son, born of a woman, born under the law . . . so that we might receive adoption as children (υἱοθεσίαν, *hyiothēsian*). And because you are children (υἱοί, *hyioi*), God has sent the Spirit of his Son into our hearts, crying, 'Abba! Father!' So you are no longer a slave but a child (υἱός, *hyios*), and if a child (υἱός) then also an heir, through God." The transition here is from being a son to being given the inheritance that belongs to the son. A restatement of this is found in Rom 8:15–17, where, as in Gal 4:6–7,

---

[10] Compare this image with the image of the vine and the branches in John 15:1–10.

the present Christian existence is described as the indwelling of the Spirit of God in the believer.

The preposition σύν thus governs the relationship between the believer and Christ, but it is not used exclusively for the ultimate reality. It is employed also for the present union with the Lord and refers to the sharing in his suffering (2 Cor 4:11–12; Phil 3:10–11) and death (Rom 6:1–14).[11] The reason for this is that full participation in Christ's resurrection entails a transformation and a conformation (1 Cor 15:49–53). At present, the believer shares in the resurrection of Christ imperfectly, by walking "in the newness of life" (Rom 6:4), by being alive to God in Christ Jesus (v. 11), by "being renewed day by day" in the "inner nature" (2 Cor 4:16). This present sharing, although still associated with the sharing in the death of Christ, is connected to the future, the full sharing in Christ's resurrection (Rom 5:5, 8–9).

When referring to the present association with Christ, σύν indicates this stage of the journey. It refers mainly to the spiritual sharing in the death of Christ. Thus in Rom 6:4 Paul, explaining the baptism "into Christ," says, "We have been buried with him." In v. 5 he explains this as being "united with him (σύμφυτοι γεγόναμεν, symphytoi gegonamen) in a death like his," while in v. 6 he states, "We know that our old self was crucified (συνεσταυρώθη, synestaurōthē) with him." The same vocabulary occurs in Rom 8:17, where Paul uses the expression συμπάσχομεν, sympaschomen: "If, in fact, we suffer with him (συμπάσχομεν) so that we may also be glorified with him." In Phil 3:10 the compound συμμορφιζόμενος, symmorphizomenos,[12] is employed to indicate a conformation to Christ's death.

The continuous sharing in Christ's death and resurrection in the present involves human cooperation: through faith, through baptism, the believer enters or is transferred into the death of Christ, sharing in its inclusive reality. It means a continuous dying to the old master, to self, to sin, and to the world (Rom 6:15–19). It means belonging to the dominion of Christ and serving Christ as the new master.[13] This sharing in Christ's death is the condition for, and the guarantee of, the end-time sharing in Christ's life: as we

---

[11] The present Christian existence is more commonly indicated by means of the preposition "in" (ἐν); cf. Neugebauer, In Christus, 148.

[12] This vocabulary occurs also in Rom 8:29 and Phil 3:21.

[13] Cf. Tannehill, Dying and Rising, 8.

have shared in his death, so we will share in his life (Rom 6:5–10). The context indicates that sharing in Christ's death means dying to the selfish self, to sin, to the world and its values.

C. DEVELOPMENT OF PAULINE ESCHATOLOGY

The many ways of being with Christ—in the present exist-ence, at one's death, at the parousia of Christ, at the resurrection of the dead—suggest a development of Paul's notion of the ultimate fulfillment. According to W. Wiefel,[14] while union with Christ is a constant in Pauline eschatology, Pauline reflections on the occurrence and nature of this union indicate a develop-ment.[15] Some scholars have noted a shift on the moment of the fulfillment from the end time to a time closer to the present, to one's death or even to present participation.[16] This shift involves more than a foreshortening of the perspective; it is a change in the notion of the fulfillment itself. In the new perspective, union with Christ occurs immediately upon death or even earlier—in one's spiritual union with Christ in this life—thus making the end-time parousia and resurrection redundant. The notion of fulfillment, it is said, also includes a shift from Jewish anthropol-ogy and cosmology to Hellenistic anthropology, which differenti-ates more strongly between the body and the soul of a person and focuses on the immortality of the soul.[17]

Thus Dupont sees Hellenistic anthropology operative in 2 Cor 5:5–10 and in Phil 1:21–26.[18] While in 2 Cor 5:1–5 Paul still looks toward the parousia and the resurrection as the mode of com-pletion, in vv. 6–10 he envisages union with the Lord immediately upon one's death. Verses 1–5 regard death with horror, but

---

[14] Wiefel, "Hauptrichtung des Wandels," 66, 81.

[15] Wiefel (ibid., 66–81) sees the first "level of reflection" in the focus on the parousia in 1 Thess 4:13–18. The second level occurs in 1 Cor 15:50–56, which deals with the motif of transformation. 2 Cor 5:1–10, dealing with individual union with Christ, represents the third level. The fourth level occurs in Phil 1:21–25 and 3:21, which concern individual eschatology (p. 80). For a contrary opinion, see Baum-bach, "Zukunftserwartung," 436–44, 451–52.

[16] The latter is the position of Dodd (New Testament Studies, 57–65). Dodd's solution, however, did not find scholarly consensus. See A. L. Moore, Parousia, 50.

[17] Wiefel, "Hauptrichtung," 66–81.

[18] Dupont, L'Union, 135–91. Dupont suggests that this probably came to Paul through the early church or through Jewish sources.

vv. 6–10 see it as something desirable, since it brings one closer to the Lord.[19] Dupont claims that the same expectation as in vv. 6–10 is also evident in Phil 1:21–26, where Paul expresses his desire to die in order to be with the Lord. All this is a change from 1 Thess 4:13–18 and 5:1–11, which envisage union with the Lord only at the parousia. The shift, Dupont states, was brought about by the influence of Hellenistic thought on the apostle[20] and by his experience of facing death in Asia, mentioned in 2 Cor 1:8–11.[21] This shift implies a different conception of "being with the Lord." While 1 Thess 4:13–18 understands this to happen at the parousia and to involve a collective, rather impersonal gathering around the Lord in the end time, 2 Cor 5:6–10 and Phil 1:21–26 place it at one's death and imply a highly personal, "mystical" union with the Lord.

But Dupont's explanation is far from obvious. It does not explain how Paul in 2 Cor 4:14 and 5:1–5 still looks forward to the resurrection and the parousia, while in the very next verses, 6–10, he abandons this expectation. Nor does it explain how the apostle continued to await the parousia and the resurrection, as is evident from Phil 3:10–11, 20–21 and Rom 6:4, 8; 8:23. Moreover, 1 Cor 15:47–56, a text close to 2 Cor 5:1–10, clearly indicates that Paul regards union with the Lord at the parousia as something more than a "mere" spatial closeness and a collective experience. He talks in vv. 47–49 about assuming the likeness of the second Adam. Love for the Lord (Gal 2:20) and spiritual union with the Lord in the present (Gal 4:6–7; Rom 8:9, 17), in fact, feed the hope of sharing in the resurrection of Christ, of which Paul speaks in Rom 6:5, 8 and 8:29. The resurrection at the parousia is the culmination of the present partial experience of the resurrection of Christ, which touches only the inner self (2 Cor 4:16–18; Rom 6:4). It is the entry into the inheritance of those who have received "sonship" (υἱοθεσία) through the Spirit of Christ (Rom 8:11, 14–17).

As A. Lindemann points out,[22] because in 2 Corinthians the apostle writes to the same community as in 1 Cor 15, his previous instruction is presumed by him. Thus, in 2 Corinthians he is not

---

[19] Cf. Plummer, *2 Corinthians*, 163.

[20] Dupont, *L'Union*, 170–71.

[21] Dupont (ibid., 171), however, does not exclude the influence of Jewish and early Christian sources on Paul's thought. When Paul departs from Jewish views, he does it under the influence of Hellenistic thinking.

[22] Lindemann, "Die korinthische Eschatologie," 392; Dupont, *L'Union*, 139.

proving again the resurrection of the dead. The new context calls for a new mode of expression.[23] He has been talking in very personal terms ever since 3:7 about his own apostolic sufferings. In the same way, Paul then talks in 5:1–10 of what awaits him after the resurrection, the heavenly and eternal house "not made with hands." He is affirming the reality of the resurrected body and its glory and expressing his desire to be in that body. When in vv. 6–8 he states that his real desire is to be at home with the Lord and, hence, away from the present body, he still hopes to be vested with the resurrected body.

It has been observed that here the apostle shifts to using personal and individual eschatology. But this scarcely means that he abandoned the collective experience of the resurrection and transformation, for Phil 3:20–21 still affirms it, as does Rom 6:4–8 and 8:23. In fact, 2 Cor 5:1–5 agrees with 1 Cor 15:50–57 about the transformation.[24] Gillman states, "There is then, contrary to the interpretation of C. F. D. Moule . . . a rather consistent Pauline view of matter in the two passages. In each case it is to be transformed. Where a shift can be noted in the two passages is from the use of a more literal, abstract, and anthropological terminology in 1 Cor 15:50–55 to a rather intricate development of metaphorical language in 2 Cor 5:1–4."[25]

Plummer also sees a change of perspective in 2 Cor 5 between vv. 1–5 and vv. 6–10. According to him, in vv. 6–10 the apostle expects a union with Christ immediately after his death. Here Paul presents the vision of future glory that outweighs the sufferings and even the horror of death.[26] The apostle suggests that "those who die before the parousia will be better off than they were in this life, for they will be nearer to Christ."[27] In Plummer's view, Paul believes that the dead Christians enjoy a conscious union with the Lord. "They are happier, because they are in closer communion with the Christ than they were in the body."[28]

---

[23] The occasion behind 2 Cor 4:7–6:2 is Paul's self-defence against the competing missionaries. According to Gillman ("Thematic Comparison," 445), the immediate context is the meaning of apostolic sufferings. Cf. also Lindemann, "Die korinthische Eschatologie," 393.

[24] Gillman, "Thematic Comparison," 454.

[25] Ibid.

[26] Plummer, 2 Corinthians, 161.

[27] Ibid.

[28] Ibid., 162.

But does the statement in vv. 6, 8—"While we are at home in the body we are away from the Lord. . . . We would rather be away from the body and at home with the Lord"—refer to Paul's desire to die, as in Phil 1:21–23? In 2 Cor 4:14 Paul still affirms his hope in the resurrection. Could it be that in 5:6, 8 Paul is again thinking of this perishable and mortal body as keeping him away from the Lord, as he did in 1 Cor 15:50? In 2 Cor 5:1–5, at any rate, he contrasts the present lowly body with the heavenly body—a reference to the resurrection and transformation (cf. Phil 3:20–21).

Hoffmann[29] makes a case for a uniform interpretation of 2 Cor 5:1–10. According to him, any interpretation of the passage must take into consideration 4:14, where Paul asserts his belief and knowledge about to his own resurrection: "The one who raised the Lord Jesus will raise us also with Jesus, and will bring us with you into his presence." This declaration clearly looks forward to the parousia and the resurrection. It suggests that the heavenly abode mentioned in 5:1–5 refers to the resurrected body. Hence, 5:6 also refers to the parousia and the resurrection. At that point the ultimate reality will be disclosed and put into effect. It is that event for which the apostle yearns.[30] He does not change his perspective in vv. 6–10, as if he now caught sight of the interim state of blessedness between his death and the Lord's coming. And he does not switch to Hellenistic anthropology. For the apostle, salvation consists in union with the person of Jesus Christ.[31] Hoffmann[32] shows that the parousia and the resurrection remain the constant referent in Paul's letters.[33] Thus, the resurrection of the dead is expected from 1 Thessalonians to Romans and Philippians. Similarly, the parousia of Christ is expected in 1 Thess 4:13–5:11; 1 Cor 1:9; 15:23–28, 50–56; 2 Cor 4:14; Phil 3:20–21; 4:5; and Rom 13:11–12. And the apostle never gives up the expectation that the Lord will come soon.

Yet Hoffmann admits that Phil 1:21–26 does deal with union with Christ immediately upon death. He does not, however, link this presentation with Paul's own brush with death in Asia,

---

[29] Hoffmann, *Toten*, 253–85.

[30] So also Perriman, "Paul and the Parousia," 521.

[31] Hoffmann (*Toten*, 318) notes an essential difference between Paul's idea and the Jewish apocalyptic ideas of association with the Messiah in the beyond.

[32] Ibid., 326–29.

[33] That is, the letters commonly accepted as Pauline. This excludes 2 Thess, Eph, and Col.

mentioned in 2 Cor 1:8–11. By the time of writing 2 Corinthians the apostle has recovered from this scare and has regained his hope. He states in 1:10, "He who rescued us from so deadly a peril will continue to rescue us; on him we have set our hope that he will rescue us again." Besides, the brush with death is nothing new for him, as is clear from 4:7–9, 6:4–5, and especially 11:22–29.

Hoffmann suggests that Paul could have harbored for some time the idea of union with the Lord immediately after death; the first mention of it in his letters need not also be the origin of the notion, and the idea itself agrees with Jewish thought. Jewish thought also maintained the resurrection of the dead in the end time. The two presentations do not rule each other out.[34] Some proponents of this development suggest that Paul did not begin to write his letters in 50/51 CE but earlier, in the forties. They arrive at this conclusion, however, by making use of the development of theology[35]—the very thing that needs to be proved. Those who maintain that Ephesians and Colossians also belong to the authentic Pauline epistles, as does P. Benoit,[36] make a legitimate observation about the development of Paul's eschatology. But then the burden of proof is on them to establish that Ephesians and Colossians were indeed written by Paul himself. Our contention here is not that Ephesians and Colossians could not be Pauline epistles but, rather, that in the commonly accepted epistles of Paul, there is little evidence of a development of eschatology.

D. THE NEARNESS OF THE PAROUSIA

Paul thus never gives up his expectation of the parousia; he shares in the early church's fervent awaiting of the Lord's coming. He discourages speculation about "the times and the seasons" (1 Thess 5:1) and counsels the faithful to live quietly, mind their own affairs, and work with their hands (1 Thess 4:10–11; cf. 2 Thess 3:6–13). But he also thinks that he is living at the end of the ages. In 1 Cor 7:29, 31, where he discourages marriage, he twice mentions that the time is running out: "I mean, brothers and sisters, the appointed time has grown short; from now on, let even

---

[34] Hoffmann, *Toten*, 323–29. See also Baumbach, "Zukunftserwartung," 436–55.
[35] This is the procedure of the John Knox school.
[36] Benoit, "Resurrection," 108.

those who have wives be as though they had none. . . . For the present form of this world is passing away."

The apostle does not claim to know the time of the Lord's coming, but he, with other Christians, fervently expects it. In 1 Thessalonians, for instance, the parousia is the constant referent of his remarks. The apostle here praises the community for their "steadfastness of hope in our Lord Jesus Christ" (1:3) and their awaiting of God's Son from heaven (1:10). His aim is that the entire community be gathered around the Lord at his coming (2:19). He comforts the Thessalonians regarding their presence at the parousia (4:13, 18; 5:9–11), counsels vigilance and responsibility (5:6–8), and prays that they be unblemished on that day (3:13; 5:23). The statement in 4:17—"Then we who are alive, who are left, will be caught up in the clouds"— suggests that the apostle himself hopes to be among those who will live to see the Lord's coming. It is clear that Paul and the Thessalonians live in anticipation of that day.

First Corinthians likewise has the parousia as its referent. In the thanksgiving section, Paul praises the community for its expectation of the Lord's coming. As he gives thanks to God for their spiritual gifts, he says, "So that you are not lacking in any spiritual gifts as you wait for the revealing of our Lord Jesus Christ. He will also strengthen you to the end, so that you may be blameless on the day of our Lord Jesus Christ" (1:7–8). In 4:5 the apostle points to the Lord's coming for judgment and cautions, "Therefore do not pronounce judgment before the time, before the Lord comes, who will bring to light the things now hidden in darkness and will disclose the purposes of the heart." When he pronounces his condemnation of the man guilty of sexual immorality, Paul again refers to the Lord's coming: the community is to hand the man over to Satan for the destruction of the flesh "so that his spirit may be saved in the day of the Lord" (5:5). In 7:29–31 the apostle twice indicates that they are living at the close of the age. In 10:11 he pointedly underscores the seriousness of his admonition with a reference to the end: "These things happened . . . [but] were written down to instruct us, on whom the ends of the ages have come (εἰς οὓς τὰ τέλη τῶν αἰώνων κατήντηκεν, *eis hous ta telē tōn aiōnōn katentēken*)."[37] In ch. 15 the parousia serves as the referent

---

[37] In the light of 7:29–31 it is not possible to interpret 10:11 as the present fulfilment in the wake of the Christ-event, as Klein ("Naherwartung," 259) does.

for the resurrection of the dead (vv. 23, 52), and in 16:22 the apostle concludes with the cry "Our Lord, come!" (Μαρανα θα, *Marana tha*).

How close is the parousia, according to Paul? As G. Klein observes, the first person plural in 1 Thess 4:15, 17 indicates that he thinks he will live to see the Lord's coming.[38] Here it is his and the community's experience of the parousia, not his own death, that is on the apostle's mind. Death before the parousia is seen as something expected.[39] And the coming of the Lord, Klein points out, means also the end of the ages. In vv. 4:13–18 the resurrection makes it possible for the deceased to share in the parousia.[40]

The situation in 1 Cor 15:50–57, according to Klein, is different. While in 1 Thess 4:15 Paul states, "We who are alive, who are left until the coming of the Lord," in 1 Cor 15:51 he asserts, "We will not all die, but we will all be changed." Here death before the parousia is seen as something likely to happen or as being in store for most of them.[41] The governing thought is change, asserted in v. 51: "We (ἡμεῖς) will all be changed." The clause in v. 52—"And the dead will be raised imperishable"—specifies one of the consequences implied by the affirmation "we will all be changed,"[42] since the need for change governs the dead and the living. Here, Klein states, the living and the dead are brought to the same level through the eschatological change, rather than through the resurrection; the latter is subsumed under the change, or implies the change. The norm and the exception of 1 Thess 4:13–18 are here reversed: death is now normal, survival is an exception.[43] And it is no longer clear whether Paul still expects to be alive until the Lord's coming.

Unfortunately, Klein overstates the case, having neglected the context of 1 Cor 15:51–56[44] and downgraded the relevance in this regard of Paul's counsel in 7:29–31. The context in 15:51–56 is the resurrection of the dead (vv. 1–34) and the quality of the resurrected body (vv. 35–57); hence, in vv. 51–57 the apostle gives to the

---

[38] Ibid., 245. Also Luedemann, *Paul*, 236. But see Lindemann, "Die korinthische Eschatologie," 378.

[39] But see Henneken, *Verkündigung*, 77; Dalton, *Christ's Proclamation*, 260.

[40] Klein, "Naherwartung," 250.

[41] Sieber (*Mit Christus Leben*, 73) speaks here of the majority being alive at the parousia. Klein ("Naherwartung," 251) disputes this.

[42] Klein, "Naherwartung," 253.

[43] Ibid., 256.

[44] See Lindemann, "Die korinthische Eschatologie," 388.

resurrection the prominence it deserves. What is astounding is that the apostle still affirms that "we will not all die." This, together with 7:29–31, 10:11, and 16:22, places the present generation near the end of time.[45]

Whether Paul[46] in 1 Corinthians still thinks that he himself will be alive at the parousia, in Phil 4:4 and Rom 13:11 he asserts the nearness of the parousia,[47] as Hoffmann rightly observes. There is therefore little evidence of a shift in this regard between 1 Thess 4:13–18 and 1 Cor 15:50–56. It is not the apostle's own thinking that has changed but the circumstances he is addressing; a different context calls for a different response.[48]

Most scholars posit a shift in Paul's thinking in 2 Cor 5:1–10 and Phil 1:21–23.[49] That the apostle reckons with his own death is clear from 2 Cor 4:14a, where he asserts, "He who raised the Lord Jesus will raise us also with Jesus."[50] But he also looks forward to the resurrection and the parousia, as the next clause—"and will bring us with you into his presence"—indicates. The striking agreement between this text and 1 Thess 4:14 has been observed earlier.[51] To apply Klein's argumentation,[52] here it is the resurrection of Paul himself that puts him on the same plane with the Corinthians. But the resurrection is taken for granted. Although the parousia is not explicitly mentioned here, it is implied with the resurrection and the verb παραστήσει, *parastēsei*, for the apostle consistently associates the resurrection with the parousia.

The resurrection of the dead at the parousia is a constant referent in Paul's letters.[53] It is clearly the main topic in 1 Cor 15,[54] although the discussion ends on the inclusive note of the resurrection of the dead and the transformation of the living (vv. 51–56). And in 2 Cor 4:14 the resurrection of Paul himself is the topic, while the bringing of the Corinthians into God's presence need not

---

[45] Ibid., 387.

[46] Caution is called for in the interpreting the "we" in 1 Thess 4 and other eschatological passages; cf. Lindemann, ibid., 389–90; Fee, *1 Corinthians*, 800.

[47] Klein's dismissal of Rom 13:11; 1 Cor 7:29–31, 10:11; and Phil 4:5 as witnesses of the near awaiting is surprising.

[48] Lindemann, "Die korinthische Eschatologie," 391.

[49] See Gillman, "Thematic Comparison," 439–41.

[50] That the "we" here refers to Paul is held by Wolff (*Korinther I*, 97–99).

[51] See ch. 3.

[52] Klein, "Naherwartung," 244–56.

[53] Hoffmann, *Toten*, 327–28.

[54] This is forcefully brought out by Perriman ("Paul and the Parousia," 512–13).

imply their resurrection.[55] The context here also is the parousia, as the similarity of this text to 1 Thess 4:14 indicates. This holds true also for 2 Cor 5:1–10, where Paul talks about the dismantling of the body and of the acquiring of another, heavenly body. Thus, the apostle does not change his view here from that in 1 Cor 15:50–57.[56] And he does not shift the occurrence of the resurrection forward to the moment of one's death.

There remains Paul's affirmation in Phil 1:21–23 that upon his death he will be with the Lord. This, however, may be less a shift in eschatology than a complementary perspective. Some scholars argue that here, at least, the moment of death is also the moment of the resurrection. This, however, can scarcely be supported in view of the statement in 3:20–21.

CONCLUSION

Being "with Christ" (σὺν Χριστῷ) is not merely a "collective" gathering around Christ; Paul has infused it with an intensely personal desire to share the company of Christ and the life of Christ. This desire is present in 1 Thess 1:10, 2:19–20, 4:13–18 and 1 Cor 16:22 as well as in 2 Cor 5:6–10 and Phil 1:23 and is not necessarily linked to a Hellenistic dichotomy between the body and the soul.

Besides the image of being gathered around the Lord, Paul employs the notion of sharing in the image of the Lord. This means becoming like him in body (1 Cor 15:49), sharing in the power of his resurrection (Phil 3:10). Paul regards this change as essential for entry into the kingdom of God (1 Cor 15:50) and as an outstanding aspect of the redemption of the body (Rom 8:23). The change entails the resurrection, which is not a return to this life, or the transformation of the living. Both the resurrection and the transformation include the adoption of the end-time body. Thus, living "with Christ" and "being conformed to his image" mean a mode of life not available to the believer in the present. According

---

[55] This aspect is neglected by Perriman (ibid., 516–18). The implied context here is the parousia, which is linked to the resurrection of the dead. The similarity between 2 Cor 4:14 and 1 Thess 4:14 is too great to be coincidental.

[56] This, however, is maintained by Moule ("St. Paul and Dualism," 118). Cf. Hanhart, "Paul's Hope," 449.

to Paul, it is the risen Lord who will bring this about: he will raise the dead and transform the living by the power given to him to put all things under his feet (1 Cor 15:25, 27; Phil 3:21).

But besides speaking of being with Christ at the parousia, Paul talks also of being with Christ at one's death (Phil 1:23). This notion means a shift in the expectation of the union with the Lord, but not an abandonment of the expectation of the parousia or of the resurrection. Paul continues to await the near coming of the Lord, and he continues to look forward to the resurrection, although the possibility of his own death is real to him. In Philippians he still talks about the day of the Lord (1:10; 2:16), of the nearness of the Lord (4:4), of his desire to share in the Lord's resurrection (3:10), and of the transformation at the Lord's coming (3:20–21). Second Corinthians 5:6–10 need not be interpreted as Paul's desire to die in order to be with the Lord. Nor is there much evidence for the notion that death before the parousia has become normal, and life until the parousia the exception: Paul continues to await the coming of the Lord in the near future. His intense desire to be with the Lord is, no doubt, responsible for the foreshortening of the perspective.

12

⁂

THE PAROUSIA OF CHRIST
AND THE CHURCH

Paul's depictions—like those in the rest of the NT—of Christ's coming in the end time employ the imagery used for the OT and Jewish apocalyptic portrayals of the day of the Lord, which had a collective significance and allocated a special place to Israel. To what extent does the apostle's imagery of the parousia retain this collective dimension by relating the parousia to the church, the new people of God? In Gal 6:16, for instance, he asserts that the church is the new Israel of God.[1] Elsewhere he talks about the church as the ἐκκλησία τοῦ θεοῦ, ekklēsia tou theou[2] (1 Thess 2:14; 1 Cor 1:2; 10:32; 2 Cor 1:1; Gal 1:13), the ἐκκλησία ἐν Χριστῷ, ekklēsia en Christō (Gal 1:22), or the αἱ ἐκκλησίαι Χριστοῦ, hai ekklēsiai Christou (Rom 16:16) or ἐκκλησία ἐν θεῷ, ekklēsia en theō (1 Thess 1:1). But this is linked with another question: to what extent is the church as a whole the subject of Paul's letters, since he writes them to local congregations or individuals in these congregations? He addresses in his letters

---

[1] Paul here contrasts the "Israel of God" with "Israel according to the flesh." According to Cerfaux (*Church*, 74), "the new people is under the influence of the Spirit, κατὰ πνεῦμα, kata pneuma, so that the Israel of the past must appear by contrast fleshly (Rom 5:5; 7:25)."

[2] On ἐκκλησία τοῦ θεοῦ ("church of God"), see Hainz, *Ekklesia*, 229–55; Merklein, "Die Ekklesia Gottes," 55, 65–70; Schrage, " 'Ekklesia' und 'Synagoge'," 200–202; Schnackenburg, "Einheit," 61–72; Schlier, *Geist*, 179–200; Beker, *Sieg Gottes*, 94–96. This expression especially might have reminded Paul of the OT expression קְהַל יהוה, qᵉhal Yahwe, the assembly of God; see Schnackenburg, "Ortsgemeinde," 37.

the church of God that is in Corinth (1 Cor 1:2; 2 Cor 1:1), or the churches in Galatia (Gal 1:2), or the church in Thessalonica (1 Thess 1:1). To what extent does he regard the whole church as the people of God and the community of salvation and hope?[3]

A. LOCAL COMMUNITIES AND THE CHURCH

One difficulty in addressing this issue is that Paul, in his writings, does not simply replace Israel with the church, nor does he derive the expression ἐκκλησία τοῦ θεοῦ ("the church of God") directly from the LXX translation of יהוה קְהַל, q^{e}hal Yahwe. Another difficulty is that he does not use "the church of God" for the church universal. According to Cerfaux, "the notion of 'the people of God' is one thing, and the history of the word ἐκκλησία is another. . . . We have no indication that the word ever connoted the universal church, directly and explicitly. We have no proof that 'church' and 'church of God' are synonymous."[4] J. Hainz, agreeing with Cerfaux,[5] states that in Paul's writings ἐκκλησία τοῦ θεοῦ means any assembly of the faithful. According to him, the notion that this local assembly is a part of or represents the universal church is not the primary meaning of this phrase.[6] But the primary meaning need not be the only meaning. As Merklein brings out,[7] this phrase

---

[3] Schnackenburg ("Kirche und Parusie," 675–78) discusses the christological, salvation-historical, ethical, judicial, and antagonistic aspects of the parousia for the church.

[4] Cerfaux, *Church*, 107. Cerfaux makes this statement against Schmidt, "ἐκκλησία," 506–7. Hainz (*Ekklesia*, 229) agrees with Cerfaux. Schrage (" 'Ekklesia' und 'Synagoge,'" 198), Berger ("Volksversammlung," 167–68), and Merklein ("Ekklesia Gottes," 58ff.) suggest that the expression ἐκκλησία τοῦ θεοῦ derives from the Hellenistic section of the Jerusalem Christian community. Merklein (p. 63) disputes that this expression is limited to the Hellenists in Jerusalem.

[5] Hainz, *Ekklesia*, 230. According to Hainz, "Paulus kennt keine Gesamt-'Kirche' " (p. 251). On the relationship between an individual community and the universal church, see ibid., 250–55; cf. Merklein, "Ekklesia Gottes," 51–55; Schnackenburg, "Ortsgemeinde," 41–45.

[6] Hainz, *Ekklesia*, 231. Hainz admits that some of these text (Gal 1:13; 1 Cor 15:9; Phil 3:6) presume a larger church than the local community, but according to him these overtones are a vestige of tradition.

[7] According to Merklein ("Ekklesia Gottes," 66–69), ἐκκλησία τοῦ θεοῦ generally means for Paul the local church in communion with the Jerusalem church, but with the connotation of the full eschatological community of salvation made up of those who are baptized into Christ. For Schlier (*Geist*, 179), the expression τῇ ἐκκλησίᾳ τῇ οὔσῃ ἐν Κορίνθῳ, tē ekklēsia tē ousē en Korinthō, found in 1 Cor 1:2 and 2 Cor 1:1, means "to the Church which is in Corinth" as it is in other places.

denotes also communion with Jerusalem and the eschatological community of salvation of those who are "in Christ."

In the Pauline letters, the risen and coming Christ does not directly address a church community, as he does in Rev 2–3. In Revelation the seven churches receive the risen Christ's messages, which mirror their spiritual condition. There the lordly Son of man, who is to come soon, speaks directly to his communities[8] as their Lord, the coming judge, vindicator, and savior.[9] He has scrutinized each of them, assessed some things in them as good, other things as questionable or reprehensible. They hear from him words of consolation, of encouragement, and of warning.[10]

Paul, however, writes to the community as Christ's apostle, and what he writes to the local community applies to the entire church,[11] to all who hope and believe in the future coming of Christ. His notion of the church as κοινωνία[12]—fellowship and participation—and as the body of Christ indicates that the church is more than the gathering or association of like-minded believers.[13] For Paul the church is also more than the OT notion of the people of God:[14] God is the God who revealed himself in Jesus Christ.[15]

The word κοινωνία is characteristically Pauline,[16] employed for the fellowship of the believer in Christ, for the mutual fellowship of

---

[8]The number seven is comprehensive; it may suggest that the Lord who addresses seven communities speaks to the whole church.

[9]The features of the Son of man who is to come are especially evident in the last promise given each time to the victor, such as "I will give permission to eat from the tree of life that is in the paradise of God" (Rev 2:7); "Whoever conquers will not be harmed by the second death" (2:11); "to everyone who conquers I will give . . . a new name that no one knows except the one who receives it" (2:17).

[10]According to Caird (*Revelation*, 27), it is not clear that all the references here to the punishment or victory of a community or individual presume the parousia as their context.

[11]For instance, the allegory of Hagar and Sarah, applied to the present and to the heavenly Jerusalem respectively (Gal 4:21–31), or the warning from Israel's history to those who rely on baptism and Eucharist (1 Cor 10:1–22).

[12]Cf. Bori, KOINΩNIA, 81–102; Hainz, *Koinonia*, 162–205; Panikulam, *Koinōnia*, 1–108; McDermot, "Biblical Doctrine," 69–77, 219–23; Schnackenburg, "Einheit," 54–57, 61–72.

[13]Schlier, *Geist*, 181.

[14]McDermot, "Biblical Doctrine," 66–67.

[15]Merklein, "Ekklesia Gottes," 67.

[16]The word κοινωνία occurs 13 times in Paul. Besides κοινωνός, *koinōnos* (5 times), κοινωνέω, *koinōneō* (5 times), and κοινωνία, Paul also employs, more often that the rest of the NT, the compounds συγκοινωνός, *synkoinōnos* (3 times) and

the believers,[17] and for participation. In Rom 12:13 and Phil 4:14 Paul calls on the faithful to contribute to the needs of other communities; in 2 Cor 1:5–7 he talks of participating in the sufferings of Christ; and in 1 Cor 1:9 he states that κοινωνία with the Son is the goal of the Christian vocation.[18] The κοινωνία in 1 Cor 1:9 involves the present and the future reality, for only the future completion at the parousia will bring about perfect fellowship.[19] In Phil 3:10 Paul states that κοινωνία in the sufferings of the Son will culminate in fellowship with him in the glory of his resurrection.

In Pauline texts, κοινωνία in centered on Christ and means sharing in Christ with others.[20] According to W. Mc Dermot, "the full theological import of κοινωνία will only be revealed in the Pauline letters as that most intimate union of man with God and his fellow-men accomplished through Christ that constitutes final salvation."[21] It has soteriological and ecclesiological dimensions: "Fellowship with Christ is for him salvation, and fellowship with one another in Christ is for him the ideal of Christian community."[22]

The faith in the return of Christ is a "constitutive element of the church as such"[23] and not merely that of a local community. It is what Paul preaches everywhere, and is part of the church's

---

συγκοινωνέω, synkoinōneō (once). According to McDermot ("Biblical Doctrine," 67–75) Paul's use of κοινωνία deviates from the common Greek usage.

[17] McDermot, "Biblical Doctrine," 65; Panikulam, Koinōnia, 5. For a critical review of literature on this topic, see Hainz, Koinonia, 162–204.

[18] Panikulam, Koinōnia, 5.

[19] Ibid. According to Panikulam, κοινωνία in faith (Phlm 6), κοινωνία in the gospel (Phil 1:5), κοινωνία in the collections (2 Cor 8:4; 9:13; Rom 12:13; 15:26), κοινωνία in the Spirit (2 Cor 13:13; Phil 2:1), κοινωνία in the Eucharist (1 Cor 10:16), and κοινωνία in the sufferings (Phil 3:10) "serve as concrete modes of responding to this call to koinōnia with the Son."

[20] Panikulam, Koinōnia, 5; Hainz, Koinonia, 16–17; Jourdan, "κοινωνία." According to Jourdan, "When Paul wished to indicate the inwardness of the fellowship for each individual Christian, he did it by means of another phrase en Christō einai" (ibid., 113); against Seesemann (Der Begriff KOINΩNIA) and Campbell ("KOINΩNIA and Its Cognates"). Conzelmann (1 Corinthians, 29) states, "It is not understood as an experience of mystical communion, but in terms of belonging to the Lord until his parousia."

[21] McDermot, "Biblical Doctrine," 65.

[22] Panikulam, Koinōnia, 5. Schnackenburg ("Einheit," 62, 71–72) stresses that "fellowship" (Gemeinschaft) is not an adequate translation of κοινωνία here, for the genitive denotes sharing (Anteilhabe) in Christ, participation in his life and in his riches. But Schnackenburg admits the presence here of the ecclesial dimension. Thornton (The Common Life, 450) states, "The precise meaning of such words as 'partake' and 'share,' as well as 'fellowship' and 'communion,' depends on the context."

[23] Rahner, "The Church and the Parousia," 297.

understanding of salvation as presently taking place but not yet completed, so that "it can be accepted by the believer as having happened only by his reaching forward in hope to its fulfilment."[24] The parousia of Christ has, therefore, a special meaning for the entire church, especially since the apostle links it with the resurrection of the dead, the transformation, the judgment, and the completion of history. What Paul says about the parousia to a local community applies to all communities, and what the apostle says to the individual is also meant for the church.[25]

Paul regards the church as the body of Christ, with its many members having different functions (1 Cor 12:12–31; Rom 12:3–8).[26] According to Beker, while ἐκκλησία almost always denotes the local church, the body of Christ has a universal dimension, since it means incorporation of all in Christ.[27] The church is the קָהָל, qāhāl, the gathering in which salvation is being realized, the ἐκκλησία of those who have been justified by God's grace, who are imbued with the Spirit of God (Rom 5:5), and who hope in the future completion at the Lord's return. This entire church, in which members and the institution are in dialectic tension, is looking expectantly and with joy toward the Lord's coming (1 Cor 16:22).

Therefore, what applies to a believer applies to the church and vice versa. Nevertheless, there is an important difference between the two. E. Schlink states, "My being in Christ, my being justified and sanctified stands or falls with my ever-new acceptance in faith of the righteousness and holiness of Christ, which He bestows on us in Word and in Sacrament. But the church does not stand or fall with my faith. She was, before the individual came to believe; and she will remain, even when the individual ceases to believe." Hence, according to Schlink, statements about the church "can never be resolved into existential statements."[28]

---

[24] Ibid.

[25] Schnackenburg, "Kirche und Parusie," 551; also Church, 83, 166–70.

[26] Other images in Pauline writings indicate the collective and organic unity of the church: the Jerusalem from above (Gal 4:26); our mother (Gal 4:26); the bride of Christ (2 Cor 11:2); the Israel of God (Gal 6:16); the people (λαός, laos) of God (Rom 9:25; 2 Cor 6:16); the circumcision (ἡ περιτομή, hē peritomē, Phil 3:3); the seed of Abraham (σπέρματι [τοῦ Ἀβραάμ], spermati [tou Abraam], Rom 4:13). Cf. Schlier (Geist, 180) for similar images in other NT writings.

[27] Beker, Sieg Gottes, 95.

[28] Schlink, The Coming Christ, 118. Schlink warns against hypostatizing the church.

The church is thus greater than the sum of all its members. Yet the church is still on earth and is at the same time holy and sinful. Schnackenburg applies to the church mainly positive statements in Paul's letters and speaks of the church as the community of salvation and of hope, while Schlink and W. Joest, by the same token, forcefully apply the negative statements to the church.[29] C. J. Roetzel even speaks of the church under judgment.[30]

B. THE CHURCH AS THE COMMUNITY OF SALVATION

The church is the community of salvation. The best example in the NT of the church's role in the ultimate reality is the depiction of the new Jerusalem in Rev 21:2. Here the seer reports, "And I saw the holy city, the new Jerusalem, coming down out of heaven from God, prepared as a bride adorned for her husband." That this indeed applies to the church in a comprehensive sense is made clear by the imagery of the city: on the twelve gates of the city are inscribed the names of the twelve tribes of Israel; the walls of the city have twelve foundations, "and on them are the twelve names of the twelve apostles of the Lamb" (v. 14).[31]

There is, as well, a highly developed notion of the church as the body of Christ in Colossians and Ephesians.[32] In Eph 2:19–22 the author assures the faithful that they have become "members of the household of God, built up on the foundation of the apostles and prophets, with Christ Jesus himself as the cornerstone. In him the whole structure is joined together and grows into a holy temple in the Lord; in whom you also are built together spiritually into a dwelling place for God." The inclusive nature of the church is brought out in 3:6, in the disclosure of the mystery that "the Gentiles have become fellow heirs, members of the same body, and sharers in the promise in Christ Jesus through the gospel."

In the hymn in Col 1:12–20, Christ is presented as the "head of the body, the church" (v. 18); through Christ, God is reconciling

---

[29] Schnackenburg, "Kirche und Parusie," 553–62, 573–78; Schlink, *The Coming Christ*, 114, 245–55; Joest, "Parusie Jesu Christi," 548–50.

[30] Roetzel, *Judgement in the Community*, 136–76.

[31] The eschatological character of the heavenly Jerusalem should not be diminished by a realized eschatology, as is done in Caird (*Revelation*, 300–301).

[32] See Merklein, *Christus und die Kirche*, 45–52.

everything to himself. The mystery that the author proclaims to the Gentiles is the greatness, the richness, and the glory of "Christ in you, the hope of glory" (1:27). Here the organic union of the church with Christ is even more intense than in Ephesians. Christ in the church is also the hope of the church. It is clear that the church figures in the ultimate completion (1:19).

But Paul, in the letters commonly attributed to him, does not present Christ speaking in his role as the coming judge and savior, as does the Book of Revelation; and he does not give us the high profile of the universal church presented in Colossians and Ephesians.[33] The elements of this profile, however, do appear here in a diffuse way. The apostle speaks of the church as the body of Christ (1 Cor 12:12, 27; Rom 12:5), constituted of those who have been baptized in the one Spirit (1 Cor 12:13). They share in the one bread, which is the body of Christ (1 Cor 10:16–17), and in the one cup containing the blood of Christ (1 Cor 11:23–26). Members of the church function as organs of the one body, performing different tasks according to the gifts of the same Spirit (1 Cor 12:4–31). Paul insists that this body is not merely an aggregate of individuals but an organic unity kept alive and functioning by one Spirit. It is the assembly of God (ἡ ἐκκλησία τοῦ θεοῦ, 1 Cor 1:2; 11:22; 15:9; 2 Cor 2:1; Gal 1:13; 1 Thess 2:14) and the temple of the Holy Spirit (1 Cor 3:16; 2 Cor 6:16). In Gal 4:26 he depicts the church as "the Jerusalem from above" and "our mother," while in 2 Cor 11:2 he portrays the church as "a chaste virgin to Christ."

The church is thus both a historical and an eschatological reality. It is not living merely from the Christ-event in the past; it is experiencing the power of the risen Christ and the Holy Spirit and looking forward to being united with Christ and sharing in his resurrection at his coming. Those who are sharing in the death and resurrection of Christ now have the legitimate hope of sharing in Christ's parousia and resurrection (1 Thess 4:13–18; 2 Cor 4:14; Rom 6:1–11; Phil 3:10–11).

The church experiences a new quality of life, forming as it does a fellowship in the Holy Spirit (2 Cor 13:13; Phil 2:1). The church is the community of salvation: the believers are οἱ σωζόμενοι, *hoi sōzomenoi,* those who are on the road to salvation (1 Cor 1:18) and who have been justified by God through Christ (Rom 3:21–26; 5:1)

---

[33] See ibid., 99–102.

and have hope of attaining the completion (Rom 5:10). It is the object
of God's love (Rom 5:5), a new creation (2 Cor 5:16–18), the new
covenant in Christ's blood (1 Cor 11:23–26), nourished by the
body and blood of Christ (1 Cor 10:16–17) until he comes (11:26).
The latter reference alludes to the eschatological dimension of
the Eucharist. The church is the family of God, and its members
are the adopted children of God and heirs with Christ (Rom 8:17).

For Paul, baptism, Eucharist, and endowment with the Holy
Spirit are ecclesial realities of eschatological significance. While
baptism, the incorporation into Christ, is the sharing in Christ's
death and resurrection now, it carries the promise of the end-time
resurrection with Christ. The Eucharist is a sharing in the body
and blood of Christ "until he comes" (1 Cor 11:26), uniting the
community and preparing it for the end-time union with Christ.
The faithful walking by the Spirit are given the promise of inheriting the kingdom of God (Gal 5:5, 16–25): those who have the Spirit
of Christ are also the heirs of Christ (Rom 8:17). The community of
salvation is thus also the community of hope.

C. THE CHURCH AS THE COMMUNITY OF HOPE

The church is the community of hope (Rom 5:1–10), and it looks
expectantly toward the coming of the Lord (5:6–10; 6:1–11; 8:18–39).
For all the fulfillment that the church claims for itself in relation to
the Israel of old, the completion is still in the future; it is not yet
realized.[34] Paul corrects mistaken notions of the present completion
(1 Cor 4:8–13; Phil 3:17–19) and points to the present experience of
the cross. The future is appropriated not only in openness here
and now to the God who is always coming[35] but also in expecting
and experiencing a definite event that will complete the present
awaiting. The parousia gives to baptism and the Eucharist a provisional character: the baptismal sharing in Christ's death and resurrection is incomplete until our resurrection from the dead (Rom
6:1–11), and the present partaking of the bread and of the cup of
the Lord is meant to "proclaim the Lord's death until he comes"
(1 Cor 11:26). The parousia stamps the church itself as preliminary

---

[34] Dodd emphasizes the present fulfillment to the neglect of the future completion; see Dodd, *The Apostolic Preaching*, 57–65.

[35] Joest, "Parusie Jesu Christi," 542.

to the kingdom of God, which it seeks. The present form of the church is not the ultimate one and will one day pass away.

The existence in faith (2 Cor 5:7) is still not the vision of the Lord (vv. 16–18), or being close to him (1 Thess 4:13–18; 2 Cor 5:6–8), or being conformed to him in the body (1 Cor 15:47–56; 2 Cor 5:7). The church therefore longs to be at home with the Lord and looks forward to the coming of the Lord, trying to make itself ready for the event (1 Thess 3:12–13; 5:6–8, 23). Paul's hope is to see the entire church assembled around the Lord at his coming (1 Thess 2:19–20). He tells the Thessalonians, "For what is our hope or joy or crown of boasting before our Lord Jesus at his coming? Is it not you?" (1 Thess 2:19).

The church takes heart at its present experience of the Spirit, knowing that this is a proof of God's love (Rom 5:5). As the dominion of Christ (Rom 8:9–11) and the temple of the Holy Spirit (1 Cor 3:16), the church is the proximate ground of hope. Its hope is not in human accomplishments but in God's love, lavished through Christ, and in the action of the Spirit in the church. Thus, the church abides in hope and fosters hope in its worship (1 Cor 1:4–9; 7:25–35). In 1 Thess 4:13 the apostle refers to the outsiders as those who have no hope, whereas the community lives in the hope of sharing in the Lord's coming and of being with him forever (cf. 1 Cor 1:7). The faithful are those who are destined to obtain salvation (1 Cor 1:18; 2 Cor 2:15; 1 Thess 5:9) and who eagerly await it (1 Thess 1:3; 4:18; 5:11; 1 Cor 1:9). They are those who are saved in hope, are justified in hope, and are being prepared for the eternal glory (1 Cor 4:16–18). They "groan" inwardly, waiting for the full eschatological endowment (2 Cor 5:4, 8)—the passing from faith to the vision of the Lord (1 Cor 4:16–18), from separation to union.

Paul consoles the Thessalonians grieving that their dead will not share in the coming of the Lord (1 Thess 4:13–18). He encourages that community to build one another up in hope (4:18; 5:11) and he speaks with authority about the quality of the risen life expected at the resurrection of the dead (1 Cor 15:35–56). And he encourages the faithful to reach their destiny: "The one who began a good work among you will bring it to completion by the day of Jesus Christ" (Phil 1:6; cf. 1 Thess 5:9–11; Rom 5:5–10).

The church in Christ thus looks forward to the transformation of the outer self, to the shedding of mortality and corruptibility, to joy that knows no more sorrow or sickness or death. The present experience is still an experience of physical death, of sorrow, of persecution, of temptation, and, yes, of sin. The full entry into salvation is yet to come. The church, therefore, does not live as if it has reached the goal: it is not the kingdom of God. It accepts the cross in the present existence (Rom 6:1–11; Phil 3:10). It lives in the power of the risen Lord, who is at present working in it and bringing to completion the work he began at Easter.[36] It journeys (περιπατεῖτε, *peripateite*, Gal 5:16) in the Spirit in order to inherit the kingdom of God.

The parousia thus belongs to the church's self-understanding as the community of hope[37] and is part of its understanding of Christ in God's plan of salvation. The God who began the work of salvation through the sending of his Son in the past, above all through the Son's death and resurrection, will complete this work through the future coming of his Son (Rom 5:5–10). The church came into being through the Christ-event in the past and will be brought by Christ into the kingdom of God. As Joest observes, this understanding of the church is connected with the identity of Jesus Christ: he is not merely a prophet of the coming kingdom but the actual bringer of the kingdom. He did not merely enter the kingdom ahead of others; in him others enter the kingdom.[38]

D. THE CHURCH AND THE JUDGMENT

In the book of Revelation the church is under the Lord's scrutiny and is accountable to the Lord. Chapters 2–3 contain a public examination of conscience of seven communities in Asia by the coming Lord. Thus the church at Ephesus is reprimanded for having abandoned the love it once had and is called to repentance. The coming Lord warns, "If not, I will come to you and remove your lampstand from its place" (2:4–5). The Lord warns the church at Pergamum, "Repent, then. If not, I will come to you soon and make war against them with the sword of my mouth" (2:16). He warns the church at Sardis, "If you do not wake up, I will come like a thief, and you will not know at what hour I will come to you" (3:2–3). And the church of Laodicea is told, "I am about to

---

[36] Cf. Schnackenburg, "Kirche und Parusie," 551.

[37] Ibid., 576.

[38] Joest, "Parusie Jesu Christi," 541.

spit you out of my mouth. . . . Listen! I am standing at the door, knocking" (Rev 3:15–20).[39] The communal aspect of these judgments is obvious.

But in the Pauline epistles the risen Lord does not speak directly to a community, although on occasion Paul claims to speak ἐν λόγῳ κυρίου (1 Thess 4:15) or to be disclosing a "mystery" (1 Cor 15:51). And the church does not stand or fall because of the faith, righteousness, holiness, or sinfulness of the believer or a local community. While this is evident in Ephesians and Colossians, it is true also for the other epistles of Paul.

Paul speaks to his communities as the ambassador of the Lord (2 Cor 5:20), as the apostle of Christ (1 Thess 2:7), as a nurse who tenderly cares for her own children (1 Thess 2:7), as a father (2 Cor 6:18), and as one responsible for the life of the spirit in the churches. He consoles and encourages, but also warns and threatens, often by referring to the Lord's parousia and the day of judgment. Thus he tells the Corinthians not to judge his stewardship "before the time, before the Lord comes, who will bring to light the things now hidden in darkness and will disclose the purposes of the heart" (1 Cor 4:5). He warns the same community not to participate in the Eucharist unworthily: "All who eat and drink without discerning the body, eat and drink judgment against themselves" (11:29). In 11:32 Paul relates the community's sicknesses to the end-time judgment: "But when we are judged by the Lord, we are disciplined so that we may not be condemned along with the world." He warns that everyone will have to appear before the throne of Christ to give an account of one's life on earth (2 Cor 5:10). Thus, at any point in its existence the church is facing its judge and savior.[40]

The church stands before the judgment of Christ, even though it is the body of Christ and the community of salvation. As Schlink points out, ecclesiology is not to be equated with Christology, for Christ also "confronts the Church as Lord and even as judge."[41] The church is judged to the extent that it does not embody Christ. As a

---

[39] In all these messages the words are spoken by the Lord, whose power and glory are depicted in 1:13–16. He is the Son of man, standing in the midst of the lamp stands. The churches are thus accountable to him. He is their Lord, confronting them but also consoling and encouraging them.

[40] Ibid., 114–18.

[41] Ibid., 97. See Rev 2:5, 20, 23; 3:1–3, 15.

community, it has special responsibilities for its members, and its leaders have a responsibility for the health of the entire body.

Paul speaks of his own accountability to the Lord as the Lord's steward (1 Cor 4:1–4) entrusted with the laying of the foundation of the church (3:10–11), and he warns other missionaries of their responsibility toward the community (3:10–15; cf. 2 Cor 11). He points to the end-time judgment and the experience of loss in those whose works in the church will be shown to be improper or unworthy. And he calls on the assembly to carry out its responsibility toward immorality in its midst (1 Cor 5:1–8). When they are assembled and when Paul's spirit and "the power of our Lord Jesus" are with them, they are "to hand this man over to Satan for the destruction of the flesh, so that his spirit may be saved in the day of the Lord" (vv. 4–5). This action in the community is to be carried out in view of the Lord's coming—to save the culprit from being excluded from eternal life.

E. THE CHURCH AND MORAL RESPONSIBILITY

In his exhortations about ethical responsibilities,[42] Paul often refers to the parousia of the Lord. In Rom 13:11–14 he concludes the long ethical instruction with a reference to the completion:[43] "You know what time it is, how it is now the moment for you to wake from sleep. For salvation is nearer to us now than when we became believers; the night is far gone, the day is near. Let us then lay aside the works of darkness and put on the armor of light; let us live honorably as in the day."[44] The closeness of the completion is thus a feature in Paul's exhortation (cf. 1 Cor 7:29, 31). We find this feature also in the warning in 1 Cor 10:9 not to put "Christ to the test" as some Israelites had tested the Lord in the desert and were destroyed. He counsels those who think they are standing firm to watch lest they fall (10:12), for the example of Israel in the

---

[42]Paul, to be sure, does not deal with ethics in a systematic way, but he does have an idea of what is right for a believer, and applies this to himself, to other missionaries, and to the church. But he advises in an ad hoc fashion, in relation to a specific situation. Cf. Furnish, *Theology*, 209–10.

[43]Eschatology is not the only basis of Pauline ethics. Schrage (*Ethics*, 172–86) brings out the christological, sacramental, pneumatic, and eschatological foundations of Pauline ethics.

[44]See also Furnish, *Theology*, 23–24; Schrage, *Ethics*, 183–84.

desert is a warning to us, "on whom the ends of the ages have come" (10:11).

And as noted above, the apostle, with a glance at the Lord's coming, also warns the Corinthian church against unworthy reception of the Eucharist: "Whoever . . . eats the bread or drinks the cup of the Lord in an unworthy manner will be answerable for the body and blood of the Lord" (11:27). And he warns against toleration of a sexual offender in its midst (5:1–5; cf. 2 Cor 12:20–21). In 5:5 he commands the community "to hand this man over to Satan for the destruction of the flesh, so that his spirit may be saved in the day of the Lord."

Paul trains the eyes of the community upon the heavenly realities that the Lord will effect at his coming (Phil 3:20–21; 1 Cor 7:25–35). In 1 Thess 5:4–8 he affirms the Thessalonians to be "sons of light and sons of the day"[45] and hence in good standing for the ultimate fulfillment, but he also exhorts them to be vigilant and sober and to avoid carousing and the like (vv. 6–7). They should vest themselves with faith, love, and the hope of salvation (v. 8). He admonishes those who act in proud disregard of the conscience of the weak that their action of eating meat sacrificed to the idols may destroy the life of Christ in a fellow Christian (1 Cor 8:1–13; cf. Rom 14:1–22). In 1 Cor 3:17 he warns that the one who destroys the temple of the Holy Spirit will be destroyed by God. To the extent that the expression "God's temple" here is a communal designation, the apostle speaks of the destruction of the community and of the one who has caused this destruction. He counsels the faithful in Rome not to pass judgment on their brothers and sisters: "For we will all stand before the judgment seat of God" (Rom 14:10).

The nearness of the completion is a factor also in Paul's advice in 1 Cor 7:29–31, where he outlines the Christian attitude toward the world that is passing away. The καιρός, kairos, the appointed time until the parousia, has grown short, and the faithful should live as if they had no ties to this passing world. They should be inwardly free of attachment to this world in order to serve the Lord better.[46]

---

[45] The NRSV translation—"children of light and children of the day"—obscures the Semitic turn of phrase.

[46] Schrage, Ethics, 182.

The believers are thus to keep the Lord's judgment in their minds. Paul exhorts them, "So whether we are at home or away, we make it our aim to please him" (1 Thess 5:10). He warns, "For all of us must appear before the judgment seat of Christ, so that each may receive recompense for what has been done in the body, whether good or evil" (2 Cor 5:9–10; cf. Rom 14:7–9). The faithful thus live in the knowledge of Christ's judgment. The awaiting of the parousia, and of an imminent parousia at that, is therefore the horizon of Paul's ethical instructions and exhortations. He repeatedly warns that those who indulge in immorality and the flesh will not inherit the kingdom of God (Gal 5:16–21; 1 Cor 6:9–11; Phil 3:17–19; 2 Cor 7:1). He calls for vigilance and soberness. Paul's hope is that the entire community will be found holy before the Lord at his coming. But he knows that the church is a mixed community of saints and sinners. And he knows that the church in the world is in conflict with certain powers.

F. THE CHURCH IN CONFLICT

The conflict motif of the Lord's coming concerns the annihilation of the powers that are hostile to God. According to the apostle, the faithful are no longer under the elemental powers of the universe, or under the power of sin and death, but in the dominion of Christ. At his coming, Christ will annihilate these powers, including the "last enemy," death (1 Cor 15:26). The parousia of Christ means the victory of Christ, but the time between Easter and the parousia is the time of battle.[47]

This antagonistic aspect of the parousia warns the faithful about certain powers hostile to God. The faithful are at present in the dominion of Christ and are fundamentally safe as long as they stay in that dominion. They should, therefore, stay away from idolatry, for behind the idols are demons (1 Cor 8:4–5; 10:14–22).[48] And they ought to know that nothing can separate them from the love of God in Jesus Christ (Rom 8:31–39).

---

[47] Joest, "Parusie Jesu Christi," 543.

[48] They should also not keep seasons or months or days or festivals, as they did in the past, for they do not owe any worship to angels or any other powers in the creation (Gal 4:8–10).

Death, above all, is regarded by Paul as a hostile power that will be annihilated. The faithful should therefore look beyond the present trials and experience of dying to the kingdom of God, in which there is immortality and incorruptibility (2 Cor 4:14–18). But above all, they should no longer be slaves to the power of sin (Rom 5:14, 17, 20). Paul reassures the Romans, "In all these things we are more than conquerors through him who loved us. For I am convinced that neither death, nor life, nor angels, nor rulers . . . nor anything else in creation, will be able to separate us from the love of God in Christ Jesus our Lord" (8:37–39).

CONCLUSION

Although Paul's ἐκκλησία τοῦ θεοῦ means primarily the local community, the overtones of communion with the Jerusalem community and with all who are "in Christ" are also heard. The church is the fellowship of all who believe in Christ, who hope to be with him, and who are sustained in this hope by the Holy Spirit given to them. The church as the body of Christ is more than a gathering of like-minded individuals. The κοινωνία extends into the future completion and is the ultimate goal of this fellowship. In certain instances, what the apostle says to individuals applies to all members in the community, and what he says to one community applies to other communities. He knows that they are all "in Christ," sharing as they do in Christ's body and blood and in the same faith and hope. As Christ's apostle, Paul talks to his communities about the ultimate fulfillment: he exhorts, warns, and encourages them, and he prays for them. Although the church is still exposed to the influence of certain powers in the world, it is in the dominion of Christ and therefore protected; and it can be confident that nothing in the world can separate it from the love of God in Jesus Christ.

The church is thus the community of salvation and hope. The existence in faith is not yet a vision of the ultimate realities: the completion is yet to come, and all in the church hope to share in it. The faith in Christ, who is to return for the completion, is an essential element of this fellowship. The parousia, or the day of the Lord, is thus a constant referent in the Pauline epistles, but especially in 1 Thessalonians, 1 Corinthians, and Philippians.

But the church in its communal dimension is also confronted by the risen Lord. According to Paul, those who minister in the church, including himself, are accountable to the Lord. The apostle calls on local communities to carry out their responsibilities before the Lord when they come together, but especially when they share in the body and blood of the Lord.

13

⚜

PAUL'S APOCALYPTIC THEOLOGY

Paul's statements concerning the coming of the Lord include imagery, patterns of thought, and a worldview that occur also in Jewish apocalyptic.[1] Ever since Bultmann suggested that this language ought to be "demythologized," questions have been raised about its place and function in today's proclamation. Should it be eliminated or not? Does Jewish apocalyptic have any place in contemporary theology? If this language is to be retained, then what can be done with it? How can it be made useful and meaningful in contemporary proclamation? On what grounds and principles can it be interpreted?

A. THE PROBLEM OF METHOD

The problem of method here is compounded by the approach of Bultmann,[2] who reinterprets not only the apocalyptic imagery but the entire gospel of Paul. His essay on demythologization has provoked scholarly discussion for some forty years since World War II. Another approach, diametrically opposed to Bultmann's, is the harmonization adopted earlier by F. Heitmüller[3] and others. A short investigation of these two approaches will stake out the outer limits

---

[1] On Jewish apocalyptic literature, see Koch, *Rediscovery of Apocalyptic*, 18–35. For a working definition of what is apocalyptic, see J. J. Collins, "Morphology," 2–12; Beker, *Paul the Apostle*, 135–181; Beker, *Sieg Gottes*, 63–66.

[2] Bultmann, "Neues Testament," 187–352.

[3] Heitmüller, *Wiederkunft*.

of the attempted solutions. Since Bultmann's reinterpretation is not only exegetical but also theological, we shall, in addition, present here K. Rahner's essay on hermeneutical principles[4] governing eschatological assertions in the NT.

1. Retention of the Existing Imagery

Heitmüller regards the disparate Pauline assertions dealing with the Lord's coming as so many pieces of a jigsaw puzzle, which only need to be put together in order to give us the entire picture. He presumes that the whole NT had the same picture of this event and that the various sketches and allusions in Pauline letters give us a section of this portrait. Thus, by combining 2 Cor 5:10, Rom 14:10, Rev 20:11, and Matt 25:31, Heitmüller obtains three different judgment thrones: Christ's "great white throne" (Rev 20:11), "the throne of his glory" (Matt 25:31), and "the judgment seat of God and Christ" (Rom 14:10; 2 Cor 5:10). In this way he comes up with a synthetic depiction of the judgment of the faithful,[5] the gathering of the rest of the Jewish people,[6] and the judgment of the Gentiles.[7] By joining 1 Thess 4:13–18, 1 Cor 15:50–53, Matt 25:6, and 2 Cor 5:1–10, Heitmüller reconstructs the scenery of the Lord's coming,[8] which contains the following elements:

   a. The Lord rises from his throne at the right-hand side of God and comes down to the sphere above the earth, the place of meeting with his community.

   b. With the call "Here is the bridegroom! Come out to meet him" (Matt 25:6), the Lord awakens his community and calls it to himself. An archangel's voice accompanies this call, and the trumpet of God gives the signal to come forth to the full and eternal redemption.

   c. At this, the dead in Christ, whose spirits are now in the Father's house in heaven, receive their new body.

   d. The surviving believers are then transformed and vested with a new life.

   e. Both groups of believers are then taken up by the clouds to meet the Lord.

   f. The entire event takes place in a split second.

---

[4] Rahner, "Hermeneutics," 323–46. See also Rahner, "Eschatologie," cols. 1096–97.
[5] Heitmüller, *Wiederkunft*, 11–13.
[6] Ibid., 13–14.
[7] Ibid., 14.
[8] Ibid., 6–7.

In this reconstruction, 1 Thess 4:16–18 serves as the frame-work into which pieces from other passages are fitted. This procedure, however, raises some fundamental problems. One is the assumption, made by Heitmüller, that all the NT writers had an identical picture of the end-time drama. Another is that Heitmüller's procedure, for all its faithfulness to the literal text, is arbitrary. Why should 1 Thess 4:13–18 be taken as the framework? And why is the context of each passage totally neglected?[9]

2. Radical Reinterpretation of the Imagery and the Framework

In 1941 Bultmann wrote his essay "Neues Testament und Mythologie,"[10] in which he gave his reasons for demythologizing the NT. According to him, not only the imagery but the entire NT kerygma is mythological language derived from Jewish apocalyptic mythology and the Hellenistic savior myth. It is thus not possible simply to remove this imagery[11] from the kerygma: the kerygma itself must be stripped of mythology. This language, which is not even Christian, is at present hindering the hearing of the word in faith and must therefore be reinterpreted for our time.[12]

Bultmann accomplishes this by interpreting the NT language in terms of Martin Heidegger's existential analytics of *Dasein*[13] and by conforming his interpretation to Marburg neo-Kantian

---

[9] A similar harmonization, only on a smaller scale, had been attempted by Teichmann (*Vorstellungen*, 20–26) and Beyschlag (*New Testament Theology*, 260–62).

[10] Bultmann, "Mythology." First published in *Offenbarung*, the essay was repub-lished in Bartsch, *Kerygma und Mythos*, 1.15–48.

[11] Ibid., 15–16. (Pages here and following refer to the translation by Fuller.)

[12] Ibid., 9–16.

[13] Heidegger in his existential analytics distinguishes between *Vorhandensein* and *Dasein*. The former refers to the given, the inanimate, the object, while the latter denotes the human being in search of being in general and reflecting on self and on personal responsibility in the world. The analysis of *Dasein* draws on life's experience and unveils the general and formal characteristics *(Existenzial)* of existence that is specific to human beings. This *Existenzial* is appropriated by the *Existenziell*, the actual life-decision by which a person effects its *Dasein*.

For a philosophical discussion of Bultmann's appropriation of Heidegger's philosophy, see Malevez, *Christian Message*, 29–49; Johnson, *Origins*, 28. According to Johnson (p. 18–29), Bultmann's reliance here on Heidegger is eclectic: he adopts Heidegger's philosophy only when it agrees with the Marburg neo-Kantianism (p. 38–86). Johnson (p. 207–31) points out that the catalyst for Bultmann's interpreta-tion of myth was Jonas, *Gnosis*.

philosophy[14] and the Lutheran dichotomy between works and faith.[15] The analysis of the *Dasein*,[16] which deals with the self-reflective existence that is proper to human beings, discloses two ways of existing in the world: one is impersonal, uncommitted, and objective *(das Vorhandensein)*; the other is personal, responsible, and authentic. The latter way is being swallowed by the former and is made unauthentic. Human beings know that they are unauthentic, but also that they can be authentic and responsible. According to Heidegger, human beings can liberate themselves from unauthentic existence by concrete, personal *(existenziell)* decisions with which they assume their responsibility.

Bultmann accepts this analysis, but with one modification: human beings are fallen and cannot rise on their own.[17] They can rise, however, by an existential *(existenziell)* decision to accept the challenge of the cross in the kerygma, which contains God's liberating judgment. Thus, when the cross of Christ is proclaimed to them, God condemns them, but also pardons them for having acted like those who belong to this world. In this way God frees them so that they may be authentic and live no longer from their own resources but from faith in God's offer of grace. In response to the kerygma presented in this form, the believer, although still taking part in the world, lives as though the world were not (1 Cor 7:29–31)—the believer is crucified to the world (Gal 6:14). To exist in this fashion, according to Bultmann, is to exist eschatologically.[18]

---

[14] The Marburg form of neo-Kantian philosophy separated the rational, objectified forms of reality and immediate religious experience. On neo-Kantianism at Marburg, see Johnson, *Origins*, 32, 38–86.

[15] On the particular form of Lutheranism espoused by Bultmann, see ibid., 84–86.

[16] Existential analysis is regarded by Bultmann as universally valid. Its usefulness is in releasing the natural self-knowledge in human beings. It furnishes us with existential universals of *Dasein*, with the constants of human personal existence. This general anthropology is preparatory to the knowledge of being in general (Malevez, *Christian Message*, 36).

[17] Malevez (ibid., 103) points out that here Bultmann follows his Lutheran interpretation of Paul: "Just as the doctrine of justification destroys, in man, the false security of his own 'works,' similarly and in a parallel way, demythologizing destroys our confidence in our 'objectivizing' knowledge *(konstatierendes Erkennen)*. . . . He alone finds security and certitude who renounces all desire for intellectual certainty, and is ready to plunge into that 'dark night' which constitutes faith." Similarly, Ricoeur, *Essays*, 63.

[18] See Malevez, *Christian Message*, 52–53.

When the message of the NT is recast in this fashion, it sloughs off Jewish eschatology and this-worldly representations of the transcendent world. It does away with the objective facts, like the incarnation, the resurrection of Christ, the presence of the Holy Spirit. And it does not speak of the transcendent world that comes down from heaven: there is no parousia of the risen Christ, no universal judgment as a cosmic event, and no objective resurrection in the end time.[19]

The church, Bultmann claims, either failed to grasp the full significance of the encounter of God in Christ or expressed it in language that is no longer meaningful to us. In Bultmann's opinion, the parousia belongs to the former: the church did not understand this aspect of the encounter of God in Christ, since history did not come to an end.[20] Bultmann therefore draws from this mythological depiction of the parousia the kerygmatic core and recasts it into existentialist language.[21] He shifts the end-time resurrection, the parousia, and the judgment from the plane of objective reality and knowledge to the plane of subjective appropriation by faith. Jesus' death on the cross[22] is given meaning in the kerygma, which speaks of the resurrection, the parousia, and the last judgment. These, however, are not historical realities but a knowledge of faith. The language of the resurrection interprets Jesus' death on the cross as God's redemptive judgment of the world.[23] Thus, according to Bultmann, Christ rose in the kerygma and only in the kerygma. Hence, through the proclamation "the cross and the resurrection are made present: the eschatological 'now' is here"[24] and in each existential moment. It is here that the

---

[19] Ibid., 52–55.

[20] Ibid., 5. See also A. L. Moore, *Parousia*, 67–68.

[21] Bultmann, "Mythology," 17–22.

[22] Bultmann (ibid., 22–23), realizing that a Christianity without Jesus is logically impossible, insists on the reality of the historical Jesus. But for some of his critics, this exception to the purely subjective analysis of the NT data raises questions of procedure and consistency.

[23] Ibid., 42. Bultmann speaks of the death of Christ, "which is both the judgment and the salvation of the world." The apostolic preaching is itself part of the Easter event, supplementing the cross and making its saving efficacy intelligible by demanding faith and challenging human beings to understand themselves as crucified and risen with Christ. For Bultmann, the word of preaching is the word of the cross. The language of the resurrection, devoid of the fact of Jesus' resurrection, expresses the saving character of the cross for the one who accepts it in faith.

[24] Ibid.

risen Christ is meeting us, the judgment is taking place, and the end time is occurring.

But as L. Malevez, Ricoeur, and R. A. Johnson point out, Bultmann does more than strip the NT message of Jewish apocalypticism or its unscientific worldview. In line with the Lutheran understanding of justification by faith apart from works, he calls for a religious commitment without the support of objective knowledge.[25] Here "apart from works" means "apart from objective knowledge." Bultmann makes use of objectifying knowledge to get rid of the objectifying dimension of the kerygma. But in doing this, he saws off the branch on which he is sitting. Ricoeur asks of the end result, "In what sense is it still a language? And what does it signify?" According to him, the demythologizing, which began as an intellectual demand to get rid of mythological components in the kerygma, ends up in a *sacrificium intellectus.* It eliminates all questions that arise from objectifying thinking, including the question with which it began.[26] And this means that the kerygma can "no longer be the origin of demythologization if it does not initiate thought, if it develops no understanding of faith."[27] Bultmann, according to Ricoeur, makes the mistake of fusing the moment of exegesis and the moment of existential decision. Exegesis brings out the meaning of the text, which embraces the objective understanding and the subjective signification. The latter is appropriated when the reader "grasps the meaning, the moment when the meaning is actualized in existence." The objective and the existential interpretations are thus not contrary but complementary.[28]

---

[25] Malevez, *Christian Message,* 103; Ricoeur, *Essays,* 65; Johnson, *Origins,* 33–35. According to Johnson (p. 35), "Bultmann's earliest appropriations of Heidegger . . . are already informed by his particular Lutheran concern."

[26] Ricoeur, *Essays,* 66.

[27] Ibid., 66–67. Ricoeur observes, "How could it do so if it were not both event and meaning together and therefore 'objective' in another acceptance of the word than the one eliminated with mythological representations?" According to Ricoeur, Bultmann does not understand Heidegger correctly, who did not emphasize in his existential description man "but the place—the Da-sein—of the question of being. . . . Consequently, meaningful statements about man and the person and, *a fortiori*, the analogies concerning God as a person can be thought and grounded only ulteriorly" (p. 71).

[28] Ibid., 68. "Therefore, the semantic moment, the moment of objective meaning, must precede the existential moment, the moment of personal decision, in a hermeneutics concerned with doing justice to both the objectivity of meaning and the historicity of personal decision" (ibid.).

A. L. Moore criticizes Bultmann for rejecting supernatural events in the name of historical criticism. He points out that the criteria for the truth of the historical and suprahistorical events must be obtained from the records of the NT itself and from the general methodology of the science of history, not from nineteenth-century ideology, as done by Bultmann. The supranatural phenomena, if they can be verified, should not be ruled out a priori from the field of the historical investigation. Nor should the historical investigation presuppose a breach between Jesus and the early church.[29] The historical veracity of tradition must not be discounted but, rather, probed.[30]

Malevez points out that Bultmann's objections to the language of the NT do not agree with contemporary scientific thinking. They reflect, rather, a rationalist bias.[31] Thus, Bultmann's understanding of myth scarcely does justice to the concept of myth.[32] Bultmann lumps together under this term such heterogeneous elements as the miracles of Jesus, the preexistence of the Son of God, the atonement, the Holy Spirit, and grace.[33] While the purpose of myth, according to Bultmann, is to give expression to man's self-understanding in the present world,[34] the NT "myth" deals rather with the encounter of God and man. It conveys a theological understanding.[35]

According to Moore, demythologizing would be called for only if the primary subject of the NT were human beings or human self-understanding.[36] But this is not the case. In Ricoeur's

---

[29] A. L. Moore (*Parousia*, 70) agrees with Cullmann ("Out of Season Remarks," 138–39) on this point.

[30] A. L. Moore, *Parousia*, 70.

[31] Malevez, *Christian Message*, 125–42, esp. 128.

[32] Ibid., 164–67.

[33] So Henderson, *Myth*, 46. According to Henderson, Bultmann does not object to these for the same reason. To the sacraments and the doctrine of the Holy Spirit, he objects that they "confuse the categories of *Vorhandensein* and *Dasein* and thus treat of spiritual factors as if they were natural entities." To the miracles, he objects that they do not fit the scientific conception of the world. And to the language about heaven, he objects because it is anthropomorphic. Cf. also A. L. Moore, *Parousia*, 72.

[34] Bultmann, "Mythology," 10.

[35] A. L. Moore, *Parousia*, 72. Here the cosmological and anthropological components are subordinated to the theological statement. Cf. also Malevez, *Christian Message*, 157.

[36] A. L. Moore, *Parousia*, 72–73.

view demythologizing[37] is legitimate on philosophical grounds, but not by taking from Heidegger's analysis only the personalist component,[38] as Bultmann does, for the meaning of the text has objective and existential components. Ricoeur states, "It is the objectivity of the text, understood as content—bearer of meaning and demand for meaning—that begins the existential movement of appropriation."[39] If there is no objective meaning, as Bultmann presupposes, "then the text no longer says anything at all." In Ricoeur's opinion, Bultmann approach veers toward fideism.[40]

The meaning thus involves religious language, experience, meaning brought to expression in that language, and concepts that human intelligence constructs in thinking about God.[41] In particular, eschatology makes use of an apocalyptic language and framework. What meaning does Paul convey through this medium? What losses are incurred when the word of God is translated into existentialism? According to Beker, not every medium is equally capable of transmitting the word of God, and twentieth-century existentialism is scarcely *the* system for this transmission.[42] The existentialism of Heidegger, employed by Bultmann, scarcely gives to a human being an adequate self-understanding. Neither the past nor the empirical future obtains here its proper relevance. The parousia deals with the last things, but, for Bultmann, futurity is simply a dimension of the present human existence: there is no particular content as the object of hope, such as the Lord's coming, the resurrection, the judgment, or eternal life with Christ. Hope is but the openness of faith to God, who is coming ever anew to the believer.[43]

---

[37] Ricoeur (*Essays*, 60–62) speaks of three levels of demythologization in Bultmann that correspond to the three definitions of myth: (1) adjustment of the biblical view of the world to that of modern science; (2) restoration of the myth's intention in terms of Heidegger's existential interpretation; (3) reduction of the imagery borrowed from Jewish eschatology and mystery cults.

[38] Ibid., 66–67. Bultmann, according to Ricoeur, moves too fast to the moment of decision, leaping over the moment of meaning, the objective stage, the exegesis (p. 68).

[39] Ibid., 68.

[40] Ibid.

[41] Malevez, *Christian Message*, 157–58. According to Malevez, these concepts are the fruit of the human mind in love with God. But these objective ideas are applied to God in a transcendental and analogical way. They are legitimate as well as necessary; they are the "bearers of transcendent significance."

[42] According to Beker (*Paul the Apostle*, 135), the resurrection of Christ can only be understood in the framework of Jewish apocalyptic.

[43] Bultmann, *Primitive Christianity*, 186.

But as Moore observes, according to the NT, "futurity is not simply a phenomenon of existence but is also God's time, time and occasion for divine action; it is subject to the Lordship of Christ."[44] It means that God in his encounter with man "does not ignore man's time frame-work. God allows succession and chronology to be really involved, and he creates salvation-history."[45] Thus, Moore states, the present life "in hope" is not merely a hope of the constant renewal of a divine encounter in Christ but also hope that the provisional relationship in faith "is *really only* provisional, being bounded by the awaited future revelation of Christ in glory."[46]

Bultmann's demythologizing raises the question of the relevancy of Jesus' historical life for the believer and for the world. If God was, in Christ, reconciling the world to himself (2 Cor 5:19), then the historical particularity and sufficiency of the Christ-event must not be abandoned, since it gives meaning to the past, to the future, and to the each "now" of human existence. Moore states, "Jesus Christ reveals himself as the One who was and who will be, as the 'preexistent Son of God' and as the 'Judge of the End-time.' In that encounter is given the impetus and authority to refer God's activity in Christ both backwards into the past . . . and forward into the future, involving some idea of a Parousia."[47] In the present epoch, "man is for the moment given time and occasion for a response of free decision to the Eschaton, inasmuch as it encounters him as yet only in a mystery, veiled."[48] Human beings are invited to anticipate a real future consummation.

Faith is therefore a "commitment to certain divine events in history and their significance."[49] But these events, Moore asserts, "have an independent status and meaning quite apart from man." Thus the cross did not acquire its saving significance only when the disciples began to believe in such a meaning for them; it signified the relationship of God to the world both before and independently of the disciples' faith.[50] Faith involves a commitment

---

[44] A. L. Moore, *Parousia,* 75.

[45] Ibid., 76. This can be maintained no matter how complicated it is for human beings to understand the relation of past to present and of present to future in regard to God and his salvation history.

[46] Ibid.

[47] Ibid., 74. See also Cullmann, *Christ and Time,* 17–33.

[48] A. L. Moore, *Parousia,* 77.

[49] Ibid.

[50] Ibid., 77–78.

to the particular action of God in history, above all to God's action in the person of Jesus Christ. It authenticates the hope of the future revelation of the end as it recognizes its anticipation in the historical event of Jesus Christ.[51]

The question comes down to the nature of biblical hermeneutics. According to K. Barth, biblical hermeneutics is unique[52] because of the sovereignty of the word of God with respect to human beings and their thinking. Contemporary concepts should therefore subserve the proclamation, rather than rule over it, and no single philosophical system should claim to be the sole medium of interpretation of the NT.[53] Barth probably overstates the total transcendence of the word of God with respect to the human mind, forgetting that the same Word also created human beings and made them capable of searching out reality, truth, and goodness. For faith to be truly a human act, it must agree with the God-given principles of truth and goodness inherent in the human mind, as Malevez points out. Where Bultmann went wrong was in making the pure decision the only referent for the word of God. He was, in fact, subjecting the word to a defective structure of the human mind, asserted on the basis of a faulty existential analysis.[54]

3. Hermeneutical Principles Governing Eschatology

What, then, are the principles of biblical hermeneutics? In particular, what are the hermeneutical rules proper to eschatology? The above discussion points out the need for some principles in interpreting the eschatological statements. In 1960 Rahner laid down several such postulates.[55] According to him, the "last things" require specific and explicit hermeneutics guided by the principles drawn from biblical theology dealing with the last things. But since to construct such a hermeneutics is too involved and time-consuming, Rahner derives principles from the methodology governing

---

[51] Ibid., 79.

[52] Malevez, *Christian Message*, 170–212. See Barth, "Rudolf Bultmann."

[53] But see Malevez, *Christian Message*, 192–212. The starting point in Barth's hermeneutic is the absolute lordship of Jesus Christ even in thought. While Barth admits that we come to the Bible with our ideas, these should not be elevated into absolutes (p. 198). Human categories should not limit the word of God, and the latter should not be reduced to the requirements of anthropology.

[54] Malevez, *Christian Message*, 208–11.

[55] Rahner, "Hermeneutics," 323–46.

basic assertions in systematic theology.[56] He lists the following basic principles:

(1) The Christian understanding of faith and its expressions must include what bears on the empirical future, on what is yet to come.[57]

(2) God is all-knowing—this is a metaphysical axiom as well as a truth of faith—hence, God knows future events.[58]

(3) (a) God has not revealed the date of the end. The completion is announced as a mystery and is essentially hidden. It becomes present to us as the mysterious, unmistakable, overwhelming, irresistible, promising, and menacing reality of God's coming to us.

(b) Human beings are essentially historical beings and cannot understand themselves at any given moment without a backward and a forward look that constitutes, as well as limits, the hermeneutics of eschatological statements. Therefore, the future is an inner component of human existence,[59] and salvation involves also our physical, spatiotemporal existence.

From (3)(a) and (b) Rahner draws three corollaries:

(4)(a) The future must be impenetrable and uncontrollable[60] so that human beings are free to believe, to dare, and to trust.

(b) The future belongs to God alone and fulfills the whole person.

(5) Knowledge of the future must be derived from the meaning of our present eschatological experience and from the Christ-event: this knowledge concerns the fulfillment of an existence that is taking place in an eschatological situation[61] and is necessary for our spiritual decision in freedom and in faith. Thus, Christian anthropology and Christian eschatology are ultimately Christology.[62]

---

[56] Ibid., 325. Rahner, however, hopes that this method would be confirmed by that drawn from biblical theology.

[57] This is called for by the self-understanding of Scripture and by the prophetic nature of the pronouncements dealing with the future. According to Rahner (ibid., 326), to reduce this to what is taking place here and now is theologically unacceptable.

[58] Hence, divine revelation is not limited by human beings, for they do not control God and prophecy is a divine prerogative.

According to Rahner (ibid., 328), the principles derived from the word of God are thus not an external limitation of divine revelation. They leave us open to God and do not restrict the knowledge of God or the power of divine revelation.

[59] Hence, the future must not be eliminated from our self-understanding.

[60] Hence, it is not a preview of what is in store for us (Rahner, "Hermeneutics," 334).

[61] Ibid.

[62] Rahner (ibid., 335) states that the mode of revelation "must be a forward looking draft of existence orientated to the fulfilment of the end of time. Otherwise the object of revelation would be the future as directly seen and decreed in itself

Rahner then draws another set of inferences from (3)(a) and (b):

(6)(a) The eschatology of salvation and the eschatology of the loss of salvation are not on the same plane. Both possibilities remain open, for the pilgrim can only make free decisions on what is open and unforeseeable.[63]

(b) All eschatological assertions concern human beings both as individuals and as members of society. Neither can be completely absorbed by the other.

(c) There is no fundamental opposition between an imminent and a distant parousia. Eschatological assertions must deal with actual events in history, with "God's action on man at any moment," and also take into account the possibility of a distant completion, for God is incalculable.[64]

(d) The present experience of salvation gives us knowledge of the genuine future in faith, disclosed in the death and resurrection of Christ as the historical event of the supreme communication of God to us. Hence, Christ is the hermeneutical principle of all eschatological assertions.

(e) By invoking certain formal principles of the theology of history, we can derive all that can be said objectively about eschatology.[65]

Finally, Rahner envisions a way of separating eschatological imagery from the content:

(7) The basic principle stated in (3)(a) and (b) above provides a fundamental criterion for distinguishing between the form and the content of the eschatological assertions in Scripture, although a perfect separation may not always be possible.[66]

---

by God, described so to speak in a narrative which moves backwards from the future into the present." This, however, would destroy the mystery and the openness of our future.

[63] According to Rahner (ibid., 339), it excludes presumptuous knowledge, the certainty of salvation before death or of damnation after death.

[64] These assertions, Rahner insists (ibid., 342), are not inside information about future events that do not affect our present. But neither are they so thoroughly existential that the whole future is taking place in the present.

[65] Rahner (ibid., 343) mentions such things as the end of the world, the accentuation of antagonism in the last epoch, the ambiguity of the temporal, etc.

[66] According to Rahner (ibid., 344–45), by correlating several assertions "the relationship between the form and content in any given assertion will be fluid: the term of the analogy to which such an assertion points will be recognizable as the consciously ensuing difference between form and content, though it remains impossible to disentangle it completely. And hence the thing intended will be conceivable under a new form of expression, though formulated once more in a new type of imagery."

The first three assertions—(1), (2), and (3)(a)—are drawn from the self-understanding present in biblical writings and from the prophetic nature of the pronouncements concerning the future. They are guided by the revelation of God through the prophets and through Jesus Christ and by the fact that this revelation did not disclose the time of the completion. Principle (3)(b), however, is taken from the requirements governing human self-understanding. But Rahner here limits himself to general hermeneutical principles as he affirms the role of the past and of the future—hence, of genuine temporal order—in human self-understanding. As Bultmann before him, Rahner is combining the self-understanding of the Scriptures and anthropology, but he is not bypassing the objective component of human knowing, nor is he reducing everything to the existential decision.

Although Rahner nowhere mentions Bultmann in this discussion, he implicitly takes issue with Bultmann's employment of a philosophical system in which not only human but also Christian self-understanding is truncated. In particular, he insists that knowledge of the future, veiled as it is, is necessary for the believer's spiritual decisions in the present.[67] He sees this knowledge present in the believer's understanding of Christ and of the present Christian existence in the light of Christ. Christ is God's self-communication to us and thus the hermeneutical principle for interpreting the expected fulfillment. Rahner is also more conscious than Bultmann of the collective dimension of Christian existence and its implications for the realization of salvation. The delay of the parousia is not a fundamental problem for him, since he understands it as intrinsically linked with the sovereignty of God.

In his criterion (7) for the steps to be taken in order to separate the image from the content, Rahner clearly expects that the form and the content can in most cases be separated. But for Pauline statements concerning the ultimate events, Rahner's procedure of disentangling the images from the content has proved to be unworkable. Pauline statements are simply too contextual to allow that. As Beker points out,[68] the apostle formulates in response to the particular problem at hand; he does not repeat on every

---

[67] But Rahner does not directly confront Bultmann about his understanding of myth, under which Bultmann includes the resurrection of Jesus, the parousia, the last judgment, and the Holy Spirit.

[68] Beker, *Paul the Apostle*, 352–55.

occasion a set description of the last things but patterns his expression to the situation at hand.

B. PAUL'S APOCALYPTIC THEOLOGY

In reaction to Bultmann's reduction of eschatology, Beker stresses the role of apocalyptic in Paul's theology. Apocalyptic deals with hope. But hope, according to Beker, is more than a "component of faith" or a "believing posture," as Bultmann would have it; hope has a specific object, and apocalyptic supplies the framework for this object. "Faith," Beker asserts, "not only is hope but it has a hope; it cannot exist without the specific object of hope."[69] And hope, as presented in apocalyptic writings, is centered on the last judgment, on the resurrection of the dead, on immortality, on eternal life, on the kingdom of God: "The apocalyptist has a profound awareness of the discrepancy between what is and what should be . . . he lives a hope that seems contradicted by the realities of his world but that is fed by his faith in the faithfulness of the God of Israel and his ultimate self-vindication. Will God keep his promises to his people? . . . Will he . . . establish his people in victory over their enemies and thus vindicate his glory in the glorious destiny of his people?"[70]

Apocalyptic, Beker insists, is not an empty abstraction or idle speculation. It provides the only appropriate medium for conveying the good news, and it is born out of a deep existential concern.[71] In agreement with K. Koch, Beker presents the following essential traits of Jewish apocalyptic: (1) historical dualism; (2) universal cosmic expectation; and (3) the imminent end of the world.[72] Apocalyptic thus sees the discontinuity between this age and the age to come, looks toward a radical transformation of the present world, which is ruled by the forces of evil, and expects an imminent end.[73] Paul relies on apocalyptic but does not use it slavishly; he adapts the traditional apocalyptic pattern to the Christ-event. Thus the apostle does not employ the terminology

---

[69] Ibid., 147.
[70] Ibid., 136.
[71] Ibid.
[72] Ibid., 135–36; cf. Koch, *Rediscovery of Apocalyptic*, 18–35.
[73] Beker, *Paul the Apostle*, 137–38.

of "this age" and "the age to come," or depict the escalation of conflict and woes in the end time, or follow timetables and periods leading to the completion.

Paul, according to Beker, has both located the Christ-event within the general apocalyptic framework and adapted the apocalyptic framework to the Christ-event. On the one hand, the notion of the resurrection belongs to the domain of the new age, which entails the transformation and the re-creation of everything. This holds true for the resurrection of Christ and for the general resurrection that is linked with that of Christ. On the other hand, the Christ-event determines Paul's apocalyptic dualism in that it "not only negates the old order but also initiates the hope of transformation of the creation." The resurrection of Christ, Beker states, "marks the beginning of the process of transformation, and its historical reality is therefore crucial to Paul because it marks the appearance of the end of history and not simply the end of history."[74]

Apocalyptic, Beker insists, is the constant in Paul's thought before and after his Damascus experience. Elimination of the apostle's apocalyptic eschatology has led to a "misconstrual of the eschatological hope in Paul's thought," for apocalyptic is not an "ornamental husk that could be removed without affecting the core of Paul's thought."[75] The language of apocalyptic "concerns the reality of the cosmic victory of the creator over his created world."[76]

C. THE RESURRECTION LANGUAGE AND JEWISH APOCALYPTIC

According to Beker, "resurrection language is end-time language and unintelligible apart from the apocalyptic thought world to which resurrection language belongs." It belongs to the new age, to the transformation and re-creation of everything, as is

---

[74] Ibid., 149. Beker plays down the difference between Jewish apocalyptic and the NT. The difference is not between the old and the new, the hidden and the public, the darkness and the light. At least in the Qumran community, the new is celebrated as a present reality and not simply as the expected reality. According to Beker, the real difference between primitive Christianity and Judaism lies not in the concept of salvation but in the role of the law (p. 150).

[75] Ibid., 140.

[76] Ibid., 141.

asserted by the apocalyptic thought. "Thus, the resurrection of Christ, the coming reign of God, and the future resurrection of the dead belong together."[77] This means that the parousia of Christ, at which the resurrection is to occur, is also an apocalyptic event. It belongs to the victory of God.

But is the resurrection the essential component of apocalyptic, and is it proper to it alone? According to G. W. E. Nickelsburg, belief in the resurrection has OT roots. In the intertestamental Jewish theology the beliefs in resurrection, immortality, and eternal life are carried within the framework of three forms already established in the OT and have specific functions within these domains. The forms in question are (1) the story of the righteous man and the Isaianic exaltation tradition, (2) the judgment scene, and (3) the two-way theology.[78]

In the first form, a wise man, member of a king's court, is unjustly accused and condemned to death, but at the last moment he is rescued from death, vindicated, and exalted to a high position, while his enemies are punished (Isa 52–53). In later development (Wis 5) the righteous man is in fact put to death; but at the moment of death he is exalted to the heavenly court, where he is given a place of honor.[79] Later on, the exaltation motif was replaced by the vindication motif: the righteous are vindicated and the wicked are condemned.[80] According to Nickelsburg, this tradition developed into the doctrine of the resurrection of the body.[81]

In the second form, the resurrection is part of the judgment that follows the persecution. Here the specific injustice is redressed through the resurrection of a particular just man.[82] This resurrection, however, is not a vindication of the righteous, as in

---

[77] Ibid., 152.

[78] Nickelsburg, *Resurrection*, 170–74.

[79] Ibid., 170.

[80] According to Nickelsburg (ibid., 171), in the Similitudes of *1 Enoch* the righteous man has been replaced by the exalted Son of man, who metes out judgment to the mighty and the kings. In Dan 12, *T. Mos.* 10, and *1 Enoch* 104 the exaltation of the righteous is one of the motifs of judgment. *2 Bar.* 51 has a description of judgment after which the righteous ascend to heaven and are given a glorious body.

[81] Ibid., 170–71.

[82] According to Nickelsburg (ibid., 171), Dan 12:2, the earliest intertestamental text dealing with this motif, alludes to Isa 26:19 but is really drawing on Isa 65 and 66.

the first form. In *1 Enoch* 94–104, for instance, the resurrection enables the righteous to receive their promised rewards, which their suffering and death denied them. *Testament of Judah* 25 promises resurrection to those who were put to death for the Lord's sake as well as to the patriarchs. In 4 Ezra 7, however, the resurrection is called for by the extinction of all human life on earth; it is still a means by which reward and punishment can be dispensed.[83] Here, however, resurrection is universal and is a means to general reward and punishment.

The third form is rooted in OT covenantal theology. The two-way theology describes the right and the wrong ways—one leading to eternal life, the other to eternal death. The judgment here is general, and the time and mode of eternal life are left vague. This theology, according to Nickelsburg, is compatible with the immediate assumption (*T. Asher* 6:6) or with the immortality of the soul (Wis 5:1, 15–16).[84]

Nickelsburg has noted Hellenistic influence in the theology of intertestamental Judaism. This literature does not speak only of the resurrection of the dead but also of the release of the spirits of the dead from the chambers in which they were kept since death, and of the ascension of the living into heaven. Thus, according to Nickelsburg, the above forms are only loosely connected with the dualistic worldview and imply neither the universal cosmic horizon nor the expectation of the imminent end of the world. The oldest traditions using the resurrection language deal with the vindication of a particular individual. This conclusion contradicts Beker's assertion that the resurrection language belongs essentially to the apocalyptic horizon.

In contrast to the three forms within which the resurrection has a function in the Jewish intertestamental literature, the resurrection of Jesus Christ is affirmed by Paul as a fact in the past and revealed and confirmed through the resurrection appearances. As such it does not fit into the apocalyptic horizon, which expected the resurrection to happen at the end of the ages, or into the forms in which resurrection language was employed. Apocalyptic, according to Nickelsburg's analysis, could only interpret Christ's resurrection as God's vindication of Jesus or as God's exaltation of the spirit of

---

[83] Ibid., 171–73.
[84] Ibid., 173.

Jesus at his death.[85] But that is not how Paul presents it. He does not speak of Jesus' resurrection as a vindication of Jesus or as a resurrection of this particular righteous man. He speaks, rather, of God's deed inaugurating the resurrection of all who belong to Christ (1 Cor 15:20–23) and of the resurrection and of the risen Jesus as life-giving power (1 Cor 15:45; Phil 3:10). And he links Jesus' resurrection to the lordship of Jesus (1 Cor 15:24–27), which will come to completion at his parousia (vv. 23–28). The resurrection of Jesus means Jesus' lordship over death—and that means the power to raise the dead and to endow the living and the dead with immortality and incorruptibility (vv. 52–55).

For Paul, the future resurrection (of the faithful) is the means of being with Jesus and of becoming conformed to him. It is not a reward for martyrdom or for the trials in this life; it is, rather, the culmination of the present life "in Christ." If Paul limits the resurrection to those who belong to Christ (1 Cor 15:23), as he does, the reason is that for him the resurrection is itself a salvific event: it brings the one who is "in Christ" to be finally with Christ, the center of hope, and it conforms the believer to the risen Christ. For Paul, the resurrection is not a means of sharing in the enjoyment of the fruits of life that were denied here on earth, as it is in apocalyptic. The apostle's hope of the resurrection is linked with the sharing in the cross of Christ, with self-denial (Phil 3:10), and with a preference for the heavenly realities.

D. THE COMING OF THE LORD AND JEWISH APOCALYPTIC

Whereas Jewish apocalyptic associates the resurrection with the final judgment, Paul associates it with the Lord's coming (1 Thess 4:16–17; 1 Cor 15:23, 52). It was established earlier,[86] however, that the coming of the Lord is rooted in the day-of-the-Lord tradition and in OT theophanies. It belongs to the victory of God, to God's

---

[85] While the vindication motif may be present in the hymn in Phil 2:9 ("therefore God also highly exalted him"), the text, strictly speaking, does not speak of the resurrection but of the exaltation, although Paul, no doubt, understood this to involve the resurrection. The vindication motif, however, is not evident in Rom 1:3–4, where the resurrection and endowment with power are simply juxtaposed to Jesus' origin "according to the flesh." Nor is the vindication motif evident in the general resurrection.

[86] See ch. 1.

enforcing his rule in the world. The day of the Lord is therefore ambivalent, an image of both judgment and salvation. In Jewish apocalyptic literature it is presented as an end-time event and as a component of the final victory of God. In certain strata of tradition it is associated with the transcendent messianic figure (the Son of man; the Elect One; the Messiah). A development of this image can be traced in *1 Enoch*,[87] *4 Ezra*,[88] and *2 Baruch*.[89]

As noted above,[90] the day of the Lord is presented in three forms: (1) as a coming of the Lord from heaven to enforce his rule; (2) as a disaster, like the flood in the time of Noah or the destruction of Sodom and Gomorrah; or (3) as a judgment scene in a forensic setting. The three forms, however, often overlap. The following examples can be singled out:

(1) The God of the universe, accompanied by a mighty heavenly army, marches out of his place to enforce his rule and to judge (*1 Enoch* 1:3–9; 10:11–14; cf. 71:13–17; Isa 26:21; Mic 1:3). The whole of creation trembles at his coming. All upon earth perish (*1 Enoch* 1:7), and everyone is judged. The righteous, however, are preserved and are given peace: they belong to God and live in the light of God. This depiction, which refers to the flood, governs *1 Enoch* 1–36 and serves as the type of the last judgment (10:11–11:2). The Watchers are imprisoned but not destroyed until the final judgment, when they are brought out, condemned, and thrown into a fiery pit (10:11–14). Here the Lord's coming is associated with the judgment and the cleansing of the earth from the sources of evil. The judgment restores creation and establishes an eternal or long-lasting life of righteousness, peace, harmony, and bliss on earth.

(2) According to the Dream Visions (*1 Enoch* 83–90), the history of mankind and of Israel ends with the last judgment, depicted as a courtroom scene (*1 Enoch* 90). The judge—the Lord of the Sheep—opens the records of deeds committed on earth. The stars (the fallen angels) and the seventy shepherds (angels) who have overstepped their authority over the nations are condemned and thrown into the fiery pit (90:24–25). The apostates are also judged, condemned, and then cast into a fiery abyss (90:26–27) specially prepared for them. After the judgment, a new and endless era of peace, harmony, and righteousness begins. The dispersed and those who have been destroyed gather in the new Jerusalem (90:33). A white and powerful bull is born—an image of the Messiah—and the Gentiles

---

[87] *1 Enoch* is a composite writing that was composed in sections between 250 BCE and 50 CE.

[88] *4 Ezra* is dated after the destruction of the second temple, about 100 CE.

[89] *2 Bar.* is dated around 100 CE.

[90] See ch. 1.

offer him homage (90:37). The Gentiles, depicted earlier as beasts and birds of prey, turn into white bulls, while the great white bull becomes a lamb.[91]

(3) While in the Dream Vision the messianic figure does not play an active role in the judgment, in the Similitudes (1 Enoch 37–71) this figure is entrusted with judgment. Here the Elect One is seated on the judgment throne by the Lord of the Spirits (45:3; 46:3–6; 48:2; 49:2–4; 51:2–3; 52:9; 61:8). The judgment is forensic, with the (arch)angels Michael, Gabriel, Raphael, and Phanuel serving as the appointed ministers of the court, although they, somehow, carry out the commands of the Lord of the Spirits. The Elect One judges the Watchers (54:1–6; 56:1–4; 61:8–9), the mighty on earth, the sinners, and the righteous. The Watchers and their progeny on earth, together with the renegades, are sentenced to eternal death—a death forever consummated in the fiery inferno. The kings and potentates are driven by the angels from the face of the earth and are destroyed (38:3–6; 46:4–5; 53:5; 62:5). The oppressors are given into the hands of the elect ones for punishment (38:5–6; 48:9), and sinners are banished from the earth and destroyed (53:2; 45:1–6). The Elect One then reveals the secrets of the righteous, for whom this day is the day of salvation (48:7; 51:2, 5).

This day of judgment is also the resurrection day. The Similitudes mention the resurrection of the righteous. The manner of their dying is no obstacle to the resurrection: those who were buried in the desert, or drowned in the sea, or devoured by wild beasts, or eaten by fish in the sea (61:5) are raised (51:1). Chariots speeding upon air bring them from east and west (57:1–3). The spirits of the dead are brought from the chambers, for the Elect One opens "all the hidden storerooms" (46:3; cf. 2 Bar. 30:2).

According to the Similitudes, a change takes place after the judgment: the righteous receive (eternal) life (62:16) on the transformed earth (45:4–5), as well as light, glory, and honor (50:1). They live in a congregation of the elect (53:6) together with the Son of man for ever (62:14; cf. 45:4), and the Lord of the Spirits abides over them (62:14).[92] The transformed earth is a paradise on earth (61:12; cf. 2 Bar. 29:5–8; 51:11). Second Baruch 73:1–7 mentions that all evil, illness, death, and sin have disappeared (vv. 2–5).

(4) In 4 Ezra and 2 Baruch occurs a further development. Here the messianic figure is given a function before the final judgment, while the latter is

---

[91] This imagery probably suggests righteousness and peace.
[92] Cf. 2 Bar. 42:8; 85:5.

reserved to God. The messianic figure is given the authority to judge and to rule for a limited period of time immediately before the end of the ages. He establishes peace and righteousness on earth for those still living and for the righteous who have died for their faith. According to 4 Ezra 7:26–30, the Messiah rules for four hundred years. At the end of this period everyone, including the Messiah, dies. After seven days of primeval silence the new and incorruptible age awakens, the final judgment takes place, the righteous are rewarded, and the wicked are punished (vv. 34–38). General resurrection occurs at this moment.

The Messiah will be revealed "with those who are with him" (4 Ezra 7:26–29)—probably with those who have been taken into heaven, such as Ezra, Baruch, Elijah, and Enoch.[93] At times this messianic figure is depicted as a mighty warrior who comes to annihilate his foes. In 12:31–33 he is portrayed as the lion who denounces the eagle—the Roman empire—for its ungodliness and wickedness and finally destroys it. He delivers the faithful who have survived, and keeps them joyful until the day of judgment (v. 34).

In 4 Ezra 13:1–4 a figure resembling a man comes out of the sea—he is mysterious[94]—and flies with the clouds carried by a strong wind. Wherever he looks, everyone trembles, and at his voice everything melts like wax before the fire. With his powerful voice he battles the assembled foes and annihilates them (vv. 8–11, 25–53), and after this he assembles a peaceful multitude (vv. 12–13). In v. 52 this figure is identified by the Most High as "my Son." The judgment entrusted to this figure is limited, and the life with the Messiah is not yet the incorruptible and immortal life, although it comes close to it: during his reign there will be no untimely death or sickness or blood or sin in the world. But the dead will rise only at the final judgment, which is yet to come.

According to *2 Bar.* 29:3–30:1, the Messiah is revealed before the end of time. Only the deceased martyrs are raised from the dead to partake of the messianic reign (30:1–5).[95] In 30:1 the Messiah returns to heaven in glory, after which the end time comes.[96] According to 72:2–6, the Messiah judges the nations, sparing those that did not harm Israel and destroying those that oppressed Israel.

---

[93] So Wilcke, *Zwischenzeit*, 45.

[94] See 4 Ezra 13:26.

[95] See Wilcke, *Zwischenreich*, 43.

[96] This verse is interpreted by some scholars as a Christian interpolation; cf. Wilcke, *Zwischenreich*, 42–44; Luedemann, *Paul*, 228–30; U. B. Müller, *Messias und Menschensohn*, 142.

According to *2 Bar.* 30:1 the Messiah returns in glory to heaven, while 72:1–6 indicates that the messianic rule culminates in the eternal age. After the Messiah's return, the dead rise and the souls of the righteous come out of the chambers, while the wicked waste away (30:1–5). Then the new and incorruptible age begins (73–74). According to 50:2–4, the righteous assume ever higher forms of glory. Their splendor increases with the transformation. The shape of their faces assumes the light of the beauty of the undying world (51:3). They are like angels and equal to the stars (51:10); they can change into any shape they desire (50:10). But the wicked assume an ever more horrible shape (51:2). The messianic figure here, as in the Similitudes, is preexistent, mysterious, and living in heaven— the one whom the Most High "has been keeping for many ages" (4 Ezra 13:26; cf. 13:52; 14:9).

The messianic reign is thus a privilege granted to the righteous— to those who have survived and those who have died. The Book of Revelation, written around the same time, maintains this notion (20:1–6). The righteous are transformed after the final judgment.

E. THE MESSAGE AND THE APOCALYPTIC IMAGERY IN 1 THESSALONIANS 4:13–18, 5:1–11; 1 CORINTHIANS 15:23–28, 50–55; AND PHILIPPIANS 3:20–21

The analysis of these texts[97] has shown that each is structured to answer the particular problem at hand. Although they all deal with the parousia of Christ, each presents its own aspect of the parousia and has its own imagery. Paul does not give a pat answer for every problem dealing with the parousia.

Thus in 1 Thess 4:13–18 the apostle makes use of apocalyptic imagery and of the spatiotemporal framework to make a particular affirmation—that the deceased faithful will share with the living in the taking up at the Lord's coming. He employs apocalyptic imagery in 1 Cor 15:23–28, 1 Cor 15:50–55, and Phil 3:20–21 to make other assertions, such as Christ's victory over death or the transformation of the living and the dead. In this way he affirms Christ's victory over the powers and over death, the resurrection of the body, the transformation, and conformity to the exalted Lord. He thereby also affirms the real, empirical future of its completion.

---

[97] See chs. 2–6.

All these passages draw on the proclamation of Christ's death and resurrection in all its meaning for the believer. They project on the eschatological screen the interpretation of the kerygma that touches the problem at hand. Thus in 1 Thess 4:14 Paul infers from the death and resurrection of Jesus that God will bring the deceased faithful with Jesus (into his presence). In 5:9–10 he points to Jesus' dying for us as the ultimate sign of God's faithfulness toward us. In 1 Cor 15:23–28 Paul is still working out the implications of Christ's resurrection for Christ's lordship, parousia, and role in the resurrection of the dead. Philippians 3:20–21 is governed by vv. 10–11, where Paul speaks about sharing Christ's death and resurrection. Thus, the eschatological completion is asserted on the basis of God's saving intent in the death and resurrection of Christ. According to Paul, from this present and past experience of God's gracious offer of salvation through Jesus Christ, the faithful can infer their own future, for they know the outlines of God's plan for them.[98] But the apostle can also resort to the word of the Lord for a prophetic assurance and disclosure; not everything can be drawn from the Easter event. He relies on this source in order to depict how, in particular, the deceased will share with the living in the taking up. But the completion is decked in the costume of Jewish apocalyptic. Thus Paul speaks about the Lord's descent from heaven, the κέλευσμα, the archangel's voice, the trumpet of God, the taking up by the clouds, the annihilation of death, etc. All this is established imagery.

But the believer also likes to know how, in particular, it will be possible for the deceased faithful to participate in the parousia. This the apostle depicts by means of an apocalyptic scenario containing the coming to life of the deceased believers and the taking up by the clouds. God is powerful and can overcome all obstacles; he can bring the dead to life again. Paul assures the faithful that they will all be with the Lord forever.

As to the time of the completion, however, the believer needs no additional instruction or reassurance, as Paul points out in 1 Thess 5:1–11. Here Paul refers back to his previous instruction of the community in this regard. The completion is totally in God's hands and bears the possibility of a painful surprise for those who count

---

[98] Rahner, "Hermeneutics," 334.

on undisturbed peace and security in this life. The faithful, there-fore, should not presume on God's forbearance or indulge in the works of darkness. They should live as they have been taught—a life of faith, love, and hope at any and every moment of their life. They must know this, but not the moment of the Lord's coming.

On the other hand, Paul here assures the faithful of their good standing with the Lord and of their well-founded hope. He does not want them to live in constant fear and trembling or fall prey to despair. He therefore assures the faithful in Thessalonica that a life of faith, love, and hope will end up in union with the Lord when he comes, for God has destined them from the first for salvation (vv. 9–10). This is a necessary, but also a sufficient, preparation for attaining salvation. The believer must understand that the present existence in faith is incomplete and is to be open-ended. The completion is yet to come, but it cannot be calculated.

Apocalyptic imagery, however, does not provide a preview of things to come; nor is such a preview necessary for authentic Christian existence.[99] Paul brushes aside the attempt to find out the date of the day of the Lord's coming (1 Thess 5:1–2) and is rather reserved in using the eschatological imagery. Thus the reference "in a moment, in the twinkling of an eye, at the last trumpet" in 1 Cor 15:52 is, in comparison with 1 Thess 4:16–17, sharply reduced in imagery. Paul does not dwell on the manner of the Lord's coming, nor on how the dead will be raised, nor on how the transformation will take place. The apocalyptic imagery in Phil 3:20–21 is somewhat more explicit in mentioning Christ's descent from heaven and his transforming our earthly bodies so that they resemble his risen body.

The apocalyptic imagery in these texts also shows discontinui-ties; it changes with the circumstances. Thus the depiction of the Lord's descent in 1 Thess 4:16 does not recur in any other passage we have examined. Perhaps the closest to it is Phil 3:20–21, which also mentions the descent from heaven. First Corinthians 15:52 only alludes to the parousia with the mention of the last trumpet. But the circumstances mentioned here do not so much depict the coming of the Lord from heaven as the instantaneousness and the wonder of the happening. And the resurrection is presented differ-ently. In 1 Thess 4:16–18 it is a return to this life, while in 1 Cor

---

[99] See ibid., 330.

15:52–56 the resurrected life is a transformed life, radically different from the present life.

The taking-up motif occurs only in 1 Thess 4:17[100] and involves the living and the dead. In the depiction, Paul insists that the resurrection precedes the taking up. The taking-up motif is not reproduced again in our texts, nor is the resurrection again depicted as a return to this life. In 1 Cor 15:52–55 Paul also refers to the living and the dead, but the point he makes there is the instantaneous change of the living and of the dead so that they can enter the kingdom of God.

The transformation is mentioned in 1 Cor 15:50–55, 2 Cor 5:1–10, and Phil 3:20–21, but each time in a somewhat different way. In 1 Cor 15:50–55 the apostle emphasizes the necessity of the change for the living and the dead: the kingdom of God demands the removal of all vestiges of mortality and corruptibility. In 2 Cor 5:1–11 Paul affirms the somatic nature of the ultimate reality and its transcendence with respect to the present physical existence. And in Phil 3:20–21 he points out the abiding and heavenly nature of the assimilation to the heavenly nature of Christ. In 1 Cor 15:23–28 he depicts the antagonism between Christ and certain powers in creation, including the power of death, but this feature is not present in other depictions of the parousia. The imagery in each case is thus made to fit the particular message that Paul is making there.

All this seems to indicate that the apocalyptic language is employed for a specific purpose, as Paul tries to solve the problem at hand. His primary aim is not consistency of thought and expression. As he gropes for language appropriate to the situation, his imagery shifts, but this does not necessarily imply that we can therefore dispense with this imagery. If we rephrase it in contemporary expressions, we have no absolute certainty that we have done the right thing, or that we have made it more intelligible to the people of the twentieth century, or that we have eliminated the anthropomorphic presentation of the transcendent.

Paul, it seems, employs apocalyptic language even when he speaks to a community that is Gentile. He seems to presume the community's familiarity with it. We can assume that his personal presentation, when he founded the community, included also a

---

[100]Although we may suspect it behind Paul's statement in 2 Cor 4:14.

more extensive instruction in the apocalyptic medium. The letters, at any rate, presuppose that earlier instructions in the fundamentals of faith and hope employed apocalyptic language.

Apocalyptic language is especially appropriate for depictions of the future completion. It is the traditional language. The discontinuities that we have observed in the imagery are part of Paul's contingent application of apocalyptic in his message of hope. This imagery has a functional significance: it provides the stage props for the theological constants. It also helps our groping imagination to express this transcendent reality in a spatiotemporal manner, conformed to our present earthly existence.

F. REPHRASING APOCALYPTIC IMAGERY

Can and may the apocalyptic imagery[101] in these passages be eliminated? Can the passages be separated from the kerygma? According to Bultmann,[102] they cannot be separated from the kerygma and, hence, the entire statement must be reinterpreted. Bultmann's reinterpretation is, however, scarcely justified on scientific, philosophical, exegetical, and theological grounds. It is questionable that his demythologization is more appealing to the man of today than Paul's language or that it helps the faithful.

Excision of this imagery is scarcely the best way of proceeding, for it only leaves a void. It also implies that the imagery is irrelevant to the message. The imagery itself must somehow be rephrased. But this means that its meaning in the context must be accurately determined. Hence, the search for an adequate understanding of Paul's thought goes on, as does the search for a more contemporary formulation.

1. The Apocalyptic Imagery in 1 Thessalonians 4:16–17

This investigation has shown that in 1 Thess 4:16 the cry of command (κέλευσμα) motif expresses the overpowering, irresistible, and awesome might of the Lord's command as he comes for judgment and salvation. The motif is best attributed to the coming

---

[101] Paul himself probably never identified this imagery as apocalyptic; to him it was simply the language familiar to him from his Jewish background.

[102] Bultmann, "Mythology," 9.

Lord and probably belongs to the antagonistic, or conflict, aspect of the parousia.

The voice-of-the-archangel (φωνὴ ἀρχαγγέλου) motif is a kindred motif. It also suggests the power and the glory of the coming Lord as he comes together with this mighty prince of angels vested with his own authority. And it also has an overtone of conflict. The presence of this motif here enhances the κέλευσμα motif. It brings out the heavenly authority and glory of the coming Lord. According to Luke 9:26, the Lord will come in his glory and "in the glory of the holy angels."

The trumpet-of-God (σάλπιγξ θεοῦ) motif suggests that the Lord is coming in God's name and with God's authority to establish the kingdom of God (1 Cor 15:28, 50) in God's creation. In the words of Luke 9:26, the Lord comes "in the glory of his Father"—specifically to carry out the Father's command to establish the kingdom. This motif thus reinforces the previous two motifs. The three images are mainly sound images, although each of them reverberates with its individual overtones. Each states in its own way that the Lord is coming in the divinely bestowed power and in the glory of heaven to bring about the ultimate reality, the kingdom of God. In the words of Phil 3:21, the Lord is coming from heaven "by the power that also enables him to make all things subject to himself."[103]

The cloud (ἐν νεφέλαις) motif, as this exegesis has brought out, is part of the imagery dealing with the taking up. It is not part of the usual presentation of the Lord's coming on the clouds of heaven. The cloud here is a means of transporting living human beings, body and soul, to heaven or to the place of meeting with the Lord, who comes down from heaven.[104] It is not an ordinary cloud. The transporting expresses an elevation of the present life on earth to a higher life, that of the risen Lord. The cloud thus depicts in a visible and concrete way the lifting of the *whole* person, not merely the human spirit, to the ultimate form of life that is

---

[103] Or in the words of Mark 13:26: "They will see the Son of man coming in clouds with great power and glory"; cf. Matt 24:30–31. Luke 9:26 mentions the coming of the Son of man "in his glory and the glory of the Father and of the holy angels." This is a fitting paraphrase of 1 Thess 4:16.

[104] Angels, for instance, are not depicted as coming on a cloud. The transportation of a soul to heaven, either in a trance or at death, is also not associated with a cloud. The cloud is associated with the body being transported from earth to heaven or from heaven to earth.

associated with the risen Christ.[105] The cloud somehow supplies the power that sustains the person in the new form of life.

The time sequence, insisted upon in this text, is connected with the taking up of the deceased. The dead must first be brought to life in order for them to be taken up. The insistence on the joint assumption of the living and the dead allays any anxiety that the deceased may be left out of this joyful meeting with the Lord.

The message in 1 Thess 4:16–17 seems to be this: the Thessalonians need not bewail the loss the deceased believers incur because they have died before the Lord's coming. God's promise of salvation, given in the Easter event, holds true, for death cannot thwart it. When, in the end time, the risen Lord will be revealed in all his power, God will keep his promise without any detriment to the dead. The dead will be raised to life again, and together with the living faithful, they will be brought to join the Lord and, in his company, enter the ultimate reality, the presence of God.

2. The Apocalyptic Imagery in Philippians 3:20–21

Whereas 1 Thess 4:16–17 assures the believers of God's faithfulness to his promise in Christ that is not thwarted even by death, Phil 3:20–21 exhorts the community to raise its gaze from the completion on earth to that which heaven provides. The present existence on earth is not yet the ultimate completion: at his coming, the Lord will transform our present body into the likeness of his own glorious body. The focus is on the goal—heaven. Heaven is the home country for the faithful.

There is little explicit apocalyptic imagery here, although heaven, the coming of Christ from heaven, and physical transformation belong to the apocalyptic world. Heaven is the transcendent, mysterious, and glorious world of God and of the risen Lord. Paul emphasizes that the risen Christ belongs to this higher reality and that those who belong to Christ will also be elevated to this world. The present human existence is a sharing in the lowly reality of this passing world. The ultimate existence will be

---

[105] In the synoptic portrayals of the parousia, the cloud is associated with the Lord's coming down from heaven. In that depiction it also serves as the mode of transportation.

a sharing in the transcendent world of God, to which the risen Christ belongs. That ultimate existence is the ultimate goal of our hope. The exalted Christ will appear in the power that enables him to raise our present lowly existence: he will transform the present body and refashion it to conform to his own glorious body. Then we will share fully in the power of Christ's resurrection. The believer's ultimate goal is thus the transcendent world of God, where Christ is.

3. The Apocalyptic Imagery in 1 Corinthians 15:52–55

This passage likewise has little apocalyptic imagery. The expressions "in a moment" (ἐν ἀτόμῳ), "in the twinkling of an eye" (ἐν ῥιπῇ ὀφθαλμοῦ) are scarcely apocalyptic. They bring out the instantaneousness and the wonder of the event: it will happen in a flash.[106] But the suddenness and the wonder indicate that this is God's doing, not man's or nature's. God will bring about the necessary change in order that the dead and the living may enter the kingdom of God.

The "last trumpet," however, is an apocalyptic referent. It was suggested that this motif here stands for the parousia of Christ. At that moment the kingdom of God will be inaugurated. The assertion "the trumpet will sound" affirms the reality of Christ's coming for the completion—the kingdom of God. Paul insists on these two realities; it is at this happening that he expects this change to take place.

The apostle thus assures the Corinthian community that at the parousia, which is certain to come, the Lord will in a mysterious way change the present human condition, removing from it all vestiges of death and dying. The dead will be raised imperishable, and the living will be transformed to immortal life. There is no place for death or dying in the kingdom of God.

4. The Apocalyptic Imagery in 1 Corinthians 15:23–28

The apocalyptic background shines through this presentation, which suggests a conflict between the risen Lord and the powers hostile to God. The rulers, authorities, and principalities are here

---

[106] Cf. Luke 17:24.

the principles of (spiritual and transcendent) opposition to God in this world. They are part of the creation opposed in principle to the rule of God, inspiring as they do false worship and false values in the world. But the imagery is not clear, and the nature of these powers can only with difficulty be obtained from the rest of Paul's writings and from other NT and apocalyptic sources. Yet the reality of these forces in our world is emphasized here.

The theological statement, made in the language of Pss 8:6 and 110:1, is that God has designated Christ as Lord above all the powers that be, including death. He will, in that power, establish his rule over all of them. In God's name and authority he will establish his rule over death by raising the dead to life, by changing what is mortal into what is immortal, and what is corruptible into what is incorruptible.

This victory over death states, in conflict imagery appropriate to the messianic tradition, that Christ will conquer all opposition to God and inaugurate a life that is free from sin, conflict, and death. He will raise the dead to life and change what is mortal to what is immortal. With Christ's coming there will be no more death or dying, for at that moment the kingdom of God will take place (1 Cor 15:50); immortality will replace mortality, and incorruptibility will replace corruptibility (vv. 52–56). The ultimate reality thus involves the resurrection of the dead and the transformation. Christ's function as Lord will not be over until he has achieved all this. When Christ reveals himself at the end of time, his God-given task of salvation will be accomplished. Then all the sources of power in the cosmos will be overcome, and death will be no more.

5. The Apocalyptic Imagery in 1 Thessalonians 5:2–3

There is little apocalyptic imagery present here. Paul is using as comparisons such images as a "thief in the night," birth pangs of a woman with child, and a catastrophe that suddenly overtakes everyone. This imagery is readily understandable today. The point he wants to make is that the ultimate event is unpredictable and threatening. The believer must therefore be totally ready at any moment of existence to face the Lord. Any attempt to live recklessly will end in disaster.

CONCLUSION

We have attempted through an examination of these texts to recast the apocalyptic language of Paul into a more contemporary idiom without jettisoning the reality of Christ's parousia, the judgment, the resurrection of the dead, and the union with the Lord. In doing this we have only attempted to provide an understanding of what we believe is Paul's thought so that the latter can be restated in our own language. The invitation to do this, and to do this better, goes to every proclaimer of the word and every interpreter of Paul.

According to the apostle, the question whether Christ will come personally as Lord to usher in the end-time completion has been fundamentally decided with Christ's death and resurrection. And the question whether the believer will in fact reach the completion of salvation at the Lord's coming has also been decided at Easter; for Christ's death is the insuperable sign of God's undying love for us, and Christ's resurrection is the promise and the guarantee of God's victory over death, a victory that will take place at the resurrection and the transformation. The apostle is therefore constantly drawing his fundamental assurance out of the Easter event. He affirms categorically that Christ in fact rose from the dead and that Christ will in fact come again. He insists on his interpretation of Christ's resurrection as the event that is meant to, and has the power to, effect universal resurrection. The truth of God and the commitment of God through Christ are, therefore, the implications of the Easter event for the faithful and for the cosmos.

The parousia is the culmination of Christ's present rule, the beginning of God's kingdom, and the moment for the resurrection of the dead. The Lord's coming is thus the culmination of Christ's own resurrection and of his lordship, which began with that event. Christ was raised as the first of the many and as the one through whom all others will be brought to life. And he was made Lord so that he may put everything under his feet. The parousia is also the culmination of the present existence "in Christ." Those who belong to Christ will be with Christ at his coming.

Through this message the apostle moulded Christian existence in his communities, and he himself died in the hope that the Lord will come soon. The moment of completion, however, is God's mystery, and the delay of the expected completion only underscores this. The mystery encounters everyone at all times and calls for vigilance and sobriety, for faith, love, and hope.

The message of the Lord's coming thus shapes the faith of the believers and raises their hope in the ultimate fulfillment, which is centered on being with Christ and in sharing the life of Christ. The future parousia expresses the not-yet of salvation. It motivates Christians ethics, and it turns the gaze of the faithful toward heaven—away from and beyond their engrossment with the life here and now.

INDEX OF MODERN AUTHORS

Delcor, M., 60
Delling, G., 13
Dibelius, M., 7, 84, 173, 176, 232
Dodd, C. H., 272, 287
Doughty, D. J., 124
Dunn, J. D. G., 260, 261
Dupont, J., 7, 8, 9, 10, 43, 89, 90, 154, 155, 265, 272, 273
Dupont-Sommer, A., 185

Eckart, K.-G., 66, 67
Eissfeldt, O., 6
Ellis, E. E., 133
Ernst, J., 250

Fee, G. D., 123, 125, 149, 150, 151, 152, 157, 239, 241, 255, 279
Feuillet, A., 4, 5, 7, 60, 255
Findlay, G. G., 51
Fitzmyer, J. A., 260, 261
Flanagan, F., 188
Foerster, W., 139, 184
Fohrer, G., 57
Frame, J. E., 45, 46, 51, 74, 86, 109, 113, 232
Freedman, D. N., 51
Friedrich, G., 57, 67, 101, 172
Froitzheim, F., 69
Furnish, V., 109, 293

Garland, D. E., 172, 173, 174, 175, 188
Gerhardsson, B., 100, 101
Gillman, J., 95, 149, 274, 279
Gnilka, J., 172, 173, 176, 179, 183, 188, 189, 190, 227, 229, 230, 234, 235, 241, 254, 267
Godet, F., 152
Greenfield, J. C., 27
Grelot, P., 25, 27
Grosvenor, M., 226
Gundry, R. H., 189
Guntermann, F., 65, 96, 125
Güttgemans, E., 124, 176, 188, 189

Hainz, J., 282, 283
Hanhart, K., 280
Harder, G., 149
Harnisch, W., 65, 67, 70, 91, 91, 100, 105, 106, 117, 118, 119
Hartman, L., 20, 66, 80, 88, 105, 118
Hay, D. M., 133
Heidegger, M., 300, 303

Heitmüller, F., 298, 299
Henderson, I., 304
Henneken, B., 71, 79, 278
Héring, J., 125
Hill, C. E., 127, 129, 132
Hoffmann, P., 65, 70, 71, 72, 73, 94, 101, 167, 237, 258, 267, 275, 276, 279
Holtz, T., 7, 9, 68, 69, 71, 72, 73, 75, 81, 89, 91, 101, 116
Hooker, M. D., 173

Isaac, E., 19, 25, 28, 29

Jeremias, J., 66, 79, 81, 90, 91, 149, 152
Jeremias, Jörg, 60
Jewett, R., 226
Jonas, H., 300
Joest, W., 287, 289, 291, 295
Johnson, R. A., 300, 301, 303
Jourdan, G. V., 285

Kabisch, R., 65, 86
Käsemann, E., 16, 117, 124, 260, 261
Kaiser, O., 14
Kee, H. C., 6, 47, 49, 37, 38, 39, 185, 186, 261
Kehl, N., 254
Kilpatrick, G. D., 174
Klauck, H.-J.,
Klein, G., 167, 277, 278, 279
Klijn, A. F. J., 34, 37
Knibb, M. A., 26, 27, 28, 29
Koch, K., 298, 311
Koester, H., 91, 124, 172, 177, 190
Kreitzer, L. J., 34, 127, 133
Kuck, D. W., 233, 234, 235, 236, 237
Kümmel, W. G., 66, 99, 118, 124, 125, 125, 127, 172, 233

Lambrecht, J., 125, 126, 127, 131, 132, 133
Laub, F., 100
Liddell, H. G., 4, 126
Lietzmann, H., 125, 126, 127, 151
Lindemann, A., 68, 273, 274, 278, 279, 279
Lohfink, G., 60, 83
Lohmeyer, E., 187, 227
Löhr, G., 82
Lohse, E., 254
Lövestam, E., 108, 109, 113
Luedemann, G., 65, 69, 70, 72, 75, 81, 82, 90, 91, 92, 278, 318

INDEX OF ANCIENT SOURCES